The Trader at

Rock Island

George Davenport and the Founding
of the Quad Cities

———

Regena Trant Schantz

Published in the United States
By Heritage Documentaries, Inc.
www.heritagedocumentaries.org

Copyright 2020

Cover image: Davenport House Site on Rock Island, attributed to
John Casper Wilde, ca 1844. Photo courtesy of the State Historical
Museum of Iowa/Kay Coats

Cover production by Chris Mandle
Interior Design by John Peragine

ISBN: 978-1-64704-119-9 (Paperback)
ISBN: 978-1-64704-120-5 (eBook)
Library of Congress Control Number: 2020900710

Table of Contents

Preface v

Illustrations xi

Prologue xiii

Chapters

   1. To America By Accident 1

   2. Into the Army 9

   3. Frontier Outpost............................ 25

   4. Domestic Life on Island 51

   5. Entering Indian Trade 63

   6. Davenport's Credit Books 89

   7. Full Steam Ahead 97

   8. New Commander, New Ideas 115

   9. To England 135

   10. Influx of settlers 143

   11. Escalation to War 165

   12. Black Hawk War 179

   13. Laying New Foundations 195

   14. The Dwindling Indian Trade 223

   15. A New Town in Iowa 237

   16. Out on the Rock 261

   17. Harnessing the Waterpower 287

   18. Digging In and Digging Out 303

   19. Assessing Success 319

   20. Wrapping Up The Fur Trade 329

   21. The Iron Horse 341

   22. Seduced by the Devil 355

Epilogue 371

Appendix I -- Will 383

Appendix II -- An Indian Ceremony 393

Notes 397

Bibliography 451

Image Credits 467

Index 469

Preface

When George Davenport was murdered in broad daylight in his own home on the Fourth of July, it was the most sensational story of 1845. It is still a good story. There is, however, much more to George Davenport than a dramatic and sensational death. The Trader at Rock Island; George Davenport and the Founding of the Quad Cities is the story of an English merchant sailor who joined the United States Army and staked his claim to the western lands of Illinois. This is not just one man's biography, but also a study of how the communities on the Upper Mississippi River Rapids used the attraction of cheap land and unharnessed waterpower to transition the country from Indian land into urban settlements.

George Davenport arrived in America at the moment when Lewis and Clark had reached the Pacific Ocean in their exploration of the Louisiana Purchase. Like many immigrants, Davenport was interested in the opportunities of the great western lands then being explored. His entry into American life was the army, in which he served for ten years in the Mississippi Valley. He fought in the War of 1812 in the Niagara theatre and then parlayed his experiences into the cut-throat business of the Indian Trade. His knowledge of the Upper Mississippi Valley and of merchandizing on the frontier helped him build a prosperous land business culminating in a town named in his honor. This is not just Davenport's story, but also the story of the settlement of the Midwest. By placing George Davenport into a national context we can better understand how one man was able to transition from life in Indian country to settled land and also how one community's development followed a pattern that was repeated across the frontier in the years after the War of 1812.

Davenport came to the Rock Island area as the Contractor's Agent for Fort Armstrong, and turned to the Indian trade with the Sauk and Fox (Mesquakie). As the Upper Mississippi Valley opened up due to steamboat travel and increased interest in the lead mines in Northwestern Illinois, Davenport transitioned to mercantile business for settlers and services such as ferries and inns. He helped organize local government and engaged in land speculation. As a land merchant, he was especially active during the boom years of 1835 - 1836, investing in all the town plats surrounding the island of Rock Island. With Antoine Le Claire and others he developed the town of Davenport, Iowa, which was named for him. Despite Davenport's deep involvement in the development in the Quad City region, no biography of him exists. Only one chapter in Franc B. Wilkie's *Davenport Past and Present,* published in 1852, provides factual information about Davenport's career. Edward Bonney's *Banditti of the Prairie* (University of Oklahoma Press) tells the story of Davenport's murder and the capture and trial of the culprits, but the full story of his life and involvement with town development has never been written.

My interest in George Davenport began as a young adult with stories of the haunting of the Davenport House. As one of the founding members of the Colonel Davenport Historical Foundation in 1977, I began researching the Davenport story for the promotion of the house as a museum, providing information for exhibits, school tours, guide training, and general publicity. In 1991 I completed my Master's degree in American Studies at the University of Iowa with my thesis on the Davenport house and family.

The search for Davenport's story has taken me to many public and private libraries, including the National Archives, Newberry Library in Chicago, and a variety of courthouses and museums. But it was in his hometown of Louth, England, where I met with Dorothy King, a collateral descendant of George Davenport, and my perspective on George Davenport changed. I realized that Davenport was recreating his past in a new land, just as every immigrant was trying to do. I am especially grateful to Ms. King for her family knowledge and gifts of books on Louth history and to Pauline Franklin, whose book on the L'Oste family gave me insight into Davenport's understanding of town development.

I have used the Davenport story to entertain countless audiences and as the basis for teaching classes on early Iowa history and the founding of the Quad Cities in the CommUniversity program (held on St. Ambrose University campus each February). My research has contributed to the documentary video on *George Davenport, The House That Courage Built* (Avolux Media, 2006), the documentary, *East Meets West* (Heritage Documentaries, Inc., 2017), and three children's books published by the Colonel Davenport Historical Foundation. I have presented papers on George Davenport and on Fort Armstrong at the Illinois History Symposium and the Midwest Archaeology Conference and my chapter on Fort Armstrong is included in *Frontier Forts of Iowa*, edited by William Whittaker (University of Iowa Press, 2009).

There are many who have contributed greatly to my research over these many years. Kathie Walch spent hours with me as I learned the process of historical research. Bill Hannan offered encouragement to write a book with all that stuff I was collecting. Dick and Doris Balzer fed me lunch and picked my brain as I honed my story. Kris Leinicke, Rock Island Arsenal Resource Center led me to the story of Ft. Armstrong and Alexandra Benedict brought the Rock River story to my research. Dr. Roald Tweet recognized early on the importance of telling George Davenport's story.

I am deeply indebted to the Staff at Rock Island County Historical Society and Augustana College's Tredway Library and Special Collections, and especially to the librarians in Richardson Sloane Special Collections at Davenport Public Library for helping me access many collections on interlibrary loan; to Professor Leigh Vandervelde for the opportunity to research at the National Archives; and to Pauline Franklin for sharing her work on the L'Oste family history.

Special thanks go to Maryann Wherry for her advice on how to write a biography; to Gayle Rein, Alexandra Benedict, Kathleen Seusy, Michael Hustedde, Ezra Siddran, Coky Powers, Kris Leinicke and Curt Roseman for their critiques, proofing and editing help. And finally, I give thanks to my loving husband and family, without whose push I would never have gotten this into print.

The Trader at Rock Island: George Davenport and the Founding of the Quad Cities is a long overdue contribution to the understanding of how the Midwest was carved from Indian land to urban settlement.

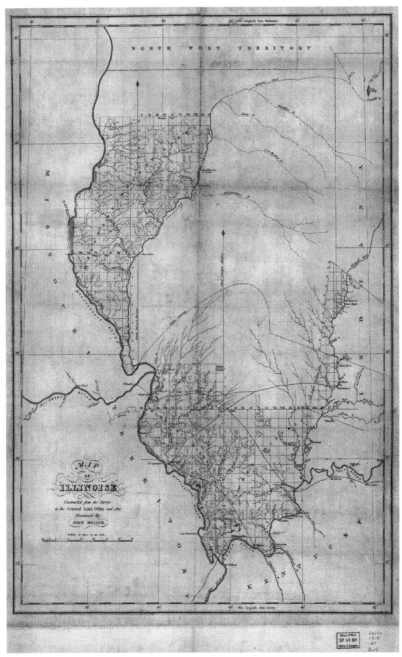

In 1818 only two areas of Illinois had been surveyed: southern Illinois and the Military Tract, which was reserved as bounty lands for the veterans of the War of 1812.

Illustrations

1. Map of Illinoise, 1818 x
2. George Davenport xxii
3. Ft. Armstrong 24
4. Susan Lewis Goldsmith 50
5. Trading Posts 62
6. Keelboat 88
7. Ft. Armstrong Walters 114
8. Indian Cessions in Iowa 178
9. Davenport House............................... 194
10. Plat of Davenport 236
11. Parker Map of Davenport, 1837 244
12. Rock Island City and Surroundings 260
13. Rock River 260
14. Moline Waterfront 286
15. Bill Senate 44 328
16. Rail roads surrounding Rock Island 340
17. Obituary of George Davenport 354
18. 1,500 Dollars Reward 354
19. Gravepost 392

Prologue

When George Davenport arrived on the island of Rock Island, or Rocky Island as he called it, deep in Indian Country, he considered himself the first permanent settler north of the Illinois River. He had come to the United States, as many immigrants before him, to find land and a new life.

Illinois Territory was, in 1816, sparsely populated with only about 34,000 persons. It was a land of opportunity, stretching from the Ohio River on the south to 42 degrees 30 on the north. The Territory was largely prairie, a vast, mostly treeless, expanse of land, which early travelers found breathtakingly beautiful in early spring.

Settlers had avoided the prairies, however, thinking them unsuitable for agriculture since they had no trees. They preferred to settle the scenic bluffs and hills of the Mississippi and Ohio Rivers and their tributaries in the southern counties of the Territory. Consequently, the majority of settlements in 1816 were south of the Illinois River. Most settlers had migrated from Virginia, Kentucky, and Tennessee, although some settlers had come through Ohio from Pennsylvania. For the most part they came on flatboats down the Ohio River into Illinois Territory through its primary port of Shawneetown, which was then the first port that settlers would encounter as they passed the Kentucky-Indiana border. [1] As pioneers who had pushed the frontier ever westward through Kentucky and Virginia, they expected, even demanded, that Indian lands would become public lands, lands that they could claim by right of preemption.

Along the Mississippi River were the French who had long been settled in Kaskaskia, which was then the territorial capitol, and in Peoria, along the Illinois River. There were also French settlements along the Wabash in eastern Illinois, which were connected to the old French town of Vincennes, now in Indiana. They had long been engaged in agriculture and fur trading. There were also small settlements of free blacks in the territory.

The majority of immigrants were farmers but the production of salt at the Great Salt Mine in Gallatin County was a major industry that attracted miners. The mines had been operated by Indians for centuries. Around 1800, the mines were taken over by the English. American operation of the mines began in 1803 when leases were authorized for the benefit of the Federal Government. In 1804 the saline lands of southern Illinois were reserved from sale as property of the United States. Although slavery was prohibited in Illinois by the Ordinance of 1787, the Legislature of Indiana had permitted slaves to work in the mines for short periods of time and the Illinois State Constitution continued the practice.[2]

The northern half of Illinois Territory was Indian Country. It was the land of the Potawatomie, Sauk, Mesquakie, Kickapoo, Ho Chunk and Menomonie. The Potawatomi were established from Green Bay on the north to the Illinois River near present-day Peoria on the south and eastward to the Wabash River Valley – mainly in the northeastern part of Illinois Territory. The Kickapoo were settled in central Illinois, one band along the Vermillion River and the other along the Sangamon River. Some Menominee had settled among the Kickapoo after the War of 1812, although the main part of the tribe lived further north near Green Bay. The Sauk and their allies the Mesquakie (or Fox) lived on the Mississippi River between Dubuque on the north and the mouth of the Des Moines River. The Sauk maintained a large village, perhaps the largest settlement in Illinois at the time, at the mouth of the Rock River near the Mississippi. The Mesquakie had their villages primarily on the west bank of the river and mined lead in the area of Dubuque, in addition to fur trading. Fifty miles or so up the Rock River was a band of the Ho Chunk, or Winnebago, who had separated from the main tribe on the Wisconsin River. This band also engaged in mining lead in the Galena area of northwestern Illinois. Neither the Kickapoo, nor the Sauk and Mesquakie, nor the Ho Chunk had entered into peace treaties with the Americans and were considered fierce fighters and anti-American.

The Sauk particularly held a grudge against the Americans because of a land cession obtained by William Henry Harrison in 1804. By this Treaty, the Sauk had sold all their land in Illinois. The tribal leaders maintained that the land cession had been made under false pretensions with members who had no authority. Their only consolation was that they could remain on their land until it was surveyed by the U.S. Government and sold as public land.

The combined population of these tribes was, perhaps, about the same as white settlers in the southern half of the territory - around 12,000 persons. Their economy was heavily dependent on trade - furs exchanged for manufactured goods supplied by British traders - although they engaged in some agriculture. After the Revolutionary War, British traders had remained in the Upper Mississippi Valley and the Great Lakes areas in order to trade for furs. These traders had a heavy influence on the tribes. In order to maintain trade relations, the British promised arms and ammunition to the warriors who would fight for them and encouraged the tribes to wage war against Americans.[3]

Despite a request from Territorial Governor Ninian Edwards for the tribes to remain neutral in a war between the United States and Great Britain, most of the tribes in Illinois allied with the British and engaged in warfare against the Americans. Sauk and Potawatomi braves were particularly successful against the Americans. They had waged successful attacks against the Americans at Fort Madison, Ft. Clark, Campbell's Island, Credit Island and Ft. Dearborn.

So hostile were the tribes, that Territorial Governor Edwards encouraged settlers to defend the Illinois Territory by pursuing and overtaking any Indian who had committed murder or destruction and to kill them. The law he signed, "An Act to Promote Retaliation Upon Hostile Indians," provided rewards for any settler who had taken captive or killed hostile Indians. The Territorial Militia was also entitled to rewards for pursuing hostile Indians and killing or capturing them.[4]

When Congress ratified the Treaty of Ghent on December 24, 1814, it marked the end of hostilities between Great Britain and Ireland and the United States, but the British made no concession for their Indian allies. Having had such success in the war against the Americans in the Mississippi Valley, the Sauk and Kickapoo in particular were reluctant to accept defeat and resisted accepting the terms of peace. The United States Government, however, was obligated to establish peace with each tribe with whom they had been at war. The Government was also obligated to restore to those tribes "all possessions, rights, and privileges, which they may have enjoyed or been entitled to in one thousand eight hundred and eleven, previous to such hostilities."[5]

News of peace trickled slowly into the Mississippi Valley where the British-allied tribes were still raiding American settlements and farms. Accordingly, a commission of three (Superintendent of Indian Affairs William Clark, Illinois Governor Ninian Edwards, and Auguste Chouteau of St. Louis) invited all of the Upper Mississippi Valley tribes to a peace conference at Portage des Sioux, a small village located in northern Missouri near the confluence of the Mississippi, Missouri and Illinois Rivers. During the summers of 1815 and 1816, tribal chiefs and representatives met with the commissioners to sign peace treaties. Governor Edwards also sought concessions of land from the Illinois tribes.

After Clark threatened military force against them and Ft. Armstrong was constructed in their neighborhood, the Sauk finally signed the peace treaty on May 13, 1816. They begrudgingly acknowledged the land cessions given to William Henry Harrison in 1804.[6]

On the 24th of August 1816 the Commissioners again met with the Potawatomi, Chippewa and Ojibwa residing on the Illinois and Milwaukee Rivers and along the southwestern part of Lake Michigan to settle a dispute between them and the Sauk and Mesquakie as to lands that had been sold to the United States. The resulting Indian Boundary Line of 1816 was surveyed between the southern-most point of Lake Michigan and Rock Island. The portion between the Lake and the Illinois River was most important for the proposed Illinois and Michigan Canal. George Graham, who was then Acting Secretary of War, stated, "If that tract of land was surveyed and settled, it would very much facilitate the migrations to the Illinois Territory from New England and the State of New York by means of the lake navigation."[7]

The immediate consequence of the War of 1812 was the pacification of the Indians. Although the commissioners were not charged with obtaining land cession during the peace negotiations, Governor Edwards of Illinois Territory was not satisfied with the lands cessions he had achieved. He wanted more, but was willing to wait. His strategy was to keep the tribes happy until they were outnumbered and persuaded to remove themselves from their lands. "If they (meaning the Indians) can be kept in a good humor for two or three years, the growth of our population, by the appeal it will then make to their fears, will prevent all future danger."[8]

According to the terms of peace, British military withdrew their troops from within American territory and the Unites States Government began to take charge of the borders, particularly along the Mississippi River. To secure the borders, and monitor the activities of the foreign traders, the U.S. military reconstructed Fort Dearborn at Chicago and established Fort Armstrong at Rock Island. One of the first steps was to wean the Indian tribes from their allegiance and dependence on their British traders by establishing trading factories in Indian Country. One particular area of concern was at the Indian village of Saukenuk, on the Rock River. In the winter of 1815 - 1816, British traders were actively engaged in the trade. The Missouri Gazette reported the following:

"An officer stationed at the cantonment near Rock river informs the Editor that the troops are healthy and in good spirits. Capt. Foulke in his rambles has discovered specimens of rich lead are in that neighborhood. Some of the British traders have built trading houses at Rock river: those fellows has (sic) been forward in leading the Indians to the massacre of our women and children, after the peace was promulgated to the Indians, and now have the impudence to ask licenses to trade with their Mississippi red companions. We learn that Governor Clark has refused them license. Buisson, another notorious British partisan has removed to the west side of the Mississippi, near the Sack hunting ground, and has opened a store,

under a license (it is said) from Governor Edwards. We expect that Gen. Smith will notice those fellows trading on the river in defiance of the laws regulating intercourse with the Indians."

To provide for the trade goods, which the Indians had previously gotten from British traders, factories were established at Chicago, Fort Edwards, and Prairie du Chien, but it would take time for the Indian Agents to know how to deal with the traders already entrenched in Indian Country. Although the intent of the law was clear, the new law caused some Indian Agents like Richard Graham to question to what extent he had authority. "Some difficulty has arisen with respect to the right I have to cause to be apprehended any Trader without licence(sic), found on the lands recently ceded to the U.S. by the Indians lying between Illinois & Ouisconsin - The law, forfeiting the goods of the Indian Traders, speaks of lands to which Indian Title by Treaty has not been extinguished. Am I authorized to prevent such traders from establishing themselves among the Indians on those lands?"[10]

The Sauk in particular were not pleased when they learned that their British traders would be removed from American territory and it was in Sauk territory where the greatest problem lay. After observing the treaty negotiations with the Sauk for a few days Indian Agent Richard Graham wrote, "There is a nest of British Traders, some have obtained licence(sic), & others are acting without licence(sic) trading among them, who stir them up to act as they do --& I believe there never will be a cordial peace between the Indians, who have been under the influence of the British, and our Government, until means are taken to put a stop to the intercourse between them & the British traders ... "[11]

As peace with the Illinois tribes gradually spread over the Mississippi Valley, settlement escalated in Illinois Territory and with the help of some creative counting of the population, Illinois was given statehood in 1818. In July of 1818, the Kaskaskia newspaper reported the census returns as totaling 34,610 - well below the 60,000 required for statehood and even below 40,000, a precedent set by Ohio in achieving statehood. By 1820, the population was over 55,000 and by 1830, over 157,000.[12]

Several factors combined to encourage eastern farmers to settle in Illinois. One was the Illinois Pre emption Act of 1813. According to Malcolm Rohrbough, "When in 1813 Congress granted pre-emption rights to early settlers in Illinois, pioneers flocked to Illinois land offices to affirm their legality. Threats of Indians did not take their minds off land, which was far more significant to them in the long run. ... So great was the interest in the public lands in Illinois that the government organized a new land office in April of 1814 at Shawneetown." Not just pioneers, but also speculators interested in rapidly rising land prices were also looking for cheap land. Even the Indian Agent for Illinois Territory, Richard Graham, was interested in buying land for speculation. "Lands are rising rapidly in this Country," he wrote his brother, " & but few chances of speculation offer."[13]

Finally, there were bounty lands set aside for veterans of the late war. By an Act of Congress, bounty lands in Michigan, Illinois and Missouri were set aside as payment to volunteer soldiers for the War of 1812. Not only would this Act pay soldiers with free land, but it would also encourage settlement in the three territories. The Illinois Tract contained 3,500,000 acres and lay between the Illinois River and the southern border of present-day Rock Island County. In 1815 - 1816, the Military Tract was surveyed and opened to settlement. Over 17,000 bounty warrants were exchanged for patents between October 1817 and January 1819. By 1816, yet another land office was needed to handle the demand, and the Edwardsville Land Office was opened.[14]

Travelers to Illinois Territory wrote letters home extolling the beauty of the prairies, but also with practical information about conditions that would affect farming. "We have all kinds of soil, " Gershom Flagg wrote to his brother, "from Midling poor to the very best it produces Corn & Wheat Country better than any other I have seen ..." Breaking the prairie would not be easy: "The Roots of the grass are very tough ... it Generally requires three yoke of Oxen or six horses to plow up the prairies & the plow must be kept at a keen edge ... but this is all that is to be done except fencing to raise a crop ..."[15]

George Davenport joined the military expedition to establish military forts in Indian Country in 1815 with every expectation that the Indian title to the land above the Indian Boundary Line would be extinguished and that he would be able to claim a parcel of the public lands under the right of pre emption in Illinois Territory. Here, he would raise his family, take advantage of economic opportunities that would come his way, and establish a life for himself that was far better than any he might have had in England.

George Davenport as Proprietor of Davenport, Iowa. Unknown artist.

CHAPTER ONE:

TO AMERICA BY ACCIDENT

IN THE SUMMER OF 1804, an English merchant ship in New York Harbor was preparing to weigh anchor for her trip back to Liverpool. As the anchor came up, one of her sailors was knocked overboard. George Davenport was standing near the stern when he saw the accident and immediately jumped into a small boat and caught the sailor by the hair as he was going down in the water for the last time. The mate survived, but Davenport broke his leg in the rescue, fracturing it badly. He was taken to the city and placed in hospital where he remained for about two months. He was then advised to go into the country to recover his health and strength. So began the adventures of George Davenport, who arrived in America quite by accident, and after many years on the American frontier, left a legacy that included a town bearing his name.[1]

George Davenport was born in the northeastern part of Lincolnshire, England, not far from the North Sea in the ancient town of Louth. He was christened in the Church of St. James and named John King, the fourth child of Joseph King, farmer, and Amy Tyson, his wife. When and why he changed his name to George Davenport is unknown. It may have been as simple as wanting to start a new life, or maybe something more nefarious. Only one thing is certain. His timing was fortuitous.

Davenport's accidental arrival came just as Lewis and Clark were trekking toward the Rockies exploring the Louisiana Purchase. A whole new world was opening up, very different from the ancient market town of Louth in northeast Lincolnshire where the economy was stagnant and there were concerns about war. But, George Davenport did not shed his Lincolnshire heritage. Instead, he chose to live in an environment that was very much like home.

The landscape of the Upper Mississippi Valley is very much like the rolling hills and small river valleys of Lincolnshire where his King families had farmed for generations. Louth is 138 miles north of London, surrounded by rich rolling hills called the Lincolnshire Wolds on one side and the Fens on the other. On the Wolds farmers raised grains, particularly wheat, barley, and oats. Today the fields are planted primarily in rape, the seed of which is used for cattle feed. The Fens were marshy areas near the sea where cattle and Lincolnshire Longwool sheep grazed. The climate helped to produce a particularly valuable type of wool that was much sought after by Europeans and enriched the pockets of the many tailors and wool producers in town.

The wool industry connected Louth to markets in Germany, Italy and other places in Europe. Power for manufacturing came from the river Lud, a reasonably fast-flowing river that ran through Louth. Exporting their manufactured goods, however, was a problem for Louth merchants and manufacturers. With no direct link to the North Sea, goods had to be transported over land until 1770 when the Louth Navigation canal was constructed, linking Louth with the North Sea. Building the canal was a watershed event for Louth that stimulated the town's commerce. Today the canal is being reborn for recreational purposes with footpaths and restored locks.

Louth itself still evokes a Georgian-period atmosphere with houses of red bricks and slate roofs, most of which date from 1700 onwards. That date, according to historian David Robinson, is when Louth began replacing older structures with Classical, Queen Anne and Georgian architecture, but there are traces of the town's medieval heritage. Narrow twisting streets near the town centre date from the middle ages, and the town is dominated by the Church of St. James, the only medieval structure remaining today. The church spire, the tallest in all England, can be seen from nearly every place in the town centre and from miles away in the countryside. Today Louth is home to 10,000 souls who value their unique history and their independent economy. [2]

George Davenport's King family had been living in Louth at least since 1551 when William King was one of the original assistants to the Warden of Louth Corporation. They were yeomen, modest landowners or freeholders, who lived in town and cultivated their own lands nearby. The King family farm was just east of Louth near St. Margaret's Church, Keddington, where Davenport's earliest ancestor, John King of Louth Park, worked as a farm labourer. Although the family managed to live comfortably, albeit frugally, for generations on ten to twenty acres, by the late eighteenth century there was no room for succeeding generations. [3]

When Davenport's grandmother died in 1784, the small farm was divided equally among her four sons, but the parcels were too small to support four families. Davenport's father, Joseph King and his wife, Amy, soon moved to town with their daughter Naomi, and changed their membership from the Keddington Church to St. James Church in Louth. They rented a house in town and owned a small parcel of land in Goosepool Paddock, just a few blocks from St. James Church. Three sons were christened in St. James Church. Edward, born in 1775, is thought to have died in childhood. Joseph Jr. was born in 1776, and John, a.k.a. George Davenport, was christened on the 29th of November 1783. [4]

All three of the King children were able to read and write, a testament to Louth's reputation for excellence in education. There had been a grammar school in town since 1551, but the King children would have attended the Petit Free School, whose mission was simply "to teach children to read, to learn their catechism and instruct them in it, to write, to cast accounts, to teach them their accidence (parts of speech), and to make them fit for the grammar school." According to Louth historian David Robinson, the building was still standing at the corner of Northgate in 1790 when George Davenport was a school-aged child.[5]   Most likely he attended school off and on until he reached the age of eleven or twelve when he was apprenticed to a tailor in the market place.

Apprenticeship was the economic reality facing many English farming families in the late eighteenth century. Political unrest in France and widespread crop failures in England made life difficult. Crop failures all over England lasted into the 1820s. For small farmers like the King family, the outlook for future farming was poor.[6] So, Joseph King did what many other fathers were forced to do: he apprenticed his sons in the trades. Son Joseph was apprenticed to a carpenter and wheelwright in addition to his duties tending a small herd of cows. George was apprenticed to a tailor.

Davenport's apprenticeship may have been arranged through his brother-in-law Frederick L'Oste, who was an important and influential man in Louth. L'Oste was a seventy-one year old widower when he married Davenport's sister, Naomi King.[7] At the age of 23, Naomi was younger than all six living L'Oste children. Socially the marriage maintained the social status that the King family enjoyed within the community. As Dorothy King, the family historian, once told me, "The King family always had more status than money." The L'Ostes lived in Eastgate in a two-story semi-detached brick house on the edge of Louth, not far from the Riverhead, and associated with Louth society. Their neighbors and friends included the Tennyson family of which Alfred Lord Tennyson was descended. Although the marriage produced no children, it lasted until Frederick L'Oste's death in 1807.[8]

Frederick L'Oste was a powerful influence on, and role model for, young George Davenport. L'Oste was a relative newcomer to Lincolnshire, who had worked himself up into Louth society. His grandmother and father were French Huguenots who had escaped to

England after the repeal of the Edict of Nantes, which had given religious freedom to Protestants in France. Frederick's father was ordained in the Church of England and became the Vicar of Louth. L'Oste himself chose to be a tradesman, a grocer and mercer in Louth. During the first of his seven terms as Warden (or Mayor) of Louth, he purchased stock in the Louth Navigation, a corporation that supervised the canal operations between Louth and the Humber River. He spearheaded the development of the area called the Riverhead where wharves and warehouses were built. L'Oste also owned pastureland along the Riverhead, where the canal industries developed. The King brothers, Joseph and George Davenport, tended their father's cows in that same area. Joseph continued to rent pastureland there throughout his lifetime. From the riverbank, the boys could watch the sloops, billy-boys, and keels sail in from the Humber River. George Davenport's career in Illinois and Iowa would later parallel L'Oste's career in Louth.[9]

Davenport never completed his apprenticeship as a tailor. Unrest in Europe because of the Napoleonic Wars produced fears in towns along the North Sea, fears of invasion by Napoleon's armies. By 1800, the threat seemed imminent, and frequent alarms caused the Lincolnshire towns near the North Sea to be on guard. Volunteer armies were raised to defend the coastal towns. By then, George Davenport was 17 and of an age to serve the military, but it seems that his father had other plans for George.

Instead of going into the army, he went to sea. The family story says his father placed him with an uncle, who was master of a merchant ship.

Life at sea was a hard way to earn a living and it is unknown how Joseph King, arranged for his son to sail. Who the "uncle" was is not known but there was emphasis on the phrase "was placed by his father." John King was no runaway to the sea, but intentionally positioned for a reason. From Louth, Joseph King and his son would have made their way to the near-by fishing village of Grimsby, or more likely to Hull, thirty miles away and the biggest harbor in the area. Both are port cities located on the Humber River with connections to London and other major ports.[10]

At age seventeen, George Davenport was old to be one of the ship's boys on a merchant ship. More likely he was one of the young apprentices to the captain, grooming to be the master of a ship rather than just another able seaman. A young man who had connections with the owners or master of the ship was more likely to be trained for command of a ship. While such a recruit was not treated with any special consideration, his prospects were higher than ordinary recruits. At sea, connections were just a beginning. How far a young man rose in rank was up to him. The surest way to become a ship's master, according to Ralph Davis, author of The Rise of the English Shipping Industry, was to be the nephew of a rich merchant. Davenport's connection to his "uncle," was enough to open the door. Still, life at sea was not easy.[11]

Rarely were these apprenticeships formally registered with the local authorities since there was a heavy fee associated with the recording of such agreements and no record of Davenport's apprenticeship has been found. Merchant seaman apprenticeships normally lasted four or five years. After two or three years in service, the apprentice had usually made several voyages and was trained enough to get employment as an ordinary seaman. Work was seasonal and each seaman, including the master of the ship, was hired by the voyage. Davenport's four years at sea gave him a basic understanding of the import-export business, the role of transportation in the international marketplace, and most importantly, how cargo was moved from the ground up. Merchant seamen were, after all, cargo movers, loading boxes and barrels onto the ship and off again. Davenport gained hands-on experience with the vast number of products that stood on the wharves of some of the busiest ports in the world.

According to family stories related by Franc Wilkie, author of Davenport Past and Present, Davenport made trips to France, Spain and Portugal, to the Baltic, and finally to New York from Liverpool. Trade routes to Spain and Portugal were short voyages of four or five month's duration and a ship could make two or three such trips in one year. By the late 1700s English merchant ships had developed a substantial trade, importing Mediterranean fruits and wine, glass beads from Italy, timber and naval stores from the Baltic. Hundreds of ships used English ports everyday during the shipping season. By 1800, the tonnage of goods entering and leaving Liverpool alone was 40,000 tons. In general the trip to the Baltic was longer than those to Spain and Portugal and would have included stops at Copenhagen and St. Petersburg. In Davenport's case, one trip was much longer than expected.[12]

In the Fall of 1800 his ship sailed from Liverpool for St. Petersburg, and shortly after its arrival in St. Petersburg, an embargo was placed on all English vessels in Russian ports. This was a result of the Napoleonic War. Letters from the British Consul date the embargo from October 1800 to May 1801 and support many of the facts related by Wilkie.

The Russian Government seized all English ships in port, including the crew, their stores and provisions, and even the cabin furniture. There was frost on the ground, but ice had not yet formed in the harbour. In all, 204 English vessels were seized. The seamen were marched on foot to various places in the interior of Russia in groups of ten to one hundred, and to different towns and villages. The distance to the different towns varied from 150 to 1300 versts. (A verst is equal to 0.66 miles, so the captured seamen walked anywhere from 100 miles to 858 miles to their place of imprisonment). Alexander Shairp, a British merchant residing in St. Petersburg, noted "every Englishman seemed to bear his situation with the spirit and fortitude of a Briton." Correspondence from English merchants in St. Petersburg expressed serious concern for their British seamen, because of their unpreparedness for the seizure as well as for the Russian winter. Most of the sailors did not have sufficient clothing, so the merchants, expecting reimbursement from the British Government, provided each man with a sheepskin coat, a cap and sash, a pair of gloves, some warm shoes and two pairs of stockings. Carts were provided for the Captains and the old men, but the majority of the seamen walked the distance to their imprisonment. The local peasants provided horses for their baggage. The weather was harsher than the seamen were accustomed to and many were expected to die.[13]

The sailors with George Davenport were imprisoned somewhere in an old stone church for the entire winter. The Russian Government provided each sailor with 5 Copecks or about 1 and 1/2 pounds sterling per day plus a small amount of rye flour and grits. Davenport complained of the severe cold. Heat in the church was dependent upon the good nature of the villagers who were responsible for their safekeeping. Lincolnshire winters had not prepared him for such intense and prolonged cold as they experienced there.

No mention was made of the captured sailors in the newspapers back home. The editor of the Stamford Mercury in Lincolnshire took the matter of embargo rather lightly, considering it a minor matter of war, hardly worthy of note. His concern was more about national security and economic effects, as well as with certain individuals who would suffer financially. All English crews were released in the spring and restored to their ships, which sailed home to Liverpool where they prepared for their next voyage. In the summer of 1804, George Davenport arrived with his ship in New York Harbor and was preparing to sail back to Liverpool when he met with his accident.[14]

Davenport never returned to the sea. Instead, he chose the United States Army as his next apprenticeship.

CHAPTER TWO:

INTO THE ARMY

WHEN DAVENPORT HAD RECOVERED from his broken leg, he went to New Jersey and stopped at what he called "a pleasant village named Rahway." It was a much cleaner and less crowded place than New York City and work associated with sea life was readily available there. Whatever money he had, was surely spent by the time he went to New Jersey. He remained in Rahway for some time, perhaps as long as a year. It is not clear from Wilkie's story if he was employed in Rahway or had gone there after working somewhere else in order to join the army. It was in Rahway where he encountered an army recruiter by the name of Lieutenant William Lawrence.

Davenport stayed in Rahway until enough men had enlisted before marching to Carlisle, Pennsylvania, with the full roster of recruits. The recruits were held together at the recruiting station until there were enough men to meet the quotas. Then, according to standard army recruiting practices, the new recruits were marched together to the training grounds at Carlisle Barracks. Davenport was recruited with the promise of the rank of sergeant, provided that the position was open in his assigned unit. His experience as a merchant seaman was useful to the frontier army. On the 23rd of October 1805, the merchant seaman John King became, according to the official army records, George Davenport, soldier.[1]

According to general recruiting instructions, new recruits were supposed to be taught appropriate behavior "by gentle methods" and drilled four hours a day. Some 200 recruits reported for duty at Carlisle Barracks, Pennsylvania, on the 23rd of October 1805 to begin basic training. They trained throughout the winter of 1805 - 1806. At age twenty-one and standing five feet eight inches tall, George Davenport met the age and height requirements of the army at that time. He was probably in excellent physical condition now that his leg had healed. Coffman, in his treatise on the Old Army, says that the average recruit was 25 years of age and had an average height of five feet eight inches. As an immigrant, Davenport should have felt reasonably comfortable among the soldiers, eighteen per cent of whom were foreign born themselves.[2] As an Englishman, he had the advantage of speaking the language.

For his willingness to enlist George Davenport was paid an incentive bounty of twelve dollars. This was a small sum, hardly the equivalent of two weeks wages, and not enough incentive to entice any man to commit to five years of servitude. But the army promised much more. It provided Davenport with a home - not just a place where he could eat, sleep, and work, but a place where he could belong. New York City had shown him how difficult it was for immigrants. The city was crowded with immigrants and the job market was poor. Despite the poor pay, the army offered steady work, adventure, security, and comradeship. At the very least the army offered free passage across America, a good set of clothes, daily rations of food, and shelter. It also offered opportunities for land. For at least the next five years, George Davenport would make the American frontier his home.

Davenport had arrived in America when the United States was on the brink of major expansion. The army was at the heart of every adventure on the frontier. Lewis and Clark were at that very moment at the furthest reaches of the continent, exploring the Louisiana Purchase, and Zebulon Pike was exploring the Upper Mississippi Valley. John Jacob Astor's men were exploring the Columbia River in the far northwest. There was land, lots of land, just waiting for development. Captain John Armstrong, recruiting many years earlier had expressed what many young men, including George Davenport, were still looking for: "Young men who wish to become Adventurers in the New Country, by joining this Command, may acquire a Knowledge of the Western World, subject to no expense: and after serving a short period, set down in their farms, and enjoy all the blessing of Peace and Plenty." [3] The ad appealed to many men like George Davenport who had little or no prospects for a future. The army was Davenport's entry into the business world of the United States.

In 1805 the United States Army was beginning to recruit soldiers in order to bolster the small army after the American Revolution. The army was needed on the frontier, but army service was not highly regarded by the American public, nor did Congress believe that a peacetime army was a necessary expense for a young nation sorely in need of money. Without public support the small army attracted mainly the dregs of society - men who wanted to isolate themselves from the rest of society for whatever reasons. They were for the most part "men in trouble, out of work, on their beam ends." According to Coffman: "For those on the bottom rung of society, the army provided relief from a life of uncertain employment at low wages with little prospect for a better future." [4]

Not all men in the army were on their beam-ends or on the bottom rung. There were some good men in the army at that time, men whose names would be remembered in history such as General James Wilkinson, Meriwether Lewis, Zebulon Pike, and some lesser known but still historical men like Jacob Kingsbury, William O'Fallon, Caleb Atwater, and Lawrence Taliaferro. These men would all touch George Davenport's career later, on the frontier.

In 1804, the army census stood at a mere 2,730 soldiers. During the next five years enlistments tripled and recruits were ordered to fortify the borders against the Spanish along the southwestern borders and the English on the north. Davenport was at the front line of frontier defense and expansion, clearing forests, paving roads, and erected buildings in the new land. Private George Davenport did well in the army, not because he was intelligent or skilled in reading and writing, but because he was a strong and healthy young man who could work hard. As a merchant seaman he had learned discipline and knew the kind of routine work required by the army. He was ready to earn his $6 per month private's pay.

While Davenport and other recruits were training at Carlisle Barracks, General James Wilkinson, Commander of the United States Army, was ordered to the Sabine River to protect the western boundaries against a possible Spanish attack. Davenport, along with the other new recruits, were ordered to New Orleans where they would defend the city against Spanish invasion. 200 strong, they marched across the Alleghenies to Pittsburgh, floated boats down the rivers to New Orleans where Davenport took his place in Captain John McClary's Company of the 1st United States Infantry.[5] His duties in New Orleans were repairing and building new fortifications and readying the city for defense. Conditions there were abominable. Recruits from northern states were unaccustomed to heat and humidity, and coupled with the long march from Pennsylvania, sick with dysentery. Davenport, however, does not seem to have succumbed to any sickness. His youth, his years on the open sea, and his naturally hardy disposition must have worked to keep him healthy.

In the autumn they were ordered to join General Wilkinson on the Sabine River. Troops went by keelboat up the Mississippi and Red Rivers to Natchitoches. After remaining there for a short time Davenport was sent on special orders with dispatches for General Wilkinson to Fort Adams on the Mississippi. With one other soldier, he set out to canoe down the Red River. Their canoe hit a snag and upset and the two soldiers narrowly escaped with their lives. They lost their canoe and all of their provisions and were forced to travel across country, over swamps, bayous, and sloughs with makeshift rafts. At night they were nearly devoured by mosquitoes and each took turn watching the fire and keeping a lookout for alligators. Food was scavenged from the forests and the two soldiers existed on berries and wild fruits until they reached Fort Adams several days later.[6]

When peace was made with the Spanish, General Wilkinson's troops returned to New Orleans where they began once again to fortify the city's defences against the Burr expedition, which was on its way down the river. Aaron Burr had had delusions of building his own empire between the Ohio River and Mexico, so New Orleans was under Martial Law awaiting the arrival of Burr and his forces. Davenport was assigned as orderly to General Wilkinson and, about the middle of December 1806, he was part of a guard detail sent to arrest Dr. Erich Bollman, Burr's confidential agent in Natchez.[7] Having been singled out of the ranks for these special details were signs that George Davenport had attracted the attention of his commanders.

New Orleans was a difficult place for the troops, not only because of the climate, but because the living conditions were poor and the supplies inadequate to sustain the army. Many soldiers were sick with dysentery and cholera and the death rate was high. Private Davenport took his turn, as did all able-bodied soldiers, at burial detail. This, according to Wilkie, was a dreadful duty. Graves could only be dug three feet down because of the high water table, and were constantly drained of water. Coffins were weighted down in order that they did not float before they could be covered. The shallow graves gave off a horrible stench in the intense heat, making for unbearable conditions in the camp. While stationed in New Orleans, Private George Davenport was promoted to Corporal.

By early March the Burr Affair was over. Burr had been arrested in January at Natchez but had jumped bail, fled toward the Spanish in Florida, but was intercepted on the way on 20 February 1807. Wilkinson congratulated his troops and announced that Burr was on his way to Washington City under military escort. No longer needed in New Orleans, the troops could be evacuated to other, more healthful locations such as Natchez and Fort Adams. Corporal Davenport's outfit, called

McClary's Company, was ordered to Ft. Adams on the 21 March 1807 under the command of Lt. Col. Jacob Kingsbury. The company marched upriver by land.[8]

Fort Adams was a palisade outpost about fifty miles downstream from Natchez and in the heart of Cherokee, Chickasaw, and Creek territory. It was located on a steep bank overlooking the Mississippi River at a place called Loftus Heights in the present state of Mississippi. In 1798, when the site was first chosen, General Wilkinson had envisioned that Fort Adams would serve as the center of all military activities on the lower Mississippi River, as an important supply point, and as an observation point of Spanish activities. But with the acquisition of the Louisiana Purchase and New Orleans, and the treaty agreements with the neighboring Indians, Fort Adams was no longer strategically located.

By the time Corporal Davenport arrived there, Fort Adams still served to maintain law and order in that area and protected the southern border of the Mississippi Territory from foreign invasion, but it was far from an important post. It was, however, a healthier location. The soldiers who had survived New Orleans and the march northward had a chance to recover their health, provided that rations could be procured. Healthy soldiers were ordered to construct the huts in which they were to live. These were not quickly thrown together, nor were they haphazardly built. Orders specified that they be sixteen feet square with a nine-foot pitch from floor to joist. There was to be a chimney for every two huts and piazzas six feet deep joining the huts together.[9]

Many soldiers survived the march only to die shortly after arrival. Not only were they still ill from the climate and conditions of the Deep South, they were also tired from the rigorous work of the army. They were also lacking good nutritious food and appropriate clothing. Daily rations, when available, consisted of one and a quarter pounds of beef or three quarters of a pound of pork, eighteen ounces of bread or flour, and a gill of liquor.[10] To that was added some salt, vinegar, soap, and a bit of candle. The problem on the frontier was availability. Government contractors were often late with their supplies and sometimes delivered rancid meat and moldy flour. By the time supplies arrived the soldiers were clothed in rags. Medical supplies, such as they were, were also in short supply. It is no wonder that so many of the First Infantry died during the years Davenport served.

Among those who died shortly after arriving in Mississippi were the commanders. Captain John McClary, commanding officer of Davenport's company, died 15 November 1807. He was buried the following day. Lieutenant Thomas Hunt died the following week.[11] Although casualty figures are not available, the description of the burial grounds at Fort Adams suggests that many soldiers succumbed to the rigors of frontier army life. Davenport was one of the fortunate ones.

For the next year Davenport's company was under the command of Captain William Swan, the company Quartermaster, and it is probable that Davenport worked in the quartermaster's store on a regular basis. His knowledge of how goods were moved, loaded, unloaded, and stored would have been useful to the quartermaster. Corporal George Davenport stood out as a promising young soldier and, he later related, he caught the attention of General William Henry Harrison, who appointed him as his personal orderly. In the 19th century world of the U.S. army, such attention brought rewards. It was the way to advancement, a chance that few men in the American Army were given.

While serving at Fort Adams, Davenport received the promotion he had been promised at recruitment. Morning Orders on the first of May 1808, noted that Corporal George Davenport was promoted to the rank of sergeant and was to be accorded all the privileges and respect of the rank. The following month, Swan and Lockwood companies were sent on detached duty to Fort Dearborn. There, on the Homichita River, they lived in tents and built a blockhouse in Choctaw Country. They remained there until August when they returned to Fort Adams to prepare for recruiting duty.

Because the First Infantry had lost so many men to unhealthy conditions and short rations, every available man of rank was sent on recruiting duty to fill the many vacancies in the regiment in the late fall, 1808. Sgt. Davenport accompanied Captains Owen and Swan to the East where the army had established recruiting stations.[12] They sailed from New

Orleans to Philadelphia, then to Baltimore, and finally to Winchester, Virginia.

Winchester was one of the places where army recruiters returned periodically. A long white weather-boarded house on Braddock Street was used as a recruiting station. The Army rented it from Jeremiah Bowling, an upholsterer and mattress-maker. One old Winchester resident later recalled the glorious days when he watched the soldiers after school. It was a source of amusement for him to see the soldiers "exercising and training their horses" and watching them "drilling, marching and countermarching to and from pegs stuck in the ground." Thirty some years later he could still remember their names: Major Joseph Kean, Simon Owen, Angus McDonald, and Hunter Holmes.[13] Over the course of the year a friendship between Sergeant Davenport and Jeremiah Bowling developed. Eventually they would be brothers-in-law.

While Captain Owens maintained the primary recruiting station in Winchester, his subordinates were assigned to temporary locations in the near vicinity. Captain Swan was sent to Washington City; others to Berryville, Virginia. Recruiting was difficult in peacetime and the soldiers depended on a good show, with a little monetary incentive, to arouse interest in the army. One soldier recalled that good music, handsome uniforms, and soldierly deportment were essential ingredients for success, but just as important were the promises of food, shelter, and clothing.[14]

Recruits of the 1st U.S. Infantry rendezvoused in Winchester. There they were inspected for their health and age requirements, clothed, armed, and equipped, and then put on drill. They remained at the central recruiting station until the rank and file of the First were filled. Peacetime recruiting was exceedingly slow work. In 15 months they managed to recruit only 24 men. Some months went by without a single new recruit. The recruiting soldiers were gone for over a year before they were ordered back to regular duty.[15]   George Davenport remained in Winchester until the spring of 1810 when he was ordered to join his company, which was then stationed at Bellefontaine Barracks north of St. Louis. Not long after he returned, his term of duty expired and he was discharged from the army on the 23rd of October 1810. Four weeks later, on the 18th of

November, Sgt. George Davenport reenlisted for a second five-year stint in the army. He was then 26 years old. He remained at Bellefontaine for the next four years.

Life at Bellefontaine must have been more routine, and perhaps easier if not more boring, than Davenport had previously experienced. The post had been built several years before, and since it was located so near St. Louis, Bellefontaine had many luxuries that most outposts did not have. Soldiers assigned there had easy access to a wide variety of goods provided by several sutlers and military stores allowed to operate near the garrison. St. Louis had been settled for such a long time that it no longer seemed like an outpost, nor was there a serious threat of Indian attacks. There were log barracks, an empty fur factory, which had closed two years before, an arsenal, and a magazine of well-seasoned timber. It was probably the first real housing Davenport had seen outside of recruiting duty since he enlisted.

During the four years George was stationed there, Bellefontaine served as the headquarters of the Louisiana Department of the Army and was used as a staging area for many outposts on the frontier, including Forts Madison, Massac, Osage, and Vincennes. The routine, however, was the same as at all frontier posts. Drums beat the hourly duty and the men performed the usual duties and job details of army life. They rose at six a.m. and had an hour for roll call, washing, shaving, and cleaning the barracks before breakfast call at seven. Mornings were spent policing the garrison, chopping and hauling wood, working in the kitchens, the gardens, at the trading post, and elsewhere on the post. At 12:30 p.m. the men returned to the barracks and prepared for dinner. Afternoon work parties began at 1:30 pm and worked until 5 p.m. Supper call was at 6 p.m. and at 7:30 p.m. the Drummer called the companies together for evening parade. At 8 p.m. the evening gun was fired, the flag was lowered, and the final company roll call was made. Tattoo was at 9 p.m. and all soldiers, except those with evening passes, were expected to be in their barracks. Then, candles and lamps were extinguished for lights out. Twice a day, each man was issued half a gill or about two ounces of whiskey.[16]

Periodically, special orders were issued and small companies of men were sent into the interior to deal with Indian troubles.

As sergeant, George Davenport earned the princely sum of $12 a month. In addition he was issued clothing and rations. Rations were determined by regulations specified by the War Department and provided by government contractors who bid annually for the right to provide beef, pork, flour, salt, and vinegar to the troops at various posts. Clothing for each soldier was distributed at various times, usually on a seasonal basis, and accounted for scrupulously. The Company Book of Captain Simon Owens charts the clothing distributed to each man in Davenport's company between November 1810 and August 1814. This book shows that George Devonport (sic) was issued the following items: 5 complete hats, 3 stocks and collars, 3 coats, 2 vests, 17 shirts, 16 pairs of shoes, 9 pairs of stockings, 7 pairs of socks, 8 sets of linens, 5 sets of woolen, 4 frocks, 4 trowsers (sic), 4 gaiters, 4 blankets, 1 knapsack, no epaulets, and 1 ??? case.[17]

In the spring of 1812, Captain Owens Company was sent up the Mississippi to an island just below the mouth of the Illinois River. Here the soldiers were ordered to build temporary fortifications to protect St. Louis and the nearby settlements from Indian attacks. They remained there until sometime in early fall when they joined Governor Benjamin Howard of Missouri Territory in his expedition against the Potawatomie on the Illinois River at Peoria Lake. The regular troops, under the command of Lt. Col. Robert Nichols, proceeded by water and were met at Peoria Lake by the rangers and volunteer militia who had arrived by land. Their purpose was to subdue the hostile Indians, build a strong garrison to impress the Indians of the strength of the United States, and to interrupt the trading channels of the British fur traders in the Mississippi Valley. The garrison was called Fort Clark, in honor of General George Rogers Clark of Revolutionary War fame. None of the troops met Indian resistance on the way and so they began to build a blockhouse on a high hill overlooking the prairie. It was protected with a double row of logs or pickets around which was dug a ditch.[18] It was while digging a well for fresh water when Davenport had one of the most harrowing escapades of his military career.

While searching for something to draw up the water from the well, Davenport suggested to his superior officer that a grapevine would work on the sweep. He had noticed some wild grapes growing in the woods nearby and took a fellow soldier with him to cut them. While trimming the vines they heard a strange sound and started for the fort. When they reached the edge of the forest, Davenport climbed a tree to see across the prairie towards the blockhouse and, to his horror, saw the prairie filled with Indians. As quickly as they could, he and his fellow soldier ran along the lakeshore trying to reach the blockhouse before they were discovered. They were not halfway to the fort when the battle began, but were unable to reach the blockhouse because the Indians were nearer than they were. They next determined to run to the gunboats on the lake. When they were about halfway to the boats, the Indians discovered them and began firing at them. The men on the boats became alarmed and pushed off from the shore. Fortunately, one of the boats grounded on the sand and Davenport and his fellow soldier were able to reach it. Wading into the water, George and his fellow soldier put their shoulders to the bow and pushed it into deeper water. All this time the Indians were firing at them and balls were whizzing by their heads. Soon they were able to get on board and under cover. Davenport, however, had had the scare of his career and wanted revenge. He pointed a small cannon at the Indians and fired, but the gun misfired. While he hunted for a primer someone aimed the gun too high and when the match was applied the cannon went off with a tremendous explosion. The muzzle of the gun had been elevated above the porthole and when it went off, the whole load struck the side of the boat. Fortunately, no one in the boat was hurt and the battle was soon over and the Indians retreated.

The fort was completed in September and was fortified without incidence during the fall. About the first of December, the Potawatomie sent a large party with a flag of truce to suggest a meeting with the commanding officer in council. At the agreed upon time about forty Chiefs and Braves under the leadership of the principal chief, old Black

Partridge, met with the commanding officer and other officers of the post. After smoking the pipe together, the Indians expressed their wish to be friends with the Americans, to stop fighting, and to make a treaty of peace with them. Since the officers at the post had no orders or authority to treat with the Indians, the commanding officer suggested that they send a delegation to General William Clark, the Superintendent of Indian Affairs, at St. Louis. Thirteen principal men and one woman were selected to go to St. Louis and the commanding officer chose George Davenport and four other soldiers to escort the Indians to St. Louis.

The party started down river in a piroque, but soon ice halted their progress and they were then forced to go by land. Each took a small amount of their provisions and stored the rest in a hollow tree. Included with their provisions was a small keg of whiskey. After giving each man a dram, they intended to hide it for their return trip, but Black Partridge insisted that they drink the whole keg. Davenport would not let them and ordered them to continue their journey, hiding the keg after the others had moved on. Later, after joining the others, he made certain that no one could go back to look for the keg. At night he positioned their camp so that no one could escape without the soldiers' knowing. They travelled for two or three days when they spotted smoke on the prairies. The Potawatomie thought it was a war party of Sauk and were certain that they would all be murdered if discovered. To avoid danger, they decided to travel near the timber away from the prairie and to make no fires at night.

As they neared the Mississippi River, the Indians were increasingly concerned about being discovered by the Illinois Rangers, who were guarding the settlement areas against Indian attacks. To help calm the Indians' fears, the soldiers placed their hats and coats on poles at night so that any Rangers who happened upon them would know that there were white men present. Finally, they reached St. Louis where they reported to General Clark.

During their visit General Clark asked Sergeant Davenport how his party had been able to reach St. Louis without being seen by the Rangers who were under orders to guard the frontier against surprise attacks. Davenport replied that they had seen nothing of the Rangers on the way nor seen any sign that Rangers had been to the mouth of the Illinois River. Some Rangers who overheard his remarks swore that they would show "whether there were Rangers on the lookout or not." [19] As a result, Davenport and his soldiers and the party of Indians hugged the Missouri bank of the river on the way back to Peoria Lake for fear that the Rangers would fire upon them.

After this incident Davenport returned to Bellefontaine until the summer of 1814 when the First Regiment was ordered to the Erie frontier to join General Brown. The War of 1812 had started and many western troops were ordered east. They travelled on keelboats down the Mississippi, then up the Ohio to Pittsburgh. From there they marched over the mountains until they reached Erie, Pennsylvania. There they sailed to Fort Erie, arriving just in time to participate in the hottest part of the Battle of Lundy's Lane. It was during this battle that Davenport picked up his Glengarian musket on the battlefield, a souvenir he treasured throughout his life. After the battle he remained at Fort Erie for a time, serving on picket duty much of the time. In October much of his company, including Davenport himself, spent about a month in the Williamsville (New York) Hospital recovering from battle fatigue and dysentery.[20]

When rested and recovered, Davenport was sent on special assignment to Pittsburgh to serve General Daniel Bissell who was preparing for an expedition against the Indians in the Mississippi Valley. Davenport was working as an orderly sergeant, involved with outfitting the expedition and arranging transportation for the troops. What his specific duties were are not known, but he maintained in later years that, should the war have continued, he would have been promoted. "I received an order and accompanied General Bissell's staff to Pittsburgh, to be in readiness to join the troops ordered for a campaign in the Upper Mississippi in the spring (1815), at which time I was to receive a commission." Service under General Bissell did not agree with him. Shortly after he arrived in Pittsburgh he was charged with insubordination and reduced to private.[21] Before he could be reinstated to sergeant, peace was declared and he was ordered back to Bellefontaine where, like most of his fellow soldiers, he was dropped from the muster rolls on 9 June 1815.

Since his arrival in America, George Davenport had crisscrossed the United States between the Atlantic coast and the Mississippi river, New Orleans and the Canadian border. He had floated rivers, sailed on the Great Lakes, marched across mountains, and trudged through swamps, bayous and prairies. He fought the Spanish in Arkansas, the Indians in the Upper Mississippi Valley, and the British in the Erie Valley. He had more adventures than most people could expect to have in one lifetime. More than once he had cheated death. He had also had ten years of good work experience, ten years of building blockhouses and soldiers' quarters, digging wells, repairing roads, ten years of drilling, marching, and army rations. He had also had ten years of subordination, of following someone else's orders, and threats of the harshest punishment when he didn't. It was time to be on his own, to be his own boss.

There were rumors about what would happen once the treaty had been hammered out, but when the cutbacks came, the First U.S. Infantry was entirely eliminated and Davenport was out of the Army. What was left of the First became the Third United States Infantry and sent to negotiate the end of the war with the Mississippi Valley Indians. Many of his friends returned to their former homes and family ties, but George Davenport did not wish to return to England.

Twice before George Davenport had found himself in similar circumstances. Both times he had turned to the army, but the army was no longer an option. What is certain is that he found work with the government contractor, James Morrison of Lexington, Kentucky.

That summer, the Army determined that three more forts would be built deep into Indian Country in the Upper Mississippi River Valley. Morrison held the contract to supply the army with rations in Indiana, Illinois, and Missouri Territories and his agent in St. Louis, George Wilson, was busy with preparations for the army expedition into Indian Country on the upper Mississippi river. The expedition was set to leave Bellefontaine Barracks in early September.[22]

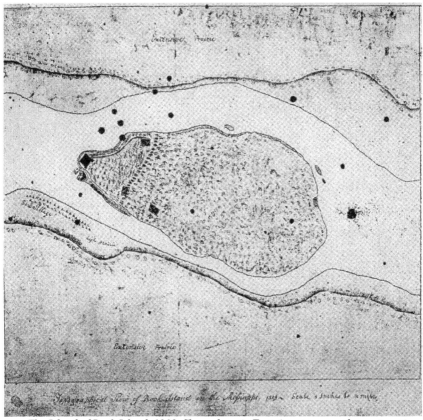

The Island of Rock Island, 1819. Shown here is Fort Armstrong on the western tip of the island, the Davenport house on the north shore and the fence line that separated the cleared area of the fort from the natural vegetation of the rest of the island. The main channel of the Mississippi River is shown on the north side of the island and runs from east to west past the island. The square on the south side of the island may be the house of trader Antoine Gokey. Drawn by John Anderson, Major M. Marston Report, 10 September1819

CHAPTER THREE:

FRONTIER OUTPOST

GEORGE DAVENPORT'S YEARS in the American army had prepared him for frontier conditions. He had seen first hand how fiercely the Potawatomie Indians fought the Americans while at Peoria Lake, and nothing had changed with the ending of war. The Sauk and Mesquakie were still strongly allied with the British and actively hostile to American settlers who had settled in Indian Country. So, too, were the Ho Chunk. The atmosphere was far from peaceful as Davenport prepared to go deep into Indian country in the Mississippi Valley with the Army.

That summer, the summer of 1815, the Indians at Rock River were dancing with American and French scalps. Indian Agent Nicholas Boilvin, who was heading for Prairie du Chien with his family, remained at Rock River for three days observing their dances and enduring insults and threats. Without presents to appease the angry braves, Boilvin was in a difficult position. Every Indian he met expressed a firm intention of keeping the land. At Prairie du Chien, Boilvin was met by the Ho Chunk, or Winnebago, reputedly the most savage of the nations, and was surprised by their compliant attitude. They were thankful for peace and expressed hope that the President of the United States would keep his promises to their people. Without supplies to give them, Boilvin realized that in a few months time ten thousand Indians, who had had no chance to raise corn during the late war, would be travelling to Fort Drummond to receive hunting supplies and food from the British Government. If Boilvin had any hope of dispelling the Ho Chunk's belief that there was deceit on the part of the American government, he would need supplies in the spring. Established American forts with their associated trading posts in the Mississippi valley would, hopefully, answer that need.[1]

As the Army prepared to build those posts, emissaries travelled throughout the valley spreading the news of peace and inviting all the nations to gather at Portage des Sioux, just north of St. Louis, for peace negotiations in early July. The Treaty of Ghent, which ended the War of 1812 in 1814, had made no provision for these British allies, so it was the United States that notified all the Indian nations in the Illinois country that they, too, had lost the war.

Many Indian nations were still in a war-like mood and hardly a week went by when some attack or murder by Indians was not reported in the St. Louis newspapers. Most tribes received their invitation to treat with the Americans "with sullen acquiescence or open hostility." Some flatly refused to come. The Sauk, in particular, expressed open hostility. They were quoted as saying "If the Americans wish to make a treaty they must send the commissioners to us at Rock river to treat; we can live without treaties, nor will we suffer an American soldier to ascend the Mississippi: traders may come and they shall be well received, &." [2]

About forty to fifty Sauk and Mesquakie finally did attend the gathering, albeit grudgingly. The Missouri Gazette reported that they " frowned and strutted about with the most insufferable impudence."[3] Thomas Forsyth, Indian Agent of Missouri, called them "dastardly," "cowardly," and full of duplicity, and, in their party of fifty or sixty warriors, only one chief was among them and he had no authority to sign any agreements. After a harsh talk by Superintendent William Clark and a thirty-day deadline to return with enough head chiefs to negotiate, the Sauk and Mesquakie party left during the night.[3]

Between July 18 and October 28, 1815, thirteen separate agreements with other tribes were concluded and signed. With the exception of the Ho Chunk, whose chiefs were at Mackinac and could not negotiate, only the Sauk and Mesquakie of Rock River refused the terms of peace that summer. Richard Graham observed that the Sauk were among "the wildest & most untracticable (sic) savages in the world – whose disposition bears a strong resemblance to the Wolf." He had doubts about being able to civilize them as he thought they were too concerned with other manners. Indeed, Graham wrote, if any innovation is made in their habits & manners, it must be a gradual one & work itself imperceptibly on them – a few may be found who may be disposed to agriculture & a fixed life – and through them the advantages of civilization may reach others." [4] The peace conference continued the following summer.

Because of their refusal to negotiate peace, the commissioners recommended that a fort be built near the Sauk villages for the purpose of subduing them. In fact, the Government plan called for three forts to be built in Indian Territory, which is where George Davenport was headed, as agent of the Government Contractor James Morrison of Lexington, Kentucky. Morrison was an experienced contractor, having been in the business for many years before the War of 1812, providing rations to the forts in the Indiana, Illinois, and Missouri Territories. Morrison's agents also established commissary and sutling stores near the posts they served, for which they were paid $27-30 per month.[5]

Until 1818, the business of feeding the frontier army was the responsibility of independent contractors, who annually submitted bids to Congress to supply the army with food. Contracts were awarded to the lowest-bidding independent contractor. In 1815, the contract was awarded to James Morrison, and George Davenport was hired to bring eight keelboats, manned by 160 French Canadians, and loaded with barrels of provisions into Indian Country with army rations. Because the frontier posts were so far from cities and often isolated during the winter months, the army required the contractor, through his agents like George Davenport, to keep a six-month supply of rations at all times. Each ration consisted of 18 ounces flour, 3/4 pound of pork or 1 and 1/4 pounds of beef, 1 gill of whiskey, and salt. For every 100 rations, the agent also supplied 4 quarts vinegar, 2 quarts salt, 1 and 1/2 pounds candles and 4 pounds soap. Officers received two to six rations per day, depending on rank. Non-commissioned officers, enlisted men, and officers' servants received one ration per day. At Fort Armstrong, the required six-month supply in 1816 amounted to 30,000 rations. That translated to about 22,500 pounds of pork, (usually salted and packed in barrels), 15,000 pounds of flour, 3,750 gallons of whiskey, 300 gallons of vinegar, 150 gallons of salt, 450 pounds of candles, and 1,200 pounds of soap. The beef, in the form of live cattle, were driven overland from Louisville and did not arrive at Rock Island until the following summer (1816).[6]

As soon as the Army's intentions were known, George Wilson began collecting the components of the rations and hiring hands to transport the rations into Indian Country. When exactly George Davenport was hired is not certain, but surely he was engaged soon after the expedition was announced, as the army's target date for leaving St. Louis was the tenth of October 1815.[7]   Morrison and Company had also been engaged in supplying the food for the treaty negotiations held at Portage des Sioux.

The expedition was much like an invasion into Indian Country, more or less organized around the establishment of the frontier forts. The large force of soldiers all the necessary support followers of sutlers and clerks, contractors and boatmen, laundresses, and their families; government agencies such as the Indian agents and subagents, blacksmiths, gunsmiths, and interpreters; the factors, sub-factors and clerks for the fur factories; independent traders with their entourage; and others intent on promoting their own special interests. The frontier fort would provide a home for many of these people, protection for those who didn't live there in times of need, and trading opportunities for the Indians. The quantity of rations estimated for this expedition was enormous: 1600 - 1800 barrels of flour, upward of 800 head of beef, eight to nine thousand gallons of whiskey, and an undetermined number of hogs and salt.[8] They were estimated to serve the troops through the winter when the river would be frozen.

Davenport and his boatmen were assigned to the combined expedition of Rifle Regiment and the Eighth Infantry under the command of Colonel Robert C. Nicholas. The expedition left St. Louis for the Upper Mississippi on schedule. They travelled in keelboats, each 70 feet long and propelled by twelve men, six on each side, who pushed the boats upstream with poles. When the wind was favorable, sails helped propel the boats. They averaged about twenty miles each day. By mid-November, the expedition had progressed as far as the mouth of the Des Moines River when ice on the river forced them to make camp, called Cantonment Davis, for the winter. Winter came early that year and was colder than usual.[9]

At Cantonment Davis the expedition began preparing for the winter, building log huts for the men to live in as well as safe storage areas for the provisions. The men had to put poles in the ground and cover them with green cowhides, on account of the lateness of the season. When the hides dried, they made "tolerably warm houses." Army Sutler John Cleves Symmes spent nearly a month living with his two assistants on the boat that housed their supplies until his cabins were finished about the middle of December. His letters to his wife, Marianne, who remained at Bellefontaine with their two children, provide some hints of what life was like. According to Symmes, he and his men were living very plain, like careless bachelors, hardly addressing their own discomforts because there was so much work to do. Mr. Davenport, he wrote, helped when his own duties permitted and was not otherwise engaged. According to Symmes, Davenport was methodical and transacted business "with a good deal of facility." Davenport supplied them with milk, good beef, venison, and bread. Symmes' business was brisk when he opened his store, selling a thousand dollars worth of tobacco, sugar, and flour in three days. Symmes did not mention whether they traded with any Indians during their time at Cantonment Davis, but he was legally licensed to trade with the "Fox on the West side of the Mississippi and with the Sioux who had already treated with the U.S. Government."[10]

Various traders and other personnel, who travelled back and forth between the cantonment and St. Louis that winter, kept communication lines open and reported the abundance of the Indian Country. Without cattle, or beef supplies that would arrive in the spring, the soldiers relied on hunting and fishing. The soldiers reported catching 7000 pounds of catfish in one day, with several catfish weighing 100 pounds or more. Deer were also plentiful and the soldiers feasted on venison.[11]

On the 1st of April (1816), when the ice in the river was expected to break, Brevet Brigadier General Thomas A. Smith, commander of the Ninth Department of Southern Division, arrived at Cantonment Davis to get the expedition moving northward. One company remained nearby on the east bank of the Mississippi to begin building Fort Edwards. The rest of the troops, under Colonel William Lawrence of the Rifle Regiment, proceeded upriver to the mouth of the Rock River to build Fort Armstrong. They expected to remain until the end of September when the "works" were to be completed. The third company travelled up the river to Prairie du Chien to establish Fort Crawford.[12]

The three forts functioned as one extended communication chain between the upper river valley and St. Louis. Fort Edwards was a small fort designed to house one company of troops. Built high on the bluff overlooking the Mississippi River, it was an ideal location to patrol for foreign traders, because it was an established rendezvous point for the Sauk and Mesquakie who hunted in the Des Moines River and Iowa River Valleys. Fort Crawford at Prairie du Chien was a government factory, designed to serve as a trading post for the region, as the location had been a trading center since 1671. The factor assigned there, John Johnson, had served at Fort Madison during the War of 1812 and was experienced in Indian Territory. Fort Armstrong, located about half way between the two forts, was the designated arms depot. It was located on the lower end of Rock Island, just three miles from Saukenuk, the largest Indian village known at the time.

Saukenuk was a city of about 6,000 Sauk, laid out much like eastern cities with street and alleys, and approximately 700 dwellings. There were two public squares, a council house in the center of the town, and a palisade surrounding the town with gates for entrances. Nearby were cornfields and pastures for their horses. With the obvious signs that the U. S. Government meant what it said when it threatened to establish a fort near them, the Sauk and Mesquakie reluctantly concluded to negotiate peace. During the winter they had sent emissaries to St. Louis to tell Governor Clark they were ready to talk. Just as the soldiers approached Rock Island, a delegation of Sauk and Mesquakie descended the river to St. Louis to make their peace with the United States, which was completed on May 13, 1816, three days after the soldiers arrived on Rock Island. The terms were much like the treaties signed by other tribes the previous year with a few added conditions imposed as penalty for their delay.[13] Although he would later claim not to have signed, it should be noted that one of the signers of this treaty was Black Hawk.

The troops arrived at Rock Island on the 10th of May and immediately began to cut trees for building. When the Sauk and Mesquakie returned to their village, they thought building a fort rather contradictory to the peace treaty they had just signed in St. Louis. To Black Hawk and his warriors this seemed "to prepare for war in time of peace," and sent a pipe to the Ho Chunk, Ottawa, and Chippewa asking them to join with the Sauk and Mesquakie in preventing the erection of the fort and driving the Americans from their country. In later years Black Hawk did not remember that his people protested the building of the fort, but the Missouri Gazette reported that the Indian chiefs warned of trouble, and that they "could not be responsible for the conduct of their young warriors." Indian Agent Charles Jouette at Chicago noted that the Sauk had gone to the British to complain of American encroachments. General Smith, however, was not dissuaded and the fort construction continued.[14]

May was a time of much activity in Saukenuk, the month of the Planting Moon. During this time the men could usually be found relaxing and trading stories after a hard winter of hunting. The women opened their caches of corn and other provisions which they had stored through the winter and were busy repairing their lodges and readying the fields for planting when the lookouts, seated on platforms in the trees, spotted eight soldiers' keelboats moving up the Mississippi toward their villages. Hardly before the runners could reach Saukenuk with the news, the forests rang with the sounds of military drums and burly voices of soldiers landing on a large island opposite one of their villages. In later years Black Hawk only remembered the noise of the soldiers. That noise, he said, had driven away their Great Spirit. Without doubt, he reasoned, only a "Bad Spirit" would replace it.[15]

Although the Indians saw only a band of noisy soldiers in 1816, they were, in fact, heralds of a greater transformation that would all but obliterate the ancestral traditions of the tribes. New peoples, thousands of them, were soon to follow the Indian trails to Rock Island and with them would come new attitudes and new values that would conflict with the old and established ways of the ancient peoples. They would shape the land to their own needs and ideas of how the land should be owned and how it could be made productive. But for now, with only 79 men at Fort Armstrong and 84 at Fort Edwards, the military was greatly outnumbered and posed no viable threat to the native people. Although outnumbered, the troops were well armed. Besides axes and mauls for building, they had one battering cannon, five field cannons (both twelve- and six-pounders), and seven howitzers.[16] The fort's design and location also helped to protect them.

Fort Armstrong was built much like forts of an earlier era with blockhouses and palisades. It was perched on a perpendicular bank of limestone, about twenty-five feet in height, on the western tip of the island. According to Major Morrell Marston, the structure was about 270 feet square, with three blockhouses, mounting three six-pounders. The barracks were constructed of hewn timber, and sufficiently extensive to quarter three companies. The magazine was made of stone and well built. The commanding officer's quarters were located in a two-story building 28 feet in length, with wings of one story, fifteen feet in length, and piazzas built in front and rear. Fresh water was supplied by a spring about 100 yards from the garrison. Provisions would come regularly from St. Louis.[17]

George Davenport supervised building the storehouse, where the rations were safe from the elements, insects, and theft by Indians and soldiers. Then, two cabins were constructed: one for a bake house, the other for George Davenport and his family who were soon to arrive. In addition to storage, Davenport kept track of the shifting numbers of military men and ordered additional supplies from St. Louis. It was a complicated business and the lives of the soldiers so far from the source of provisions were dependent on his attention to their needs.

Within a month of Davenport's arrival on Rock Island, James Morrison's contract expired and the contract for the next year, 1816 - 1817, was awarded to a different Morrison, William Morrison of Kaskaskia. There is some evidence from William Morrison's ledger accounts that George Davenport was his agent at Fort Armstrong. What Davenport might have earned for this job is not known. James Morrison's agents (of Lexington, Kentucky) were paid $27 per month (or $340 annually), but agents of William Morrison (of Kaskaskia) were paid as little as $250 for the year.[18]

Who owned the post store that had been opened by George Davenport is also unknown although Davenport continued his store-keeping activities after his services as contractor's agent were no longer needed. In such a remote location a civilian-operated store was immensely useful to the army and potentially lucrative. Besides being a healthy competition for the army sutler, the contractor's store offered different goods like coffee and tea, eggs and cheese, dried fruits, tobacco and wine. These foods supplemented the soldiers' rations and were not readily available so deep in Indian country. Such independent shops were usually encouraged by post commanders in order to keep the prices competitive for the soldiers. [19]

The specifics of Davenport's early store business are few, but through a quirky chain of events that resulted in a published account of a feud between two of the officers in charge, we get a glimpse of Davenport's post store business on the Island.

In August of 1819, recruits of the Fifth Infantry and their supply boats were moving toward the St. Peters' river in Minnesota to establish a new fort there. They stopped at Rock Island for a few days of rest before travelling farther and camped just outside the walls of Fort Armstrong. Three detachments of recruits were under the leadership of Recruiting Officers Captain Peter Pelham, 2nd Lt. William G. Oliver, and Lt. William Downey and had left Bellefontaine Barracks well supplied. But by the time they had reached Clarksville, they were destitute of tobacco and sent someone to purchase a supply there. By the time they reached Rock Island, they were again in need of supplies. Taking advantage of Davenport's store, they bought supplies of tobacco, coffee, and sundry other goods for the duration of their journey. They also arranged for supplies of sugar, coffee, and tobacco from the store to be delivered to the St. Peters later in the fall. A list of names of all who purchased goods and the amounts they owed George Davenport has survived in court records and the accompanying record of testimony provided at the trial of one of their captains offers some insight into the difficulty in procuring payment from military personnel.

In all, one hundred and five men and women purchased goods on 5 August 1819. All purchases, including fifty-six pounds of tobacco and thirty-four pounds of coffee that were to be delivered in October, were sold on credit with the promise of payment whenever the paymaster next arrived at Fort Snelling. The charged amounts ranged from fifty cents to $4.75 and totalled $349.00. Captain Pelham, however, could not promise to collect money from all the men, because he knew that by the time they were paid, the men would be scattered to other posts. Collection of monies for their debts, then, would be dependent on other officers and it appears that Davenport received most, but not all that was due him. Some men were either discharged, transferred to other posts, or had died by the time the regimental paymaster arrived at the fort St. Peter's River the following January. In all thirty-one of the one hundred and five accounts were never collected; twelve of them because the men had died.[20]

The collection of the Fort Snelling accounts illustrates the risks involved with the credit system. At frontier outposts such as Fort

Armstrong, the paymaster personally brought the payroll, but his arrival was unpredictable and irregular. Sometimes the soldiers were not paid for six months. The army allowed the sutler and other post merchants to sell on credit and then sit at the pay table to collect their debts from the soldier's pay. The Army set the Interest rates and did not allow the storekeeper to extend more credit than the soldier's pay. Uncollectable debts was not unusual for the frontier army storekeeper and one reason why frontier goods were so expensive.[21]

Davenport should have had his stores and living quarters arranged by the time his family arrived in the summer of 1816, although the living quarters may have been rather rough and temporary. Davenport could easily have apprised Mrs. Davenport of the existing conditions on the island, so that she could bring much-needed supplies from St. Louis with her, just as Army Sutler Symmes' wife Marianne had done.

As the fort took shape, the land began to yield to a new order. The west end of the island was cleared of shrubs, trees and undergrowth and, under Davenport's supervision, storage and food facilities had been constructed. Somewhere near Davenport's cabin were two ovens for baking bread built by an old French baker named Baptiste LaMott. The construction methods used by LaMott were unlike anything Susan Lewis had seen before and she recalled them in detail. The ovens were prepared in the following way:

[LaMott] placed twelve blocks of wood endwise in the ground, and then placed small hewn logs upon the blocks for a bed for the ovens. Upon this bed he put about sixteen inches of caten clay, made by mixing cut grass with the clay, smoothing the surface over with clay alone. While the clay was drying, he went into the woods and cut hickory poles which he formed the arch for the ovens, placing poles close together, with each end set firmly in the bed of clay. He then spread over the poles, evenly, wet grass, and then put on layer after layer of ctaten clay, giving time for each layer to dry, pursuing this until the walls of his ovens were about twelve inches in thickness, and leaving an opening in one end for a door. After the walls were thoroughly dry, he built a slow fire in the ovens and burnt out the grass and poles. Then the ovens were ready for use. This

mode of building bake ovens, without lime, stone, or brick, was something
new to most of those present.[22]

Brigadier General Smith's correspondence with Fort Armstrong
focused on the problems with the contractor in getting sufficient supplies
to the troops on the Upper Mississippi, with problems in communication
from all the outposts, and in keeping within the budget for erecting the
post. The first drove of cattle, about 500 head from Kentucky, arrived in
August of 1816. This was the last year, according to Susan Lewis, that
bison were seen on Rock Island, putting the cattle at risk from the Indians.
Occasionally, Sauk and Mesquakie stole cattle from the fort's pastures, a
common problem in Indian country. The contractor's agent at Prairie du
Chien reported that in July Indians had led off and slaughtered 69 head
of cattle. Contractor William Morrison estimated that these beeves would
have provided a five-month supply of rations for Fort Crawford. At Fort
Armstrong twenty-one fat cattle, which would have made approximately
11,340 rations, had been stolen from Davenport's pasture and found in
the possession of the Rock River Indians. Horses were stolen at Fort
Clark. Government surveyors were roughed up a little by Indians, either
Sauk, Mesquakie, or Ho Chunk, but there is no evidence that the soldiers
at any of the forts did more than increase their practice time on the
cannons and strengthen their guard.[23]

Brigadier General Smith was of the opinion that the Sauk and
Mesquakie would attack if they ever found the troops off-guard or
unprepared. Only fear, he believed, would keep them from attacking, not
friendship. He ordered the western tip of the island cleared in order to
reduce the chance of a surprise attack by hostile Indians. Though at first
hostile, by mid-summer the Indians seemed to be reconciled to the
American soldiers, who bribed their friendship by inviting them to dance
and giving them presents. A few days after one such present-giving event,
the soldiers were out cutting timber when a large party of warriors headed
by Ne-ha-le-quat came to the island in canoes. They landed on the north
shore, and danced up to the entrance of the encampment, wanting to
dance for the commander. About the same time someone discovered
another group of warriors, led by Keokuk, approaching the south side of

the island. The bugle was sounded to recall the men from the woods, the cannon moved to the entrance, and all the men stood ready to fire their weapons. The quick action of the colonel saved the encampment from surprise and massacre.[2]

Increasingly, there were friendly relationships between the new inhabitants of the island and the Sauk and the Mesquakie. The Indians brought some of their surplus sweet corn, pumpkins, and beans to the Davenports and to the soldiers who had had no opportunity to raise any food of their own that year. The food was welcome, adding to the meager food supply of army rations, especially for those engaged in the hard work of felling trees, hewing logs, and constructing a defense facility. The Ho Chunk were a bigger threat than the Sauk and Mesquakie and were often incited against the Americans by British traders in the area. Fort Armstrong, however, was without an interpreter and unable to communicate with them. Major Marston called them the most lawless set of beings in the world.

During the first few years, then, the atmosphere in the Upper Mississippi Valley was one of studied peacefulness. Underlying the serenity, however, was an undercurrent of anxiety, but no overt action against the fort was ever made. The soldiers pursued their construction activities, and by July 1817, the fort was nearly finished, and attention was given to the interiors. Brigadier General Smith gave instructions for the completion of the officer's quarters and furniture for the soldiers' barracks. The barracks' furniture was made according to regulations. Wooden bunks, sleeping two soldiers per bunk, were constructed. The soldiers would each be issued blankets and forty-four pounds of straw every month for their bed ticks. Comfort on the frontier was relative, usually relative to the bunkmate.[25] The officer's quarters were more spacious and home-like, and the commandant's quarters were the best that could be found on the frontier. By the middle of August, Smith was complementing Major Willoughby Morgan on the handsome and elegant commandant's quarters that had been completed and finished off.

That first summer, according to many sources, Davenport purchased lead from the Sauk and Mesquakie and took a boatload of lead to St.

Louis. Lead was an important product for the Sauk and Mesquakie economy. James Lockwood, who visited the Upper Mississippi Valley in 1815 looking for a suitable place to build a sawmill, noted that traders from St. Louis often took lead in payment for goods bought by the Indians. Indian Agent Nicholas Boilvin had reported that the Mesquakie had nearly given up the chase (hunt) in order to produce nearly 400,000 pounds of lead in 1810, but since the death of Julien Dubuque that year, the tribes had not had an outlet for their lead. During the war years there had not been many buyers for this commodity, so with the war over, the tribes were eager to trade their lead for supplies. Mining the lead was done by hand, using tools such as hoes, shovels, pick-axes, and crowbars that were obtained from traders. According to Schoolcraft who visited the mines in 1820, the tribes were paid a rate of two dollars for a hundred and twenty pounds. The traders then ferried the lead to St. Louis.[26]

It is not clear under whose direction George Davenport initiated this trade in lead. It is doubtful that he would have attempted to trade on his own, and would have needed a good boat for the task. Davenport's boss for 1816 - 1817, Government Contractor William Morrison of Kaskaskia, had previously inquired about a lease of the lead mines, but not much is known about Morrison's business in lead. It is possible that Morrison had directed Davenport to investigate the prospects of establishing trade in the lead district on the Upper Mississippi. Or, direction may have come from Colonel Willoughby Morgan, commander of Fort Armstrong, in order to establish relations with the local Sauk and promote civilizing the tribes. It was generally believed at the time that, as the tribes grew to know the Americans, their customs and manners, they would forego their hunts, live in fixed villages, and take up agriculture and domestic arts. Rather than trying to force the tribes to change their traditions, it was believed by many who knew the Indian customs and beliefs that a better approach would be by example. A man like Davenport was needed to set good examples. Regardless of whose direction he was following, this first boatload was an important step in establishing Davenport in the Indian Trade.[27]

During the second summer on the island, the fort's relationship with the local Indians was still uneasy. Late in August, a large gathering of Sauk, Mesquakie, Ho Chunk, Kickapoo, and Potawatomie assembled near the fort. The fort's commander, Major Willoughby Morgan, learned that they intended to attack the Sioux after their corn had been planted. A party of braves went to Mackinac for a supply of gunpowder for that purpose, but Major Morgan was not convinced that they really intended to attack the Sioux. Morgan's efforts to communicate directly with the Indians were greatly hampered by his lack of an interpreter and he wrote to Brigadier General Smith that he was desperately in need of one, as well as an Indian Agent on site to help with mediation. Smith responded with permission to hire an interpreter but it was too late in the season to hire one, since all qualified persons in the French community of the Portage had gone already.[28] Without an interpreter or Indian Agent, Morgan was powerless to dissuade the Sauk and Fox from attacking their enemies.

Rumors that British subjects had established trading houses at Rock River and were leading the Indians in massacres of women and children was a great concern to both government officials and residents. Indian Agent Boilvin at Ft. Crawford warned officials in Washington of danger. Richard Graham, Indian Agent in Illinois Territory, expressed the same sentiment. Many chiefs, according to Graham, were at that time on their way to St. Joseph in Ontario, Canada, in order to know the wishes of the British government. Their traders were using all their influence to promote the Indians' distrust of the American government.[29] Rock Island was a targeted area because of the continued allegiance of the Sauk and Mesquakie to the British, whose traders still influenced them.

The presence of an Indian Agent would have been useful to the situation at Fort Armstrong. The Indian Agent supervised the political relations among and between tribes and with the United States, an essential element in establishing and maintaining good relations with the Indian nations. He was a mediator, especially in treaty negotiations, who granted independent traders licenses to trade, received Indians who visited the fort, gave them presents, settled their differences, and performed a variety of other services for the Indians. The Sauk and

Mesquakie Indian Agent, Richard Graham, and his sub-agent, Thomas Forsyth, would periodically travel to Fort Armstrong to issue trading licenses and conduct other business pertaining to the Sauk and Mesquakie, but there had been no provision to house the Agency with its interpreters and blacksmith at Fort Armstrong. Consequently the burden of diplomacy fell on a fort unable to interact with the Indians on any meaningful basis. It would have been to the advantage of the Indian Department to have eyes and ears on the ground to monitor the activity of the local tribes, dispel rumors, and determine who the British traders were and with whom they were trading. It would also be an advantage to the fort commander, like Fort Armstrong's Morgan, who was generally unfamiliar with the Sauk and Mesquakie trading community. Having a trader near the fort would be an advantage to him as well. It is almost certain that all three men, Graham, Forsyth, and Morgan encouraged George Davenport to enter the Indian trade in order to help them identify the loyal British subjects. Davenport's British looks and Lincolnshire accent gave him an edge over American traders, and his service in the War of 1812 had proven his loyalty to the American cause. Davenport was also out of a job. In the spring of 1817 Congress restructured the army supply system by removing private contractors from supplying military posts and establishing a Commissary department within the Army to purchase rations. The proposal passed in April 1818 and was put into effect on the first of June 1819.[30]

Left with the prospect of supporting his family, who had arrived the previous summer, as an independent shopkeeper whose only customers were infrequently paid, or finding a new source of income, Davenport turned to the Indian trade on a full time basis. Wilkie says that George Davenport sought permission from Colonel Willoughby Morgan to select a location on the island that would not interfere with the garrison, and then proceeded to build a home for his family at the place designated by Morgan. Davenport selected a quartersection of land on the north shore of the island. Following protocol, he notified Secretary of War, J.C. Calhoun, concerning his presence and his improvements on the island and received written instructions concerning his plans for settling there.[31]

It was unusual for a commander to encourage or even promote such settlement, but Colonel Morgan must have had his reasons for allowing, even encouraging, Davenport to remain. Trade was a key element in relationships with the native people, a vital element in the winning their trust and friendship, and controlling their warring traditions. Until the country could be rid of the British traders and replaced with Americans, their military efforts at border security were doomed.[32]

Wilkie says, "He now, with what little money he had saved, purchased a small stock of Indian goods, and commenced the 'Indian Trader.' " The structure he built was described as a double-log cabin with a chimney between them. One room of the cabin provided living quarters for his family, and the other was used for storing goods and furs. That same summer (1817), Indian Agent Thomas Forsyth made his annual visit to Rock River and brought annuity payments to the Sauk and Mesquakie. He had recently been formally assigned to the tribes and expected them to be moving to the western side of the Mississippi, out of the jurisdiction of Illinois. Davenport had the opportunity to obtain a license from him and to discuss how best to trade with them, while Forsyth was taking note of the Indian situation.[33]

Forsyth's observations on the Sauk and Mesquakie Nation were intended to give Army personnel information for the purpose of defense. Forsyth had supplied such information for Illinois Governor Ninian Edwards during the late war while working as a trader for Kinzie & Forsyth in the Illinois Indian country. His report reveals the insecure situation that Davenport faced as he initiated trade with the Indians. At the old Sauk village on the Rock River, Forsyth estimated that the village had one hundred lodges with about one thousand warriors. Although he had seen many Indian villages, never before had Forsyth seen such a large or populous village as Saukenuk. He noted construction activity in the village, repairing old lodges and building new ones, and sensed that there was no plan to make a new village on the west side of the Mississippi. The Sauk also had other villages downriver from Fort Armstrong. At the Mesquakie village, just a few hundred yards across the slough from Fort Armstrong, Forsyth counted twenty lodges and about two hundred warriors, which he estimated to be about half the population of the whole nation. The Mesquakie's main village was at Turkey River where there were 280 braves and 820 family members. A third village located at the Dubuque mines, housed 80 braves and 240 others.[34]

Forsyth learned that many Sauk had recently visited the British at Fort Malden on the Canadian bank of the Detroit River, where they received many presents, as was the custom of the British. They had been advised to be quiet and peaceable towards the Americans. If they did so, said the British, the Americans would move away on their own in time. Continued reliance on the British was troubling news to Forsyth and the knowledge that the Sauk were planning another trip to Fort Malden at the end of the month, this time with Osages and Kansas, confirmed his worst suspicions. It had recently been reported by Charles Jouette, Indian Agent at Chicago, that "the rapid settlement of the Rocky River ... have excited the Saukes to the highest pitch who are gone to the British to complain of American encroachments."[35] The American forces at Fort Armstrong were put on guard just as George Davenport prepared to begin trading.

Another visitor to the fort that summer was Lieutenant Stephen H. Long who inspected the new construction as well as its neighbors. Long's estimates are a little different from Forsyth's, as he estimated that the Mesquakie village had thirty cabins, each with two fires and a population of about five hundred. The Sauk village, Long reported, was much larger with two to three thousand people. Long estimated that the Sauk had one hundred cabins, each having two, three, and sometimes four fires. Despite the disagreement in numbers, Long and Forsyth agreed that this was the largest concentration of hostile Indians in America.[36]

The Indians were seasoned traders, as well as warriors, accustomed to trading for American and British goods. The late war, however, had disrupted their supply of trade goods and they had had few chances to sell their furs. Davenport was already seeing these people as an eager audience waiting to buy his wares. Trading with the Indians was a relatively easy business to get into and did not require a large amount of capital. With a license and a small supply of goods from St. Louis, whose merchants Davenport knew from his army days, one could begin trading for lead and furs. They were relatively easy to sell at a profit.[37] For security on his license, Davenport contacted George H. Kennerly.

Kennerly was the government's transportation agent for the fur factories on the Mississippi and Missouri rivers and had been a licensed trader with the Sauk and Mesquakie. He was then trading with the "Indians of the Mississippi River," the Sauk, Mesquakie, Ioway, as well as Ho Chunk, and some Kickapoo.[38] He was well connected to the Indian Trade, since his wife was the daughter of Pierre Menard and his sister married to William Clark, Governor of Missouri and Superintendent of Indian Affairs. Kennerly also operated a mercantile store in St. Louis in partnership with his brother James. Kennerly supplied Davenport with some trade goods in those early first years as he ventured up the Rock River to initiate trade with the Ho Chunk. The Kennerly-Davenport partnership lasted until 1822, during which time George Davenport learned the basics of the trade and built up his own inventory of merchandize.

A month after Forsyth's and Long's visits, Davenport purchased 16 beaver traps and 12 large mining picks from William Morrison's Kaskaskia store.[39] This is the earliest documented evidence that Davenport had entered the Indian trade on his own and supports the idea that his initial venture was related to the Indians at the lead mines in what is now northwestern Illinois. Pick-axes, crowbars, hoes, and shovels were the tools of the Indians who mined the lead. Davenport took his trade goods, along with two trusted men named Gokey and Degre, into the Rock River region near what is now Prophetstown, Illinois. There he traded with the Ho Chunk who had not had a trader visit them for some time. It was an opportunity for adventure and profit, especially since the Ho Chunk also mined lead.

Gokey was Antoine Gothier or Gauthier, commonly known as Antoine Gokey, a French Canadian who had once worked for the Hudson Bay Co. Gokey may have been sent to Rock Island by the trader James Lockwood to trade with the Sauk and Mesquakie (Fox) for Indian corn as there was none being grown in Prairie du Chien and the Sauk and Mesquakie often had corn to trade.[40] He had settled on Rock Island sometime after 1812 and was married to Rosa, an Indian woman by whom he had at least four children. Davenport hired him as interpreter and clerk, and they remained close friends until Davenport's death in 1845.

The identity of Degre is less easy to ascertain. He may have been Charles Degre who later worked for the American Fur Company as an interpreter and on the steamboat *Yellow Stone* on her 1832 trip up the Missouri.[41] Under the tutelage of these three men, Davenport the novice became a seasoned trader. Davenport began to trade in earnest with the Ho Chunk on the Rock River, fifty miles away from Fort Armstrong. Trial by fire was the quickest way to learn.

Davenport had been fully warned about the Ho Chunk on the Rock River whose unpredictable and treacherous behavior was well known among Indian traders. They were a splinter group of the main tribe in Wisconsin, usually referred to as renegades. During the War of 1812 they had fallen under the influence of the Shawnee Prophet with whom Black Hawk sometimes consulted and made scattered raids against the frontier settlers. Although they had little interest in peaceful relations with anyone on the frontier, they were eager for trade goods.[42] Davenport had been warned that they would steal his merchandize and try to kill him, a prediction that came true. Davenport's relationship with the Ho Chunk was punctuated by one harrowing escapade after another.

An event that occurred in the fall of 1817 sent shock waves through the trading community when an American Fur Company trading expedition was arrested at Fort Crawford. It was a large party consisting of two boatloads of trade goods manned by traders Russell Farnham and Daniel Darling, two clerks, and fourteen boatmen. The traders under Ramsay Crooks, the acting manager and right hand man of John Jacob Astor, were hoping to expand the company into the region between Prairie du Chien and St. Louis, an area that had not had consistent trading activities since the beginning of the War of 1812. The arrests stunted the activities of the American Fur Company in the Upper Mississippi Valley for a year, but it provided an opportunity for Davenport to step into the Sauk and Mesquakie trade.

Russel Farnham was a seasoned employee of John Jacob Astor's American Fur Company, one of the original Astorians who went overland to the Columbia River to establish a trading post in the Northwest. Darling was inexperienced, being on his first trading venture. The two traders intended to trade above the Indian Boundary line which lay on the east side of the Mississippi in the vicinity of Riviere de la Roche (Rock River) or Rivere du Main where the Sauk's main village lay.[43] Because Farnham did not know the language and Daniel Darling was new to the business, two Frenchmen, St. Jean and Lagoterie, were sent along in the capacity of clerks.

Both Lagoterie and St. Jean were crusty old French Canadian traders, married to native women, and associated with British trading interests in the Rock River area before and during the War of 1812. Eduard LaGoterie, sometimes LaGuthrie, was known to have been trading among the Sauk for the American Fur Company in the Rock River area in 1816,1817, and 1818, and had once been a trader at Black Hawk's village.[44] He knew the territory, the Indians, their languages, and their customs. St. Jean, too, was experienced among the Sauk. Much of the success of Farnham's party rested on these two men, but both were highly suspect characters whose allegiance to the United States was uncertain.

The expedition's route from Mackinac took them to Prairie du Chien, where seizures and arrests of illegal traders had occurred, most recently in the previous year, when Brigadier General T. A. Smith had seized the goods and property of illegal traders working for British companies. American authorities in Prairie du Chien were sensitive to the fact that British traders still influenced the Indians, and were therefore suspicious of this party of traders. The party had been licensed in Mackinac by a military commander not known for his discrimination in licensing. Furthermore, the party consisted of foreigners with notorious reputations as British sympathisers with cocky attitudes. The commander at Fort Crawford, Colonel Chambers, ordered the entire party to go directly to St. Louis for proper licenses and with instructions to check in at each military post along the way. He forbade them to have any contact with the natives. As the party left the fort, Lagoterie was overheard saying that nothing could stop them from trading below the Rock River. Colonel Chamber sent orders to Colonel Morgan at Fort Armstrong to confiscate all goods and escort the party in leg irons to St. Louis. Ramsay Crooks was outraged because the whole incident wasted a year's work and delayed any American Fur Company trading activity in the Rock Island area for a full year. Lagoterie and Darling were dismissed from service; Lagoterie because he was too dangerous to American Fur Company purposes and Darling, for being incompetent. Crooks and the American Fur Company filed a lawsuit against the U.S. Government. to recover losses. The incident eventually proved embarrassing for the American Army when Crooks won the lawsuit against the U.S. Government, but in the meantime, Farnham was cooling his heels in St. Louis, complaining of his lost wages, and eager to get back into the business.[45] Lagoterie, having been dismissed by the American Fur Company, probably returned to Rock River and worked for Davenport, as he was known to have been secretly hidden at Saukenuk that winter and the mercenary Lagoterie was not known for his company loyalty. He continued in the trade for several years, sometimes with, but often in competition to, the American Fur Company.

Had there been an Indian Agency at Fort Armstrong, wrote the Governor of Illinois, the whole affair might have been mitigated. He had a point. There was no Indian Agency at Fort Armstrong and the army was neither trained nor equipped to protect the Indian rights or to establish diplomatic relations with hostile nations. In fact, diplomacy was somewhat contrary to the concept of a standing army. As a direct result of this incident, the Fort Clark Indian Agency at Peoria was closed and Agent Forsyth transferred to Rock Island.[46]

Forsyth proved to be particularly sensitive to the Indians and their needs for the next twenty years. He had been involved with Indians of the Illinois country long before the War of 1812, and his personal opinion was that if agents knew the native languages and their duty to the native peoples, Indian affairs would be smoother. Forsyth knew both. He recommended that Indians be treated well, with fair laws, "presents every

September ... for fall hunting, and a little liquor every spring and autumn for a frolic ... ", listen to their complaints and render them justice, never promise more than you mean to perform, allow them a free trade to all places, and encourage as many persons as possible to engage in Indian trade.[47]

Establishing an agency at Fort Armstrong would mean hiring a small staff to help with the many needs of the Indians: an interpreter, a blacksmith, a gunsmith, and their families, many of whom were a mixture of French and Indian. Interpreters, especially, were the key ingredient to establishing and maintaining good relationships with the Indians. A good interpreter - one who could communicate with the proper words and phrases - needed to be intelligent, tactful, and courageous.[48] The Indians had practical needs, for blacksmiths and gunsmiths, but the fort had no time or money to provide any of this.

It was several years before an agency would be built. This did not bother Forsyth who was not convinced that his presence was needed at Fort Armstrong on a full-time basis. Because the Indians were in their village only about four or five months out of each year, Forsyth thought it prudent for him to visit Rock Island in May through September rather than risking his life, and that of his family, full-time in Indian Country. He therefore spent his winters on his farm near St. Louis. When he was present on Rock Island in the summers, Forsyth conducted his business from the fort and lived with the Davenport family, at least until the time when their growing family crowded him out.[49] Forsyth and Davenport worked well together and became fast friends.

By the end of the second summer, life on the island began to settle down to a routine for the sixty-two men and two women at Fort Armstrong. Guarding the frontier was often monotonous with little but strenuous work to break up the time. Short bursts of frenzied activity were often followed by long stretches of inactivity and boredom. Periodically small groups of soldiers took their turn guarding the lead mines of northwest Illinois. Occasionally the Indians stole horses, or slaves, or attacked settlers, but Fort Armstrong never sustained an attack.[50]

For diversion some soldiers at Fort Armstrong engaged in odd jobs for the officers and the Indian Agency, as a way to work off debts accumulated at the post store as well as for buying extra supplies in the Davenport store. In later years Susan Lewis recalled that she once owned a stand of pit-sawn lumber that the soldiers had cut from local cherry trees and Mrs. Davenport used a sewing table made for her by the soldiers at Fort Armstrong.[51]

On the forty acres of cleared land adjoining the fort the soldiers began to cultivate Fort Armstrong's gardens. Caleb Atwater described the gardens on Rock Island. "The officers have adjoining the fort, a most beautiful garden regularly laid out, with gravel walks, in which are cultivated beets, carrots, onions, potatoes, corn, and every vegetable growing in this climate."[52]

The Davenports, too, cultivated gardens on the island and raised their own cattle. The gardens were productive, "abound(ing) with the choicest fruit and vegetables" such as potatoes, beets, cabbages, and asparagus. George Davenport began planting an orchard around 1820 with apples, pears and peaches, the latter of which were said to grow well in this region until about 1848. That year there was a particularly severe cold snap in the spring and the peach trees died. George planted fifty peach trees near his house and engaged in a little winemaking from time to time. Barrels of apples were sold now and then and provided a little needed cash.[53] The Davenport cattle, about forty or fifty head, roamed on the island and mingled with the public cattle that provided beef for the soldiers.

Visitors to the fort provided distractions from the ordinary routines on the island. Occasionally the fort was visited by delegations of local Indians who came to trade their surplus corn, beans and squash for flour, salt and tobacco and also by other military units travelling on the river. Sometimes parties of Government surveyors or geologists and other scientists who were examining the Upper Mississippi river valley stopped for a time at the fort. They paid their respects to the commander and also visited Davenport's store to share the latest news and learn about the surrounding country.

During those first years the Davenport's lives became interconnected with the native people, with the military, and with their own efforts to establish themselves in a new environment. As Davenport grew to know the Sauk and Mesquakie, who had once been the most hostile tribes in the Mississippi Valley, he gained their confidence and respect. In the years to come, he would often be called upon to settle disputes among them and to persuade them to accept the ways of the United States Government. The place where they all came together was at Davenport's Indian Lodge.[54]

Often called Mrs. Lewis by the early settlers, Susanna M. Lewis was the daughter of Margaret Bowling Lewis Davenport and the mother of George Davenport's two sons, George L'Oste Davenport and Bailey Davenport. Daguerreotype from the Hauberg Collection, Augustana College Special Collections.

CHAPTER FOUR:

DOMESTIC LIFE ON ISLAND

IN THE SUMMER OF 1816, George Davenport's wife, Margaret, and her fifteen-year-old daughter, Susan Lewis, embarked from St. Louis on a keelboat bound for Rock Island. They passed through terrain that few non-native women had ever seen before. The women had left behind friends and family to settle on an island in the Mississippi River surrounded by unfriendly neighbors, dangerous river waters, and wild beasts. It would be some time before any woman would pass this way again. According to family stories, the Davenport women saw no other white woman for five years. Accustomed to strong kinship ties and the company of other women as the Davenport women seem to have been, life on the frontier must have been extremely lonely. During their years on Rock Island, their relationship as mother and daughter must have grown extraordinarily close as they shared all aspects of making a home on the frontier.[1]

The women arrived at Fort Armstrong just three months after building had begun. What quarters Mr. Davenport had obtained for them is uncertain, but based on accounts from other frontier forts, they were cramped, crude in nature, and had little privacy. Since the fort was unfinished, they might even have had to live for a time in a tent. Fortunately, their quarters were temporary. Family stories suggest that they lived together within the walls of the fort for just over a year, until they built their own home half a mile away from the fort.

One can only wonder how prepared the Davenport women were to follow the rhythm of military life at Fort Armstrong, whether it was a familiar routine or a radical departure from what they had known in Erie, Pennsylvania, or in St. Louis. Most certainly, they had never before been so deep in Indian country or experienced the remoteness of Rock Island. Eventually they learned the dialects of the Sauk and Mesquakie to communicate with the native women.

Although one might question Davenport's wisdom in bringing his family to the frontier so soon after the War of 1812 when the Indian situation was so unsettled, the practice was well established. Margaret Davenport, like many army wives since the Revolutionary War, followed her husband into the heart of Indian Country where they had a chance to create their own version of the American Dream. They ventured into Indian country in hopes of securing not just a place for themselves in terms of a plot of land, but also a place where they could earn some measure of the good life to support them into their old age. The arrival of the women was the first sign that Davenport intended to stay in the Rock River region.

We know little about Mrs. Davenport's background, but what little we do know suggests that she was prepared for frontier life. Margaret Bowling Lewis Davenport was born in 1769 in Virginia. She had at least two brothers, Jeremiah and Ambrose Green Bowling, and at least one sister who later joined her at Rock Island. Her brother Jeremiah was an upholsterer and mattress maker in Winchester who rented one of his buildings to the First U.S. Infantry as a recruiting station. Winchester may have been where Margaret Bowling Lewis, a widow with a daughter, met George Davenport during his recruiting mission. Her brother, Ambrose Green Bowling, was a rope-maker in Arlington Heights, Virginia, before the War of 1812. He served as a substitute during the war and afterwards moved his wife and family to Ohio where he farmed just east of Cincinnati.

When and where the Davenports were married, however, is not known. Although there has been speculation that they were married in Cincinnati, it is more likely that they married in Missouri, perhaps even after Davenport was discharged from the Army.

Mrs. Davenport was living on the western Pennsylvania frontier in 1801 when her daughter Susan was born.[2] At that time, there were settlers opening farms in Erie, as well as a military presence at Fort Presque Isle, but whether her husband was farmer or soldier is not known. What is clear, however, is that Mrs. Davenport had learned how to survive on the frontier near such an outpost and was able to help her new husband as he moved into the Indian Trade business.

For fifteen-year old Susan Lewis, life at a frontier fort was exciting, as evidenced by her strong memories of those early years. She remembered even the smallest details into her old age and told and retold her stories to everyone who wanted to hear them. It was she who told how the bake ovens were built in the first days of the soldiers arriving on Rock Island. And she recalled with fondness how the Sauk and Mesquakie played their games, as the family watched from the bluffs above. Her stories about how Davenport charmed the Ho Chunk and how Black Hawk had a favorite tea cup in the Davenport home are stories that add to our understanding of what life was like on Rock Island in those early days.[3]

Life at a frontier outpost was a difficult place, especially for women who had few places in the military system. Army regulations provided employment for married women to serve as laundresses and matrons in the hospital. Soldiers' wives could earn supplemental pay, sometimes more than their husbands, as well as drawing their own rations. Did the Davenport women, perhaps, work as laundresses for the soldiers or as matrons in the hospital?   Such work could have supplemented

Davenport's wages, but the earliest records of Ft. Armstrong have been lost. We can only guess, based on the records of women at other frontier forts, what their daily life was like.[4]

In such a male-oriented world, the Davenport women were separated from their own kin and from other women who shared a common background and reactions to their new surroundings and experiences. There must have been times when their loneliness was almost unbearable. Cultural diversions at the fort were few and communication by mail with friends and family was irregular at best.

Even soldiers found frontier posts to be isolated and lonely. The nearness of the Indians, so recently hostile to Americans, and the presence of wolves, snakes and other wild animals only heightened their sense of vulnerability, until friendships could be forged with the Native Americans. Major Morrell Marston expressed it well: "Altho' we have no fear for the safety of the garrison, yet it is rather unpleasant to be surrounded by hostile savages: indeed it is making no small sacrifice, in the best of time, to be stationed at a post like this two or three hundred miles from civilised society. The ice now begins to form in the Mississippi & I presume that the navigation will soon close, & we of course be cut off from all intercourse with the world ... "[5]

Amos Farrar, who operated one of the post stores under cover of the fort's guns, expressed somewhat the same sentiment, but hinted that there were social gatherings from time to time. The Davenport women, then, could have had occasional opportunities to get to know their neighbors at the fort. "I enjoy good health and live in a perfectly easy manner," he wrote to his brother in Massachusetts, "but I've had to deplore the want of society for its like Banishment to live in wilderness country surrounded by savages without it but in the meantime I enjoy myself Tolerably well in the society of the Officers of the post and one family which lives on the island & cultivating the friendship of the Indians as much as I can with safety."[6]

Wild animals presented another problem. Although they lived on an island, the dense underbrush provided habitat for a variety of critters, including snakes. In later years, Bailey Davenport told tales of finding huge snakes in the grasses and laughing at the horrified reaction of his friends. His mother and grandmother may have had similar reactions.

Wolves were common. Farrar wrote that they were common as squirrels in Massachusetts. In one season alone he had trapped seven wolves and thought he might make a decent living as a trapper. John Spencer also told of wolves prowling about in the night, and about the Indian dogs barking.[7] Davenport family stories, however, do not dwell on fears.

At first, life on the island revolved around the fort and its established routine. From wake up to retreat, the day was broken into segments by the roll of the drum or the musician's bugle. Women were not involved with the soldiering business of the fort, so they are beyond the scope of ordinary recordkeeping and there are no letters from Fort Armstrong that illuminate women's lives around the fort. From court martial records, just two women accompanied the soldiers to Fort Snelling in 1820 and camped briefly near Rock Island before continuing northward.[8] Most frontier forts had women in residence once the initial construction was completed. Officers' wives were allowed to join their husbands, but officers complained that they weren't paid enough to support their families on the frontier. Enlisted men could live with their families outside the fort walls, but construction of the fort took precedent over building enlisted men's houses. At Fort Armstrong, this was after 1820, four years after the fort's construction.

The first official reference to women in the post returns for Fort Armstrong is in the third quarter of 1821 with two unnamed women employed as laundresses. Not long after that, Factor Robert B. Belt was transferred from Fort Edwards to Fort Armstrong with his wife and family. Mrs. Belt was possibly the first white woman the Davenport women had a chance to visit with.[9]

About that same time, the wife of William Downey, the post sutler, arrived. By this time families of officers and other enlisted men were living outside the fort and the Downeys lived in their own cabin. Doctor Sprague, the post surgeon, and his family also lived in a cabin outside the fort walls, as did the family of William Gooding. This is the first evidence that a small community of military families was present on the island and living outside the fort walls. Whether these women socialized with the Davenport women is not known.[10]

Sometime around 1820, Antoine Goque or Gokey settled on the island. His house, as described by early settler David Sears, was a one and a half story log building with a dirt floor and a fireplace on one end, located near the center of the island, not far from the Davenport house. Gokey was a French Canadian interpreter who became not just an invaluable employee of George Davenport, but a life-long friend. Mrs. Gokey was a Fox or Mesquakie woman, whom Sears described as being sociable and very pleasant and usually had a houseful of guests, most from the Mesquakie village across the Slough. According to Sears, she made soap and maple sugar, which she saved for treats for the children and others who visited. She was a gardener, especially fond of her gooseberry bushes and small apple trees that she had planted near her home. The Gokeys became close friends of the Davenport. It may have been the Gokeys who taught the Davenports the Mesquakie language, The Gokeys had at least four children, among whom were Joseph, Antoine Jr., and two daughters. Both Sears and Bailey Davenport were frequent visitors to their home and close friends of Joe and Antoine Gokey Jr. [11]

Not until steamboats began regular trips to the northern posts did women become regular visitors to the Upper Mississippi Valley. At least two women died and were buried on Rock Island. We know only their names, Maria Hewet and Mary Beston, from newspaper stories. David Sears, an early settler who knew the island well, remembered the graveyard as being near the old fort site on the south shore of the island, "about 150 feet long, east and west, and from 60 to 75 feet wide. It was enclosed by a dry rubble stonewall, with one or more timbers along the top. One narrow gate near the west end ... gave entry and ... in the southwest corner ... was a smaller enclosure surrounded by a fence of hand-made pickets. This was known as the women's corner and contained several graves."[12]

Also living at the fort was a small number of slaves of officers who performed a variety of daily tasks like cleaning, cooking, and sewing.

Slaves of medical personnel, like the famous Dred Scott who accompanied Dr. John Emerson, assisted in treating the sick both at Fort Armstrong and later at Fort Snelling. Based on the number of officers, there may have been as many as ten slaves living at Fort Armstrong in any given year. A few may have been women.[13] The Davenports, too, had slaves or indentured servants, to help with the farm, the new trading business, and household work.

As family of the contractor's agent, Mrs. Davenport and her daughter may have helped with the management of the soldiers' rations. The flour and salt had to be kept dry and the flour checked for worms. Pork, stored in wooden barrels, required careful storage and frequent checking to make sure that the brine had not soured or that maggots hadn't settled in. From time to time the meat was repacked so that the brine was evenly spread over the meat. It was a time-consuming and unpleasant task, but it is likely that Mrs. Davenport and her daughter assisted with this task.

The women undoubtedly helped with the butchering and the salting of the beef. Army regulations specified the process and the Davenports would have followed the same procedure: three hundred pounds of beef, required seventy-five pounds of common salt and thirty-four pounds of Liverpool salt. This dried the beef, which could then be stored until it was needed. The Davenports' diet was similar, if not identical, to the soldier's diet, and supplemented with wild game, wild fruit, and vegetables from their garden.[14] It is certain they had milk cows, but how many and whether they made their own butter and cheese are not known, although these were tasks that pioneer women often performed.

Home life for the Davenport women changed only slightly when the family moved away from the fort and they engaged tasks like other pioneer women on the frontier. They grew, prepared, and preserved most of their own foods, tended the garden and orchard, and looked after the livestock -- the cattle and hogs and a few chickens. Rock Island County pioneers remembered the jars of quince that Mrs. Davenport had prepared for them and the wine that Mr. Davenport had made himself from the peaches and pears planted in 1820. Susan Lewis told how they preserved their grapes in cotton and peaches in alcohol such as brandy or sherry.

Fruit pies and preserves would have been welcome additions to their diet. Visitors to the Island noted Davenport's beautiful and well laid out gardens and orchard on the island.

Unlike other traders' wives, Mrs. Davenport and her daughter did not follow their husbands into the field to help collect furs or distribute hunting supplies. Nor did they set up camp in the Indian villages. Instead, Mrs. Davenport and her daughter remained at home near the fort on the island while Mr. Davenport travelled to the various villages and temporary trading posts. Theirs was a much easier life when compared with wives such as the one described by Caroline Phelps, who followed her husband William Phelps up and down the river and into the interior of Iowa. Mrs. Phelps rarely saw another white woman as she followed her husband into the field, often pregnant and nursing a baby. She lived with the Indian women, travelled by canoe with them on the rivers, and experienced their help. But, Caroline Phelps also saw the darker side of tribal living -- the drunken frolics that sometimes erupted into fierce fighting among the men and lasted into the wee hours of the morning. She often hid children under her bed to keep them safe during such times Like Caroline Phelps, Mrs. Davenport and her daughter were often left alone when Davenport visited the lead mines or St. Louis or his various posts in the hunting grounds. Caroline Phelps depended on the Indian women to protect her. Mrs. Davenport and her daughter relied on the soldiers at the fort.[15]

More than likely the Davenport women made most of their clothing and household linens and bedding, or employed seamstresses to help with the annual clothing of the family. It was usual for such women to come and stay at the Davenport house until the sewing was completed and the family supplied with new clothes for the next season. It is doubtful that the Davenport women engaged in spinning and weaving their own cloth, since Davenport regularly carried bolts of yard goods in his store. His ledgers indicate that specialty orders for cloth and trimmings were occasionally obtained from merchants in St. Louis. Heavy annual tasks like making candles and soap were not necessary at the Davenport house since Davenport procured candles and soap for the fort. Certainly he could provide these for his family as well.

The Davenports were no different from other pioneers on the frontier at the time, with the same sense of wonder for the land that surrounded them. At the same time, life on the frontier was fraught with fears and uncertainties. Beneath the beauty of the prairies and the river landscape lurked a savage land. One can only question how they dealt with wolves howling in the nights. Were the beasts ever so close to their door that they could hear their teeth snapping and twigs snapping under the feet? Did they encounter bears and the hordes of mosquitoes that most pioneers complained of, and the aches and ailments that came seasonally? How did they prepare for sudden summer storms, the winds, sleet and hailstorms of the winter?

Susan Lewis never mentioned the prairie fires in her stories, but they were annual events, usually in the fall. More than one writer has recorded their awe and wonder at such a force. Fire was always a danger on the frontier, and at the fort, barrels filled with water were always in readiness in the barracks and other places, just in case. One particular year, 1823, was noted in the post surgeon's weather diary kept for Ft. Armstrong. The fires that season were visible on all directions for nearly two weeks. High winds only added to the excitement before a hard frost put an end to the autumn fires. George Davenport made only a brief note to prairie fire in his memorandum for November 1, 1826: "Great Fire across river - all our hay stacks burnt."[16] Separated from the mainland prairie by the slough, the Davenports could view the fires from a safe distance, but the fires were destructive and more than one pioneer family had been caught unaware of their powerful force.

The rivers were their best means of transportation and contact with the outside world, but they separated the family from the mainland and carried with them their own dangers. George Davenport was away from home for long periods of time with infrequent letters to his family at home, travelling by horseback and by the rivers. How many times did the women wonder when he would return or if he would return at all? Of all the deaths recorded at Fort Armstrong, drowning was the most recorded cause, and even men with many years of experience on the frontier were drowned.

With the exception of the Ho Chunk, who never really accepted white men in the Davenport's lifetime, the Indians who at first seemed so hostile and threatening grew to be friends. How much influence did the women and children have in forging these relationships? The Indians regularly visited Davenport's trading post on the Island and their women often accompanied them. Susan Lewis, and perhaps her mother, learned to speak the language of the Sauk and Mesquakie and allowed her children to spend their days in the Indian villages, playing with other Indian children. Her son, George L'Oste Davenport, was said to be a favorite with the Mesquakie, excelling in their sports, and was officially adopted into the tribe. The Davenports were honored guests at feasts and Susan Lewis spoke of visiting the villages and watching their ball games at such times.[17]

For the Davenports, family was an important aspect of their lives. Although physically separated from their kin during their early years, they never lost complete contact with England or Virginia. There were letters, but they came at rare intervals, and visits back east were infrequent. Until Margaret's family could be reunited on Rock Island, as they eventually were, the Davenports had to create new ties, new support groups, and new ways to support them on the frontier, even using unconventional means to do this.

Perhaps it was Mrs. Davenport's age, or the remoteness of their situation that prompted the unusual relationship between Davenport and his wife's daughter. At age sixteen, Susan Lewis was at the general age when girls at forts often married, according to Fort Wayne historian, Willa Cramton. Amos Farrar also addresses the early age of marriage for women on the frontier. Writing from Galena in 1827 Farrar says, " There are but comparatively few females. Hence every female unmarried who lands on these shores is immediately married. Little girls fourteen and thirteen years old are often married here." [18] Although Susan Lewis bore George Davenport two sons, she did not marry him. She was generally known to settlers as Mrs. Lewis.

In November 1817, the Davenport family welcomed George L'Oste Davenport, named in honor of Davenport's brother-in-law, Frederick

L'Oste. For the rest of her life, Susan Lewis remained the mother in the family. Mrs. Davenport took the role of grandmother, and George Davenport himself was Pappy.

The relationship of Mrs. Davenport, her daughter, and her husband has always given rise to questions and speculations. How each one felt about the situation is evidenced only in the remarks of the pioneers who recalled that they all lived happily together. In many ways, the relationship of George Davenport to the women in his household was like the relationships he formed in the Indian Trade and his later businesses in service industries and land development. There was a clear division of labor. Mrs. Davenport and her daughter managed the household, keeping household accounts, cooking cleaning, and gardening, supervising the slaves or servants, and attending other domestic duties while Davenport concentrated on the non-domestic businesses. The women raised the children until the sons were sent away to schools for further training. Then the sons took their place alongside their father in the family businesses.

This first-born son was Davenport's link between the old world and the new, a continuation of the family traditions, and an investment for their future. It was a signal that the Davenports had arrived and were prepared to take their place on the frontier, to claim their land and their fortune, and to make a lasting impression on Rock Island. The timing of this birth was no accident; it justified Davenport's decision to put down stakes on the Island.

Six years later, Bailey Davenport was welcomed into the family. In the grand scheme of estate building, it stood to no purpose if there were no heirs to inherit the land and carry on the work. George L'Oste Davenport and his brother Bailey were destined to carry on their father's work and carry on the family name.

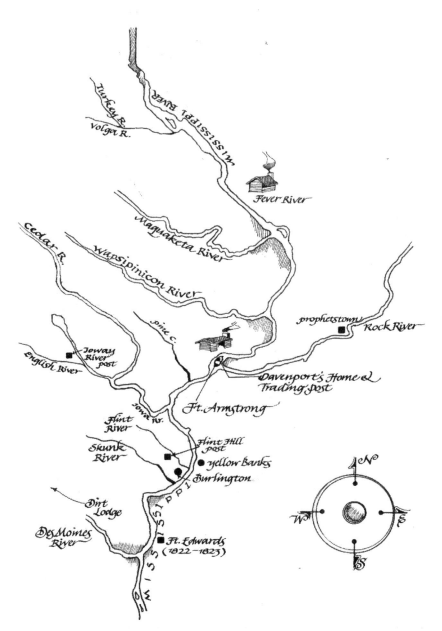

George Davenport's three permanent trading posts at Fever River, Rock Island, and Ft. Edwards, were positioned to accommodate his trade with the Sauk and Mesquakie. Temporary winter posts, identified by squares, were established in agreement with the tribal elders for each winter hunt.

CHAPTER FIVE

ENTERING THE INDIAN TRADE: The Early Years, 1818 - 1822

GEORGE DAVENPORT HAD MUCH to learn about the Indian trading business: the language, the local customs, and the personalities of his new customers. Where the Davenports had been accustomed to following the drum and bugle of the military day, their lives now began to revolve around the agricultural and hunting seasons of the Indian cycle. Perhaps because of his success with trading in lead, he was ready to take the step towards expanding his trade. According to Wilkie and Davenport family stories, George Davenport went to St. Louis in 1818, purchased a small keelboat that he called the "Flying Betsy" and loaded it with goods and provisions in order to enter the Indian Trade. Davenport first began his trading business with the Ho Chunk, or Winnebago, on the Rock River. Of all the tribes in the Mississippi Valley, they alone had not signed peace negotiations with the United States Government. They had, therefore, been neglected by the U.S. Government and did not have an Indian Agent assigned to them. Nor had they been given any Government presents as other tribes had, as noted by Richard Graham, who suggested to John C. Calhoun that $1,500 worth of presents be sent to them to curry the tribe's friendship. These were good reasons for Davenport to choose this tribe to begin his trading.[1]

Trade in Indian Country was regulated by the United States Government and required both a license and a security bond to prove financial capability. The license specified the tribes with whom Davenport could trade, but the location to trade was not designated. Davenport could follow the tribes into their hunting grounds to collect his furs and peltries, but he was restricted from trading anything that suggested loyalty to another country. No uniforms other than those of the United States were allowed to be given or sold, nor were "medals, flags, arm bands, or any other ornaments" of foreign powers, since those were given to the Indians as badges of loyalty. Nor could Davenport send to or exchanged spirituous liquors with the Indians and a complete inventory of goods was submitted to the Indian Agent as proof of his compliance.[2]

As Davenport began to trade with Ho Chunk (or Winnebago), and then the Sauk and Mesquakie, the entire Davenport family grew familiar with the Rock River life cycle and the traditions of these people. Most of the year was spent in hunting and trapping as the Sauk and Mesquakie depended on their hunting for food and clothing. They traded only for goods that they could not produce themselves. Their annual cycle began in April when the two tribes began to gather when the hunt was over and they came in from their hunting grounds. Then they prepared to return to their villages. While the women opened their caches of corn and other foodstuffs stored the previous fall and began repairing their lodges, the old men had a frolic with the few kegs of rum they had gotten from the Indian agent or the traders. Then came the Medicine Feast and the burial of those who had died the past year. They repaired the fences around the fields and the women began to prepare for planting. As the women worked, the men rested, feasted, and told hunting stories. After the corn was planted the Sauk and Mesquakie feasted and danced the Crane Dance. This dance lasted two or three days, after which there was the national dance for the warriors. During this time the courting began and young braves selected their wives.

The ball games were especially important to the Davenports because they were often invited to the village at this time, an honor that they accepted. The games were held on the prairies where Chippiannock Cemetery in the city of Rock Island is today and involved hundreds of players who gambled for stakes such as horses, buffalo robes, and blankets. Susan Lewis remembered this as a time of great excitement when spectators numbered in the thousands. Black Hawk says that there were from three to five hundred ball players on a side, a spectacle rarely observed by most European settlers.[3]

When the cornfields were hoed and the corn was about knee-high, the young men prepared to head west to hunt deer and buffalo by visiting their traders for supplies. In order to be competitive, Davenport's stock of goods needed to be complete at this time, so he could supply the tribes with hunting supplies or lose business to other traders. Black Hawk said that everyone left the village for about forty days before returning. Some of the old men and women went to the lead mines and the remainder of the tribe fished or collected cattails in the swamps for the women to make their annual supply of mats. Until the corn was ready for picking they feasted again, held their ball games, horse races, and other dances, and visited among themselves.[4] It was a relaxed time for the tribe, and they often visited with the Davenports during this time.

The goal of the summer hunt was buffalo and for this hunt the braves usually went to the Des Moines River Valley in central Iowa. Sauk enemies, the Sioux, also hunted these buffalo grounds and contact between the tribes often ended in warfare. Davenport understood that even the slightest chance of meeting the Sioux was enough to make his hunters stay home. He had to work hard to persuade them to go on the hunt, because the tribes depended on them for food to feed the tribes until the corn was ripe. The hunt also provided some buffalo skins and red deer hides for trade, but never was the summer hunt as important as the winter hunt.[5]

While the hunters were away, Davenport ordered his goods for the coming winter season from his suppliers in St. Louis. He wanted to have them delivered to Rock Island by August, the time of the summer harvest, so that he would have on hand whatever clothing and hunting supplies the Indians might require for the winter. Late in September Davenport and all other traders established with the tribes were invited to meet with the tribal elders or chiefs. In council they agreed on the prices of trade goods as well as the prices each trader would pay for the furs. They also decided on the location of that winter's trading house where additional supplies could be obtained, and where the furs would be collected.[6] Afterwards Davenport delivered whatever goods the hunters required, and his clerk recorded the goods sold on credit in ledgers. Black Hawk decided what the chiefs or elders would tell the trader as to which men were good risks and which were not. Within days of this council the whole tribe would be ready to set off for the winter hunting grounds.

A few weeks after the tribe departed, Davenport sent his men to the hunting grounds to begin collecting the furs. It was important that they be at the agreed-upon place early in the hunting season to collect the furs and peltries, because the hunters were sometimes tempted to sell them to any trader whose post was closer to them, or who offered whiskey, or a better deal. Davenport's men took with them additional hunting supplies such as powder, flints, and new guns and traps, in case the hunters had lost or broken their equipment. They established temporary structures, or winter posts, at the agreed-upon places and waited for the Indians to bring in their furs throughout the winter and into the spring. In February, the month of the Cold Moon, the trappers prepared for the beaver hunt, as well as raccoon, muskrat, or bear. In early March part of the tribes went to the maple groves to collect the sap for making maple sugar. Generally the hunting season was over by the 10th of April when the cycle started all over again. Black Hawk says: "After this trade was over, the traders would give us a few kegs of rum, which was generally promised in the fall, to encourage us to make a good hunt, and not go to war."[7]

In the early years of his involvement in the Indian Trade, George Davenport travelled to the mines, to Fort Edwards, and to the Des Moines River post, supervising the trade. Sometimes, says the family, he went on foot. Other times he would go by canoe or horseback, but he was often travelling, visiting the various villages where he had established trade.[8] Eventually, as he built up his business, he hired clerks, interpreters, and others to do the day-to-day business, but Davenport supervised the work himself.

Davenport hired French Canadians called in French, engages, or in English, hirelings, to do the packing and transporting. Following in the tradition of fur trading since the early seventeenth century, Davenport hired men with names like Baptiste, Michel, Antoine, and Jacques. These men brought with them a rich cultural tradition in the fur trade industry and a long history of good relations with the Indians. Such men were invaluable in the Indian trade because they ate, drank, and slept with the Indians. They learned their languages and often married into Indian families, which gave these men valuable family ties with the Indians in the trade. Such men were by nature physically well suited to the many requirements of the trade as they were short, stocky men with great upper body strength and able to withstand the rigors of outdoor life. They served as boatmen, as clerks and interpreters, and as runners between posts and were loyal to whoever made them the best offer.[9] Short-term contracts helped to channel their independent natures.

A standard printed contract, usually written in French but occasionally written in English, was used. Some of the surviving contracts used by Davenport and other traders illustrate how the traders demanded complete loyalty from engages in an attempt to insure that trade secrets were kept from their cutthroat competitors. The voyageur, hivernant or hireling, agreed "to take good care of everything belonging to the said Farnham and Davenport such as merchandize, peltries, provisions, utensils, etc. ... to obey all lawful commands of the said Agents, also to use to my best endeavors to make his profits and evade his losses and to inform them of any thing touching their interest which may come to my knowledge ... " The contracts usually covered a period of one year, for salaries that ranged from one hundred twenty-five dollars to two hundred dollars, payable at the end of the contract period. In addition, French hirelings were given rations of meat and flour per day, a three-point blanket, soap and tobacco. Lodging was provided in the men's house at Rock Island or at the designated post near the hunting grounds. Most workers stayed for just a year or two before moving on, but a few, like Antoine Gokey, stayed for life. Gokey was probably Davenport's most loyal and trusted employee and the Davenports' closest neighbor outside the fort. Whenever George Davenport was away from his family and trading post for a time, according to old settler David Sears, Gokey was placed in charge. [10]

Family stories suggest that Davenport's capital investment was initially rather modest, but his activities seem to have expanded rapidly, perhaps due to his energy and ambition, and more perhaps to the lead trade. Unlike the old French traders who were content to stay at their posts and let the Indians come to them, Davenport set off across the prairie and visited every encampment he could find, a method called "en derouine." It allowed him flexibility in his trading and helped him get to know the Indian communities.[11] Blessed with a healthy constitution, disciplined from his years in the army, and energized by his new-found mission, George Davenport, now thirty-five, focused on expanding his trade.

Davenport had entered the trade at an opportune time. Although the business was rife with pitfalls and risks, it suited him. He established his post on Rock Island and encouraged the unpredictable Ho Chunk to come to him. It was a strategy that probably saved his life. His house on Rock Island, called Indian Lodge, was a central location that was convenient not only for trading, but also on the well-beaten path between Malden, where the British were based, and the western hunting grounds between the Mississippi and Missouri rivers. By 1819, Davenport was conducting trade in three areas: Rock River, Rocky Island, and Fever River near Galena. Early licenses and ledgers show that he dealt with six of the Mississippi river tribes: the Sauk and Mesquakie, Ho Chunk,

Ioway, Kickapoo, and Menominee. But he was far from the only trader in the region. There were many others fighting for a share in this lucrative business and the tactics they used were not always ethical or legal.

To further complicate the business, the U.S. Government had established a branch of the Fort Crawford Factory at Fort Edwards to compete with the independent traders. The Fort Edwards trade was particularly lucrative because it was located near the mouth of the rich Des Moines River Valley. Indian Agent Thomas Forsyth had noted earlier that a group of Sauk and Ioway Indians were settled near the fort site and planted corn there. The Mesquakie villages were not too far away on the Ioway River.[12]

One competitor there was John Campbell, a veteran of the war of 1812 who had been wounded during a dangerous mission on the Mississippi near what is today called Campbell's Island. Campbell had been appointed both post sutler and contractor's agent at Fort Edwards, and was also a licensed Indian trader employing at least fourteen men in both Illinois and Missouri Territories. His company had posts at Flint Hills, Fort Edwards, on the Des Moines, at Two Rivers, Bay Charles, at the mouth of the Little Maquoketa River, and at other places. Campbell's was no small trading outfit, and for George Davenport, who was just getting started, Campbell was a primary competitor. Not only was Campbell's business bigger and targeting the same Indians, but his men were found in all the places where Davenport had sold his credits. And, most importantly, Campbell was not above using whiskey to lure the trade away from others. According to one man who knew him, Major Campbell was "a great spendthrift who was fond of drinking" and his habit of using whiskey as a lure caught up with him at an opportune time for Davenport.[13]

In the spring of 1818, Captain James Ballard arrested Major Campbell and his partner Elisha Moore at Fort Edwards, and confiscated their merchandize for violations of the laws governing trade with Indians. Based on the testimony of other traders, this meant he was selling whiskey to the Indians. Among others, Edward Lagotherie testified that he had actually seen Campbell trading pelts for whiskey in the Mississippi area.

Campbell's "large and confident speech," was an attempt to hold his ground, but Captain Ballard held his ground as well.

Civil authorities in St. Louis refused to hear the case, as it appeared that the violations had occurred in Illinois Territory and was, therefore, beyond the jurisdiction of Missouri courts. Campbell escaped prosecution, but was forced to forfeit his bond when the matter was turned over to the District Attorney, which put him out of the business for a short time.[14] Campbell moved out of the Illinois country and into northern Missouri, but the vacuum created by his absence was quickly filled by George Davenport and other traders already in the field. Fort Edwards remained an important trading site for Davenport for all the years he was involved in the Indian Trade.

Another vacancy was created at Prairie du Chien when veteran British trader, Colonel Robert Dickson, was arrested at Fort Crawford. Dickson had operated there under a license from Mackinac for years and had actively promoted the British during the War of 1812. The Sauk in particular were susceptible to his promises and presents, and for this reason, he was considered especially dangerous to American interests. During the spring of 1818 he was transported to the Civil Authorities in St. Louis by Benjamin O'Fallon, U. S. Indian Agent. As they slowly travelled down the river to St. Louis, only the Sauk of Rock Island showed any displeasure at one of their British traders being removed from their country. Both the Sioux and the Mesquakie had expressed pleasure that this dissident was being removed from their midst, but among the traders, no one regretted his removal.[15]

With the arrests of these men, the American government signalled that it was clearing the Indian country of foreigners, cracking down on violators of the law, and taking over the Indian trade. By securing the borders, the government hoped to reduce foreign influences, and keep the peace among the various Indian tribes. It was a break for Davenport, who quickly moved in to fill that void, but it also served to teach him, and everyone else in Indian country, the rules of the Indian trade. Alcohol was one lesson that he paid particularly strict attention to and he was never accused of using it in his trade.

As in the previous year, the year-round presence of an Indian Agent was warranted for a stricter enforcement of the laws, and in the following month, the Illinois Indian Agency in Peoria was closed and the agent transferred to Rock River. Sauk and Mesquakie movement, however, delayed any building on Rock Island. Indian Agent Forsyth reported that the tribes were intending to move their villages to the Ioway River, sixty or eighty miles west of the Mississippi, well beyond the jurisdiction of the Illinois Governor. Forsyth was comfortably settled in St. Louis and not eager to live at Rock Island. He successfully argued, as he had in the past, that the Indians were in their villages for only about four or five months out of each year and that it would be prudent for him to visit in May and September rather than risking his life, and that of his family, in Indian Country.[16] Plans for the Fort Armstrong Agency were put on hold and Forsyth rented a cabin from the Davenports when he visited Fort Armstrong. The much-needed interpreter, however, was hired during this summer. Antoine Le Claire, whom George had met during his assignment to Peoria Lake, was sent to Rock Island for a brief time.

Le Claire was the son of Antoine LeClaire Sr., a French Canadian trader associated with the trading firm of Kinzie & Forsyth at least since 1800. Both father and son had worked with Forsyth at Peoria since 1809. Antoine junior had been schooled in languages and had been the Potawatomie interpreter at the Illinois Indian Agency in Peoria since June of 1816, serving under Thomas Forsyth. He probably worked at the fort for just a few months before leaving with a party of commissioners and government surveyor John C. Sullivan, who were to survey the boundaries of the Osage lands that winter. In the spring, Le Claire was assigned elsewhere, and T. Honorie, also a U.S. interpreter at St. Louis, was hired to accompany Forsyth. Other interpreters were used at the mines and at Prairie du Chien.[17]

Several events that summer offer a glimpse into Davenport's life at that time. Although still loyal to the British and not overly friendly to Americans, the Sauk were beginning to accept the American presence. Davenport had found some friends among them. One day when he was searching for stray cattle on the island, an old Indian rescued him from an attack by some rowdy Indians. The old man recognized him as being British and called out "Saganosh," meaning "he is an Englishman." The attackers stopped immediately, and the name stuck.[18] It should be noted, however, that the name was not unique to George Davenport, but a way of identifying all British persons whose ways were familiar to them. Still, it was an important point with the Indians with whom George traded.

Not long after Davenport had begun trading with the Ho Chunk villages on the Rock River, George had a narrow escape from certain death. He had gone to the Prophet's Town on the Rock River with Antoine Gokey and four or five horse packs, but when they arrived at the lodge of an old friend, the old man said that he was sorry that they had come at that time. He was afraid that the traders would be killed because there was a war party starting from the village at that time. He invited them in, however, and told them to show no signs of alarm. In a few minutes, a large crowd surrounded the lodge and the old man stepped to the door to see what they wanted. They answered that they wanted to kill the white men, but the old man spoke to them about the rights of hospitality and the sacredness of his lodge. He also told them that they had plenty of time, since the traders were planning to stay for several days. When the crowd dispersed, the old man told Davenport and Gokey to set up camp as if they were preparing for several days' trading, and then steal away in the night. Following the old man's instructions, Davenport and Gokey were able to escape in a canoe, although they saw several campfires along the river during the night and had to float by them without noise. Some time later, Old Wataico, the man who had helped Davenport and his men escape, told what happened next. The next morning the whole village headed by the Crane turned out, armed with tomahawks, bows and arrows, war paint, and singing their war song while dancing and beating their drums. They soon discovered that the white man was unpredictable. After this Davenport declined to visit the Rock River villages, and restricted his trade with them to his home post.

A second attempt by the Ho Chunk, this time at Rock Island in the fall of 1819, involved the entire Davenport family. A war party led by the same chieftain named Crane, arrived at Davenport's store about sundown and wanted to trade. Davenport refused to open his store until the next morning, but invited them to stay the night in the room occupied by his men. This room was separated from the family quarters by a chimney wall that had a short passage from one room to the other, with a door at each end. One of George's men, named Jerome, was suspicious that the Ho Chunk hadn't taken off their moccasins before lying down to sleep, and so it was decided that the men should keep watch until morning. Shortly before the men went to sleep, one of the Indians asked permission to sleep in the same room as the family, since the other room was crowded. In the middle of the night, Jerome turned over and rattled his powder horn. This alarmed the Indian who sprang to his feet, yelled, and rushed into the other room. When the Indians came rushing into their room, Davenport and his men levelled their guns at them, and the Indians retreated into their room, barricading the door. No other sounds were heard for the rest of the night, and in the morning, they could see that the Indians had left. Some time later, the Davenports learned that the Crane's party had intended to murder the whole family and loot the store. Failing this, the Ho Chunk party lurked about the area for any opportunity to kill someone. They soon succeeded in shooting and scalping two soldiers who had gone into the woods to make axe-handles.[19]

The Ho Chunk were openly hostile to all inhabitants of the island. They were silent, treacherous foes who hid in marsh grasses and sprang at unsuspecting victims. Davenport's stepdaughter, Susan Lewis, had her own personal encounter with them. The following story is a rare example of the Davenport women's experiences with dangers on the frontier. It was interpreted by Mary Brackett Durham, who retold many of Susan's tales in verse:

> *Some tribes were foes of ours; I'll tell*
> *A tale - to show you_ of what befell*
> *Me, one time in the early spring,*
> *If left alone I was apt to sing;*
> *By the window, singing, I went to spin*

When a tall Winnebago stepped catlike in.

Make me coffee, he wickedly sneered; I knew
That if hostile to Black Hawk, he was to us too;
But I rose to obey, and had scarce turned round,
When he seized my arm with a noiseless bound.
I screamed with despair, as he felt for his knife,
It was gone; which saved me my scalp and life.

The pouch that hung from his neck had worn through,
And the knife dropped out where he hid his canoe
Near the cave. The traitor was seen no more
By living man; he had vanished before
Our men ran in, - for they heard my scream.
The Sauks and Foxes searched isle and stream.[20]

During the summer and fall of 1819, there was a lot of troop movement on the Mississippi. As mentioned in the previous chapter, a new fort was established at the St. Peters River, in what is now Minnesota, and the troops stopped for the night at Fort Armstrong. Another visitor was a Methodist circuit rider by the name of Peter Williams, who preached the first sermon in the area. Reverend Williams was an occasional visitor to the settlements along the Mississippi, because he regularly carried the mail between Clarksville, Missouri, and Rock Island every three months. It was on one of these occasions that he stayed long enough to offer a little religion to the few residents of the island, perhaps at the urging of the Post Commander or maybe even the Davenport women. Reverend Williams considered himself a "preacher on his own hook," although most reminiscences suggest he was Methodist. He had settled with his wife, Rebecca, in the vicinity of Fort Edwards and was known to be something of a botanist. He operated the first ferry in the vicinity of the fort and speculated in land, buying sections offered at the annual tax sales. His knowledge of how the tax sales worked would prove useful to the Davenports in acquiring land for themselves.[21]

During this time, Farnham was still in St. Louis and having problems getting licenses to trade in Missouri and Illinois. Despite a circular sent by the Secretary of War John C. Calhoun, the American Fur Company was still trying to get clearance for their employees before another year was lost. Farnham's detainment had already cost the Company $2,721.09, and he especially was eager to get back in the field. One of the sticking points for the American Fur Company was Mackinac Island, which happened to be the best place for illegal aliens to enter the Great Lakes-Mississippi Valley for trading purposes. The American Fur Company used Mackinac as their supply depot, and the company complained that they were being sanctioned for this as well as for using men who had once worked for the British. Eventually, the American Fur Company ceded this point and moved their headquarters to St. Louis.[22]

Farnham continued to experience a number of difficulties, primarily from rival traders who had headquarters at St. Louis, but also from the military. Rumors had been circulating about the American Fur Company, stirring up suspicion and fear about the company's tactics and ambitions. There seemed to be a concerted effort to keep the company out of the Indian trade. Farnham must have heard about this new trader, Davenport, who was working in his territory. David Lavender, in The Fist in the Wilderness, suggests that the ambitious George Davenport was probably the main competition to the American Fur Company with the Rock River Indians and that the partnership with Farnham was a workable solution to the competition. Farnham, according to Lavender, had two choices: either force Davenport to dissolve his business, or incorporate him into the Company. It was a recruiting strategy often used by the Company.[23]

After a wasted year in St. Louis, Farnham was cleared to trade for the winter of 1818-1819 on the Mississippi below Prairie du Chien, but the Sauk, Mesquakie, and Ioway were hunting in northern Missouri and on the Des Moines River. Farnham was needed there, so Ramsay Crooks sent Farnham to the Missouri River and brought in Maurice Blondeau to supervise the trade at Rock River under Farnham's direction. General Clark, Superintendent of Indian Affairs in St Louis, would not allow Farnham to take his old crew with him to the Missouri River. After another delay, Farnham found a new crew of fourteen boatmen with no suspicious foreigners and proceeded to row his barges up the Missouri to the Grand River and the Des Moines River Valley.[24] He intended to follow the previous year's instructions, giving credit north of the Indian boundary line near Rock River and establishing his winter camp to wait for the furs to come in from the hunt. Instead Crooks instructed Farnham to spend the winter at Rock Island where Maurice Blondeau was living with the Sauk. Blondeau had recently been recruited by Crooks to work with Farnham, although he had been an employee of the Cabanne and Co., a company also supplied with goods by the American Fur Company. Though it had been understood that the American Fur Company would not compete with Cabanne, the lost revenue of the previous year gave Crooks the justification he needed to recruit Blondeau and send Farnham into the territory.

Blondeau was part-Sauk and part French. He had grown up in the Indian trade and acted as Indian Agent for the Sauk during the late war, but the Governor of Illinois had disapproved of his trading activities on the side. He had then been appointed Indian Agent for Missouri Territory before his association with Cabanne & Co.[25] His defection to the American Fur Company was typical of those who worked in the industry.

With Blondeau and Farnham positioned in the Des Moines and Rock River areas, Crooks believed that the American Fur Company was well represented to all the natives in the Upper Mississippi Valley.[26] Farnham's share of the profits from his trade with Sauk and Mesquakie in 1819 was $768.54 -- not a bad sum considering the problems of the two previous years, but the company had higher expectations for profits from the Mississippi Indians.

Farnham, as the main decision-maker for the company in the field, expected to expand the company's influence and profits among the tribes. He was also looking for new men to bring into the company. Crooks authorized Farnham to make whatever arrangements he needed to hire any person he thought "safe," in order to further the company's interests. A regular assortment of goods would be furnished at 100% to those traders who would come to Mackinac for them and pay one half of the total at the time of the purchase. Once the new recruit was considered "safe" Farnham could offer him an Outfit of his own. George Davenport was one of those under consideration.[27]

Although he had been a trader only a short time, Davenport had already established himself as a man the Indians trusted and could rely on. For that reason alone he was the kind of man the American Fur Company wanted. He had good credentials. He was also energetic, a self-starter who needed no prodding from the Company. He also had connections to the military, with a well-established post at Rocky Island, a choice location with military protection nearby. Davenport had the approval of the military to be in the trade, and Farnham had need of a good relationship with the local commanders after his recent experience. Davenport was also an excellent judge of furs and Crooks demanded only good skins, preferably beaver, otter, and muskrats and they were not to be second quality. Davenport also had experience in accounting and transporting goods on sea and in the army. All he had to do was prove his loyalty to the Company.

Loyalty in this business was an issue and the loyalty of new men had to be cultivated carefully. The stakes were high, competition fierce, and the profits attractive. Crooks wanted only loyal men, not traders who jumped ship whenever a better offer came along. He was, therefore, cautious in his hiring of new traders, often watching a trader for two full seasons to assess the trader's intentions and loyalty. The tactic was pretty standard and Davenport was drawn into the Company in this way: by a simple agreement, Farnham sold goods to Davenport in exchange for a comparable amount of furs at the end of the season. The risk was on Farnham rather than the Company. Davenport remained free to purchase goods from other suppliers with similar arrangements, and he could be relatively independent as long as he could pay his creditors. Then, after a period of time, probably two or three seasons, a contract might be offered, should Davenport prove himself to be a loyal and successful trader for the Company and both parties could agree on terms.

Crooks had another reason for getting good men in his camp. The Company was expanding and the new trade area was large, too large for one man to oversee. Russel Farnham was in charge of this district, but he still had obligations to appear in court on the unsettled suit against the government. He was summoned to appear in St. Louis on four different occasions, in April and August 1819, and in March and October 1820.[28] These were critical months in the Indian Trade and the company needed someone in the field who was trustworthy during Farnham's absence. Sometime in 1819, Farnham and Davenport began just such a trading relationship. It was not yet a partnership, but it would be profitable and evolve into a close friendship.

Until 1822 when the American Fur Company established a branch in St. Louis, the American Fur Company was supplied with goods from Mackinac and, according to family stories recorded by Wilkie, George Davenport ordered an assortment of Indian goods, camping equipage, four hands, and a Mackinaw boat. They were delivered to Rock Island from Mackinac in time for the winter hunt of 1819 - 1820.[29] After this time, goods were readily available from merchants in St. Louis and Davenport shifted his purchasing habits to St. Louis merchants, many of whom he probably knew from his army days at Bellefontaine.

Davenport had been doing a brisk business in lead since the summer of 1816. That he had confidence in this aspect of the trading business is evidenced by his invitation to Crooks to become his partner in the mines, even before he was under contract with the American Fur Company. Crooks, however, was reluctant to make such a commitment until he knew the parameters of the deal: the amount of capital required, Davenport's expectations of his share of the profits, and the prospect of success.[30] Although Davenport sold some lead to the Company, the amounts in the American Fur Company ledgers do not reflect the quantities coming from the mines at that time, suggesting that other St. Louis merchants bought his lead. It was, however, a major component of his trade with the natives who depended on the lead to provide their people with necessities from traders.

During the summer months Sauk, Mesquakie, and Ho Chunk all worked the lead mines in northwestern Illinois and northeastern Iowa. During the War of 1812, the tribes had been unable to market their lead, and so the tribes were eager to begin trading their lead after 1815. There were, according to Thomas Forsyth, seven mines readily producing lead just two to four feet below the surface of the ground.[31] The mineral was easily extracted from the ground by the women and old men who did not go on the summer hunt. Before being sent to St. Louis, the lead was smelted to remove impurities and formed into pigs. The business was so good that Davenport formed a partnership with Dr. Samuel Muir at the mines.

Dr. Muir was a medical doctor originally from Washington, D.C., who had served as a young surgeon with the 1st United States Infantry. Perhaps Davenport had met him while in the service. More recently Dr. Muir had served as post surgeon at Fort Edwards then at Fort Armstrong. When orders to disassociate with Indian women were announced in July 1819, Dr. Muir chose to leave the army rather than leave his Indian wife. The legend of his being saved from certain death at the hands of the Winnebago by an Indian maiden who hid him and brought him food until danger had passed has often been told. Muir, in gratitude, married her and they had five children before he died in 1832. The story has been much romanticized, but is illustrative of the anti-Indian attitudes in the military at that time. Muir's marriage to a Mesquakie woman was an asset to his trading activities, and he had the added advantage of speaking the language.[32]

When the partnership was formed is unknown, but in the fall of 1819, miner Jesse Shull found Muir already established at the mines with a supply of goods furnished by George Davenport. Noted frontier historian Henry Schoolcraft said that Dr. Muir offered to accompany him to explore the Indian lead mines during the summer of 1820.[33] Later Muir had a partnership with Shull at the Portage Farm or Place (Galena) where he continued to practice medicine in addition to his trading with Davenport. Forming partnerships was a way for Davenport to expand his business to widespread locations.

That year, nearly all the Sauk were living in the village on the Rock River, even the so-called Missouri Sauk, a band of the tribe who planted their corn at Saukenuk but wintered in northeastern Missouri. The

Missouri Sauk had some political differences with the Rock River Sauk. In general, the Missouri band was friendly to Americans and open to American ways. They were even in favor of the surveying of their lands and assigning of small parcels to each family. They were also excellent hunters. The Rock River bands were more traditional in their thinking, and Black Hawk's band, in particular, was still attached to the British at Malden. The result was a rift in the tribe as a whole.[34] The combined strength in numbers that year was considerable, about five thousand strong.

By the following year, the Sauk and Mesquakie were living in several summer village sites. Two Sauk villages were located in Illinois near the mouths of the Rock and Des Moines Rivers. The Mesquakie villages were on the Turkey River, at the mouth of the Wapsipinicon River, at the Dubuque Mines, and across the slough from Fort Armstrong. The Ioway and Missouri Sauk had villages on the Des Moines and Grand Rivers. Where these bands hunted during the winter dictated where traders would position themselves and establish posts.[35]

The Indian tribes of the Upper Mississippi Valley began to escalate their hunting practices and expand their hunting territories in the early 1820s. To accommodate the Missouri Sauk, Davenport began to look for a new post location more convenient to their wintering grounds. Fort Edwards, located near the Lower Rapids of the Mississippi River, was closed in the spring of 1819, when the Rifle Regiment was ordered to the Yellowstone. Without soldiers to enforce the laws, Davenport had no secure place for collecting his furs from the Des Moines River Valley. A small band of perhaps six to thirteen lodges of Sauk lived in the area and several traders had already staked out the trade.[36] Until the Fort Edwards site was made a fur factory site, Davenport chose a new town just being developed at Clarksville, Missouri, as a potential trading post.

Clarksville was founded by John Miller, who later became Governor of Missouri, and Richard Graham, who had been Indian Agent for the Illinois Territory and was then Indian Agent for the Osage. Their town site offered many advantages to Davenport. It was, first of all, accessible to the Missouri Band of the Sauk who were moving back to the Missouri

Valley, near the Grand River, where they had lived during the War of 1812. The area was a favorite hunting ground of theirs and they had always been responsible hunters and repaid their credits. It was reason enough for Davenport to have a post there.[37]

The new town was close enough to the villages to collect furs, and the lots Davenport purchased were suitable for establishing a storehouse with room for a fur press and a counting room to pack his furs for shipment to St. Louis. It was also positioned close enough to his competitors to keep his eye on their movements. John Campbell, who had been removed from Fort Edwards, had his new post just a few miles upriver in nearby Louisiana, Missouri, with his two sons and their employees.

The location of Clarksville on the Mississippi River offered a good landing for boats. Recently, the steamboat General Pike had come up the Mississippi as far as St. Louis, and other steamboats expected to be landing at Clarksville on a regular basis within a year. Having his own property in town had the added advantage of security, and the experience Davenport gained in watching the town develop were lessons he would use later in his career.

The town lots were sold at public auction on the 15th of May 1819. On that day Davenport bought two lots, lots sixteen and eighty-five, for which he paid two hundred and fifty dollars and two hundred dollars respectively. That was a rather large sum considering that most of the other sixty-two lots sold that day averaged about one hundred and twenty-six dollars per lot. Perhaps there was stiff competition for the lots close to the river, which were among the choicest lots in town. Several lots had been reserved for promotional reasons. One lot was reserved for the original owner and ten other lots were donated to a number of tradesmen and professional men, such as the doctor, surveyor, tailor, blacksmith, joiner, and brick-maker, in exchange for their promise to remain in the town for a certain length of time and help to encourage settlement.[38] Whether or not Davenport actually constructed buildings there or rented the property to others, is not known, but it is probable that he built storehouses there of one kind or another. He sold these two lots later and bought another town lot that he retained as late as 1830.

Davenport may have had high expectations for the trade with the Missouri Sauk, but there were pitfalls. The Sauk and Mesquakie were at war with the Missouri tribes - Otoes, Omahas, and Osages - in an effort to procure more furs, especially buffalo. Although the Sauk and Mesquakie had agreements with the Ioway to hunt across Iowa to the Missouri River, these hunting grounds bordered those of the Sioux and the Missouri tribes. Any contact between enemy tribes in the hunting grounds potentially ended the hunt for the year.[39]

The Ho Chunk were also restless, particularly around Rock Island. They had killed a number of hogs and cattle, and destroyed nearly a thousand bushels of corn stored by the Sauk and Mesquakie in the fall, and the following spring, they turned against the Americans. Two soldiers from Fort Armstrong were found murdered a mile and a half from the walls of the fort. Their bodies were "shot, scalped, and mangled." Amos Farrar, who clerked in the post store at Fort Armstrong, casually mentioned to his brother that a third soldier had been missing and eventually found in the river, shot, scalped, and stabbed in September of that year. The effects of the attack were felt up and down the river.[40]

Robert Belt, the government factor who remained at Fort Edwards with military protection, wrote: "My situation here is critical. The Winnebago are determined to destroy this place. They are rendered more desperate on account of the Foxes having taken side with the Americans for the murder of the two soldiers at Fort Armstrong ... I have now about thirteen thousand dollars worth of the public property in my charge which must fall a sacrifice to the Indians unless taken from this (place) soon ... Mr Blondeau has this moment returned from Rock River & says the whole Indian village is in commotion, and that the Indians are ripe for any mischief. ... I do not put much faith in the promises of the Sacks - within the last week the Sacks & Foxes have sent out large war parties against the Winnebagos, Siouxs & Osages... " For safety, Mrs. Belt and her children were sent to Louisianaville and then on to St. Louis.

In response to the Ho Chunk outbreaks, troops were again stationed at Fort Edwards. On the 10th of May 1820, a lieutenant with twenty soldiers arrived to take possession of the fort. New orders restricted the Indians to conducting business outside the fort walls, but Belt reported that they came to trade a little each day, and that the trade for the year had been in his estimation "handsome." The Indians who had been given credit the previous fall had paid very well. Fortunately, the Indian storm ended quickly when the murderers were given up by the Ho Chunk and confined. With the return of the soldiers, however, Mr. Belt had had to move out of the fort and return to his cabin which was, according to Mr. Johnston, "like pig pens on a gentleman's farm."[41] Despite the reduced living conditions, life around both forts returned to normalcy for the summer.

Manning Fort Edwards seemed to help quiet the countryside but only temporarily. A council held by Colonel Leavenworth in the summer seemed to pacify the Ho Chunk, but peace was short-lived. Another Fort Armstrong soldier, John Haines, was murdered in the fall. The surgeon's report, made public in the St. Louis Enquirer, graphically illustrated the atrocities that could be committed upon anyone living on the frontier. It not only served as a warning to all prospective travellers, but also exacerbated the fear of Indians in the Mississippi Valley. John Haines' body was not a sight for the squeamish:

One tomahawk cut directly on the right side
of the skull, in a line with the tip of the right ear,
another very similar cut on the left side of the skull
inclining towards the left eye, the hairy scalp
completely taken off, one stab on the right cheek,
one stab on the right jaw near the chin, seven stabs in
the hollow of the back very near each other, three
stabs on the back of the left shoulder, one stab on
the top of the left shoulder, one deep stab in the left
side near the region of the heart, one very extensive
and deep stab directly below the breast bone, one
buckshot above the left eyebrow, three buckshot
directly below the left ear in the left temple, three

> *buckshot in the left armpit, several scattered*
> *buckshot lodged in the left side, and left arms.*[42]

The restlessness was contagious. The Ioway began to move south westerly into the area between the Iowa and Missouri rivers. The Missouri band of Sauk and Mesquakie, having disagreements with the Rock River Sauk under the leadership of Keokuck, separated and moved into northern Missouri and southern Iowa, and hunted in the Des Moines River valley in the area of the Fox and Calumet Rivers.

The movement of these two bands, the Iowa and Missouri Sauk and Fox, presented some logistical problems for George Davenport. His partnership with George Kennerly ended after the 1821-1822 hunting season, when Kennerly was appointed Indian Agent on the Missouri River. How Davenport carried on his Des Moines River trade with the Missouri Sauk is not known for certain. County histories suggest that in 1820 Dr. Muir had built a log cabin in what is now Keokuk, about a mile from the trader Maurice Blondeau and six miles from Lamoliese, an old French trader well-established at Sandusky (Illinois). Other sources indicate that Dr. Muir was trading in the Galena area. It is possible that he worked for Davenport at both places, at the mines in the summer and Keokuk in the winter, but this would have taxed him considerably and the Des Moines trade was too good for Davenport not to have someone operating in the area. About this time, Major Morrill Marston entered into some kind of arrangement with Davenport and Farnham.[43]

Marston had been commander of Fort Armstrong (1819-1821) and at the reopened Fort Edwards (1822-1824). He had engaged in trading on the side, as many soldiers on the frontier did, and settled near the Fort Edwards site after being dismissed from service. So, Marston was in an ideal location to collect the Indians' credits as they came in from their winter hunt. He could also keep an eye on the village where other traders were peddling their whiskey.[44]

At the mines, Dr. Muir withdrew from partnership with Davenport and Amos Farrar, who had clerked at Fort Armstrong's post store, became Davenport's new partner at Fever River. Farrar was a young man from Massachusetts (b.5 March 1796). After marrying a Mesquakie woman named Maganno, with whom he had three daughters, Farrar settled in the lead mine region. By late 1820 he was in charge of the Fever River trading post on a full-time basis. Fever River was a permanent post, operating under the name of Davenport and Farrar at the Portage Place, about two and a half miles below present-day Galena. The portage was used as a cut-off between the Mississippi and the Fever Rivers, and an ideal place for a trading house for the miners. Davenport was now well positioned in the Upper Mississippi Valley.

The Indian Trade was a fiercely competitive business, in large part because there was money to be made. How much money depended to a large extent on the investment, how much time a trader was willing to spend in collecting furs, how well he could work with his customers and outmaneuver his competitors. Davenport was said to have been more energetic than the French traders, personally visiting the Indian villages and advocating against whisky and fighting with enemies. Partnering helped him expand his business and keep his Indians productive and honest in their commitment to him.

A comparison of wages on the frontier at that time illustrates the lure of the fur trade. The average soldier made seventy-two dollars per year (plus clothing and daily rations). Unskilled workers, or engages, in the Indian trade earned around one hundred and twenty dollars per year, plus rations and clothing. Interpreters commanded a dollar per day, or about three hundred and sixty-five dollars per year. The Indian Agent, whose salary was at the top of the governmental scale for those in the field, was twelve hundred dollars. Davenport, as an independent trader, could expect to clear upwards of four hundred dollars profit in even the slimmest years, and over a thousand in a good year. By keeping his store on the island for soldiers and occasional visitors, he could do very well for himself and family.

Using his knowledge of the Illinois Indians and a common sense approach to trading with them, Davenport began the physical aspects of building his business. Soon a small village developed around his home on Rocky Island as he constructed storehouses, or stores, in which to house his goods, furs, business records, and employees. He had brought cattle, then oxen, horses, and hogs to the island, and built barns and stables to house them. The structures he built were as comfortable as any could be for that time and place. After traversing the prairies and rivers of the Mississippi Valley, experiencing every kind of miserable weather imaginable, he understood the need for comfort and a good stove to keep them warm. To reduce his overhead as well as to save time, he purchased canoes and keelboats for transporting his goods to and from St. Louis and expanded his side businesses, such as cutting hay and raising livestock for sale to the U.S. Government for use by the soldiers at Fort Armstrong, for added security for his family. Although the Indian Trade had high profits, it also had high risks. So much of his profit depended on factors he could not control: weather, the availability of game, conflict among Indian tribes, and the price of furs on the international market.

The demand for furs remained high during the early 1820s, particularly because of the European market, where fashion demanded beaver and other furs not available there. But the situation was changing. The Indians ranged farther and farther from their own village sites to obtain more and more furs and invariably intruded upon the hunting grounds of others. Conflict among competing tribes escalated, as settlers moved into the traditional lands of the Indians, the wild game moved further west, or were reduced in numbers. Yet the demand for furs continued.

Davenport had entered the business at an opportune time. He had drawn on his military connections and used his connections to key St. Louis people, like the Hempstead and Kennerly families, who provided him with security and bonds, with goods, and with links to other people and places. It was an effective networking system that served Davenport well. By the end of the 1820 season, Davenport had developed a reputation for honesty in selling his goods and was a familiar, even welcomed, visitor to the Indian villages of the Upper Mississippi Valley, particularly Saukenuk. Son Bailey Davenport used to point out the spot where his father built his trading post near Black Hawk's watch tower and where his father often sat in council with the Sauk and other hunters as they prepared for the winter hunts. No one expected the trade to last, so

Davenport used the opportunities that came his way as stepping-stones to others.[45]

The most common type of travel on the western rivers was the keelboat. It required ten boatmen plus a patroon, or steersman, who watched from an elevated position and led the songs that kept the boatmen in sync as they poled along the rivers.

CHAPTER SIX:

DAVENPORT'S CREDIT BOOKS

GEORGE DAVENPORT WAS A consummate record keeper. Unfortunately, relatively few of his record books, often referred to as ledgers, have survived. He kept daily logs, usually referred to as daybooks, credit books that itemized individual accounts, and memoranda books that recorded a wide variety of information including inventory, cash payments, notes taken and paid, and even steamboat arrivals and departures from Rock Island. Completely absent from the Davenport Collection are the lead books, records of furs and peltries collected, records of land purchased and sold, and household accounts. Despite this, the surviving books show how Davenport's attention to detail and record keeping made him a valuable agent of the American Fur Company.

In the Davenport Collection are two credit books that illustrate how the credit system worked, the kinds of goods bought by the Indians, the furs that were brought to Davenport to pay the credits, and how the business changed over time.[1] The goods and supplies that traders and hunters supplied to one another did not change much over the years, nor did the method by which accounts were kept. The earliest credit book in the Davenport Collection, though unidentified as to whose trade it was, shows how promising the winter trade was in the winter of 1819 - 1820 and why Davenport wanted to break into trade with the Rock River tribes.

The Credit book recorded the hunting supplies given to each hunter just prior to the winter hunt. After the tribal elders and traders met in council to discuss the prospects of the coming trade, they agreed on several points: the location of that year's hunting grounds, and the place where the furs would be collected, how much credit would be given to each hunter, and how much the trader would pay for each pelt in the spring. It was a system that had been used between traders and hunters since the seventeenth century.

The credit book entitled 1819 Indian Accounts with Kickapoo, Renard, Fals Avoins, Algonkian, Iowas is a small book, written in the French language by the trader's clerk, and contains 195 separate accounts with a total of $11, 651.75 given on credit.[2] Unfortunately, there is no identifying clue in the book as to whose trade it records. Wilkie suggests that Davenport was, in fact, trading with the Sauk and Mesquakie by this early date, and Indian Agent Thomas Forsyth noted that the Sauk, Mesquakie and Iowa were all together at Rock River in the summer of 1819. That would account for the wide variety of tribes represented in this book. Regardless of whose book this is, it provides insights into the trade for the 1819 - 1820 season.

With the exception of the last three entries, the accounts were generated on one day, 7 October 1819. Each account identifies the hunter by name and lists the supplies he purchased, such as guns, powder, traps, and spears. There are two values given to each article, one is the cash value of the item, and the second is the amount charged the hunter on credit, which would be repaid with furs in the spring.

The mark up on trade goods was high, sometimes as much as 400 per cent, but that does not translate directly to high profits for the trader.

Rather, it reflects the percentage of interest the trader owed to the company for the initial inventory, plus transportation costs to the post from Mackinac Island, as well as a small mark up to cover the trader's potential losses. Not all credits were repaid, as can be seen in accounts that are not balanced. This was predictable in the Indian trade and due to a variety of reasons, such as poor hunting conditions, attacks by enemy tribes, or illness and/or death of the hunter.

Consumable goods, such as tobacco and vermillion, which could not be returned or reclaimed by the trader in lieu of payment, had a higher mark up than goods such a rifles and traps, which could be used and returned. The following are some examples from the 1819 Ledger that show not only what the hunters were buying but also the mark up on individual items.

Couverte, or blankets, sold at $5.00 on credit, a 122% mark-up from the $2.25 cash value. The blanket was the standard item of clothing for the hunter and served not only to keep him warm but also to keep the rain off of him.

Vermillion, a red paint used by the Sauk and Fox for ceremonial decoration, held tremendous symbolic significance and was an essential part of the hunter's wardrobe. It was sold on credit for $4.00, a 220% mark-up from its $1.25 cash value.

Tabac, or tobacco, was every hunter's essential ingredient smoked in ceremony before the hunt began and also at the conclusion of a successful hunt. Tobacco was sold in varying quantities at a 200% mark-up.

Fusils, or long-barrelled rifles, commonly called Kentucky rifles.

Carabines, or short barrelled, large bored rifles, sold at $35.00 on credit and $30.00 cash, for a relatively small mark-up of 16.67%. This type of gun was preferred by the Indians over the long rifle, or Kentucky rifle. No lead for bullets was sold because the Sauk and Fox mined their own lead and made their own bullets.

Flint and gunpowder, two essentials for hunting with guns, were sold at substantial mark-ups: flint at 433% and powder at

200%. Flint was imported from England, easily broken or lost, and an item that was never returned for credit against the hunter's account. Items such as guns and traps could be, and often were, returned at the end of the season for full credit.

Other non-perishable items, such as looking glasses, horse bridles, knives, and kettles, could theoretically be returned or confiscated by the trader in lieu of payment and therefore commanded a lower mark-up percentage than perishable items.

Knives, both large and small (gros or fins couteaux) were used by the hunter for skinning and carving game meat. The smaller ones were more easily broken and consequently had a higher mark up of 220%. The larger knives sold for $.50 cash and $1.00 each on credit for a 100% mark up. The smaller knives sold for $4.00 credit and $1.25 cash.

In addition, yard goods such as calico, buttons, and other supplies for clothing production, and small amounts of personal items such as combs and looking glasses were considered essential for daily living and are found in the ledger. The total amount of credits given in these two days was $19, 641.75, a significant amount of credit.[3]

After the credits were given and supplies handed out, the trader sent his clerk and his men into the field to the agreed-upon collection point. The men constructed a winter camp and waited for the hunters to bring in their skins and peltries. The clerk was supplied with additional hunting supplies, such as gunpowder and shot, in case the hunters needed more during the hunt. It was important that the trader's men have enough supplies so that the hunters would not find it necessary to go to another trader.

In 1819, The American Fur Company discouraged its traders from accepting any deer and bearskins, as the market was saturated and prices low for them. "Get rid of deer if you can - deer will not do well and Bear, even worse," wrote Ramsay Crooks to Russel Farnham. Instead, the traders were encouraged to obtain beaver and otter, as the prices for those were high. Farnham was instructed to pay $3.50 for beaver and $4.50 for otter. In addition to beaver and otter, the American Fur Company was willing to pay that year the following prices: muskrats, 25 cents, raccoons, 50 cents, and buffalo robes, $3.25.[4]

Despite the instructions to Farnham, repayment was most often made with deer hides, both male and female, according to the 1819 Credit Book. Bucks were valued at $1.00 each; does at $.50 each. Les grandes castor or larger beaver were the most highly valued furs at $6.00 each for prime quality, and three dollars for average-sized pelts. Loutres, or otter, brought three or four dollars depending on the quality and size of the fur. Reynard (or fox), Chat (cats), and vision (mink) were less common and paid only $.25 to $.50 apiece. Especially fine bearskins brought two dollars apiece, while common quality brought a dollar per hide. Notably absent from these accounts is muskrat, which became a substitute for beaver in later years. In 1819, beaver were still plentiful enough and the price paid for each skin was high enough that these particular Indians gave almost no attention to the muskrat.

During the late winter and early spring of 1820 the hunters began to come in from their hunting grounds with their furs and peltries. The clerk recorded the kind and quantity of furs each hunter brought and the value of the furs applied to the amount owed. Of the 195 accounts, 69 or 35% of the total, were paid in full and marked "a tout paye" or "paye." Those paid with a surplus were marked "solde." One account was marked "ren paye," indicating that the goods had been returned to balance the account. A few accounts were marked with a promise to pay after the summer hunt, which generally was held in July while the corn was ripening. Generally credits due over a year were disregarded, with no attempt to collect them.

The rest of the accounts were either partially paid or left unpaid. Ninety accounts, or 40% of the total, had nothing applied to them whatsoever. 36 accounts, or 18.46% of the total, were partially repaid in some fashion. The remaining accounts were marked "de lette ete" and the credit was extended to the summer hunt with varying degrees of successful repayment.

How typical the returns were for this group of Indians in the year 1819 - 1820 cannot be assessed with any certainty, but the picture they show helps to explain what the risks were for the trader and why his goods were marked up so high. If a trader could only expect 35% of his credits to be repaid, then the mark-up had to be enough to help the trader meet expenses. Traders paid high interest themselves on goods extended on credit, and getting the furs ready for market was time-intensive and expensive. There were many hidden costs just as in business today.

If we compare these results with the trade of U.S. Government Factor Mr. Robert Belt in the same year, we can see what a goldmine in furs could be found in the whole Mississippi Valley. Belt was posted at Fort Edwards, a government operated trading post. His books for the same season show that the Sauk and Mesquakie had five licensed traders who employed nine clerks and interpreters and forty-three engages. They had collected a total of 980 packs of skins (60,082 skins) valued at $58,800 at Fort Edwards alone. On average this would mean approximately $10,000 - $12,000 per man, at 1819 valuations. In addition to furs, the Sauk and Mesquakie produced 286,800 pounds of tallow, 3,000 pounds of feathers, and 1,000 pounds of bees wax. Tallow, feathers, and beeswax were valuable trade goods with a ready market.[5] Because Fort Edwards was a very small post, it can readily be seen that this was a very lucrative business indeed.

The trade goods Davenport stocked were similar to those handled by the factors at the government factories at Fort Edwards and Fort Crawford. It is worth noting that these goods were, first and foremost, supplies for the hunt rather than luxury, or even everyday, items. What the credit accounts do not tell us is how much was sold to the Indians on a cash basis. It is possible that in the fall, at least, there were no cash sales. By that time, the annuity money that were paid annually to the tribes by virtue of treaty agreements, had been spent and the tribes depended on credit. Cash was probably reserved for times when the hunters had more furs than debts or shortly after the annuity payments had been made.

Unlike the 1819 Credit Book, the 1824 Credit Book is written primarily in English rather than French and has an inventory of goods in storage at Fort Edwards, left over from the previous year at the Des Moines Outfit. Instructions are included for some of the goods to be delivered to American Fur Company traders Palen and Mitchell at the

Des Moines Outfit for the present year and others to be brought up by Farnham to Rock Island. There is also a list of cooking utensils and other supplies for the clerk's use at their winter post.

The Credit Book contains 281 accounts with credits amounting to $13,074.00. This is an increase of 86 hunters and $1,422.25 in credits given. By 1824, Davenport had a formal contract with the American Fur Company and was sharing the Sauk, Mesquakie and Ioway trade with Russel Farnham. Together the two traders managed four posts on the Mississippi as well as one on the Grand River in northern Missouri and one on the Des Moines River. They employed between twenty-five and thirty-four clerks and hired hands that year.

The hunting supplies furnished in 1824 are virtually the same as those supplied in 1819, with one exception. In 1824, the Indians bought lead from the traders where they hadn't in 1819. Credits were noted as having been collected at Fort Edwards and Flint Hills, and often listed as "sondryes" rather than with itemized lists of furs. There was a significant decrease in beaver skins in 1824, only 44 beaver collected, but muskrats, not seen in the 1819 Credit Book, numbered almost 2,000.

Of the 281 accounts in 1824, only 75 or 26.69% were paid in full. Sixty accounts, or 21.35%, had no returns whatsoever. The remaining 146 accounts were partially repaid with varying degrees of returns. To repay the trader a significant number of accounts showed rifles, traps, and copper kettles being returned to satisfy a portion of the credit due. One hunter sold his horse to satisfy his account.

All in all, business was good. The high percentage of paid and partially paid accounts indicated willingness on the part of the Indians to hunt and make good on their debt. It also indicated that there was a plentiful supply of animals, but that situation could change quickly and without predictability. Good trading one year might be followed by several years of poor hunting. It all depended on the weather and the mood of the Indians and the price of furs on the international market.

CHAPTER SEVEN:

FULL STEAM AHEAD

ON THE 10TH OF MAY 1823, little George L'Oste Davenport was playing near the fort when he heard a loud and frightening sound coming nearer and nearer to the Island. It was so terrifying that all the Indians ran shrieking to the head of the island to see what it might be. He was not yet six years old but he remembered the day well into his old age, running to his mother and hiding his face in her skirts. Only after a great deal of persuasion by his mother and father would he pull away from her safety to see what kind of beast made such an awful noise.[1] A small steamboat called the Virginia was chugging up the river and about to dock near the Davenport's home. The whole community had heard the chug of her engines and seen the great billowing black clouds of smoke streaming out of her stack long before they could see the boat herself. Her whistle echoed through the valley and bounced off the bluffs heralding her arrival. The Virginia was the first steamboat to reach so far up into the Upper Mississippi Valley.

At Rocky Island the Virginia took on a supply of wood, and, according to family tradition, was guided through the upper Rock Island rapids by George Davenport and his patroon, Henry Debutts. As patron, or steersman on Davenport's keelboat, Debutts was experienced in taking boats through the rapids. After a rest of two days she continued her voyage to Fort Snelling. Among the passengers were Lawrence Taliaferro, Fort Snelling's Indian Agent who was supervising the transfer of military goods, a woman missionary heading for northwestern Illinois to work among the Indians, and a family from Kentucky planning to work the lead mines. There was also a small Italian man by the name of Giacomo Beltrami who called the event "an epoch in the history of navigation ... an enterprise of the boldest, of the most extraordinary nature, and probably unparalleled." He was not exaggerating. It was a daring, seven hundred mile voyage made in twenty days, which proved once and for all that the Upper Mississippi River was navigable by steamboats. The Virginia made two more trips above the Lower Rapids that year, establishing the practicability of steamboat trafficking.[2]

In 1823 the economic life of the frontier revolved around the rivers, and the arrival of the Virginia promised to improve transportation and marketing conditions for the Upper Mississippi Valley. Where George Davenport's keelboats usually took forty days, and sometimes sixty, to go to St. Louis and back, the Virginia had taken twenty. Spurred by sense of competition and profit, riverboat captains looked for ways to cut the travel time in half and improve their service.[3]

One serious problem remained, the Rapids. There were two stretches of rapids on the Upper Mississippi above St. Louis, the Lower Rapids at Keokuk, and the Upper or Rock River Rapids at Rock Island. They were narrow, with fast currents and dangerous eddies in good times, and shallow during times of low water. Only keelboats and barges had been navigated through them before now. Within the year Congress passed

The Act to Survey the Upper Mississippi, but the hazards of the Mississippi River rapids plagued the riverboat industry throughout Davenport's lifetime, and beyond.⁴ Even with such hazards, fourteen more steamboats ascended the river, navigated her rapids, and delivered troops and supplies as far as Fort Snelling within the next three years.

With the coming of the Virginia, the Upper Mississippi River was now officially opened to faster and noisier, though still not totally reliable, methods of transportation. Rarely did one slip by Indian Lodge on Rocky Island without the Davenports' notice. In fact, Davenport kept a log of the boats going up and coming down the river, even noting the time of day. The steamboats were a welcome sight, bringing needed goods and news from St. Louis and points east. It was an advantage for Davenport who had transferred his entire business from Mackinac to St. Louis merchants.

Word of the opportunities in the beautiful Mississippi Valley went with every trip of the steamboats. Not only could lead, furs, and other goods be sent down river faster, cheaper, and in larger quantities now, but also people, in greater numbers than before, gained access to the Upper Mississippi Valley. New business opportunities arose, such as woodlots for providing wood to the steamboats and forwarding and commission businesses for merchants. Davenport took advantage of those opportunities by establishing a woodlot of his own near the steamboat landing. A bonus to the improved travel was that interest in the fur trade was renewed and increased the price of lead and furs on the international market.

During the Davenports' early years in the fur trade, business ties with the Sauk and Mesquakie developed into friendships. That the Davenports genuinely liked the Indians was readily apparent to the Mesquakie. Son George L. Davenport often accompanied them on their summer hunting trips, which was more for food than for fur gathering. Though it was not their custom to permit outsiders into their lodges during feasts, the Mesquakie made an exception for Davenport and his son. Later, son George L. Davenport recalled that he had witnessed many scalp dances and ball games that ordinary folk had never seen. One of the Mesquakie elders told this story: "There was once a white man who was our friend.

His name was Davenport. He spoke some Fox. He liked us, and there was always truth in what he said. For these and other reasons we used to ask him into the lodge; he came, and was glad to be there." The honor was reciprocated. The Indians were frequent visitors to the Davenport home. Black Hawk, especially, was an esteemed friend to whom Susan Lewis often served tea in his favorite red cup.[5]

Even with periodic threats from the Ho Chunk, and conflict among the tribes, prospects for trade were generally good as they approached the mid-1820s. The Indians brought some of their best furs to Davenport who had a reputation for knowing good quality fur. The prices for furs remained high on the international market, and with credit readily supplied by Farnham and Davenport, the Sauk and Mesquakie lived well. Settlement in the northern part of Missouri had dislocated the Missouri band of Sauk and they had moved further into the Des Moines River Valley where game was plentiful.[6] When the hunters could avoid their enemies, they brought in deer, otter, bear, mink, raccoon, beaver, and muskrat. Muskrats were especially plentiful in the Upper Mississippi Valley, more so than beaver, and easily trapped with traditional spears and specially modified iron traps.

Davenport's Indian trappers were skilled and particular in their requests for good equipment. They wanted the best rifles and better traps, and Davenport seemed eager to accommodate their special requests. They asked for a modified trap with bigger aprons than usual, which Davenport hoped the St. Louis blacksmiths could make to their specifications. Anticipating that the blacksmiths might balk at such a request he slyly mentioned that he was sure that Cincinnati blacksmiths could, if the St. Louis blacksmiths could not. With such traps, he wrote Oliver Bostwick in St. Louis, his band of Indians would surely have a good hunt. It is probable that Davenport did not have to send away for his traps. Fort Armstrong's blacksmith, George Casner, was able to make 200 traps for Davenport of foundry iron and steel.[7]

One continually nagging problem for Davenport was transportation. Although steamboats were beginning to negotiate the Upper Mississippi River, they were irregular and unreliable in their schedule and unable to negotiate the smaller rivers. Too often the water level was too high or too low, and there were never enough boats available for Davenport. It was not unusual for one of his skiffs or piroques to be stolen by the Indians, or for his men to wait until more piroques or canoes were built to bring in the furs from the outposts. "I loaned a canoe to Keocuck(sic) to come down to Flint Hills. You can probably find it. If so make use of it. The very large canoe I purchased of L. Lot Pashe-to-a-wat stole in the fall, if at Flint Hills secure it for me but do not send it to St. Louis ... I ordered a boat. Did they receive my letter?" [8]

Purchasing a keelboat was an enormous expense, about two thousand dollars each, but it solved some of Davenport's transportation woes by doing so. There were few boats that could be rented or chartered, and a trader could not afford to waste time in getting his furs to market. The longer the furs were stored, and the warmer the weather, the more time the worms had to eat them or rot to set in.

No description of Davenport's first keelboat the Flying Betsy exists, but she was probably an older boat, perhaps a little leaky, but good for a few more years on the river. As a rule, keelboats and steamboats had a very short life span -- on average about four to five years -- and they leaked like sieves. The Flying Betsy was probably like other keelboats on the rivers at that time, eighty to one hundred feet in length, about twelve feet in width, and two feet six inches deep. Keelboats had flat bottoms with a keel on the front end.[9] After a few years she was replaced with a series of other keelboats, but the Flying Betsy was the first to get Davenport's furs to St. Louis until he could afford to buy a new boat made to his own specifications.

The year 1822-23 was a critical one for the Davenports economically. The trade had been disastrous, largely because the Sauk and Mesquakie had sent out war parties against the Sioux. In August Blondeau kept Farnham and Davenport apprised of the situation while waiting at the Des Moines River post for news. One war party, he wrote, had reached the Riviere au Calumet without having discovered any traces of Sioux, but two other war parties had not been heard from. Blondeau hoped that the war party would return with good news and require many carabines and traps for hunting. The hunters, he said, planned to go to western Missouri to hunt north of the Riviere des Kans where there was a small American settlement. This was probably at the confluence of the Kansas and Missouri rivers where Kansas City is today.   Several traders had established posts in the area, among them Francois Chouteau and his wife Berenice, and Joseph Robidoux whose post was located near present-day St. Joseph. Blondeau thought that he and Farnham should also settle there. They could enlarge the house Blondeau had built the previous winter (near the Grand and Missouri junction), construct other storehouses, and hire some trustworthy persons to remain there. The house, or post, could then be used as a base from which they could move nearer to their hunters, toward the Black Snake Hills and the Kansas River. But when the runner arrived, Blondeau realized how grim the situation was. Four Sauk had been killed and twenty wounded. In addition, the Sauk had killed six Sioux in a battle about a hundred miles from the Riviere a la Roche (Rock River), and war parties were still at large. Not only would those twenty-four Sauk be unable to hunt in the coming season, but also the Sioux were certain to retaliate.[10]

Davenport was unable to pay off his debts again that year and looking for new ways to earn cash. His family was growing, bringing additional responsibilities. His second son, Bailey, was born that fall to Susan Lewis. For the birth, the Davenport family had travelled to Clermont County, Ohio, just east of Cincinnati where Margaret's brother, Ambrose Green Bowling, and his family were living. The visit provided them with a chance to renew family ties, to hear of news from home, and to have a brief respite from the cares of life on Rock Island. Susan received care during her lying in time, and George L., who was not yet six years old, had a chance to meet his Bowling cousins. After a short visit, Margaret and George Davenport returned to Rock Island with George L., in time for the fall hunt. Susan Lewis and the baby returned to Indian Lodge the following spring.

Davenport now had two sons to carry on his legacy. Their future roles were already determined. At the age of six, George L. was preparing for the Indian trade and a mercantile career. His mother taught him reading, writing, and basic arithmetic. His father let him play in the trading post and accompany him to the Indian villages on business. His Indian playmates taught him the language and customs that he needed to interact with them. Baby Bailey's future was in the family's agriculture, keeping livestock and gardening. Although he, too, would have Indian playmates, Bailey would grow up in a different world from that of his older brother, choosing his close friends among the sons of the French Canadian workers on the island and the children of settlers yet to come. He would spend time at the fort where the soldiers would encourage his love of horses, horseracing and horse-trading.

To help with the growing domestic duties, Davenport contracted with Charlotte, a free woman of color with a small child, to work in the house. It was common on the frontier to hire occasional help within the household, but usually frontier families looked to their neighbors who had young daughters available for such work. The Davenports, however, had no close neighbors. An indentured servant solved the problem. A formal indenture document was drawn up and witnessed by Major Josiah Vose, the newly arrived commander of Fort Armstrong.

Who Charlotte was and where she came from, we can only guess. She may have been a servant of one of the officers at the fort, or she could have been brought up river from the St. Louis slave markets for Davenport. Because the transaction took place at the fort, she may have been a slave of one of the officers. Charlotte bound herself for seven years, promising to serve all her master's and mistress' commands, cooking, cleaning, laundering, and gardening. In general, she helped Mrs. Davenport run the house. In exchange she received meat, drink, washing, lodging, and apparel, both linen and wool, for herself and her child. With this indenture, the Davenport women began a tradition of having hired women to help them with household duties while they remained on the island.

What cannot be determined about this indenture is whether Charlotte was, in fact, owned by the Davenports as a slave, or whether she had, in reality, freely indentured herself for the seven years outlined in the signed agreement. Historians have argued that many of these indentures were thinly veiled legal maneuvers around the issue of slavery, so the subject of slaves in western Illinois is difficult to document. Slaves were, indeed, an integral part of army life throughout the early nineteenth century, and many civilians owned slaves in Illinois, some working at the lead mines. Although the recording of black persons was required in Illinois, there are few written records in the northwestern part of the state before the establishment of Jo Daviess County in 1828. While the Federal census recorded such persons, there are no enumerations for Rock Island and Galena before 1830, a fourteen-year gap in information for Rock Island.[11]

Davenport's attitude toward slavery is not documented, but Charlotte was just the first of many black persons to join the Davenport household. She lived and worked in the Davenport house from 1824 until 1830, during which time she had other children. There is evidence that she was still there as late as 1836, usually being referred to as Davenport's cook. She remained there at least until her indenture was completed in 1831, when the indenture was recorded in Jo Daviess County, Illinois, but she may have remained in the Davenport household after that time. At least one of her daughters, Mathilda, remained there until her marriage in the 1850s. Household accounts show that Mathilda was paid a wage for her services. Pioneer reminiscences make no mention of slaves, only black servants in connection with the Davenports, but the census called them slaves.[12]

The 1830 Federal census enumerated one male slave under 10 and three female slaves (1 under 10, 1 10-24 years, and 1 24-36 years) in the Davenport household. It is likely that Charlotte is the female slave found in the 24-36 age category, but unclear who the others might be, perhaps her children. It should be noted that no free colored persons were enumerated in the Davenport house at this time.

Ten years later, the 1840 Federal census showed no slaves, either male or female, and four free colored persons (1 male under 10, 2 females under 10, and 1 female 10 - 24) within the Davenport household. If Charlotte is the woman in the 24-36 age group in the 1830 census, then she had either moved or died by 1840. Nowhere else are slaves mentioned with regard to the Davenports. Charlotte played a crucial part in the voting during the great Scott county seat war in 1836, casting George Davenport's vote for him at the election poll.

With the addition of Charlotte and her child, the Davenport family numbered four adults and three children. While Charlotte and her daughter may have lived in the house with the Davenport family, it is more likely that they had their own cabin on the site. Also living on the site in their own house, on a seasonal basis, were Davenport's workers in the fur trade, and the Indian agent, Thomas Forsyth, who recorded the population in the Davenport neighborhood as thirteen souls.

The birth of his second son marked a turning point in Davenport's approach to business. Profits in the trading business were low, despite his best efforts, and he had many people to support. Because he still needed to buy goods for the coming winter's hunt, Davenport was forced to sign a $5,000 note to the American Fur Company in order to keep trading. Remaining independent was increasingly more difficult. A formal contract would not only give him some security, but it might also discourage new rivals for the Sauk and Mesquakie trade. He continued trading, but he also began to expand into services that would pay him cash.

The arrival of The Virginia offered one new business opportunity to him, maintaining woodlots. Steamboats devoured great quantities of wood and supplying cords of firewood as fuel became an important aspect of steamboat transportation. After this time, according to historian Willard Barrows, Davenport maintained a woodlot on the island, bringing wood from Maple Island and other places to supply the steamboats.[18] Besides being a cash business that supplemented the trading business, it was also another step away from reliance on the fort.

With more and more people coming into the Upper Mississippi Valley on steamboats, everyone, soldiers and traders alike, expected that the fort's days were numbered. It was a reasonable expectation with settlers moving into the Valley, with the paucity of Indian attacks on them, and also with the condition of the old fort itself. A military presence was no longer necessary. When Major Josiah Vose assumed command of Fort Armstrong in June of 1823, he was appalled at the deteriorated condition of the fort. He estimated that eight hundred and forty-one dollars worth of repairs were needed to make the fort liveable. Congress, however, was unwilling to appropriate money for those repairs and that seemed to confirm rumors that the fort would be evacuated the following spring. In fact, Fort Armstrong had never seen much activity in its whole history, and with other forts closing in the Mississippi Valley, closing Fort Armstrong seemed a reasonable possibility.[14] The rumour, however, proved to be premature as the Secretary of War, Congress, and the Bureau of land Management could not decide whether the fort should be closed. The issue of defining Rock Island as military reserve dragged on for several more years.

One question that did not rise in the discussion about Fort Armstrong's future was the problem of the escalating boundary disputes between the allied tribes of Sauk and Mesquakie and the Sioux, or the detrimental effect it was having on the Sauk and Mesquakie, or the role of the military in settling those disputes. By the mid twenties the need for western hunting lands brought the Sauk and Mesquakie into conflict with the Missouri river tribes, particularly the Sioux, Osages, Omahas, and Otoes. Without military intervention, the Indian wars would only escalate. Farnham and Davenport were cautious in their expectations for the 1823-1824 season, mainly because of the almost certain possibility of Indian wars.

The Missouri Sauk had already seen a decrease in their hunt after settlement in northern Missouri pushed them into the interior of Iowa. Writing from the Des Moines post, Farnham assessed the situation as dire. Farnham and Davenport's hunters on the Ioway River were attacked by the Sioux. Seven or eight braves had been killed, and the rest had been driven away from the hunting grounds. Farnham had given credits to everyone in this party and already he knew there would be no payment from them this year.[15]

Other areas were more promising. At the Fox Channel in northeastern Missouri, a two days journey from the Grand River, Farnham reported that prospects for the season were, "tolerable good" as respects the Sauk, but the Ioway were not expected to make more than one hundred packs, far less than he wished. Farnham had found about thirty lodges of the Sauk on the Missouri, about two days above the Platte River, and collected one hundred and forty packs around the first of the year, enough to pay their credits. Blondeau had about one hundred and fifty or sixty packs on the Grand River, so Farnham figured that they might have six or seven hundred packs for the season. That was a good, but not great, season. Farnham thought he could deliver the packs to St. Louis as he had planned by the 1st of April, but it was too early yet to determine the final amount.

The Missouri Sauk, who had always been responsible hunters, had been annoyed by drunken Indians who had purchased whiskey from Colonel Saurny at the Two Rivers post in exchange for guns, blankets, and peltries. This had also affected the trade. At Mr. Corran's house at the mouth of the Grand River on the Missouri, only eight or ten packs had been collected by the twentieth of that month. The hunt was not as good in that area as they had expected, because about sixty lodges had been driven in from their hunt by the Sioux and six Mesquakie had been killed in the past fall on the English River, a branch of the Ioway.[16]

On the Des Moines and Raccoon Rivers in central Iowa a good number of beaver and deer had been spotted in the late summer. The problem with the Des Moines River Valley, however, was protecting the hunters and their families from Sioux attack. Davenport and Farnham's clerk, Joshua Palen, had reported that the Sauk would hunt on the Raccoon only if forts were built for their protection as Davenport had promised. The nearest military fort, Fort Osage, was not regularly manned, and there was no other law enforcement in the area. Without protection, the Indians were vulnerable to attack by their enemies and they expected their traders to provide for them.[17] The summer hunt was especially disrupted by such warfare, and after 1824, summer hunts became less prevalent because they often resulted in a loss of revenue for both hunter and trader. Davenport explained what happened in 1824.

A war party of Sauk and Foxes left Rock Island in July 1824, and shortly thereafter met five Americans and two Frenchmen who were driving cattle on the north side of the Des Moines River. The Sauk party assumed they were heading to the St. Peter River, but none of the drovers could speak Indian languages. The war party continued toward the Missouri River, but after a few days they had not found any Sioux, so they turned toward the St. Peters. There they came upon a Sioux trail, and after following it some distance, they came upon slain cattle with their tails and hooves cut off. In the distance they heard a drum and believed that the Sioux were dancing over the scalps of the cattle drivers. Later that night the Sauk war party attacked and killed three lodges of Sioux, except for a little girl whom they took as prisoner. When the Sauk realized that there were over one hundred lodges of Sioux camped nearby, they made their escape, but not before being discovered by their enemies. They were chased by the Sioux, some riding the mules of the drovers, and surrounded. Eight of the Sauk war party were killed; two were wounded. In addition the Sauk lost several horses, blankets, leggings and moccasins.[18]

Hunting was frequently interrupted by war parties like this one, sometimes with devastating results on both sides. In order for the tribes to get enough meat for their people to live on, the United States Government attempted to negotiate boundaries between the tribes with a series of treaties in 1824 and 1825. They were only partially successful. Agreements between tribes were more complicated than simple treaties could address.[19]

Resolving the boundary disputes and settling old scores between tribes was a difficult job that required the combined effort of Indian Agents, Military Commanders, and others, but the job was hampered by the reduction of the military in the Mississippi Valley in 1824. In western Missouri, the only military outpost was Fort Osage, which had been a government factory since 1808. The small company of the Sixth Infantry, however, was not present on a regular basis and unable to enforce any peace treaties. Alexander McNair operated the Indian Agency there with interpreter, Antoine Le Claire Junior. Le Claire was an old friend of Davenport and Farnham, and an important link in the communication chain between the Missouri and Mississippi Rivers. With strong connections to St. Louis, Le Claire was a good source of Indian and military news.

Both Russel Farnham and Antoine Le Claire attended treaty negotiations in St. Louis when the Missouri Sauk and Mesquakie ceded most of their Missouri lands. Le Claire, as interpreter, attempted to reserve for Farnham and Davenport a small strip of land in the northwest corner of Missouri between the Little Platte and Missouri Rivers (the Platte Strip), which the Missouri Sauk shared with the Ioway.[20] Davenport owned land along the Grand River, but this was too far to the east for convenience of the Missouri band. Instead the partners built a post near the Black Snake Hills, where Blondeau had suggested just the year before. The post served Davenport and Farnham for several more years.

On the Mississippi that year, the situation was similar to that on the Missouri. The government closed Fort Edwards permanently at the end of June 1824. There seemed no need for the post, which had never been threatened by Indian unrest and few white settlers were in the vicinity. Because the location was ideal for collecting furs, the American Fur Company applied for, and was granted, a lease of the fort buildings for use as a trading post. From that time until his death in 1832, Russel Farnham used this as his main post and supervised the Des Moines River trade where many Sauk and Mesquakie were hunting.[21]

The following year, the Sauk and Mesquakie wintered closer to Fort Armstrong, on the Ioway, Rocky, and Wapsipinicon Rivers. The Mesquakie also wintered on the Wapsi. Not only were the hunting prospects good, but the winter camps were further from the Sioux that winter as well. This was important for the subsistence of the tribes who had not had any meat from the previous summer. Davenport, who supervised the posts on the Mississippi River, adjusted his posts. The most recent law on the Indian trade restricted traders to specific locations and no longer were they permitted to follow the Indians into their hunting grounds as they previously had done. Neither the Indians nor their traders agreed with this law, because it was an inconvenience for the Indians to lug their skins and peltries greater distances to the trading post than previously. The disadvantage for the trader was that he ran the risk of losing his credits to Indians who might use a more conveniently located trading post. Davenport was not as affected by this new law as others since all three of his posts provided him easy access to the hunters -- an advantage that he surely would not have dismissed.[22]

Competition among traders remained high and William Downey, who had been trying to steal some of Davenport's trade for some time, had formed a partnership with John Connolly, a former subagent to Thomas Forsyth at Fort Armstrong. This was a potential threat to Davenport as Connolly had previously worked for Davenport and knew some of his strategies. Connolly had found his Subagent's job to be somewhat boring, being accustomed to a much fuller schedule at Fort Edwards. He admitted that the job paid well with a five hundred dollar salary and many benefits, such as respectability among the Indians, rank among the officers, comfortable quarters, a soldier as a waiter, and plenty of firewood, but it was not enough for him. He viewed the trading partnership with Downey as an opportunity to earn a little extra money. Davenport saw this new partnership as a viable threat to his livelihood. With a debt hanging over his head, Davenport was not willing to lose any business to even the smallest of traders.[23]

Fortunately, the lead business began to boom around this time. Increased production of lead meant more miners, and more demand for Davenport's goods. His partner Amos Farrar was doing a brisk business at Fever River near the mines and, more than once, Davenport had been caught short on supplies. That was a good problem. Emergency supplies from Samuel Abbott, in addition to the usual assortment of goods he had obtained from Farnham's agency, had gotten him through the season.[24] The biggest drawback to increased business was that his presence was needed at the mines from early June until the latter part of July.

In addition to the Indians, about one hundred miners were working in the lead mine district in 1824, and the numbers were climbing. In the previous three years (1822 -1823), the total combined output of lead had been 335,130 pounds, but in 1825 that production almost doubled when 664,530 pounds were produced. Again, in 1827, production rose and 5,182,180 pounds of lead were sent down to St. Louis. The miners needed food, clothing, tools, and other supplies, and the business of Davenport and Farrar increased so much so that they took in a third partner, Charles D. St. Vrain. St. Vrain was a brother to Felix St. Vrain, who later became Indian Agent at Fort Armstrong, and to Ceran St. Vrain of Bent's Fort fame. The new partnership was called Davenport, Farrar & Co.[25]

Increased business required better boats for transporting the lead and supplies. His old boat had sprung leaks on the top and sides, so Davenport bought a new one. Whether this was his Flying Betsy or the Adam is not known, but rather than buying a used boat as in the past, he had a new one made to order. His personal instructions for the new boat offers a picture of what kind of craft he required. He wrote: "... I Shall be in want of a Boat in the Spring and will be Glad to Get one Built of twenty Tons Burthan, to be Strong Timbers and Good plank to be made not to draw much water on account of the rapids, with a good roof, to have a Bulk head next the Bow, and hatches to Shut down when the men Rows - four Oars on a Side ..." New boats were a luxury, however, that he could not always afford, and so the following year he purchased a used keelboat, the Phoenix for $578.55. In 1826 he purchased still another one, the Missouri, for $700.[26] It is probable that Davenport owned at least three keelboats for his business in the mid- to late-1820s. Often he needed two boats to carry his lead down to St. Louis and carried his own goods from St. Louis in return rather than paying someone else for the service.

By 1824 the Indian trade was well entrenched in the Davenport life-style. They had survived Indian attacks, the vagaries of isolation, and the fickleness of the international market. Life was never secure on the frontier, but stable for the time being. They were making a modest living, and could see significant and concrete progress, especially in the changing landscape around them.

As the family's needs changed and the business grew, the Davenports built a series of structures on their property. They had started with a double-log cabin that provided shelter for the family as well as for their trade goods and workers, and then added a separate house for the men and at least one other cabin to use as store and tavern. Around their house they had planted an orchard of apple and peach trees. A large stock of cattle and hogs, which they sometimes sold for cash, grazed in the fields nearby. They maintained a woodlot from which to sell firewood to the new steamboat traffic on the river, and additional business came from the Fort Armstrong Indian Agency. Son George L. was now seven and baby Bailey nearly a year old. Charlotte and her family worked for the growing family. The Davenport family was well, even thriving, but they had a tenuous claim to their island home. Changes in the military were about to shake the very foundations on which they lived.

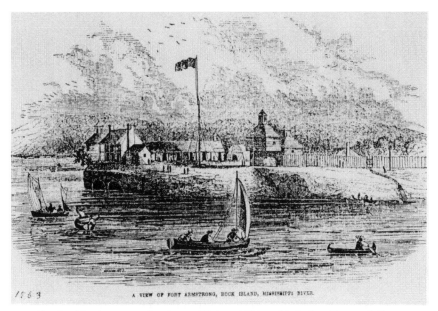

A VIEW OF FORT ARMSTRONG, ROCK ISLAND, MISSISSIPPI RIVER.

Sketch of Ft. Armstrong by George Walter, 1852, published in Gleason's Drawing Room Companion, 2 March 1853.

CHAPTER EIGHT:

NEW COMMANDER, NEW IDEAS

SETTLEMENT AROUND THE FORT was growing, a clear sign that everyone was feeling secure at Fort Armstrong. Although the Indians were at war with one another, their attacks had been at some distance from Rock Island and directed toward one another rather than at soldiers or settlers. With some sense of security then, some of the officers built small log houses outside the fort walls for their families to live in. Doctor Sprague was one of those, as well as the fort's sutler and sometimes trader, Lieutenant William Downey, whose wife joined him in 1825. In all, there were four log houses and a stable outside the fort walls at that time.[1]

Davenport prided himself on his good working relationship with the military and particularly with its commanding officers. Whenever the subject of his land claim was discussed, he expressed appreciation for the opportunities that the U.S. Army had given him and reciprocated by working to establish peaceful relationships with the Indians. His claim to his island home was tenuous, primarily based upon Major Willoughby Morgan's selection of a portion of the island for him. Davenport also understood that he had the right of pre emption guaranteed by the State of Illinois, but until he could be granted that pre-emption status, he depended on the goodwill of the commanding officer at the fort. When Major Josiah Vose took command, relationships between Davenport's trading post, the Indian Agency, and the fort grew contentious. At the center of the controversy was the issue of Indian relationships.

Because of the escalating Indian conflicts, the War Department finally agreed to locate an Indian Agency at Fort Armstrong. Despite his arguments against living there, Thomas Forsyth was ordered to Rock Island. He arrived to find his subagent comfortably settled into the fort, but no living place for himself. Fortunately, Davenport had a spare cabin that Forsyth could rent, for five dollars a month, while he conducted business from the fort. Forsyth wasted no time in hiring workers, blacksmiths and interpreters, and met with the Indian chiefs as they came to express their concerns. Louis Pettle was hired as interpreter, George Cassner as blacksmith, and Midi Beaulius as gunsmith for the new Agency.

During the winter, Forsyth drew up plans for the agency buildings, which included a house for himself, as agent, a Council House where he and large numbers of chiefs and others could meet, a house for the Blacksmith, one for the interpreter, and a Blacksmith shop. By using the services of the two companies of troops then stationed at Fort Armstrong, he figured that the government could save half of the estimated $788.25 it would take to construct the Agency buildings.[2]

Major Vose, however, was not pleased with this plan, mainly because it took soldiers from military duty. He already had nine of his men working on other non-military projects. But there were other reasons for his displeasure. Unlike his predecessors, Major Vose did not recognize the value of Davenport's and Forsyth's working relationship with the Indians and did not want the Indians to have any more reasons to come to the Island. However, the agency plan was approved, and Vose was notified that his men would erect the proposed agency according to instructions. Building would begin in the early summer.[3]

Major Vose had reasonable objections to this added responsibility. With only about 70 men assigned to Fort Armstrong, he had few men to spare from military duties. Monthly returns for the summer of 1824 show that a detachment of 27 men had been sent on special orders to the mines, one man had drowned in June, and one other was on recruiting duty at Bellefontaine. That left just 43 men to man the fort. Because there were hardly enough men to carry on the daily duties of running the fort, training was suspended for the summer -- training that Vose considered essential to the undisciplined troops he found at Fort Armstrong. Grudgingly, Vose assigned nine men to begin construction of the first of the agency buildings during the month of July.[4]

Almost immediately, a small community grew up around the Indian agency, and the island began to take shape as a small village, at least for the summer months. The blacksmith and gunsmith, with only five-month contracts, did not remain year-round on the island, but housing was required during their stay. They brought with them their entire families, and while they worked on the island, their children made friends with the Davenport and Gokey children. Louis Hebert, for instance, came with his uncle, one of the gunsmiths at the agency. Louis and George L. Davenport became life-long friends. Subagent John Connolly's three children were all born while he worked for the agency and lived on the island with their mother, even after Connolly's death in 1832. Not much is known about the family of Interpreter Louis Pettle, but his successor Antoine Le Claire Junior lived on the island with his wife and other members of their families, who were also employed in the Indian trade.[5]

From his new agency, Forsyth kept abreast of the Indian population within his jurisdiction, their military strength, and the location of their villages. The Sauk, for instance, had increased in numbers from about a thousand warriors in 1818 to about twelve hundred warriors in 1824. About two-thirds of the Sauk warriors were well armed.[6] The Sauk villages that Davenport personally visited from time to time were scattered throughout Forsyth's agency. Their principal village called The Great

Sauk Village or Saukenuk, remained about three miles from the agency. A second was located at the head of the Des Moines rapids, about one hundred and forty miles from Rock Island, and a third village was located on the Henderson River, about seventy-five miles south of Rock Island, in Illinois.

The Mesquakie, numbered about 400 warriors, or about 1,600 "souls" as Forsyth reported them, but only about one hundred to one hundred and fifty of their warriors were well armed; the rest badly armed. Forsyth added that the Mesquakie were generally addicted to "spirituous liquor" - whiskey. Forsyth found them in six locations: at a village of the principal leaders just across the Slough from Fort Armstrong, at a village twenty-five miles north on the Wapsipinicon, and another 45 miles higher on the Mississippi at Striking Prairies. Twenty-five miles beyond Striking Prairie was a fourth village. A fifth was located on the west bank of the Mississippi at the Dubuque Mines, and the final village lay on the east bank of the Mississippi, forty-five miles above the mines.

In addition, Forsyth estimated that there were approximately two hundred men, women, and children of the Ho Chunk living in villages on the Rock River, and about one hundred Kickapoo and Pottawatomi from the Spoon and Sycamore Rivers. All in all, he estimated that about six 6,700 Indians visited his Agency each year. What he did not note was that these Indians also visited Davenport's trading post.

Davenport looked forward to having the Indian Agency on Rock Island, but the agency building had not progressed very far by April of1825 when Forsyth reported that the agency site had "not as yet a Stick of Timber." The soldiers were occupied that spring in cutting and hewing timber for his buildings, but Forsyth was anxious for a roof over his head. Davenport's house was no longer available and had it not been for the generosity of Dr. Sprague, Forsyth would have had to lie in the woods until the agency was completed.[7]

Forsyth's presence was helpful in keeping peace and harmony within the Sauk and Mesquakie. The tribal leaders came to him to settle arguments amongst their members, to have their guns and equipment repaired by the gunsmith and blacksmith, and for presents. The Indian

Agency was also good for Davenport's business. It put Davenport at the center of the conversations between the Indians, the military, and Governmental agencies, an empowering situation. With his trading post close by, he often sold goods to the Agency whenever the Agency entertained tribal delegations. On such occasions, food, gifts of tobacco, blankets, and other items used by the Indians were expected by the guests, and Davenport kept those on hand for this purpose. Although the agency was not well funded, and Forsyth was careful of his expenditures, the Agency business provided a little cash for Davenport.

Major Vose, however, objected to the Indian Agency. Besides the fact that the fort was in danger of falling down around them, his prime concern, Vose was concerned with his budget. His men were engaged in extensive, and expensive, repairs on the fort. Two masons had recently been engaged to reconstruct the chimneys, oven, and walls of the fort, and the quartermaster was considering a thorough repair of the entire fort. Many other buildings were in need of considerable repair, maybe even replacement, so the order to assist with the Indian Agency at the fort's expense did not sit well with him.[8]

But another concern was the Indians. Major Vose was not comfortable with Indians. He did not know their languages or their customs, and lived constantly in fear of an attack on the fort. Having the Indian Agency so near the fort might allow for better relations, but it would also attract more Indians to the island. Vose preferred to keep the Indians as far from the fort as possible. Besides, he did not like the Indian Agent, and thought that Forsyth and Davenport were too cozy, siding with one another against him and threatening his authority. He had no control over the Indian Agency, so he began to look for ways to remove Davenport and his business from the island.

Davenport's presence on the island was dependent on continuous agreements with Fort Armstrong's commanders, on permission from the Secretary of War, and on current fur trade licenses from the Indian Agent. Without these, any government official could order him to leave the island. Davenport had carefully cultivated the friendship of prior commanders to show his willingness to affect good relationships with the local Indians. Major Vose was the first serious threat to Davenport's settlement on the island. A vigorous conflict between Major Josiah Vose, George Davenport, and Thomas Forsyth sent Davenport looking for new arrangements.[9]

From the moment of his arrival at Fort Armstrong, Major Vose had seemed different from the past commanders at the fort. Where others had been accepting of the Indians, respectful of their ways, and somewhat relaxed in their attitude to military rules and regulations, Vose was not. He had come up through the ranks of the army, rather than as a graduate of the academy, which may have contributed to his inflexible attitude. He complained he could not afford to support his family on the frontier, from whom he had long been separated. He visited them in Massachusetts on rare furloughs. He was a strict disciplinarian and religious man, concerned with morals and high standards. He declared the troops at Fort Armstrong to be highly undisciplined, and began immediately to try to shape up the lax soldiers. He restricted the number of Indians that could be admitted inside the gates at any one time, in order to strengthen the fort's security. He enforced the dress code, and ordered regular dress reviews and inspections. He forbade card playing for all men, including commissioned officers, and reduced the amount of whiskey in the men's rations. The purchase of whiskey also came under new orders. Only with written approval by the commanding officer could any soldier purchase whiskey, and this extended to the Indian Agency, to Interpreter Pettle, to occasional visitors to the fort, and to George Davenport, even though all were quartered well outside the fort's walls. His orders, and general attitude, were designed to force George Davenport and Thomas Forsyth to submit to his command.

Although this new rule was not pleasing to Davenport, it affected his business only slightly. For Indian Agent Forsyth, however, the ruling directly affected his interaction with the Indians when they came to his agency. Forsyth had been accustomed to giving the influential chiefs a small amount of whiskey when they visited him. The chiefs also, according to Forsyth, used whiskey in their religious ceremonies, and Vose's orders prevented him from continuing this custom. He wrote the Secretary of

War, John C. Calhoun, for advice, especially as the Indians were coming frequently to discuss their revenge attacks on the Sioux and the theft of their corn by the Winnebago. Because the Sauk and Mesquakie were facing a hard summer, the added denial of a little whiskey was upsetting to the chiefs.[10]

But Vose held firm. He believed that anyone who worked in the Indian trade attracted a worthless class of men whose very presence was a bad influence on his soldiers. This included Davenport and Thomas Forsyth. Furthermore, having a trading post on the island only attracted more Indians, and starving Indians in particular, whom he would have to feed. The Ho Chunk had been menacing of late, and he was afraid that another war between the Sioux and the Sauk and Mesquakie would break out soon. Also, Davenport had a valid tavern license and could legally sell whiskey to the soldiers if he chose.[11] Vose admitted that Davenport had never actually sold whiskey to Indians or to the soldiers without his authority, but the potential was there and Vose could not control Davenport's activities. Vose was not at liberty to express his personal views about the Indian Agency, although they were clearly there for anyone to see, but he was convinced that the Indian situation would only worsen when the agency was completed. The final straw came when he was ordered to assist in the agency construction by putting his men on extra duty. Vose looked anxiously for ways to get rid of at least one of these nuisances.

One transgression Vose noted was that Davenport grazed a large herd of about forty or fifty cattle on the island. Those cattle, Vose said, mingled with the public cattle and competed for the same grasses. In times of drought when the dry grass would be in short supply, the military cattle should have priority. Vose's quartermaster supported his position. When Vose learned that George Davenport was claiming his part of the island under the Illinois preemption laws, he threatened to have Davenport evicted from the island, citing infringement of the military reserve.[12]

Major Vose's argument was an old one, one that had been used at other frontier military sites for the purpose of extending boundaries. Infringement on the military reserve was an important issue of the time.

Commanders of military posts were especially sensitive to their role on the frontier as protectors of settlers, but protection often led to encroachment on the military space. Settlers, anxious to take advantage of the fort's protection and other social amenities, moved as close to the fort as they could, sometimes onto military reserve land. Davenport argued that he had adhered to the law of 1818 respecting settlers, that he did not live in Indian Territory but in the state of Illinois, and that he had a right, by means of a valid liquor license, to keep in his possession and sell spirituous liquors. His arguments fell on deaf ears.[13]

John W. Johnston, the factor at Prairie du Chien, had some years earlier requested a similar ruling, because his commander had claimed an area of nine square miles around the site of Fort Crawford. That was a difficult rule to enforce at Prairie du Chien because it included 50 civilian families, all of whom rebelled against the use of martial law as a legal loophole under which they had no legal civil rights; they could not collect debts or enforce compliance to their contracts. At Fort Snelling, too, settlers built so close to the fort that there was competition for the natural resources, especially wood, between settlers and soldiers.[14]

Vose wrote to the Secretary of War, John C. Calhoun, to ask whether he had the power to remove Davenport from the island, whether the island was still reserved for military purposes, or whether he could get rid of him by some other means. Calhoun replied that Vose could "take the proper steps to remove Mr. Davenport from the island," if Davenport was not licensed in the Indian trade and assigned by the Agent to Rock Island (March, 1825). If, advised Calhoun, Davenport were properly licensed, then Vose should complain to Governor Clark, Superintendent of Indian Affairs at St. Louis, to ask for Davenport's removal. Since he held a valid license, Vose pressured Clark to consider revoking Davenport's license at Rock Island for the following year or two. But what was not answered was the question of what constituted the military reserve. The question would remain unanswered for almost twenty years.[15]

The bad blood between Vose, Forsyth, and Davenport escalated with an incident involving the agency's interpreter, Louis Pettle, who had been caught selling whiskey to one of Vose's soldiers. That in itself was bad enough, but in exchange for the whiskey, Pettle had taken the soldier's uniform, a flagrant violation of military law. Vose ordered Pettle discharged from his duties and ordered him to leave the island. Davenport, however, knew how valuable an interpreter Pettle was, since he could speak both French and Indian. Because his skills could be used by his competitors, Davenport encouraged the American Fur Company to hire Pettle. That infuriated Vose, who saw it as a flagrant disregard for his authority on the island. [16.] To add fuel to the fire, Forsyth had recently placed his own son as a clerk in Davenport's trading business. Vose saw this as patronizing and a further threat to his authority.

A few months later Vose challenged Forsyth to a duel. Forsyth agreed, but only after Vose explained that Forsyth had "acted ungentlemanly " towards him, and when Vose was no longer commander of the fort. That effectively allowed a cooling off period for all concerned and before a duel could be arranged, Vose was furloughed and remained away from Fort Armstrong for nearly a year. Pettle was replaced with Hyacynthe Lucier who served as the Agency's interpreter for the next two years.[17] The federal order to remove the Davenports from the island was never carried out, but it caused Davenport to look beyond the island for an even more secure place to operate his businesses and raise his family.

In the summer of 1825 Davenport began to invest in land beyond the military boundaries. His action was explained in a letter to O.N. Bostwick, district agent of the American Fur Company: "... not having heard from Washington respecting my removal from rock Island and wishing to provide for the worst I have sent Col Kinney to purchase two holding claims in Illinois one will be laid on surveyed lands in the vicinity on the Best Spot for a Trading establishment which cannot be controlled by commanding officers or Indian Agents."[18]

Holding, or floating, claims refer to lands issued to the veterans of the War of 1812 as payment for their service. These claims designated the amount of acreage in the grant, but were not specifically located. The claimants had certain rights with these claims, which were granted by the U.S. Government.[19] Davenport was specifically looking at land in the Illinois Military Tract, which was then being offered for sale to the public.

The Military Tract was a triangular piece of land bounded by the Mississippi and Illinois rivers that contained 3,500,000 acres of public land intended for distribution to veterans of the War of 1812. The lands had been surveyed and warrants issued to qualifying veterans between 1817 and 1819, but migration to these lands was not as successful as the government had anticipated. Even with the incentive of having to pay no taxes for three years, many warrants remained unclaimed or unsettled. The State of Illinois seized the lands on which taxes had not been paid and offered them at public auction. It was a good way to acquire cheap land for speculation.[20]

Davenport saw this as a viable solution to his dilemma with the military. It was also the beginning of a new venture into land speculating. Davenport joined a growing group of small businessmen, bankers, editors, lawyers, politicians, and government officials who bought land at low prices and hoped to sell quickly and for a profit. In the summer of 1825 he bought eighteen quartersections and one 159-acre tract from the Reverend Peter Williams, who was then living with his wife Rebecca at Fort Edwards, and who was also speculating. The nineteen sections were variously located in Adams, Hancock, Henderson, Madison, McDonough, Mercer, Pike, and Fulton counties.[21]

Initially Davenport's objective was to locate a choice yet secure spot to carry on his well-established trade with his customers, the Sauk and Mesquakie and Ho Chunk, without interference from the military or any other political body, but it became much more. Investment in land became a means of security for Davenport and a generous income. He was, by no means, a large-scale speculator, nor was he a big gambler. His investment of five hundred dollars (for 3,039 acres) amounted to about sixteen cents per acre - a sum that he could reasonably recoup without difficulty. The small profits that he might realize would supplement his unpredictable trading income. Through the end of the 1820s, Davenport bought land throughout the Military Tract, some from Williams and some at the annual tax sales at Vandalia. Some of it he sold, some of it would be improved and rented for a time; the rest would be deeded to his son Bailey and remained unsold at the time of Davenport's death.

The Indian situation did not improve and the United States Government finally called all tribes together for the Great Council of 1825. At first the council site was set for Fort Armstrong, but some of the Indians objected, opting for a more neutral location. Prairie du Chien was then selected and the council scheduled immediately after the summer hunt. Davenport did not attend, but remained on Rock Island and supplied provisions. It was the largest and most impressive gathering held in the Upper Mississippi Valley.

By mid-July all interested parties began to assemble. From Fort Snelling, Indian Agent Lawrence Taliaferro came with four hundred Sioux and Chippewa. From Sault Ste. Marie came Henry Schoolcraft and one hundred and fifty Chippewa. Nicholas Boilvin, Indian Agent at Prairie du Chien, gathered hundreds of his Ho Chunk. Menominees, Potawatomie, and Ottawa came from Lake Michigan and Green Bay. Thomas Forsyth came from Rock Island, along with sub-agents, Robert Forsyth and W.B. Alexander. Major Thomas Biddle served as secretary, and General William Clark, Superintendent of Indian Affairs, and Governor Lewis Cass of Michigan Territory represented the United States Government. Representing the army was Captain R.A. McCabe, commander of Fort Crawford, and one hundred soldiers of the Fifth Infantry. Last to arrive were the Sauk, Mesquakie, and Ioway, dressed in their finest wardress. The warriors reportedly wore tufts of red horsehair tied at their elbows and necklaces of grisly bear claws.[22] They wore their headdresses tied to their scalp locks, and their heads were shaved and painted. The white clay print of a hand marked many backs and shoulders. Some carried lances; others clubs, guns, and knives. With their arrival, the council began with all the pomp and ceremony that could be mustered to impress the attendees.

Fort Crawford's cannon summoned all to the council (on the fifth of August). General Clark spoke first, explaining the reason for the council. He addressed the need for peace, and explained the benefit of setting clear and certain boundaries between warring tribes. On the second day each tribal leader addressed the assemblage, and on the third the tribes expressed their desire for peace, but disputes arose when they began to describe their territorial boundaries. For days, the Sioux, Sauk, and Mesquakie argued over which point of the Missouri should be the boundary between them. After two weeks of arguing, it was settled between them. On August 19, 1825, they signed the treaty, passed the wampum belt among them, and smoked the pipe as a sign of peace. Then, one by one, the tribes departed and officials and traders alike breathed a collective sigh of relief. They were cautiously optimistic that peace would hold throughout the hunting season.[23]

The winter hunt that year had promise, wrote Russel Farnham from his post at Flint Hills (Burlington): "There are a large number of Indians that are hunting beaver ... We have one hundred sixty bundles of furs ... From Mr. Davenport's last report they had eighty more ... And Mr. Blondeau said that all indications showed business to be good." In preparation, both partners obsessed about what color of strouding to stock. Their concern was not as frivolous as it may at first seem. In the previous year, Farnham complained, their strouds were too light for the Indians' taste, and they didn't sell very well. Their competitor had the darker strouds. It was a tenant of the business. They would lose their credits if they didn't have what their customers wanted. The Indians were, after all, sophisticated shoppers who knew the value of the products they bought, and their tastes changed from season to season, just like the most fashionable Europeans who wanted their furs. In another year the Indians had wanted black silk handkerchiefs, and Davenport had none. The following year he had plenty on hand but he could hardly give them away, because then they wanted white ones.[24]

Davenport's ledgers for 1825-1826 confirm that business was very good that year, considerably better than the previous one. He had purchased over $19,000 in goods - almost double the amount of the previous year - and taken in $35,000 worth of credits. That was enough to pay off his debts to American Fur Company. In spring the water in the rivers and ponds had been high and the muskrat hunt had been good. The take was again good. Nearly 50,000 muskrat pelts had been collected.[25]

Business with the miners was good as well. Having Farrar embedded at Fever River was paying off for Davenport. He had sent 304 bars of lead to St. Louis the previous September, and again, had run short of goods. Lead production had increased because Davenport's Indians had discovered a new vein and the summer of 1826 was even better. By January of 1826, Davenport reported to Bostwick that he had enough lead to fill two boats in the spring and good prospects at the Dubuque mines, too. He had about fifty thousand pounds of lead already and expected six to eight thousand pounds more. Already there was a new town in the mineral region, appropriately called Galena, the Latin word for lead.[26]

On a bigger picture, George Davenport operated a number of trading posts on nearby rivers, owned his own canoes and keelboats, and had been appointed U.S. Postmaster for the region. In May he had invested $6,000 in the 2nd U.S. Bank, a move that was calculated to give him purchasing power and credit on a national scale.[27] He had had his ups and downs, but had weathered them better than he might have foreseen. Such success had not gone unnoticed by the American Fur Company and he was finally offered a contract as agent with a salary. His risks now were the risks of the American Fur Company. It gave George the security he had wanted.

Davenport was officially notified on the 17th of June 1826 that his agreement to trade for the American Fur Company had been confirmed. Unfortunately, Oliver Bostwick did not mention the terms, but it was probably similar to Farnham's contract with the company. Contract terms for agents were not standard, but tailored to the man and the situation. Farnham, for instance, had been placed on a salary of $1,000 in 1822. Joshua Palen and Maurice Blondeau were each paid $1,200 in 1823. Others were paid on commission, a calculation according to Lavender, to stimulate them to work harder.[28.] In addition to his salary, Davenport also earned an additional percentage of the profits when the furs were sold on the international market and given his own "Outfit."

Lavender explains the outfits as "semi-independent 'dealerships' " through which Astor preferred to operate his company.[29] Accounts for Farnham and Davenport's partnership were referred to as the Sauk/Sac

Outfit by year. Each partner had his own private account as well. The private accounts were on the risks of the individual and not the Company.

The Sauk Outfit employed six men: John Connolly, J.K. Forsyth, Maurice Blondeau, Samuel Muir, Antoine Gokey, and Pierre Sausignon. At Rock Island, were Antoine Gokey, Baptiste Barte, Joseph Joinville, and Nicholas Hebert. (Note that Gokey was listed on both licenses). Farnham also had a number of men at Fort Edwards, some of whom had been long-time associates of both Davenport and Farnham, evidence of the loyalty that both men commanded. J.K. Forsyth, the son of Indian Agent Thomas Forsyth, served as clerk for the outfit. Connolly had come back into the fold, after defecting for a short time with Downey in opposition to Davenport. Presumably, Connelly had mended his ways and was now firmly allied with Davenport and Farnham. It should be noted that Blondeau had been employed with Farnham, and Samuel Muir with Davenport, for many years now. Antoine Gokey, who served both men, was the right hand man of George Davenport, and remained so until his death. These men were kept employed year-round, rather than on a seasonal basis, and were paid well with annual salaries that ranged from $120 to $170 plus rations, clothing, and other supplies. In many ways these loyal employees contributed to Davenport and Farnham's success.

Now that he was under contract, Davenport set his men to work building a new store for the safekeeping of goods and furs. His stores, as remembered by Old Settler David Sears, were large two-story buildings, made of hewn logs, and measuring approximately twenty-four feet by forty to forty-four feet. Finished in late July 1826, the storehouse was inspected by Ramsay Crooks, Astor's field manager, who stopped at Rock Island while on his way upriver that summer. The Company was looking for efficient and cost-reducing methods, and Crooks was pleased with Davenport's arrangements: "Mr. Davenport has everything very snug here, and I am much pleased with his intelligence & general arrangements."[30] Snug facilities were important, but they could not offset the uncertainties of the business.

Competition for the Sauk and Fox trade was fierce, because they had a tradition of being good hunters. Farnham and Davenport monopolized their business but never commanded 100% of their trade. There was always someone trying to cut into business, like William Downey who had built his own trading house on Rock Island.[31]

Lt. William Downey resigned as Fort Armstrong's sutler in June of 1826 and went into the trading business on a full-time basis. Davenport considered him more of a nuisance than a serious competitor, but he had to be dealt with just the same by furnishing him trade goods. With a store on the island Downey was preparing, as Davenport said, to help him in collecting his credits from the Mesquakie, but in a surprise move, Downey decided that year to concentrate on the six hundred Ho Chunk who planned to hunt muskrat in the wetlands along the Rock River and in the Meredosias.[32]

To counter Downey's encroachment on his territory, Davenport made a number of changes for the trade that season. He replaced old Lamoliece, whom Davenport thought was worth nothing, with a new man to take charge of the Rock River trade, and established three temporary posts close to home, two on the Rock River and one on the Mississippi. Because the water level was low that season, Davenport expected the Ho Chunk to kill all the muskrats in the first hunt, and did not expect a second hunt that winter. He decided not to furnish Downey with any more goods than he would need for the first hunt. Then, Farnham and Davenport decided to establish a store near the Muscatine, about 30 miles below Rock Island, either on the Illinois side or on an island, That, they strategized, would be an ideal place to intercept the Mesquakie before they travelled to Rock Island, and would thwart Downey's activities, because Davenport was sure that Downey could not afford to move to the same location. Davenport's own profits would be much better if they could keep Downey out of Indian country, but such an opening would only allow others to move in. If he and Farnham could secure the trade to themselves for two or three years, it would pay for their losses in the Ho Chunk trade.[33]

This was a typical kind of strategy that traders employed. There were few secrets about anyone's business in the Indian trade and every bit of news about a competitor's business was fair game -- one reason why traders demanded complete loyalty from their workers. Traders sought information about their rivals in order to develop ways to reduce any potential advantage they might gain. Letters from the field manager Ramsay Crooks to workers in the field were frequent, carrying news about the opposition, sizing them up, offering advice on how best to alter company strategies, and encouraging his agents to do their best, especially against former partners or employees. The situation of Francois Labussierre, who decided to go into business for himself with partner Pierre Cerre, is a good example. Labussierre's trade goods for the season had been delivered inadvertently to Rock Island instead of Fort Edwards, which had alerted the Company to his plans. Crooks imparted the following information to Farnham and Davenport about Labussierre's trading plans.

Labussierre intended to get his credits from the Fox or Mesquakie at Rock Island and then proceed to the wintering grounds. His partner Cerre planned to winter on the Ioway, and Labussierre himself planned to winter "at or near the Raccoon forks of the River des Moines ... " which is today the city of Des Moines, Iowa. Crooks, writing from Rock Island, was not terribly concerned, as long as his traders moved in ahead of Labussierre: "On the whole I do not think this opposition VERY formidable, but as Francois knows all the Indians well, he will naturally bestir himself to secure as many of the best (furs) as he can, and I therefore think that the earlier Mr. Farnham is on the ground the better so as to thwart whatever he may attempt in that way - .... " [34]

Competition for furs was fierce, even among traders working for the same company. One American Fur Company trader in particular, Joseph Rollette, often infringed on Davenport's territory, and Davenport expected the Company to do something about it. Jean Joseph Rollette was a veteran fur trader in Prairie du Chien since 1804. He was known to be tough and unscrupulous. He also recognized no territorial boundaries, even to his fellow company men. Davenport complained bitterly: "Mr. Rollette sent me word that thier was nothing in his contract to prevent him from Selling Goods to com in to this part of the Mississippi - Mr. Kinsey of Chicago has sent men and horses on Rock River close to my trading house ..." He urged Farnham, as the senior partner, to speak to Crooks on his behalf in order "to Impress on the company that they must Give particular directions to the diffrent outfits to keep with in thier limits and not to Sell Goods to com in our district ... Those things is verrey Injoures to us and a great disadvantage to the company." If the practice were not stopped, Davenport warned, "Whe must use the same means and sind goods whear whe please if the other traders for the company is not Restrained." The American Fur Company, however, did nothing. Rollette ran one of the most successful and profitable outfits in the American Fur Company and Crooks would not curb his enthusiasm. If George Davenport were to be successful, he would have to do it on his own initiative.[35]

Even with such stiff competition, Davenport did well in the Indian trade, building his reputation on fair and honest trading practices, and relying on loyal and trustworthy employees. He was loyal to the American Fur Company, even before he had a formal contract with them. When Louis Pettle was dismissed from the Indian Agency at Fort Armstrong in the Vose dispute, Davenport was anxious that the American Fur Company hire Pettle before he went to his competitor, Mr. Downey. "Respecting Pettle I advised that he should be Imployed by Mr Farnham to prevent Mr Downy from holding Councils with the Indians and advising them to trade thier credits as Pettle is the only Interpreter that can Speak English and Indian and would so will answer Downeys purpose ... if this is affected, Downy will be compleatly crippled and must give up the Ship - for with out pettle he will be compleatley a drift= but with pettle he will Sertainley Collect a great many of our credicts, if whiskey and Lying will have any affect."[36]

Davenport's methods had paid off. His financial situation had improved remarkably since 1822. In 1823 he received $5,435.77 worth of furs and peltries and the company paid him nearly a thousand dollars in cash to pay his men, even though he could not repay the debt for his goods. In 1824, he collected $9,390.88 in furs and peltries and $2,457.89 in lead, and though he made money this year, he was still in debt. In 1825, he collected $22,165.38 in furs and peltries and $4,318.64 in lead, and was finally out of debt to the company. In 1826, he collected $3,915.07 in furs and peltries and $7,034.49 in lead. Cash payments were made to him each year, about $1,000 in both 1823 and 1824. In 1825, the American Fur Company paid him nearly $4,000 in cash, and in 1826, Davenport received $2,260. Before he left for England in 1827, he received $3,200.[37]

Whether it was out of necessity or an understanding of cycles in economy, Davenport understood the value of diversifying his business interests and was involved in a number of cash-producing enterprises, so that he was never dependent on any one means of income. While supplying the troops, he sold trade goods to the Indian Agency and established an inn where he could legally sell spirituous liquors. He expanded his trading territory by taking into partnership a number of men to man the outposts, and was one of the earliest traders to exploit the lead mines of Fever River. His financial success had steadily risen.

As he planned for the Indian Trade in the coming months, George Davenport also began to make preparations for a well-earned vacation. News from his sister in Louth prompted George to return to England on family business. He had talked about going for a few years, but had not had someone to hold his place in the business. By 1826, loyal employees, good partners, trust among the Sauk and Mesquakie, and his position in the American Fur Company all worked to give Davenport time to visit his family in England. The Company agreed to send trusted men to run the business during his absence, so Davenport had his men build a store house for the purpose of storing the American Fur Company goods and furs while he was gone.[38] Then, he took his family to Cincinnati, where they stayed during his absence, and sailed to London.

While the Davenports were away from Rock Island a natural phenomenon was observed at Fort Armstrong. At seven o'clock in the evening of the 2nd of August, a "very brilliant meteor" was observed in the sky. It was "so luminous as plainly to discover objects at considerable distance."[39] To the soldiers who observed it, the meteor was a scientific marvel. For the Sauk and the Mesquakie it was a warning from the Great Spirit, a sign of a bad Manitou in their village. Had the Davenports seen the meteor, they, too, might have recognized it as an omen, for there were more changes to face when George returned from England.

CHAPTER NINE:

TO ENGLAND, 1827 – 1828

IT WAS AN OPPORTUNE TIME for the Davenports to be away from Rock Island. The Ho Chunk were once again threatening. Encroachment by miners on Ho Chunk lands had irritated the band and provoked them to hostile acts. Their threats had compelled Colonel Snelling to reinforce Fort Crawford where three companies of the Fifth Infantry, with 176 officers and men, offered Prairie du Chien its largest military presence in years. However, they did not stay long, because they were soon ordered to Fort Snelling and Fort Crawford was abandoned. The remaining garrisons at Fort Armstrong, Fort Snelling, and Fort Howard were considered sufficient to keep any hostilities from the Ho Chunk in check.

At Fort Armstrong, Major Vose continued to be uneasy about the natives. A large number of Ho Chunk had gathered in the vicinity of Rock Island for their winter hunt. They professed to be peaceful, but Vose had reservations. He ordered his men not to trust these people whom he considered treacherous and more savage than any tribe in this part of the country. No man was allowed to leave the island alone. Instead, he ordered them to leave armed and in groups of three. The same rule applied to parties going to the far parts of the island.[1] Later, Vose suspended the issue of extra rations of whiskey, except for unspecified extraordinary occasions. He cited the health and morals of his men as his concern, but in actuality he was fearful of whiskey getting into the hands of the Indians. Four canoes of intoxicated Ho Chunk Indians had recently visited the fort, and their whiskey was furnished by Vose's own commissioned officers at the fort. Reminding his men that the Ho Chunk were the most troublesome Indians to his knowledge, he reiterated his order on whiskey, hoping to keep it from the hunters. To insure the safety of the fort, no "Indian man, woman, or child will be allowed to come within the walls of the fort" during the winter.[2]

Throughout the winter of 1826-1827 many traders on the Upper Mississippi expressed fears that Ho Chunk uprisings would increase in the coming spring. The more optimistic among them did not believe that the Ho Chunk would seriously consider starting a war against the settlers, but in the spring, the hunters returned from their hunt with fewer furs, and correspondingly, were less able to repay their credits. They were also surly.[3] To complicate matters, greater numbers of miners were heading to the mines.

Reportedly, the immigration to the U. S. Lead Mines was "immense." By the middle of March one steamboat had already left for Fever River and was advertising regular passage to and from the mines. Three other steamboats had the same plan. Estimates of the numbers miners reached several thousands, even though the Government rents were "considerably increased."[4]

The Ho Chunk saw this as infringement on their land and struck back with two gruesome murders near Prairie du Chien. Both involved French settlers who had long lived peacefully among the Indians. In the first, the bodies of a man named Methode, his wife, and five children were found horribly mangled and burned. In the second instance, Registre Gagnier, a part French-part Indian man, his wife and two children, and an old soldier named Solomon Lipcap, who lived with them, were attacked in their log cabin.[5] Mrs. Gagnier and her oldest child escaped, but Mr. Gagnier and Lipcap were murdered. The youngest child survived, although she had been scalped and her throat severely cut. The Ho Chunk seemed guilty of both attacks.

On the same day as the Gagnier murders, two keelboats on the Mississippi were attacked and several men aboard were killed. When the boats arrived in Galena, news of the murders spread rapidly throughout the mining region. In panic, miners flocked to the safety of the town with their families, expecting to be assaulted, scalped, or tomahawked at any moment. The American troops were called to calm the countryside.[6]

On Rock Island the Davenports had not been immune to Ho Chunk hostility, despite the nearness of the fort and its soldiers. They had been the victims of many attacks by the Ho Chunk and did not underestimate the dangers. One story, often told by Susan Lewis Goldsmith, recounted a visit by the Ho Chunk chief called Jerro in the early summer of 1827.

Jerro arrived at the Davenport home one day with thirty warriors, all of whose faces were painted black. They entered the house without knocking or speaking and placed themselves around the room with the stocks of their guns resting on the floor. The family was taken by surprise and feared they would be murdered at any moment. Because Davenport was not at home, a messenger was sent to summon him from the fort. When he entered the house, he greeted the warriors in their own language and offered his hand in friendship, but they refused to take it. While the Indians remained silent and motionless, Davenport went into his storeroom and returned with thirty small looking glasses, one for each Indian. Jerro asked what they were for, and Davenport explained that they were for seeing how pretty they looked. Jerro laughed at that, picked up his gun, and motioned for his men to follow him. Then he marched out of the house and left the island. Why these Ho Chunk entered the

Davenport home, and why they left so abruptly is unknown, but sometime later an old Indian told Davenport that it had been the Ho Chunk intention to murder him and his family and to carry off the goods from his store. Instead, they left because they were afraid of the soldiers at the fort who had been alerted to their visit. After this, Black Hawk placed a guard around the Davenport house each night to protect the family from being murdered by the Ho Chunk until they left for Ohio.[7]

This incident convinced George to remove his family from the island for the duration of his visit to England. Even with protection from the Sauk warriors, his family was not safe. Davenport finalized arrangements for a lengthy absence. He made new arrangements at the mines when St. Vrain left the partnership with Davenport, Farrar & Co., and the company with Farrar was dissolved.[8] In its place, a new partnership with Russel Farnham was formed (May 1827). The new partnership signified the extent of their presence in the Upper Mississippi Valley. Their influence now stretched from the Fever River in northwest Illinois down to the lower rapids of the river at present day Keokuk, Iowa, and across northern Missouri to the Black Snake Hills and the Kansas River.

Confident that the trade was in good hands, the family departed for Cincinnati in July. Mrs. Davenport, Susan, the two boys, and Charlotte planned to stay in Cincinnati where George L. attended his first formal school.[9] Davenport proceeded to Philadelphia where he sailed to England. He arrived in London on 10th of August (1827) and sometime later travelled to Louth.

Letters home kept the family informed of his travels. In Louth he visited old friends and family, particularly his brother and sister. His reactions to seeing his old home and familiar landmarks have been lost, but Davenport must have been happy to see his hometown and to note all the changes that had occurred in his absence. Some things had not changed.

On the surface the town looked very much the same as it had in 1804 when last he saw it. The 12th century spire of St. James Cathedral still towered above the town. Surely he visited the local pubs --Eve and Ranshaw, The Swan, and Wheatsheaf Inns -- and reacquainted himself with old friends. The Old Wool Mart, found through the narrow Pawnshop Passage at the junction of Kidgate, may have seemed smaller than he remembered and, on closer inspection, Davenport may have noticed a little more prosperity than he remembered. Many of the mud and stud cottages with thatched roofs that provided the English village ambiance had been replaced with brick structures boasting red tile roofs. These new dwellings were harder to heat than the old ones, but brick was considered a great improvement in safety, being less susceptible to fire. Brick was one of the most important products of nineteenth century Louth and by 1827 it was being used all over the town.

Louth was undergoing change and improvement when Davenport visited. It was part of a movement, officially called an Act for Paving, Lighting, Watching, Cleansing, Regulating and Otherwise Improving the Town that had been passed in 1825.[10] The Old Town Hall had been demolished and lighting at night had been added. Just the year before, the Gas Works had been formed and the town center lit with gaslights. The event had been celebrated by sending up a hot air balloon from the Gas Works and people were still talking about the spectacle. Communication all over this part of England had improved and Louth even had its own post office with regular mail delivery.

Something that hadn't changed was the nature of the marketplace. The markets were still held on Wednesdays and Saturdays for everything but animals, which were sold on Fridays. Even the Fish Shambles remained, as it still does today. Louth had grown from a small, but important market in the center of an agricultural-based population, to a small industrial center that catered to the needs of its agriculture. Louth also supplied the far corners of the world with its products. With prosperity had come an increase in population. When Davenport left home in 1800, Louth had been about 4,000 strong. Now there were over 6,000 people, almost as many as the county seat of Lincoln, and still growing.

What had made such a difference in Louth was the opening of the Louth Navigation, a canal that connected the River Lud to the North Sea, and it was there, in the area east of town called the Riverhead, where the most changes had taken place. They were also the changes that would most impress George Davenport and remain in his memory for many years. What he saw and experienced there would serve as inspiration for his own river development when he returned home to Rock Island.

Louth had been the location of several industries connected to the wool industry before the eighteenth century. After the Navigation opened in 1770, a great many trades and industries related to the wool and shipping industries had gravitated to the Riverhead, which in turn had stimulated more growth and development. Here was the Louth Carpet Manufactory, started in 1787, which spanned the River Lud and was driven by large waterwheels, and the familiar Pack Horse Inn. Now there were many other industries. Where Davenport and his brother had once grazed their father's cows and where they had spent many lazy summer afternoons lying on the banks of the Navigation, the land was dramatically changed. By 1827 the Navigation area was a vital business center and the many industries located there used both wind and waterpower. Davenport must have remembered the carpet mill and tanneries for which Louth was especially well known and the windmills, but he would have marvelled at the big five-sail windmill that had recently been built there and the huge warehouse where goods were stored awaiting shipment on the canal. Where once there were pastures and open fields in his childhood, there was now a mixture of brick tenements, mills, warehouses, counting houses, wharfs, ship yards, granaries, and coal yards which made the Riverhead one of the more important streets in Louth for employing and housing the trades and professions. Louth was not, George Davenport found, "a sleepy, forgotten, backwater market town," but a thriving urban center full of life and connected to the greater world of England.[11]

This mixture of trades and professions, industries and residences, gardens and coal heaps which seems so strange to our twentieth century notion of separate spaces for residential, industrial, and commercial activity was hardly a new and revolutionary approach to development, but it would have been exciting for Davenport to see the progress that Louth had made. He may have been prepared for such changes through letters from his sister, but actually seeing them must have triggered some new ideas in his mind. At the very least he must have seen the similarity to the river's edge at home on the Mississippi and observed how such a mix could serve a wide variety of people.[12] One other innovation that must have played on Davenport's imagination was the railroad.

After spending some time in Louth, Davenport returned to London. How he spent his time can only be conjectured, but one thing surely caught his eye: the opening of the first railroad had taken place in England on the 27th of September 1825. Races between footmen, men on horseback, and stagecoaches had demonstrated the speed of the locomotive, 15 miles per hour. Although there were problems that would have to be overcome in extending rails across difficult terrain, including changing public opinion, it had been proven that this form of transportation was feasible.[13] It was the latest craze all over England and Davenport's interest would have been piqued by the attention since he was always interested in the latest technology, especially when it could be applied to transportation.

Davenport wrote to Bostwick that he had enjoyed seeing England but he was already anxious to get back home again. If it had not been for the dangers of the seas in winter Davenport might have returned sooner. He finally arrived in New York on the 12th of May. He could hardly wait to see his family, his business and his home, but he was also anxious to put some of these new ideas to work at home. By the time George returned to Rock Island he had been gone for nearly a year.[14]

When Davenport left for England the island was little more than wilderness, inhabited in only three areas: Ft. Armstrong where 90 men were stationed along with a few women and children; the Indian Agency surrounded by its small community of workers and their families; and the residences of Antoine Gokey and George Davenport. The Sauk and Mesquakie still returned each summer to their villages and to their cornfields on the mainland. The vast prairies were covered with grasses and wild flowers, and the forests filled with ancient trees. Thick undergrowth thrived beneath them and the forests teemed with wildlife. Davenport was eager to see what had changed in the past year.

Business, during his absence, had been respectable. Hardly had George arrived in London before St. Vrain sent a sizable boatload of furs down to St. Louis. Included in the shipment were 1,140 muskrat skins, 46 otter, 38 mink and 13 packs of red deer skins. With the exception of Farnham's illness with the ague, business was, indeed, good and the future, though always uncertain in the fur trading business, looked bright.[15]

CHAPTER TEN:

INFLUX OF SETTLERS, 1828 - 1829

GEORGE DAVENPORT RETURNED from England in the summer of 1828, happy to be home and anxious to see his family, especially his sons. They had grown during his absence and George L., now nearly 12, had learned enough at school to begin work in the Indian trade. He began observing the rudiments of the trade by sitting with his father in council, giving out credits for the fall hunt, and collecting them at the end of the season. Bailey was four and a half and still too young for schooling, but he was developing an interest in horses and was fascinated by the soldiers at the fort. Another change in the family was the marriage of Susan Lewis, the boys' mother, to a Mr. Goodale. Little is known about this man, but he returned to Rock Island with the family and took his place as son-in-law, working on the island with Davenport and operating the woodlot business.[1]

After a year away, Davenport was anxious to get back to work. Farnham's health had not been good throughout the winter, and he had been unable to go to the Missouri for some time. Palen and Mitchell had gone in his place but they had found it difficult to locate their house on the Grand River because of increased competition in that area. In fact, competition had been strong at all their posts, and Farnham had even struck a deal with Joseph Rollette at Prairie du Chien in order to neutralize Rollette's opposition near the lead mines. The past season's trade had been poor with few rats and little or no beaver. Even deer had been scarce.[2] Farnham had also exchanged some skins with Gratiot and Co., but they had been unable to reach an agreement on the price. Davenport's negotiating skills may have been missed more than anyone realized.

The Ho Chunk had indeed been at war during his absence and it was directly related to the intrusions of miners on their land at the mines. Indian Agent Joseph M. Street believed the Ho Chunk had been goaded into a state of high excitement after being forced out of their mines and robbed of the profits of their lead. They had preyed on travellers heading to the Fever River area, attacked settlers in their homes, and threatened the miners. They had also attacked keelboats above Prairie du Chien, killing and wounding crewmen. Every attempt to pacify the Ho Chunk had been unsuccessful. Not until both the Regular Army and the Militia were called up did the leader Red Bird surrender. He implicated the Sioux as instigators of the attacks. Two other Ho Chunk were taken into custody and with that, peace was declared by General Atkinson.[3] By the time the Davenports returned to Rock Island, the Ho Chunk had been temporarily pacified.

There was a still greater problem to face, a problem which had a direct effect on their Indian friends and on the Davenport's livelihood. While the Davenports were away, settlers had arrived in Rock Island. Their arrival had long been anticipated, but it must have come as a surprise to see smoke from their chimneys throughout the neighborhood.

Davenport did not waste any time getting back to work. There was much to do. It was time to collect the credits from the previous fall, to sort the furs and peltries, and to plan for the next hunting season. First, he and Farnham renewed the contracts of their workers, and then Davenport visited each post to see for himself how business was. Accompanied by Farnham, he went first to the Dubuque Mines to see what damage had been done by the spring floods to their "mineral and Ashes" at the mines. Much had been covered with water and subsequently washed away. Before going to England, he had obtained the license and made all the necessary arrangements for his men and he expected profits from the mines, so it must have been disappointing to see the damage.

Davenport spent three weeks at the mines, collecting the lead and getting it smelted before heading home. From there he made a quick stop at home, just an overnight stay, before leaving again. This time he went to Fort Edwards. There he wanted to consult with Farnham on goods that they would need for the coming year before going to the Des Moines for a few weeks.[4]

One bright bit of news was that the Sauk and Mesquakie agreed to let them build a house to store their trade goods on their land, as long as their clerk lived in one of the Sauk and Mesquakie lodges. This may have been the house at the Watch Tower that Bailey often spoke about. Even better news was that the Sauk and Mesquakie were planning a summer hunt. His post was crowded with Indians and he gave out $1,900 in credits.

By the middle of August Davenport had again returned to Rock Island and employed his men in building new sleeping quarters. Their old one was falling down and this kept them busy earning their pay. He was anxious to get back to the mines as the Indians had done little since his earlier visit and were nearly finished for the season. His top priority, however, was getting the annuity payment. It was expected any day at Rock Island and he needed to be present when it was given to the chiefs. That way he could collect at least some of the money they owed him. Although Davenport's letters did not express concern, he must have been considering the restlessness of the Indians. They had done little hunting on their summer hunt and the young braves were becoming mischief-makers. His stacks of hay, put up by his hired men, had been set on fire by the Beaver's Son. It was a constant battle on his part to keep his Indians hunting rather than fighting. Rumors were still rampant that Morgan and his band of Mesquakie had gone to war, but by the end of October Davenport was still insisting to his St. Louis contacts that the Sauk and Fox would remain at peace.

Prospects for the coming hunts were gloomy at best. Out on the Rock River there were neither Indians nor muskrats and Davenport continued to worry that his Indians were too lazy to go to the hunting grounds, preferring to fight. Because the summer hunt had produced very little for their effort, the tribes had little fresh meat. As a result, many people would starve or succumb to sickness in the coming winter. The poor hunt also meant increased debts to their traders, so Davenport worked extra hard to convince them that they needed to hunt. He sent Palen and Mitchell to the hunting grounds early that fall. From Dirt Lodge they sent word of the situation in the field before continuing to the Raccoon River. They had sent Indian runners to as many hunters as could be found to encourage them to hunt. The weather was mild and the Mississippi was rising, good signs for hunting muskrats, but by the end of December 1828, their worst fears had been realized.

From the Raccoon River, Palen and Mitchell reported that the Mesquakie war leader Morgan had indeed led his war party against the Sioux and his warriors had killed two Sioux braves. The Sioux had retaliated against the Sauk, killed the Stealing Chief and his wife, and taken a number of horses. The Sauk were all in one camp and starving. The Sauk were planning to hunt, but there was no guarantee that they would not come into contact with Sioux parties again, as no peace had been settled between the tribes.[5]

Adding to the frustration of the Farnham and Davenport men, a new competitor had opened for business in their area. The Phelps brothers, Stephen and William, had opened a post at Oquawka, Illinois, and were challenging their trade. Farnham's and Davenport's concern was well founded. The Phelps brothers were ambitious and in the next few years they opened posts on the Ioway, Skunk, and Des Moines rivers.[6]

The most unsettling realization of all that year was that settlers were pushing into the entire Upper Mississippi Valley with alarming speed. Several thousand diggers had migrated to the mines and, even though the lands surrounding the mines were still officially Indian lands, the would-be settlers had taken little notice.[7] On their way upriver the miners, and their families, noted places that they might wish to settle on, but continued to the mines hoping to make enough money in one season to pay for land that would soon be available for purchase.

The Rock River region was particularly beautiful and it was one of the first places where many families wanted to settle. They expected that those lands would soon be vacated by the Indians, because 1828 marked the last of the twelve annuity payments promised to the Sauk and Fox by the Treaty of 1816. By the terms of the treaty, the Indians then would leave. Would-be settlers not only expected, but insisted upon, the removal of the Indians, so that they could move in. Governor Ninian Edwards, himself no Indian lover, agreed with them. Edwards demanded the removal of all Indians from Illinois, but the Indians were not yet ready to move, and in fact, were given an extension until April 1, 1830.[8]

Settlers came nevertheless. They came from all directions: on steamboats up the Mississippi, overland from the South and the East, and by way of the Great Lakes. Settlers separated the Indians from the land they once roamed freely, following game. They cleared the land and fenced in their fields, preventing both hunter and deer from crossing their property. Their livestock competed with wild animals for grazing land and the wild animals moved off to open land. Some fur-bearers, like the beaver, were already close to extinction in the Mississippi Valley from over-hunting and the arrival of settlers further deteriorated the hunting situation. Only the muskrat were relatively safe, since they lived in swampy areas considered unsuitable places for settlement. Alienated from their traditional hunting grounds and finding the hunt already difficult, the Indians moved into areas used by other tribes, causing even more conflicts as well as further reducing game populations.

The settlers also competed with established traders like Farnham and Davenport. They even attempted to undermine the agreements made between Indian hunters and traders in the fall council by trading whiskey for the Indian furs and pelts. The newcomers had no understanding of the way the frontier economy worked, as Davenport explained to Pierre Chouteau: "Besides The Indian dificulteys a number of persons have Settled on the bank of The Mississippi and have goods and whiskey and will Trade our Credicts." [9] Davenport's business with the Sauk, Mesquakie, and Ho Chunk was based on trust and reciprocity, and the Indians returned the favor. The tribes were not usually inclined to sell their credits to others, but the lure of whiskey was a powerful inducement. On the other hand, the settlers had few other means to sustain themselves until their farms began to produce. It was a difficult situation for Davenport as well as for the Indians, but these settlers were not competitors that he could eliminate like small traders.

Davenport had no wish for the future that he and Farnham could foresee for his Indian friends. In the opinion of Farnham and Davenport, whiskey was the single most important problem from which the Indians needed to be protected. They believed it degenerated Indians and made them lazy and unwilling to hunt and provide for their tribe. Unfortunately, whiskey was an easy commodity to make from corn and it provided some much-needed revenue for some settlers. One such man was Joshua Vandruff who had settled on an island in the Rock River within sight of the Sauk village. He had a large family and used every means to support them, including making whiskey. Black Hawk, who discouraged his warriors from partaking of whiskey, once went to Vandruff's house, broke in the head of the whiskey barrel and let the liquor run out onto the ground. [10]

By 1830 settlers occupied the entire eastern bank of the Mississippi River. Inevitably there were conflicts with the Indians, but there were not enough soldiers to protect both settler and Indian. Ironically, as the numbers of settlers increased, the numbers of soldiers at the Mississippi Valley forts dropped. In 1830 for instance, Fort Armstrong had 88 men and 6 officers; in 1831, 62 men and 7 officers, and in 1832, only 43 men and 5 officers.[11]

The mineral lands were the first lands at risk. The Sauk and Mesquakie had managed to protect some of their interests in the mineral lands, particularly those on the western banks of the Mississippi river around Dubuque, Iowa. These mines were an important source of income for the tribes, especially in light of the dwindling supplies of furs. In June of 1830, a group of miners moved into the Dubuque mines, under the assumption that the land had been vacated, because the village was not inhabited at that time. It was a common misunderstanding. When the Indians returned, they found their mines being stripped of lead. Their call for help was answered by a detachment of soldiers from Fort Crawford who removed the trespassers and guarded the mines. Military guards remained there until 1832.[12]

At Rock Island, settlers had moved into the Sauk and Mesquakie villages while the tribes were still at their winter camps. Some settlers, like Judge Spencer, were even living in Indian lodges, and were disturbed when Black Hawk showed up one day shouting to get out, that it was his house. Returning to the cornfields each spring was more important to the tribes than the settlers understood. Without their cornfields, the Sauk and Mesquakie had no means of subsistence. They could not live on the hunt alone.

With their hunting grounds disrupted and their cornfields taken over by settlers, the Sauk and Mesquakie, like all the other eastern tribes, ranged farther and farther west in search of game, and were coming into more frequent conflict with their traditional enemies, the Sioux, and other western tribes. The Missouri Sauk and Fox had an uneasy alliance with the Ioway, but were often at odds with the Osage and other Missouri tribes, and there was no fort or agency to mitigate their differences. Farnham and Davenport, represented by Palen and Mitchell, continued to trade at their house near the Black Snake Hills with strong competition from companies of Robidoux, McLoud, and others.[13]

Knowing that their Sauk and Fox hunters were travelling further and staying away for longer periods of time, Farnham and Davenport advised the U.S. Government to buy the Sauk and Mesquakie lands. This would, according to Farnham and Davenport, settle their debts and move them away from the whiskey influence. Along with the Indian Agent and his interpreter, they presented their idea to the tribes, and after many councils with tribal elders and chiefs, the Sauk and Mesquakie decided to establish new villages on the Ioway and Cedar rivers. As soon as the Indians left for their winter hunting grounds, many more settlers moved into the Sauk lodges, assured that the Indians would not return again.[14]

An influential voice joined Forsyth's Indian Agency that year when the old interpreter at Fort Armstrong died and Forsyth offered the Fort Armstrong job to Antoine Le Claire, an old friend of Farnham and Davenport. He arrived on Rocky Island, with his wife Marguerite, in March 1828. Le Claire was an experienced and gifted interpreter, having worked for many tribes during the past ten years. Most recently, Le Claire had been at Fort Osage, but he had also worked as the interpreter to the Pottawatomi, the Illinois, and the Kickapoo as well as the Kansa. His fluency in Sauk made him especially valuable to the Fort Armstrong Indian Agency at a time when negotiations were critical and sensitive. His influence on the Indians at large would be put to the test over the next few years as they worked together with Indian agents and military commanders.[15]

The arrival of new settlers became a weekly event in Davenport's neighborhood. By the end of December 1828, there were ten new families staking claims in the valley. Judge Pence and his son had arrived on the 9th of December. Following them were Judge John Spencer, Jonah Case, William Brashar, Rinnah Wells, Joshua Vandruff, Archie Allen, George Harland, Thomas Hubbard, and John Danforth. Davenport kept track of the new arrivals in his Day Book with such entries as: " on the 27th of December, Davenport wrote, "George Wells came down for provisions, he having settled on the rapids. He makes the tenth settler in our neighborhood."[16]

Many of the early settlers were from the northeast, particularly Vermont and Pennsylvania, and attracted to the waterpower and the lush vegetation of the Mississippi River valley. They brought their families and all their earthly possessions, their cows, hogs, sheep, oxen, and chickens, and proceeded to build log homes around Rock Island. For George Davenport, they were a new source of business, although there were some threats to Davenport and Farnham's livelihood. One such threat was the family headed by Captain Benjamin W. Clark.

When Davenport returned from England he found the Clark family had claimed the land around Davenport's trading post on the bank of the Mississippi directly across from Fort Armstrong. Clark had previously been engaged in cattle farming near the old Fort Edwards, so he had some connection to the U.S. Government. He was considered to be a man of "bold, and almost unflinching, uncompromising sternness and perseverance" and he was not willing to give up his claim to the land. He told Davenport that he would fight him for it.[17] According to some of the old settlers, Davenport did everything possible to drive the Clarks away from the area by refusing to sell them provisions, even bribing the Indians to scare them. Clark retaliated with a few tricks of his own. Despite the animosity, the Clarks stuck it out, although they did eventually elect to move themselves a little further downriver.

Adjoining the Clark property was Pvt. John Haney, recently discharged from the service at Fort Armstrong. According to Judge John Spencer, Haney also settled for a time near the Farnham post, but died before he could make any formal claims to Rock Island County land.[18]

With the settlers came a new kind of religion. It was not the Algonquian spiritual belief in Manitou that the Sauk and Mesquakie had practiced, but it was spiritual nevertheless. The Methodist circuit rider, Reverend John Kinney, who had settled near Rapid City, visited in January 1829 and preached a sermon at the Davenport house. It had been ten years since Reverend Peter Williams had preached there. Many of the new neighbors came to hear Reverend Kinney. The gathering provided some welcomed social activity as well as a chance to meet the new neighbors.

Davenport accommodated the new settlers at his post by increasing his inventory with goods that the settlers needed. Unlike American Fur Company traders in the north, particularly Green Bay and

Chicago who were not allowed to sell to settlers, Davenport had no such restriction from the Company. His post store was already well established and well stocked by the time he joined the Company and that part of Davenport's business remained independent of the American Fur Company. His semi-independence from the Company was one of the ways Davenport was able to stay afloat.

During the slack times in the fur trade, Davenport kept his employees occupied, anxious to get every penny's worth of work from his men. This was a tactic fostered by the American Fur Company to reduce costs by keeping men continuously employed, and Davenport was rewarded for his diligence by giving him a salary of $1200. The salary itself is a good indication just how valuable Ramsay Crooks considered Davenport to be. Company policy was generally to hire traders on a profit-loss basis and offer salaries on an individual basis to give a trader incentive to stay in the Company or work harder to pay his debts. Davenport needed no incentive, however, since he had no use for lazy men given to periods of drunkenness. He put them to work cutting hay and building their own quarters. "I am determined to make every man that's under my contract work for is(sic) wages. I have had three Stacks of hay made for our Oxes & horses - and have the men build a house for their Selves to Live in, the Old House having fallen down."[19] He also hired some of the newcomers for good wages or payment in kind from the goods in his store. Even Davenport's older son was ready to work.

After having spent a year away at school, George L. Davenport, now eleven years old, entered into partnership with his father as a clerk and was put in charge of the trading store on the island. Sometimes he made trips into Indian country, delivering goods and collecting payments from the Indians.[20] As was common on the frontier, where there was too much work and not enough hands to do it all, children grew up early. At age eleven George L. was no longer a child, but a useful and productive member of the Davenport family, and a partner in his father's business.

With his son in charge of the island store, Davenport concentrated on his businesses away from the island. Early in February, Davenport left for Flint Hills (near present day Burlington, Iowa) and then went to the Des Moines to see for himself what the trading situation was. Two weeks later he was at Fort Edwards, still not having returned home. The war between the Sauk and Sioux had continued and was threatening to end business on the Mississippi.[21] There was little he could do to prevent the warfare, and Davenport, ever looking to the future, prepared for his own future financial health.

Two years before, Davenport and Farnham had built a log house on the mainland near the Mesquakie village and cornfields and directly across the Slough from the Fort Armstrong. This had been a major step, according to local historian John Hauberg, to distance himself from the fort. It was also a major investment of $2,000.00. But in light of the government action to remove the trading business from the island, it was a necessary move. Moving onto Mesquakie lands was risky as it could have been construed by the tribe as an attempt to get the Indian lands -- an affront to their friendship.[22] The post served dual purposes. As a post it allowed Farnham and Davenport to carry on trade away from the control of the military leaders at the fort. As an inn, it attracted the trade of travellers passing through the country on their way to the mines by providing food, drink and lodging at this site. Davenport licensed the inn with the Jo Daviess County Commissioners as a tavern and a ferry station.

According to law, the rates for such inns were set by the county commissioners, and posted for all customers to see. Lodging per night was twenty-five cents and each meal was thirty-seven and one quarter cents. John Barrel was hired as tavern keeper, and required by law to provide food and lodging for a minimum of four persons. He was not permitted to serve liquor by the glass, but only by the half pint. Brandy and gin were sold by the pint; cider, porter and ale, by the quart. The Barrel House, as it was later called, also stabled horses at the rate of seventy-five cents for a day and night.[23]

Food at such inns was simple fare. Corn bread was commonly served with pork, hominy, buttermilk, and clabber (curdled sour milk). Wheat bread and chicken were reserved for Sunday or special occasions. Wild game or fish was served on special occasion when a local brave or settler provided some for trade. Vegetables, especially asparagus, were grown at the site, as well as wild plums and currants, which the old settlers remembered growing there.[24]

This mainland house, variously known as the Barrel House, Copp House, and Spring House (depending upon its current resident), eventually would see many uses over time -- as trading post, tavern, stage coach station, court house, post office, and election center -- before being returned to its original use as a family dwelling. As the first public house in Rock Island, it did indeed attract many travellers going up and down the river. Old Pioneers remembered that the second floor accommodated the male lodgers in one large room, which was reached by an outside ladder. Ticks filled with straw and laid on the floor were the only beds. A sign at the foot of the ladder reminded them to remove their boots before climbing to the room. A pump in the yard with towel and washbasin was for the use of all.[25] A village called Farnhamsburg grew up around it and became the center of the community.

Perhaps this house was originally intended for the Davenport family's own use, since it was constructed at a time when the Davenport's future on the island was uncertain. The general description of the house resembles the house Davenport would later build on the island. Sears remembered the house as very large for its time, two stories high, with the main part of hewn logs and a frame addition built later. Overall, Sears estimated the size to be about 30 feet by 50 feet, approximately the same size as the Davenport house that stands on the island today. Davenport's use of this building as a store is documented by notations in his 1829-30 ledger.[26]

Davenport considered the location of this mainland house very beautiful. A spring nearby provided fresh water and the house itself was situated above high water, at the foot of a bluff. It was also on the only road to the lead mines. The adjacent cornfields, which had been abandoned by the Mesquakie, were fenced so Davenport could grow his own corn. For many years he had purchased surplus corn from these fields and, if the Indians came back, Davenport said he planned to offer them compensation for their land.[27]

In the spring of 1829 some of the Sauk did return to their villages on the Rock River.

Trouble between Indians and settlers was well underway when Indian Agent Forsyth returned from St. Louis in the summer. The outrages the settlers had experienced were described in petitions to Illinois Governor Ninian Edwards with their demands that the governor immediately remove of the Indians. The Indians, however, held their ground. They did not believe that they had sold their land or that any land could be sold. As Black Hawk explained: "The Great Spirit gave it to his children to live upon, and cultivate, as far as is necessary for their subsistence; so long as they occupy and cultivate it, they have the right to the soil ... Nothing can be sold, but such things as can be carried away."[28] Black Hawk's people were determined to plant their corn again that summer.

The Ho Chunk were not happy either. Encroachment on their mining lands had only escalated as more and more people hoping to make a quick profit came to the lead mines. The agreement made in Green Bay the previous summer had been too late to call a gathering of all the tribes, so formal agreements on the lead mines were delayed. President Jackson appointed General John McNeil, Colonel Pierre Menard and later, Caleb Atwater, to call another treaty session. Charles Hempstead, an old friend of George Davenport, served as secretary.

The principal task of the treaty negotiations was to extinguish the Indian title to mineral lands east of the Mississippi and south of the Wisconsin claimed by the Ho Chunk, Potawatomi, Ottawa, and Chippewa. Secondarily, the commissioners would attempt to settle boundary disputes among all the Mississippi valley tribes. So, all the tribes in the Mississippi Valley were called to gather for negotiations. Originally the meeting place was set for a place on the Iowa side of the Mississippi opposite Rock Island and Fort Armstrong, but the Ho Chunk objected strongly to that location, preferring Prairie du Chien. The entire summer was filled with preparations for the largest gathering of Indians since the Treaty of 1825.[29]

The commissioners left St. Louis on the 30th of June 1829, and gathered the various tribes with them as they proceeded upriver. When they reached Fort Armstrong they met Indian Agent Forsyth, the Winnebago Prophet, and about two hundred of his nation. To appease the Ho Chunk and convince them to accompany them to the council, they purchased extra provisions from George Davenport: eleven barrels of flour, several barrels of pork, two hundred pipes, and plenty of tobacco. At Galena another large gathering awaited them. They bought five hundred pounds of corn more and proceeded to the treaty grounds.[30]

The treaty, or rather a series of treaties, concluded without delay. On the 29th of July, the Chippewa, Ottawa, and Potawatomie concluded their agreements. On the first of August the treaty was completed with the Ho Chunk. About 8 million acres were added to the public domain from the upper end of Rock Island north to the mouth of the Wisconsin River, in exchange for money and goods plus annuities for a set period of years. In addition there were several reserves awarded to related members of the tribes.

One such reserve was awarded to Antoine Le Claire and another to his brother Francois. Because their mother was a Potawatomie, they were entitled to such consideration. Each was given a section of land lying on the bank of the Mississippi River north of the present Indian Boundary line, but because the brothers wished to establish their homes in Portage des Sioux, Missouri, they sold the land to Farnham and Davenport to raise cash for that purpose.[31] Davenport and Farnham agreed to keep this land for use by their Indian friends as long as they were allowed to remain in the area, and grow corn and hay there for their own use.

The question of boundaries now seemed to be settled and the U.S. had acquired new land for the settlers. After the Chippewa, Ottawa, Potawatomie, and Ho Chunk departed, the commissioners met with the Sauk and Mesquakie to discuss their mineral lands. Keokuk complained about white infringements on their lands. To appease them the commissioners gave them presents, but delayed the whole subject of Sauk and Mesquakie boundaries for a later time. The Sauk and Mesquakie departed in a friendly manner, but the two tribes were still in a warring mood.[32]

Not long afterwards, a war party of 80 Sauk and Mesquakie warriors started out from the Mississippi to go against the Sioux. They found a drunken party of Sioux near the Missouri and killed five men, seven women, and four children. Despite the hopes of acculturation for the native people, warring among tribes was still a way of life and their justice system seemed quite foreign to the new settlers. How the tribal leaders handled tribal business was novel enough to appear in newspapers and reaffirmed to the settlers that these people must be either converted or evicted. In one story, a young woman was killed by her jealous husband because she had gone to trade moccasins and mats among the whites. In another, a wife was murdered near the mouth of the Ioway River. It was a difficult situation for the tribal leaders, who counselled many days before they could agree on what was to be done. In the latter case, they agreed that the murderer should wear the skin of a crow suspended from his right ear for two years.[33]

Hardly had the treaty sessions concluded, when President Jackson approved a land sale in Illinois: six townships plus six fractional townships adjacent to the Mississippi River and north of the Indian Boundary line. The Galena Advertiser noted that the march of population was northward, that Hancock county had already been organized, and that Warren county was nearly populated enough to do so as well. The land for sale was fertile and well timbered, and supplied with spring water. The editor noted was that fifty families had already settled in the vicinity of Rock Island and predicted that within a year a new county would be laid off.[34]

Included in the sale was the land where the Sauk village stood, as well as their Watch Tower and cornfields. Farnham and Davenport bought as much of the land as they could, in all about 3,700 acres. The Indians, particularly Black Hawk, could not understand this. How could a man who professed to be a friend build on another friend's land? Black Hawk explained: "We learned during the winter, that part of the lands where our village stood had been sold to individuals, and that the trader at Rock Island had bought the greater part that had been sold. The reason was now plain to me, why he urged us to remove. His object, we thought, was to get our lands."[35] Davenport and Farnham understood, as Black Hawk never would, that the coming settlers could not be stopped from taking the best of the Indian lands for themselves. One way to slow them down was for the two partners to purchase the land themselves and reserve the land for Indians for as long as they wished to live on it or the Government allowed them to stay. Black Hawk was not convinced. "We held several councils that winter to determine what we should do and concluded, that if we were removed by force, that the trader, agent, and others, must be the cause; and that, if found guilty of having driven us from our village, they should be killed ... Ne-a-pope promised to kill him, the agent, interpreter, the great chief at St. Louis, the war chief at Fort Armstrong, Rock Island, and Ke-o-kuck ... "[36]

Mapping the land purchases of Farnham and Davenport at those first land sales show clearly that the lands they bought were indeed the village site and cornfields of the Sauk. What is not clear is whether these lands included the Sacred Burial Grounds of the Sauk Dead. This seems to have been a transgression on the Indian beliefs that they were not willing to make. The parcel of land containing the known burial grounds, in the NE quarter of Section 14, remained open for many years. Only one other settler, William T. Brashar, purchased some of the cornfields and In 1831, Davenport and Farnham agreed to sell 320 acres adjoining Brashar's farm to Louden Case, Brashar's brother-in-law.[37]

Of course the land was valuable. Davenport and Farnham knew this, but they had another plan. They reasoned that the Sauk and Mesquakie could circumvent the American Government and the terms of the 1804 Treaty by letting them live upon their private lands for however long they wished. Davenport told Black Hawk that if he had not bought the land, someone else would have.[38] But Black Hawk did not understand the concept of selling land and blamed the traders, the agents, the interpreters and others for forcing him to move from his land. Black Hawk put Davenport at the top of his hit list and Neapope promised to kill him.

Black Hawk wanted the land on his own terms. To accept Davenport and Farnham's offer would have meant that the Sauk and

Mesquakie would have to acquiesce to the Government wishes, to acculturate enough to live peaceably among the white settlers and their communities. Agriculture would then become more prominent in their economy and hunting less so. Other tribes were doing this, but Black Hawk had no wish to become a farmer, at any price.

The public land sales were held at the Vandalia Land Office on the third Monday of October 1829. Davenport was not optimistic that the Sauk would go quietly, but during the Indians' absence that winter, settlement proceeded. Davenport obtained a license to operate a ferry from his house or trading post on the bank of the Slough, which had always required boats for crossing. Despite its narrowness, the waters were deep and dangerous with changing currents.

Davenport was certainly anticipating an increase in his tavern business, from the soldiers at the fort as well as from travellers heading for the mines. Although the soldiers had flat boats for transporting hay and wood, the garrison boats were not to be used for private ventures. Instead, his ferry would provide transportation to and from the island for anyone. Davenport established a stable at this location, too. As more and more prospectors and families passed through Rock Island on their way to the mines, Davenport prepared to meet their needs for transportation across the river, food, drink, lodging and care for their horses and the post grew into a small settlement generally known as Farnhamsburg. The setting of ferry rates by the Jo Daviess County Commissioners, illustrates some of the changes that were occurring around Rock Island.

The following were the rates to which George Davenport subscribed:

For man and horse   *.50*
Man without horse   *.25*
For each four-wheeled carriage   *1.00*

If drawn by 4 horses   *1.50*
For each head of cattle   *.12 1/2*
For each head of hogs   *.02* [39]

The rates of exchange were set in the standard monetary values of the day, rather than in furs or peltries, and reflect a growing business in transporting people and domestic livestock across the river. Davenport's ferry employed full teams of crewmen at the slough and also at the main channel of the river, located in front of his house. Each crew consisted of two oarsmen and a man at the helm who operated the ferry from sunrise until 8 pm, which was the time limit set by order of the county commissioners. Although he never traded with the Indians after sunset, Davenport was allowed to charge double rates for travellers arriving after dark.[40] The new settlers had different needs and expectations from the Indians, the fur traders, and the soldiers at Fort Armstrong who had provided their own solutions to such problems. Crossing rivers had become a public service, and a matter for government regulation.

Miners still flocked to the mineral region in northwestern Illinois, where the government had obtained a temporary agreement with the Indians allowing settlers to occupy the lands where they worked the mines. This was good news for trading posts like Davenport's, whose business in Galena had grown immensely. Lead miners were an eager market for all the goods they could obtain. Amos Farrar's ledgers show how different the miners' needs were from the Indians. Miners bought tools, ready-made shirts, pants, and boots, as well as domestic items and foodstuffs rather than traps and gunpowder.[41]

Davenport's houses at Fever River and Farnhamsburg attracted so much trade that Farnham finally bought into the business. When Charles D. St. Vrain left the partnership of Davenport, Farrar & Co., the firm dissolved and a new partnership with Farnham was formed. By the terms of the new agreement each partner was invested with a third interest in the property at Portage Place (now Keokuk, Iowa), including the house and lot in town formerly owned by Dr. Muir, a third interest in the lot with building occupied by Farrar on the bank of the river, and a third interest in the lot lately purchased by Farrar.[42] Farrar, whose Indian wife and two of his children had recently died, remained in Galena to carry on business for his two partners.

The Farnhamsburg site was equally successful. Positioned high on the bank of the slough, it was visible from the river and convenient for travellers to stop and rest before they tackled the difficult Rock Island Rapids. It was not long before the Indian trail linking the trading house at Farnhamsburg and the lead mines in Galena was officially designated a mail route and named a public highway. Surveying of the land was moving northward and new settlements were popping up along the river below from Rock Island. Perhaps Davenport was thinking of ways for the Sauk and Mesquakie to survive this new and alien lifestyle when he participated in a Fourth of July celebration in the town of Keokuk aboard the steamboat Missouri.

Keokuk was located near the foot of the Lower Rapids in a square mile of land called the Half-Breed Tract. It was a tract of land set aside for the so-called half-breeds of the Sauk and Mesquakie in 1824. The town site itself was held in common by all the mixed-race Indian claimants in the traditional tribal fashion. Several families of mixed French and Indian descent resided there as well. Situated at the lower rapids Keokuk was an ideal place to portage around the rapids. Steamboat passengers sometimes had to spend days here waiting for passage up or down river, and many businesses stabled here, catering to the comfort of travellers, as well as storage facilities for the shipping industry. A few businesses, including Davenport's, were already in operation there and the potential for further growth in the town was high.

Farnham operated a warehouse there for the American Fur Company's Des Moines River trade in the interior of Iowa. The Company built a row of warehouses, called "Rat Row," for storing the muskrat pelts, deer hides, and other goods for the trade. Many of Davenport and Farnham's friends were here as well: Joshua Palen, Mark Aldridge, and Edward Brishnell worked as clerks; Francis Labushure and Baptiste as interpreters; John Connolly, John Forsyth, James Thorn, and John Tolman as collectors of the furs.[43]

On the Fourth of July the town was filled with an illustrious gathering of gentlemen from far up and down the river. It was both social and political in nature and provided the men a chance to congratulate themselves on progress in the river valley. They expressed their hopes and grand schemes for the future in speeches and toasts, both prepared and impromptu. The prepared toasts celebrated the American Independence, national unity, its leaders both past and present, and its military power, but the impromptu speeches related to the regional interests: hope for prosperity of the land and lead mines of northwestern Illinois, agreeable treaties towards extinguishing Indian titles to the land on which their claims were based. Davenport, too, proposed a toast - to Keokuk, a new town on the river in which he had some business interest. "May the town of Keokuk flourish, being connected with the true system of civilizing the Indians." Was Davenport proposing a blending of the two cultures? If so, there could be no better place than in Keokuk, which was an established reserve for the mixed-bloods, or so-called half-breeds, children of Indian and white parentage."

Davenport's toast reflected a popular sentiment of the time, and perhaps Davenport's personal hopes for the Indian's future: that the interbreeding of races was the best way for the Indians and whites to live together. A key phrase was "true system of civilizing." Many Americans at that time were looking for ways to teach civilizing qualities to the Indians. Davenport had already observed that the Indians could not live among the European settlers and still maintain their traditional way of life. Intermarriage, however, held the potential of blending both cultures with the hope of preserving the best of both worlds. One inescapable fact was that the Indians' tradition of holding tribal land in common held no clout in the American legal system. Indians would have to accept American ways, or move westward.

CHAPTER ELEVEN:

ESCALATION TO WAR

DESPITE HIS PROMISES not to return in the spring of 1830, Black Hawk and his band <u>did</u> return to their Rock River village and the Sauk women began to cultivate their old fields. Black Hawk was in a surly mood and furious that George Davenport, who had professed friendship all these years, now owned his village. It seemed that nothing could make Black Hawk understand the impending crisis.

Black Hawk says the Agent, meaning Indian Agent Forsyth, reasoned with him and explained that if they did not move the military would drive us off. The interpreter, Antoine Le Claire, gave him "so many good reasons, that [he] almost wished [he] had not undertaken the difficult task that [he] had pledged [him]self to his brave band to perform." He went to his old friend, George Davenport, who Black Hawk said, was "fond of talking," but he, too, offered the old warrior the same advice -- leave his village. Davenport argued that Black Hawk's resistance was only bringing distress to his women and children and asked if there was any amount of money that would help him to give up his fight honorably. Davenport offered to make such an offer to authorities for Black Hawk, but in the end, the proposal made to the U.S. Chiefs was rejected. When settlers again ploughed up Sauk cornfields, Black Hawk was more determined than ever to clear the country of intruders.[1]

Now recognized as a respected man among the Sauk, Davenport was called upon to exert his influence upon Black Hawk. His arguments to Black Hawk, recorded in his 1828 Day Book, elaborate on Black Hawk's story. Governor Edwards, as Chief of the Illinois country, had sent a message to the Sauk through Mr. Forsyth, ordering them to move out of their villages by 1st of April 1830. They had had sufficient time to make their preparations and had not requested of the Governor any more extensions of time. This was an indication that the Sauk were willing to abide by the order. Davenport explained that he was not a chief, only a trader, and had no right to interfere. He was speaking to them because of their friendship. If, Davenport said, they saw him and Le Claire going to cross the river on the ice and knew the ice would break, the Sauk would tell them of the danger. This was the same kind of warning. The Sauk should not return to their village.[2]

Had Black Hawk fully understood what was about to happen, in terms of settlement upon the lands his people had long believed to be theirs, he might have taken other action. Davenport, Le Claire, and Forsyth were only partially successful in their arguments. What Black Hawk did not understand was that a general preemption law was being discussed in Congress at that time. The law would approve land claims for anyone already settled on public land. Settlers who had cultivated a portion of that land could claim up to 160 acres at the Land Office and purchase that land for $1.25 an acre on easy credit terms when that land had been surveyed and put into the Public Domain. Proof of the claim was based primarily on written affidavits submitted to the Registers and Receivers at the local Land Office and was a relatively easy process with which to comply. The law encouraged more settlers to enter the public lands before the land had been surveyed or officially opened for settlement. That included the Sauk lands. The law was approved by Congress on May 29, 1830.

Passed by Congress just the day before was President Jackson's Indian Removal Act. Considered by the President to be a benevolent policy by the Government, the Removal Act sought to push the Indian tribes beyond white settlement by treaty agreements in exchange for the Indian lands. In his address to Congress Jackson said, "It will place a dense and civilized population in large tracts of country now occupied by a few savage hunters ... and perhaps cause them gradually, under the protection of the Government, and through the influence of good counsels, to cast off their savage habits, and become an interesting, civilized, and Christian community." Forcible removal only caused anger and resentment among those who did not wish to go and caused even more conflicts among the tribes. [3]

Rumors that the Sauk were already at war with other tribes ran rampant throughout the countryside. Fearing attacks by the Indians some settlers left the country and returned to their former settlements for safety. Both sides sought help from Fort Armstrong for weapons and guards. Indian Agent Forsyth, having exhausted his arguments to convince the British Band to vacate their Illinois lands, appealed to William Clark, Superintendent of Indian Affairs in St. Louis, for help.[4] Wapello moved his village to the Muscatine slough and Keokuk, with part of the Sauk, moved to a village site on the Iowa River. But Black Hawk and his loyal band stubbornly refused to go and took their frustration out on their enemies, the Sioux and the Menominee. Gen. William Clark blamed the issue on lack of clearly defined boundaries, but that was an oversimplification of the issue. Clark failed to understand, as did President Jackson, how deeply the old tribal rivalries ran.

In May (1830) the winter hunt was over and the Sauk and Mesquakie women were back in their summer village and planting the corn while the men were free to frolic and even old scores among their enemies. A war party of Sauk and Mesquakie attacked a hunting party of Sioux up on the Blue Earth River in southern Minnesota. Ten women and two boys were killed. In an effort to make amends in the Indian way of covering the dead and establish some peace among the tribes, the Mesquakie from the Dubuque mines were invited to meet with the Ho Chunk at Prairie du Chien. At the last minute, unknown to the Mesquakie, the Menominee were also included. In retaliation for a Mesquakie attack on the Menominee two years before, the Menominee attacked and killed all but one of the Mesquakie peace party. The lone survivor warned his tribe at the mines, who quickly moved to the west bank of the Mississippi near Fort Armstrong. Sauk braves took out their frustration on the new settlers, stealing their cattle, tearing down fences, and generally harassing the new settlers.

The Company of Farnham and Davenport wrapped up their business from the winter hunt, and after delivering the year's trade to St. Louis, took a rare break from their work. They went to Portage des Sioux to attend the wedding of the daughter of their old friend La Perche. The whole company had gathered to wish the newlyweds well: Joshua Palen, David Mitchell, and John Forsyth, Thomas Forsyth's son who worked as Farnham and Davenport's clerk. It was a festive occasion and all the distinguished guests signed the marriage record before heading back to Rock Island to get their Indians prepared for the summer hunt.[5]

Thomas Forsyth took a deputation of Sauk and Mesquakie to St. Louis, in an attempt to defuse the animosity between the tribes. Superintendent William Clark described the Sauk as having more "National Character" than any other tribe in his jurisdiction and more determined than ever in going to war with the Western tribes, namely the Western Sioux, Mahas, Otoes. Clark attempted to be decisive and firm but was sure that, if the Sauk and Mesquakie could not be restrained, the Ho Chunk, Chippewa, Potawatomi, Kickapoo, and Ioway would join them. That would be an all-out war. To make matters worse, a party of settlers had moved across the river from Galena and taken possession of the Mesquakie village vacated just a few days before. Clark called upon Colonel Atkinson to send in his troops and remove the intruders. This appeased the tribes for a time and the Sauk left for their summer hunt.[6]

When the hunters returned, they were in no better mood than they had been in the spring. They resumed their harassment of the settlers, turned their horses loose into the cornfields of their neighbors, and committed other depredations against the hogs and property of their neighbors. Fortunately no murders were committed. Despite Clark's repeated orders to Forsyth to go to Rock Island and settle the increasingly dangerous situation between Indians and settlers, Forsyth did not. Forsyth had virtually given up any hope of appeasing Black Hawk or finding any solution for the situation. Forsyth was also preoccupied with his own problems. He was grieving for his wife Keziah, who had died the previous fall. So he remained in St. Louis well into the spring.[7] Needing a resolution to the Indian crisis, Clark removed Forsyth from his position as Indian Agent and replaced him with Felix St. Vrain. This sudden change of agents confused Black Hawk, who had grown to trust Forsyth and did not like change, any change. In addition, he did not know or trust St. Vrain. The change only reaffirmed his resolve to stay at Saukenuk.

The issues were more complex than boundaries or terms of a treaty for Black Hawk, who followed the path of the traditional Indian way of life, a path worn deep over many generations. The Illinois lands were the burial grounds of his ancestors and had been for nearly a hundred years. They were sacred lands, gifts from the Great Spirit, and must not be abandoned. In his mind, the land had never been sold. His own father and children were buried at Saukenuk. His friends slept there. But a more pressing problem was the corn on which their whole economy depended. Black Hawk understood perfectly well that if they moved before harvest, his people would starve. His complaints of intrusions upon Indian lands fell on deaf ears. There was only one option for him: stay and fight for the land.

Settlers saw Black Hawk in an entirely different light. He was in their eyes a cunning and shrewd man who attempted to provoke the Americans into a war while seemingly defending his Indian rights and the graves of their fathers. He trained his braves to destroy the property and livestock of the settlers, but not to attack or kill any persons. Tribal leaders had placed Keokuk, the great orator of the Sauk, in the difficult position of staying at Rocky River to keep the peace, but Black Hawk's followers were not swayed by Keokuk's oratory. Neither were they swayed by Davenport or Le Claire.

Clark's choice for Forsyth's replacement was, perhaps, an ill-advised choice. Commonly called St. Vrain, Felix de Hault de Lassus de St. Vrain was descended from a distinguished French family and well connected in St. Louis fur trading families, but he was inexperienced in negotiating with Indians. He was a youngish man of about 31 years, described as being "tall and slightly built with dark eyes and black curling hair worn rather long." Although Black Hawk did know him or trust him, he was generally recognized by the Indians as "a man of bravery and devotedly attached to their welfare." St. Vrain bravely attempted to carry on where Forsyth had left off, but it was a difficult time to step into a new position, even for a more experienced man.[8]

Because of the constant wars between the Sauk and Mesquakie and their enemies, Farnham and Davenport's hunters had been unable to pay their credits for the past few years. Farnham went to St. Louis to apprise Pierre Chouteau in regards to their declining trade and explained that he and Davenport had furnished "almost their entire supply of clothing, utensils, and ammunition" to the Sauk and Mesquakie. The tribal leaders agreed that the debt to Farnham and Davenport alone amounted to $40,000, an amount that allowed for no profit for either trader, and they were anxious to make the treaty commissioners aware of their agreement.[9] Even if peace were established it was doubtful that the tribe could ever repay their entire debt. The Chiefs and tribal leaders had repeatedly offered to settle their accounts with cessions of land to them, but it was illegal for individuals like Davenport and Farnham to receive such cessions. The best solution was for the Indians to hunt, but with all the distractions, it was a difficult situation at best. It seemed that the only way the Sauk and Mesquakie could settle their debts was to cede their lands to the U.S. Government and to have the debt written into the treaty.

Despite anticipating failure of the hunt, Farnham and Davenport applied for licenses from St. Vrain for the coming season. Two new competitors, Stephen Phelps and Edward Stocking, had moved into their territory. Despite the proximity of these new traders, Farnham and Davenport decided to locate their posts in the same general locations as in years before: at the Flint Hills, at the Dirt Lodge, at a little prairie on an island in the Mississippi, at the mouth of the Maquoketa, and at a point fifty miles up the Rock River at a place chosen by the Ho Chunk. For the Missouri Sauk and Ioway, they designated a post at the Black Snake Hills and for the Ho Chunk, a post on the headwaters of the Rock River three miles above the mouth of Sugar Creek.

According to the information St. Vrain collected for the licenses, Farnham and Davenport were by far the biggest operators in the area, employing 34 men and $30,000 in capital investment. Stephen Phelps and Company employed 8 men and $16,000 in capital. Edward Stocking employed 4 men and $4,500 in capital. Only Davenport and Farnham reported $27,000 in their returns for 1831, a $3,000 loss in credits. Farnham also had another license, issued by William Clark, showing that Farnham also engaged 21 men and $33,667.52 in capital. No other license for Davenport has been found.[10]

There was little expectation that all the Sauk would engage in hunting, so both Davenport and Farnham had begun to supplement their income with other, settler-oriented businesses. Like Davenport who operated inns, ferries, and stores, Farnham operated a store in Hancock County with a tavern license at Fort Edwards. Farnham, however, was less able to sustain the losses from the Sauk and Mesquakie than Davenport, since his accumulated wealth was tied up in land. He had been investing in real estate since 1821 and had a large household staff to support. That often left him strapped for cash. It was the biggest difference between the partners. Reports from Ramsay Crooks in New York suggested that Farnham was also gambling more than was "prudent" in an effort to meet expenses. Crooks urged Pierre Chouteau to try to dissuade Farnham from such a damaging practice, but to no avail. Farnham was land poor, but too proud to ask for a loan. The debts in his Indian Trade preyed on his mind and he was frequently ill.[11]

Black Hawk's band, according to St. Vrain, was planning to return to Saukenuk in order to keep up their fields, lodges, and graves. Unknown to Black Hawk, Davenport purchased another 1,644.44 acres of Sauk land from the Land Office. With Farnham as partner, he also purchased the Le Claire brothers' reserve, two sections of riverfront land in what is now Moline and East Moline at the standard government rate of $1.25 per acre. Anticipating the removal of the Sauk and Mesquakie, he explored the Ioway and Cedar Rivers for new locations for his trading posts near Poweshiek's village. He placed John Gilbert in charge of this post and established another ferry - this one across the "Marais d'Ogee" where the road from the Galena mines crossed to Rock Island. It was a marshy area that was difficult to navigate, but being used more and more by people going to and from the mines wanting to avoid the river and its rapids.[12]

The population in Rock Island had increased enough by 1830 to warrant the establishment of a special district for the " election of Justices of the Peace and Constables in Jo Daviess County." The district was officially named The Rock Island Precinct. Elections were planned at Farnhamsburg and George Davenport, John Barrel and George Casner were appointed judges of election. The precinct was set apart as a separate county in 1832, but it would be three years before the Sauk and Mesquakie could be quieted enough for the county to organize any government. Transformation of the land, however, had begun[13]

The Sauk continued to live as if nothing had changed. After their corn was harvested the Sauk left as usual for their winter hunting grounds. That winter was a particularly hard season, one of the most severe ever recorded in the United States and all the tribes suffered. Blizzards covered much of the plains with deep snow that obliterated the familiar landscape. Freezing rains in January provided a crust on top of the snow that the wolves could run on, but heavier mammals broke through and were helplessly mired down. Deer and elk could not browse because all the twigs and shrubs were under deep snow. That was the last year that elk were seen in Illinois and Missouri, never to return.[14]

On Rock Island the Davenports were comfortable, but many of their new neighbors were having a difficult time surviving. The Goble family were especially in need of help, because the head of the household had died. Davenport offered the Goble's son Benjamin a barrel of flour that was on a keelboat frozen in the ice. If Ben could carry it home, said Davenport, he could have it. Davenport also hired Ben to cut firewood and paid him with goods from his store, without which the family might have starved before the winter was over. Ben Goble recalled that he was employed to cut hay for George and to work on building Davenport's new home.[15]

News that Black Hawk's British Band was determined to return to Saukenuk again in the spring caused Davenport to call his son, George L., home from Jacksonville, Illinois, where he had been attending school at the new Illinois College. Davenport expected trouble and wanted his family all together. More importantly, son George L. was an adopted member of the Mesquakie tribe, fluent in the local dialects, and his presence could afford the family some protection. It is also possible that Davenport feared that his elder son might become a target if the Indian situation escalated.[16]

Because of the hard winter, the hunt had been unsuccessful and returns were poor in the spring. Farnham was ill again, so Davenport himself went down to the mouth of the Ioway River to collect the furs. There he found lots of Indians, but no skins. Within a couple weeks, he was able to send some packs to St. Louis and expected about a hundred more, but that was nowhere near the bountiful harvest of just a few years before.[17]

In Galena, Amos Farrar, publicly blamed Davenport and Farnham for the Indian problems. Farrar accused Davenport of encouraging the Sauk hostility for his own selfish purposes and deliberately construing Black Hawk's actions as hostile. Publicly, Farrar said that Davenport was hoping for the Sauk defeat so that he could recoup his losses in the Indian trade. To no one's surprise, the partnership between Davenport, Farnham and Farrar was dissolved by mutual consent not long after the accusations. Farnham and Davenport settled with Farrar by paying him $3,000 in cash, and the property called Portage Place became the property of Davenport and Farnham.[18]

After the hard winter Black Hawk's band returned to Saukenuk with 300 or 400 warriors and perhaps 900 to 1200 women, children and elderly. This time he was more than ever determined to remove the settlers from their land. They needed their old cornfields to survive another winter and were angry at the increased settlement on their lands. Agent St. Vrain reported that the Sauk had "pulled down a house, and some fences, which they burned, they have also turned their Horses in wheat fields & say that they will destroy the Wheat, so that the White People shall not remain amongst them."[19] They destroyed Davenport's wheat, something that shocked the settlers since Davenport had once been on such good terms with Black Hawk.

The settlers were just as resolute as the Sauk, feeling justified in their own claims to the land. They demanded that the Governor remove all Indians from Illinois. Governor Reynolds called out the Illinois Militia, about 700 strong, "to protect the citizens of this state, who reside near Rock Island from Indian invasion and depredation."[20] Reynolds alerted the volunteer militia to be prepared to remove the Sauk and Mesquakie to the western side of the Mississippi, dead or alive.

In response to Reynolds's move, Major General Edmund P. Gaines, Commander of the regular army, ordered six companies of troops stationed at Jefferson Barracks and four additional companies from Prairie du Chien to Rock Island. Not being able to determine the exact number of Indians involved, Gaines sent ten companies, which he considered to be sufficient to "repel the invasion & give security to the frontier inhabitants of the State." Major General Gaines and his six companies left Jefferson Barracks on the 30th of May 1831 and arrived at Fort Armstrong on the 4th of July. All settlers in the area were moved into the fort and the livestock driven onto the island for protection as Gaines moved his headquarters to Fort Armstrong.[21] Thirty-four of the thirty-five families living on the Mississippi above the mouth of the Rock River responded.

Fifty-eight volunteers from the Rock Island Precinct also responded to Reynolds's call. They called themselves Rock River Rangers and were mustered in on the 5th of June 1831 for one month. Black Hawk, fearing that the volunteers would show no mercy on his people, quietly moved across the Mississippi to the Iowa shore during the night of the 25th of June. A few days later, Gaines' soldiers brought him back to Rock Island to council. It lasted three days. The military, traders, interpreters, and Indian agents attempted, once again, to convince Black Hawk of the futility of his stand. Black Hawk said later that he was promised as much corn as was growing in their fields and that he touched the quill and was determined to live in peace after that. It was the Militia that Black Hawk feared. Then he "went to the trader, and asked to be buried in the grave-yard at our village, among my old friends and warriors; which he gave cheerfully."[22]

Black Hawk confessed that the show of force by the military and mounted militia was so much greater than his own that he had surrendered. Had it been just the regular army, he said, he would have stayed and held his ground, but the militia were an undisciplined lot who would show no mercy to the Indians. The militia had camped in the Sauk village, burned many of the lodges, and desecrated the cemetery. Some militia dug up the graves and scattered the bones of the dead. Later, St. Vrain and Le Claire visited the village to see what damage had been done. It was complete demolition.[23] Years later the scattered bones of the dead were still visible in the old village.

Gaines brought Black Hawk and his band back to Rock Island for a second council. After considerable talk Black Hawk signed the orders drawn up by General Gaines, admitting that he had violated the terms of the treaties signed in 1804, 1816, and 1825 by remaining on and cultivating land that belonged to the United States. He agreed to end all communication with the British, to submit peaceably to the authority of the Sauk nation, and to remain on their own lands west of the Mississippi. He also agreed to allow the military to build roads and posts in the lands in question.[24] With this capitulation, the situation was thought to be at end. The soldiers mustered out and returned to their families and homes.

Davenport was deeply involved in Indian affairs that spring and early summer, primarily in convincing the peaceful Sauk and Mesquakie to continue hunting rather than fighting the Sioux and to remain in their new villages in Iowa. Davenport also remained home all summer waiting for the annuities to arrive. Fortunately, Farnham was well again and expected to be able to travel to St. Louis to conduct their annual business with the Company. Like others on the frontier, neither partner was convinced that peace would hold and they prepared themselves for a fight between the Sauk and the Troops.[25]

Black Hawk had capitulated, but he was not pacified. He spent the rest of the summer and fall settling old scores with other tribes and wooing alliances for his band in resisting removal. In late July the Sauk attacked the Menominee in retaliation for the massacre of the Mesquakie Peace Delegation the previous year. The attack came just before dawn on July 31. Twenty-five were killed and many others were wounded. Major John Bliss, Commander at Fort Armstrong, was outraged and called for a council. He demanded an immediate surrender of those responsible, but Keokuk explained to the Commander the Indian way of settling scores and concluded by saying that he could not comply with the Commander's demands. As spokesman for the whole tribe, he could do nothing.[26]

Black Hawk had expectations of winning his war. He was elated by the predictions of Wabokieshiek, the leader of the Ho Chunk called the Prophet, who foretold that Black Hawk would lead the nations and win back the homes of the people. When the battles began, the Prophet said, the dead would arise and the warriors would be plentiful, the game and buffalo would return, and the white man would be driven back across the ocean.[27] It was a beautiful dream that Black Hawk cherished.

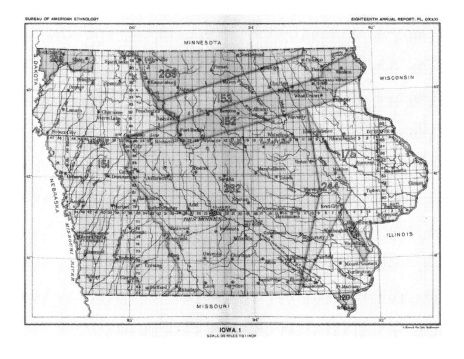

IOWA 1

SCALE 36 MILES TO 1 INCH

Indian Cessions Map. Gradually the Sauk and Mesquakie were removed westward. The Black Hawk Purchase of 1836 is identified by #175.

CHAPTER TWELVE:

THE BLACK HAWK WAR AND THE END OF THE INDIAN TRADE

DESPITE THE UNREST in 1831-1832, Davenport and Farnham again obtained licenses to trade. This time however, Indian Agent St. Vrain granted general licenses because the Indians were hunting as much as 200 miles away from the established posts. Davenport and Farnham decided to build a post near Muscatine in order to intercept the Indians before they traded away their credits.[1] Records are incomplete for this year, but it is almost certain that there were few returns. With the removal of the eastern tribes already in progress, the days of any trade at all with the Sauk and Mesquakie were dwindling quickly.

Davenport had already accepted the changes. As his fortunes turned more and more to the settlers in the area, he did what he could to help them. Indian depredations had put many of the settlers in precarious circumstances. He hired Benjamin Goble again and a Mr. Davis that winter to deliver twenty cords of hickory wood to him, a job that paid $1.30 per cord from goods in Davenport's store on the island.[2] It was a principle of George Davenport that he did not give hand outs, but offered his neighbors a way to earn a wage. In that way, his neighbors could maintain some dignity.

As the population of Illinois increased, Davenport anticipated that more land around Rock Island would soon be offered for sale. Surveying the Island had not yet been done, but he worried about his own claim on the Island. He sought letters from past commanders of Fort Armstrong for support and then, in January, travelled to Washington City to submit his claim directly to Congress. He remained in the city for several months waiting for news that Congress had taken up his case.

Davenport's petition outlined his unique position. He could not take advantage of the pre emption law which Congress had recently passed because his land had not been surveyed, even though hundreds of his fellow settlers in the vicinity had been able to do so. All he wished was to be granted the right to purchase his claim on which he had made improvements since 1816. The petition was delivered to the House of Representatives on the 30th of January. The House Committee gave a favorable report on his petition and his bill, numbered 337, was referred to the Committee of the Whole.[3]

Knowing that Davenport would be in Washington City, the Sauk and Mesquakie asked Davenport to forward a message to the President on their behalf. The letter explained that the Sauk and Fox nations had been applying for permission to come to Washington City to see their Great Father concerning their lead mines and described the wealth of those mines. It outlined the difficulties experienced by the Sauk and Mesquakie at the hands of their traditional enemies, the Menominee and the Sioux, and complained that the citizens of Illinois and of Michigan Territory had taken possession of the lead mines and carried away thousands of dollars worth of lead. Although the soldiers had removed the intruders, the Sauk and Mesquakie did not expect full time guards at the mines. Instead, they proposed to sell their lead mines to the United States as a means of preventing all future difficulties.[4]

Illinois Representative Joseph Duncan presented Davenport's letter, calling Davenport a gentleman of high standing and one who was in a position to have reliable information on the Indian situation.[5] President Jackson, however, did not receive George Davenport, nor did he respond to the Sauk and Mesquakie. Jackson had no wish to see the tribal leaders or anyone who might sympathize with their cause.

Jackson's appointees were also anxious to get the Indian situation behind them. Elbert Herring, the new Indian Office Superintendent, ordered William Clark to take whatever steps he needed to arrest all participants in last year's Menominee massacre at Fort Crawford. Not only was this an effort to reduce Indian wars, but also to remove the tribes further from lands that settlers wanted. Troops from Jefferson Barracks were made available for Clark's assistance and Brigadier General Henry Atkinson took charge of the six companies of the Sixth Infantry.[6]

But Black Hawk, more than anyone else, was not so compliant to removal. When Agent St. Vrain visited Keokuk's village on the Ioway, St. Vrain learned that Black Hawk's band, accompanied by Neapope's band, had crossed the river at Yellow Banks into Illinois, contrary to Black Hawk's promise the previous year. (15 March 1832). The Commander at Fort Armstrong, Colonel Bliss, informed General Atkinson at Jefferson Barracks that Black Hawk planned to return to Saukenuk to grow corn. Bliss repeated a conversation overheard by Charles St. Vrain, brother to the Indian Agent, between Black Hawk and Russell Farnham at the Lower Rapids. Black Hawk planned to kill St. Vrain, Wells, and Davenport once he got to Rock Island. There were signs that Black Hawk meant war. St. Vrain had also observed that the warriors of the band only danced the War Dances. Not long after receiving this information, General Atkinson left Jefferson Barracks and headed for Rock Island. The troops arrived four days later. Again the settlers moved into the fort for protection.[7]

With the Sauk back in Illinois, a second call to the volunteers went out from Governor Reynolds. General Atkinson began gathering information about the Indians' intentions. Davenport's informants believed that many young braves had been induced to join Black Hawk's band and that they had about five hundred horses, seventy pack horses, and old men, women, and children with the warriors. It was generally suspected that the British Band would be joined by Ho Chunk, Potawatomie, and others.

In a council, concerned leaders all seemed to agree with Davenport: the British Band of Sauk was determined to make war. The tribes were divided: Keokuk, Pashepaho, Wapello and their followers had separated from the British band and were still at peace, but the Ho Chunk were restless. They had taken fifteen hogs from a drover on the road to Galena and had shot at a white man.[8] Hoping to explain to the general public about the nature of the Indian conflicts, particularly the Menominee situation and in ways that Keokuk could not, George Davenport wrote to the editor of the Missouri Republican.

Davenport explained that during an attempt to establish a peaceful meeting between the Sioux and the Sauk and Mesquakie, the Menominee had also been included, unknown to the Sauk and Mesquakie delegation. Together with the Sioux, the Menominee had attacked the Mesquakie, scalping and murdering most of the delegation. Then they had returned to Prairie du Chien displaying the scalps and the head of the Mesquakie Chief Pamosky. To add further injury to the Mesquakie, William Clark was demanding that ten Mesquakie be surrendered to answer for their crimes. These men would probably all be brothers and sons of the chiefs who had been slain. Although three men had been surrendered to General Atkinson, the ones most responsible for killing Menominee were with Black Hawk's British Band, preparing to lay waste to the frontiers of Illinois and Michigan Territory.[9] It is doubtful that the newspaper readers really understood the point, or cared. What they wanted was to be rid of all Indians.

Black Hawk was indeed traveling up the Rock toward the Prophet's village, but he had not yet laid waste to anything. Black Hawk says that the

Prophet advised him that the army would not harm them as long as they were peaceful. Later, when the recruits had joined them, they would be able to withstand the army.[10]

The Davenports took seriously Black Hawk's threat to kill George and others if the band was prevented from returning to Saukenuk. The Davenport house became a veritable arsenal. Every table and sideboard was covered with powder horns, cartridges, pistols, and other paraphernalia. There were guns in the corners and a swivel gun at the door.

Nearly one thousand and seven hundred volunteers responded to Black Hawk's threats, concerned that these wars would become annual events. Their solution was to exterminate the Indians once and for all time. They were mustered in at Beardstown and arrived at Fort Armstrong on the 7th of May. Two days later the combined forces of regular Army and volunteer militia headed up the Rock. It was a formidable army. The regulars were in boats and the militia on horseback travelling along the shore. All were geared for action, or as the *Galenian* reported, to "humble our invaders."[11]

The Rock River Rangers were mustered in on the 20th of May and ordered to join Captain Moore's regiment. They marched to Dixon, Illinois, where they were assigned to guard the frontier. Benjamin Goble recalled that he remained at Fort Armstrong where he stood on picket duty.[12] For his part, Davenport served as assistant Quartermaster, procuring supplies for both the Army and the Militia. He served under Colonel Enoch C. March who was hailed after the war for his heroic efforts to keep the troops supplied.

The first bit of real news to come to public attention was at Stillman's Run, a rout on the part of the Sauk and a major embarrassment for the militia. Thomas Forsyth followed the news from his home in St. Louis through newspapers and letters from his friends in the field. He maintained for the rest of his life that Black Hawk had had no intention of fighting prior to this event, but now it was completely out of his hands. Forsyth blamed the Winnebago Prophet as the man to be reckoned with, but it was too late in his opinion, to undo the damage done by men who should have known more about Indian Affairs, particularly General Clark. Had Clark followed Forsyth's recommendations of April 1830, he wrote to Davenport, the Indians would be peaceably settled on their own lands. Forsyth had heard that the militia were sick and tired of the campaign, giving up, and returning home.[13] In fact, many militiamen had returned home at the end of their month's contract. Only three hundred agreed to stay, and Indian raids increased noticeably after this.

As the Sauk travelled further north, William Clark was particularly concerned with protecting the mines. Indian Agent St. Vrain and six men were sent with instructions from the army to Dixon's ferry. About half way there, they were attacked by about thirty Indians. Only three men escaped. St. Vrain's headless body, minus his feet and hands, was found later. The gruesome details, designed to rouse even more sentiment against the Indians, appeared in the Galenian.[14]

When news arrived at the Davenport house that St. Vrain had probably been murdered, Davenport knew that Black Hawk had reached a point of no return. His immediate concern was for the safety of Mrs. St. Vrain and her three young daughters, aged ten, eight, and seven, who were living in the Agent's house just a short distance from his own. St. Vrain's widow and her children were sent immediately to her parent's home in St. Genevieve for safety. Davenport's family, however, remained on the Island despite Black Hawk's threats.

Knowing that the volunteer militiamen would take revenge on Keokuk's band, Davenport promised Clark that, in the absence of an Indian Agent, he would do everything in his power to keep the peaceful Indians in the their own villages. Not until the 8th of June did Davenport write to Farnham with the news that a new, temporary agent, Joshua Pilcher, had arrived to take over the Indian Agency.[15] Thomas Forsyth was right about one thing: it was now war, not just another Indian uprising.

The settlers of northwestern Illinois saw this conflict as more than a fight over land rights. It was war against a foreign nation and a matter that could have no compromise for a solution. National honor as well as ownership rights were at stake. There seemed to be no room for both groups to live together. The *Galenian* reflected the settlers' viewpoint:

"Something has to be done. The Indians must be exterminated, or sent off; or we must look for such a war every season. Our government must acknowledge herself beat, or she must humble our invaders, and give up that we are completely conquered and vanished."[16]

Davenport still called this just another Indian uprising rather than war, but one that had carried on too long. The death of St. Vrain was unsettling to him. In letters to Davenport, Forsyth predicted that Black Hawk would fight with desperation. He expected Black Hawk to head for Milwaukee and then push on to Canada now that General Winfield Scott had been ordered from the East. He strongly advised his friend "to keep a good look out, and any Indians who call to see you always give them some tobacco, and something to eat, beware of treachery." Forsyth bitterly blamed General Clark for gross mismanagement of Indian Affairs, as well as St. Vrain's death.[17]

Down at Fort Edwards, Farnham was keeping a good lookout, too. He wrote: "We are all in our guard at this place ... we are not bad frightened but think it best to keep a good lookout ... " On Rock Island a stockade was erected around Davenport's store on the mainland and was filled with settlers and their families. A swivel gun, brought from the fort, stood ready in case the enemy appeared, but it was never needed. For many settlers isolated from one another and far from the security of a fort, danger lurked in every thicket. Forsyth scoffed at the strange ideas of people who knew about as much about Indians as a "cow does of a new shilling (sic)."[18] But unquestionably, there was a culture of fear on the Illinois prairies. Stories of settlers being murdered and scalped by Indians on the warpath abounded, and there was a general uneasiness and fear among them. Settlers erected forts in their neighborhoods and ran to them whenever they thought there might be an Indian attack. The massacre of St. Vrain and two of his men had only added fuel to the fire.

Black Hawk and his British Band headed north into Wisconsin with the Illinois Militia pursuing them, but the "Other tribes" alluded to by George Davenport several months before - Potawatomie, Kickapoo, Ho Chunk, Omahas, and the Sioux - failed to join them as the Prophet had predicted. In the end, some of the Upper Mississippi tribes saw a chance to revenge themselves against the Sauk. The Sioux and Omahas fought against Black Hawk. The Potawatomi sounded the alarm to warn the white settlers of the Sauk attacks. Despite delaying tactics employed by Black Hawk's warriors, the militia finally caught up with the Sauk at Bad Axe on the 2nd of August. Many of the Indians were massacred.

Black Hawk, his two sons, and others were taken prisoner. One month later, the Illinois volunteers were mustered out and sent home. Black Hawk was sent to Jefferson Barracks where he was imprisoned for a year. Davenport wrote to Farnham, "Wat a lot of fuss There is in putting down a bout five hundred Indians, their has been all readey in the field twenty five hundred men but they would not fight."[19]

With Black Hawk captured, life returned to normal. Davenport's attention returned to his trade - obtaining goods in anticipation of the seasonal hunts, settling accounts, and supplying his outfits. He and Farnham worked with the Indian Agency throughout the summer providing corn for friendly Indians, provisions for the Interpreter, and presents for visiting Indians. Presents often took the form of basic living requirements such as blankets and cooking utensils rather than frivolous baubles. Farnham and Davenport provided for Black Hawk and the other Indians in prison, too, -- blankets, tin pans and kettles, frying pans and spoons. It was all part of the business, but especially important with the changes in the Indian Agents who controlled the payment of the Indian annuities. Davenport did not trust the new Indian Agent Joshua Pilcher, and the feelings appear to have been mutual. Pilcher seemed wary of the influence Davenport had over the tribal leaders.[20]

The general unrest of the country had cut deeply into the trade for that year. Although they talked a good talk to their Indians, little hunting had been done in the entire season and the partners sustained another $5,000 loss. Nevertheless, Farnham and Davenport were already planning for the coming year, albeit with changes. The treaty had not yet been held so there were many unknowns as to Indian Country.[21]

Farnham now had a wife and baby and was thinking about retiring from the trade altogether. He had been in the business for many years and the work had affected his health. Hints of how much Farnham's health was affected came when he contracted with competitor Stephen Phelps and Company for an 8-month partnership. Farnham and Davenport had never had a friendly relationship with the Phelps Company and the agreement was for the Des Moines River trade, which had been Farnham's main responsibility. Phelps and Farnham agreed to furnish equal shares of stock and share equally in the expenses and profits of the trade.[22] Farnham did not retire completely, but continued his partnership with Davenport to trade with the Sauk and Mesquakie who were now settled on the Ioway River.

On the 11th of August, General Winfield Scott finally arrived at Fort Armstrong to negotiate the peace treaty. The Army, Illinois Militia, and Indians all began to gather and army personnel started the long process of interviewing prisoners, writing final reports, and preparing for the Treaty Council. Eventually there would be an official removal of the Sauk and Mesquakie, but before the negotiations could start, cholera broke out at the Fort. The first two cases came in Captain Ford's company of mounted rangers, and the disease spread quickly to the 4th Infantry. General Scott, fighting intemperance among the soldiers, ordered every man found drunk or intoxicated to dig his own grave. Davenport reported that of the four hundred men on the Island at that time, nearly one hundred had died.[23]

Until that summer, the island had provided a healthy environment without the usual seasonal outbreaks of disease found in many places on the frontier. Davenport had seen cholera before and knew how quickly it would spread. One morning he and Antoine Le Claire were standing outside Davenport's store talking with a young officer from the fort when an orderly came with a message from General Winfield Scott. They were requested to go to the fort as soon as possible. "Mr. Le Claire looked at Mr. Davenport to know what excuse to make. Mr. Davenport, after a moment, replied to the orderly to tell the General that Mr. Le Claire could not come, as he was quite sick. The officer and the orderly laughed heartily at Mr. Davenport and Mr. Le Claire being so much alarmed, but the next morning the first news they received from the fort was that those two men were dead." The disease raged for ten days. Of the 150 individuals buried at Fort Armstrong, one hundred and three had died of cholera in a span of eight days. Davenport, too, thought he might die of this dreadful disease. He wrote: "Our onse helthy Island is now a Buring Ground More than one Sixt of the Troops stashond here have died during the last 6 days. The disease is yet Raging. I am not verrey well, if I do not see you again God bless you."[24]

Around the first of September, the Commissioners began to arrive, but because of the cholera, Black Hawk and the other Indian prisoners were sent to Jefferson Barracks and the peace negotiations delayed until the middle of September. Joseph M. Street, Indian Agent for the Ho Chunk at Prairie du Chien, arrived late on the evening of the 5th of September. He planned to stay with George Davenport for the duration of his stay on Rock Island.[25] Where Governor Reynolds was housed is not clear although he may have been hosted by the Davenports as well. General Scott remained in a new house built that year for the fort's commandant just outside the fort.

The opening of the Treaty negotiations took place on the western bank of the Mississippi across from Fort Armstrong near the present Fifth and Farnum streets in the city of Davenport. The "war" was formally concluded on the 21st of September with the signing of the Treaty of 1832. Davenport was present with his son, George L., as well as representatives of all companies who had debts to collect from the tribe. He had been asked by the Sauk and Mesquakie to negotiate the terms of the treaty between themselves and the Government. Davenport believed he had done justice to them. The partnership of Farnham and Davenport, in response to their petition to the government, was awarded $40,000 to settle the trading debts of the previous years. Davenport was pleased. He believed he had been successful in getting his debts accepted by the Government because the tribal Chiefs, headmen, and warriors had fully acknowledged the debt certified the year before by the late Agent St. Vrain. Agent Pilcher was opposed to the claim, but there was nothing he could do about it, although he tried.

When the annuities arrived, in the sum of $7,800, Pilcher did not pay the tribes. His excuse was that their hunters had already left on their summer hunt. However, before leaving, they had signed a document that the annuities should be paid to Farnham and Davenport. The document had been witnessed by the Treaty Commissioners, General Winfield Scott and Governor of Illinois John Reynolds, but Pilcher did not accept this and placed the money in the fort's magazine. Then, being replaced by a permanent Indian Agent, Marmaduke Davenport, Pilcher left Rock Island with the annuity issues still unresolved.

The fort commander did not wish to take responsibility so the newly appointed Indian Agent wrote to William Clark for instructions and offered to return the money by the Steamboat Winnebago. Pilcher, who was also on board the Winnebago, found the six boxes and the letter to Clark, which he opened. Recognizing that he was at fault, he had the money returned to Rock Island and the debt to Farnham and Davenport was paid.[26]

With his debts paid, Davenport made an advance to the Indians on the next year's annuity payment. Farnham arrived later, congratulating Davenport for his success. David Lavender says that George Davenport made no effort to add the $5,050.03 loss for the 1832 year to the $40,000 for which the partners had agreed to settle. Instead, they claimed the balance of their debt when the annuities were paid. When the Government eventually authorized the $40,000 awarded to Farnham and Davenport by the 5th article of the Treaty of 1832, the Western Department of the American Fur Company claimed every penny. Pierre Chouteau had been anxious to get his due, even attempting to draw on the Department of Indian Affairs for the money. [27]

Another claimant to the Farnham and Davenport award was Mrs. Amos Farrar, who thought part of that money was due her late husband. Her brother, H.H. Gear of Galena, wrote to Lewis Cass, Secretary of War, to see if the money had already been paid. Although she had not been married to Farrar when he was partnered with Davenport and Farnham, Mrs Farrar was determined to get what she thought was her share of this payment and pursued the matter, unsuccessfully, for many years.[28]

Le Claire, too, had been successful in the negotiations. He had been granted two sections of land on the west side of the Mississippi river. It will be remembered that just three years before Antoine and his brother Francois Le Claire had been granted two sections on the east bank of the Mississippi and had sold that land to Davenport and Farnham with the claim that they had no interest in relocating from their homes in Portage des Sioux. Le Claire had evidently changed his mind. The land he was awarded this time was prime real estate on the west side of the river, a section located in Iowa at both the head and the foot of the troublesome Rock Island Rapids.

At the conclusion of the treaty council, General Scott presented Keokuk with a gold medal and made him head chief of the Sauk and Fox. Then they all feasted, as was the custom. There was much frivolity and merry making on both sides. Keokuk joined in a pantomime of Indians on the warpath and afterwards there was a war dance and the Indians and soldiers danced together.[29] Afterwards the Sauk and Mesquakie began to move to their villages on the Ioway and Des Moines rivers just beyond the fifty-mile border of what was called the Black Hawk Purchase.

The Black Hawk War had been a clash of ideas and vision for the future of this country. American settlers and speculators wanted the land to make it productive in ways that agreed with their own concept of how the land should be used. For the militia, they scouted the countryside to discover what rich resources the Upper Mississippi valley had to offer. In the camps at night they sat around the campfires and shared their hopes and dreams and expectations. Many militiamen returned to settle near Rock Island when the war was over.

It was just a matter of time before the prairies were filled with speculators, surveyors and lawyers -- all looking for ways to change the landscape and put the land to use in ways that the native peoples could not understand. As the Sauk and Mesquakie moved west, they left behind their village sites, their cornfields, their sugar groves, and the burial grounds of their ancestors. In their place would come cities and towns, mills, factories, and farms. Rocky Island, which once was at the very edge of the frontier, would soon be the center of urban development.

Davenport had started building a bigger and finer house before the Indian troubles had begun in the spring, and with the treaty commissioners as his houseguests, Davenport had the opportunity to discuss the merits of the countryside and opportunities for developing the land. The sections being granted to Le Claire were particularly favorable for development. Sometime during the treaty talks, Davenport met with Illinois Governor John Reynolds, Quartermaster for the Illinois Militia, Enoch C. March, and his friend Antoine Le Claire to discuss future ideas for the area. Le Claire and Davenport had already developed a working relationship together, but Reynolds and March provided some outside perspective.

Governor Reynolds was a key figure in this endeavour. His connections to Illinois politics and his views on internal improvements for the State of Illinois were already on the public record. In his 1830 address to the State of Illinois he had laid out his vision for the creation of three major roads to the mines of Galena and his vision included railroads. Reynolds was eager to capitalize on the lead in the northwestern corner of the state, but was well aware of the difficulties to shipping presented by the rapids on the Mississippi. Reynolds' plan also called for both canals and railroads throughout the state with access to the lead mines of prime importance. Whatever he shared with Davenport, Le Claire and March, it must have included solving some of the transportation difficulties. Perhaps it was Reynolds who had encouraged Le Claire to choose his reserve lands at each end of the rapids, which seemed ideal for transhipment businesses and towns.[30]

March was a young New York merchant who had come to the Illinois frontier in the early 1820s looking for new trade routes across the Great Lakes and down to St. Louis. Before being appointed Quartermaster of the Illinois Militia for the Black Hawk War, he had published the results of his own private experiment that had proven to himself and his partners that transportation costs could be reduced, even to St. Louis, by building a canal at Chicago.[31] He already had been involved in the founding of three towns in central Illinois: Naples in Sangamon county, Exeter in Scott county, and Beardstown in Cass county, all located near the Illinois River.

The four men selected a townsite in the new Black Hawk Purchase. chose the upper end of the Rock Island Rapids on one of Le Claire's grants. The plan to develop a town, named Le Claire, was the first indication of what George Davenport and Antoine Le Claire planned to do after the Indians' removal. Although premature in view of the Treaty Agreement, this town plan was the blueprint to change the cultural landscape.

As exciting as town planning might have been, Davenport was still engaged in the Indian Trade, but with the death of Farnham and other friends that fall of 1832, Davenport was forced to wrap up the business, which had sustained him for so long. Dr. Samuel Muir died in Keokuk in September. John Connolly, the Indian subagent who had worked for Davenport in the Galena post from 1827 – 1829, died of cholera. Joshua Palen, who had been Davenport's trusted clerk in the Des Moines River trade, died the following summer. Ironically, the day Davenport learned of Farnham's death was the day that his former partner in the lead mines trade, Amos Farrar, died in Galena. Ramsay Crooks wrote: "Poor Farnham! He has paid the debt of nature after a life of uncommon activity and endless exposure - Peace to his maner(sic)!"[32]

Some traders, who had been so entrenched in Indian ways, would have packed up and moved to more prosperous places, but Davenport chose to stay on Rock Island. He began to close the Fort Edwards Outfit, at first hoping to wrap up the business by the following spring, but trade that year was too good to let go. He contracted with Stephen Phelps and Co., as had Farnham the year before, to furnish goods on the Des Moines River as well as for the posts at the Iowa, Skunk, and Cedar River posts for the next eight months. Like the previous agreement between Farnham and Phelps, the profits were to be split equally. It was an uneasy alliance, but it freed Davenport from the southern portion of his trading territory. The American Fur Company sold their buildings that Farnham had managed, commonly called "Rat Row," in Keokuk. [88]

Davenport also closed the Fever River trade in Galena and petitioned the Jo Daviess county commissioners to divide the Davenport-Farnham lands held in partnership. The commissioners, however, were unable to divide the lands equitably and the deed remained in both partners' names until they were auctioned at public sales two years later (January and May 1834). Their town lot on Bench Street was purchased by a private individual, who in turn, sold the land to the County Commissioners. Portage Farm was bought back by George Davenport for the sum of $805, but there is no evidence that he continued to trade in Galena. The price of lead had dropped considerably and his Indian suppliers were no longer there to mine it.

Only the post at Rock Island remained. Where once he had prospects of furs to repay the credits, he now expected treaties would pay his debts. Fort Armstrong remained, now under the command of Colonel William Davenport (no relation to George Davenport) and the First Infantry, but for how much longer was anybody's guess. A military presence was no longer needed. Davenport continued to provide the Indian Agency with corn and presents for the Indians as he always had: blankets, ribbons, calico, strouds, and other dry goods for clothing as well as tin kettles, frying pans, tin cups and a coffee pot. For the time being, the Indian Agency itself would remain on Rock Island, now under the direction of Agent Marmaduke Davenport (another unrelated Davenport), although the Sauk and Mesquakie lived fifty miles away.[34]

For the past twenty-three years, Davenport had been engaged on the frontier in various capacities. Since 1816, he had lived on Rock Island, establishing his home and farm, raising his family, and building his trading business into a lucrative enterprise. It was a hard life, but he had done well. The next few years would find him caught between two worlds, and his high energy and strong ambition would come into conflict with the expectations of the newcomers.

Davenport House ca 1880

CHAPTER THIRTEEN:

LAYING NEW FOUNDATIONS

IN THE YEARS after the Black Hawk War, George Davenport was at the top of his career: trading to both Indians and settlers, opening new service-oriented businesses like taverns, stables, and ferries, buying and selling land, developing rental property, and organizing town sites. He entered these new ventures in much the same way he had entered the Indian Trade: observing the landscape, testing the waters with tenuous steps, and then taking the plunge. In the next three years, Davenport would help shape the local landscape into his own vision of westward expansion by promoting the natural riches of the land as well as its potential for development. He found new partners who shared his vision, some of them among Mrs. Davenport's family who were still living back east. But, the first order of business was securing a real home for his family.

Rock Island had remained in Indian Territory much longer than anyone had expected, but finally, in the spring of 1832, it seemed certain that the fort would be closed. Davenport then made arrangements to build a bigger, finer house. Generally known as the Davenport House today, it symbolizes the maturing of Euro-American possession both on the island and in the Upper Mississippi Valley. By the yardsticks of the day, it was a grand house. Although modest by our twentieth century standards, it once was the most famous and finest mansion between St. Louis and Galena, "surpassing in natural beauty and attractiveness, indoor spaciousness, comfort, and luxuriousness, and outdoor tasteful embellishments and productiveness the far-famed residence of Blennerhasset as described by Wirt."[1] No matter how grand the house seemed to others, to George Davenport it would always be "Indian Lodge."

The house gave the Davenports permanence and a sense of belonging that they had not achieved before. When he returned to England in 1827, Davenport had realized that home for him was on the Island. From London he had written, " ... England is a fine country but I am verrey anxious to get back ... "[2] They built their house in a style that meant success and comfort to them. For Mrs. Davenport, the house gave her the opportunity to use her homemaking and hostess skills in ways that a one-room log structure never could. It was warm, spacious, and above all, comfortable.

The building of this house also showed how radically the Davenports' lifestyle had changed. Economically, socially, politically, they were now the "old" settlers, well established as business operators and landowners. This house put them in the forefront of progress and established them as social leaders.

Construction began in the spring of 1832, after the winter hunt had ended. Benjamin Goble recalled that Gentry McGee and Martin Smith took the contract to build a two-story dwelling on the island about the first of May. They went up the river opposite Port Byron to the Iowa side of the river to get oak logs. Goble, then a young man of about nineteen, was employed to help them. At that time the soldiers were pursuing the Indians up the Rock River and the fort was being guarded by a company of Rangers from Sangamon County. Goble joined their company. He stood guard duty every other night and hewed logs for McGee and Smith for the Davenports' house during the days. By the first of July the framing of the house was completed. Removal of the siding during restoration in the fall of 1989 revealed those oak logs, notched with v- or saddle-notch configurations at the corners, which is typical of many early Illinois log structures.[3]

Though grand in its symbolism, the actual house was a modest structure with four rooms, two on each floor. The entire house measured 46'7" x 18'10". The first floor contained a parlor and a sitting-dining room, separated by a central hall. The second floor was comprised of two bedrooms and a small room or closet in the upper hall.[4] How magnificent and grand this house must have seemed, compared to their old log house! Its dozen or so windows made it light and airy. The four large rooms were finished with plaster and pine plank flooring and must have made it smell fresh and clean and new.

As Davenport's family and businesses expanded, so did the house. By the time of Davenport's murder in 1845, the house had more than doubled in size with the addition of two single-story side wings, a two-story kitchen wing at the rear, and a small rear porch. The site also had at least two storehouses and two small cottages that were later used by immigrant families who worked for the Davenports. There was also a brick structure of unknown size for use as a store.

Details about the construction of this house have survived in the business records of George Davenport, in pictorial records from the 1860s, and in other scattered records. The interior walls were lathed and rough-coated by October of 1833 and finish-plastered the following spring [5] This was a refinement not many of the other settlers could afford at that time.

Supplies from St. Louis merchants document not only the construction materials used in the Davenport house, but also the materials available on the frontier at that time. Accounts with St. Louis merchant Henry Shaw document Crown and Pittsburgh glass, and hardware such as nails, screws, cupboard latches, bolts, and butt hinges in several sizes. A note included on one invoice indicates that Davenport had also ordered Venetian shutter hinges, but they were not available at the time. Bills of lading show that bundles of shingles and pine planks were sent up the river to Rock Island, as they were not available locally.[6]

Since the house has been heavily restored, little of its 1833 hardware or glass remain in the house today, but those that can be identified as original offer more insight into the Davenport's lifestyle. For instance, the original front door lock, now housed in the Putnam Museum, suggests that the Davenports were aware that some things would need to be kept under lock and key. The lock itself is a modest combination of iron and brass, reflecting the Davenports status in the community without being extravagant. Other locks and keys were ordered for the interior cupboards as well. A safe, which was a noteworthy object in the house at the time of Davenport's murder, was a safety deposit for important papers as well as cash. Other important papers were kept in locked trunks.

Davenport's matched duelling pistols were placed either on the mantel or in the cupboards flanking the fireplace. He was not known to have been involved in duels, preferring to use the courts instead to solve his differences, but he could have stood as second during his years in the military. The pistols denoted his social position on the frontier as well as giving a sense of manliness to the house.[7]

The furnishings provide further clues to the Davenport lifestyle. Davenport ordered one dozen Windsor chairs of good quality, two high post beds, two with low posts, and two washstands in May 1834.[8] It is significant that the bedroom furnishings were ordered by mail, rather than personally selected. Some items, intended only for family use, were not so important and the Davenports accepted whatever was available. Bedroom furnishings, for instance, were not usually seen by any visitor to the house and, as such, would not make a statement about the family and the status they had achieved. However, for public rooms like the parlor, the furnishings required more careful selection, probably in person.

It is possible, however, that the family had seen similar items on their travels and written home to tell of their findings. Davenport's son, George L. and his mother, Susan, were in Cincinnati at that time.[9] George L. was probably attending school again, and Susan may have purchased some furnishings for the house then or at least selected some potential purchases for Davenport to make. Granddaughter Naomi Davenport believed that the family piano (now housed in the State Historical Society of Iowa, Museum Division, Des Moines) was purchased in Cincinnati and sent by steamboat to New Orleans, and on to Rock Island by way of St. Louis.[10] It is an excellent example of parlor furnishings of the 1830s made in that city. Crafted of solid mahogany with heavy turned legs, its short keyboard is perfect for occasional parlor entertainment rather than the serious musician.

Other pieces of Davenport furniture in the State Historical Society of Iowa include: one mahogany sideboard, one tilt-top table, one grandfather clock, and three straight chairs, believed to have come originally from the Davenports' island home. Sideboards, for instance, were mentioned as having been in the log house during the Black Hawk War, and indicate a lifestyle that was changing to greater consumption of goods, as well as public display.

Other items in the collection suggest time for leisure. Books and references to magazine and newspaper subscriptions suggest time for reading and a concern with people and events beyond the immediate area. A scrapbook, which appears to have been started in the early 1830s, has an assortment of clippings, pictures, etc. concerned with national events and foreign places, as well as local and family-related interests. The sewing table, made for Mrs. Davenport by the soldiers at Fort Armstrong, was an essential piece of equipment for any middle-class lady of the nineteenth century. References in the ledgers to skeins of silk purchased for his own household use also suggest that someone in the house was spending some time in embroidery or other such needlework. A cherry teacart, said to have come from the Davenport's house on the island, suggests that teatime was an English tradition still observed in the Davenport daily routine.[11]

The five Davenport portraits of George Davenport, George L. Davenport, Sarah Clarke Davenport, Bailey Davenport, and Susan Lewis give testimony to the family's awareness of their social and economic importance. In particular is George Davenport's portrait, painted in 1844 by an unidentified artist named Haydon, which commemorated Davenport's role in founding the city that bears his name. All five portraits, which are housed in the museum of the State Historical Society of Iowa, are large paintings in wide gilt frames, a sizable investment for any frontier family. Of the five portraits, three can be dated. Susan Lewis's portrait was painted in 1861 by Philadelphia portrait artist, S.J. Ferris, and may have been commissioned to commemorate Bailey's first election as mayor of Rock Island city. Bailey's portrait was painted in 1871 by W. Hunt and hung in his parlor on Eagle Street. The portrait of George L. depicts him as a young man, but Sarah Grace Clarke Davenport's portrait was almost certainly painted later than 1860. With the exception of Davenport's portrait, none of the others were done while Mrs. Davenport (Margaret) was still living, a fact which might explain why there are no known images of her.[12]

Mr. and Mrs. Davenport were remembered as gracious hosts by some of the pioneers who ferried across the slough for parties and special get-togethers. They remembered the house was lit by candlelight, which glittered off the silver and brass candlesticks, and the furniture pushed back so they could dance the minuet and Virginia reel. Another old timer remembered that "Rare old silver and china adorned the table and the house contained beautiful mahogany furniture and a quaint spinet (sic), brought from England, which delighted me very much at that time - there was but one piano in Rock Island."[13]

Some pioneers also remembered that the home was filled with colored china. Hundreds of shards of pottery have surfaced at the house site, documenting the many types of porcelain and pottery, including utilitarian wares that the family used. There are also many parts of small bottles and tableware, as well as large bottles, flasks, and champagne bottles. As his business turned more and more to trade with the settlers, Davenport obtained such wares, as documented in his account books. Perhaps Mrs. Davenport was particularly fond of this brightly colored ware, or perhaps she salvaged pieces from sets intended for sale that were broken in shipping.

Entries in Davenport's account books hint at continuous building on the site, until it took on the image of a country estate. As his house neared completion, George Davenport built a new storehouse in the summer of 1834. This time the materials were purchased entirely at the local saw mill.

Just two years after having his house built with hewn timbers, he now was able to buy sawn lumber locally from a mill. It appears from ledger accounts that the wings were already under construction by this time. Ledgers show purchases of plank and nails, and payments for additional lathing and plastering.[14]

The west wing has generally been identified as Davenport's office. At the time of his murder newspaper accounts mentioned that an office located in one of the wings had been broken into and trunks and papers strewn about. Mrs. Totten, a granddaughter of a family who lived in the house briefly, also identified the west wing as the office of George Davenport.[15] Photos taken around the turn of the century seem to confirm Mrs. Totten's information. She recalled that the wing was divided into two parts, the outer space serving as an anteroom where visitors could wait to see Mr. Davenport. From this office, rather than the posts buildings on the site, Davenport could operate his new ventures.

Until recently, the east wing has been something of a mystery. Archaeologist Frederick Lange suggested that this wing might have predated the rest of the house. Further archaeological investigations conducted in the summer of 2003 suggest that this wing may in fact have been part of the original double log cabin in which the family had lived for so long. It was attached both to the house and to the kitchen wing and had disappeared long before the house was restored in 1906. It had a fireplace opening into the main chimney on the east side of the existing house, as well as a storage pit dug into the ground. It would have been convenient for living quarters, being isolated from the main house but still linked to it, and perhaps used by George L. and Sarah after their marriage in 1839. They lived in the Davenport house for a time before settling in the town of Davenport and it was here, where their first two children were born.[16]

The kitchen wing was a two-story, timber-frame stand-alone structure with servants' quarters on the upper floor. At some time, the kitchen was connected to the main house. It had its own chimney with two openings for cooking. Pioneer A. Allen recalled how cooking was done by Rock Island county women in the early days. "Then our wives would literally roast their brains to cook our grub over a large fire or log heat in a big fireplace ... at one end of the log cabin as a cook stove was unknown ... " As the Davenports always had "help," such as Charlotte and later, Catherine, it is likely that the servants prepared the Davenport meals along with Mrs. Davenport and her daughter, Susan, during the time that they lived in the log house. By the time they had moved into their new home, cooking responsibilities were almost exclusively those of the serving women.[17]

Architect George Gleason suggested that the kitchen wing was at one time detached from the house, and at some unknown point after the house was built, was attached to the house and to the east wing. The connecting hallway is visible in photos taken around 1900 and appears as a separate structure between the kitchen wing and the house. Later, the kitchen wing was connected to the main house by a small porch that stretched across the entire back of the house, and a back stairway that led to the east bedroom. Water was carried to the house from springs on the island and, perhaps, from the river. To carry heavy buckets of water, enough for a day's use in the house, required the use of yokes such as one uncovered in the Lange archaeological survey. Although a mound just outside the kitchen was thought to have been a well, infrared photography of the area does not confirm this belief. How and where water was stored has not been determined.[18]

Heating the house may have been by the four main fireplaces, although Davenport did purchase stoves for his trading post in the 1820s. Ellen Lloyd Lynch, whose family lived in the house in 1865, remembered that the fireplaces were boarded up and stove pipes fitted into the chimneys when she lived there.[19]

The orchards that Davenport had established in 1820 and the gardens that had produced food for the Davenports over the years were given to the care of son, Bailey, when he was old enough to handle this task. There were arbors of Catawba and Isabella grapes, Morello cherry trees, and numerous peach trees to care for. By the age of twelve, Bailey was experienced in cultivation and a shrewd horse trader, interests he pursued his entire life.[20]

This house, larger, more comfortable, and more refined than their log dwelling, continued to serve the Davenports' economic and cultural needs and to prepare them for their retirement years. Davenport operated his businesses from the office in the west wing and the outbuildings held his stores of trade goods and merchandise for the local settlers. Only one thing was missing from their idyllic setting: clear title to the property in which they had invested so heavily.

Davenport had claimed his island property by right of preemption from the moment Colonel Morgan designated it a place for his settlement. But, as long as the island was held for military purposes, Davenport could not buy any of it until it was designated as public land. Now that the Sauk and Mesquakie were soon to leave for their villages further west, there would be no further need for Fort Armstrong. Like other settlers in the neighborhood who looked longingly at the island, Davenport expected that the government would relinquish its claim to the island as a military reserve. Had he known that the island would remain a reserve into the twenty-first century he might have made other arrangements, but he gambled that the land would be entered into the Public Domain and sold. It became an ordeal that would leave the Davenports and others who pre empted land on the island, uncertain about their own future on Rock Island for many years. Despite the uncertainty, Mr. and Mrs. Davenport continued with the building of their house and settling into a new lifestyle.

In the early spring of 1833, Davenport travelled with the Indian Agent, Interpreter Le Claire, and many chiefs and braves to visit his old friend Black Hawk in prison at Jefferson Barracks. Also accompanying the group was Black Hawk's wife, Singing Bird, and one of his daughters. Davenport brought him dried venison, killed and cured by some of Black Hawk's friends. Black Hawk very much appreciated the gifts and Black Hawk was happy to see his friends, especially his wife and daughter. He and the other Sauk prisoners had spent the winter making pipes.[21] There is no record of Davenport's reactions to this visit.

More and more of Davenport's interests were focused on the hundreds, even thousands, of people making their way toward Rock Island. The Davenports' house would serve as a gathering place for some of those new settlers. Here many plans and schemes would be hashed out, deals made and developed, and the family would live and die. Two events in particular would be remembered for their historical significance: the platting of the city of Davenport, Iowa, in 1835, and the formation of what would become the Rock Island Lines railroad company in 1845. Both would serve to further the development of communities beyond Rock Island and for the next twelve years George Davenport would be at the very heart of it all, beginning as an elected official.

Rock Island County was now ready to organize. The boundaries of the county had been set before the Black Hawk War, but no elections of officials had yet taken place. Three Commissioners were appointed by the State Legislature to locate a county seat. They were charged to meet around the first of June at the house of the Indian Agent, Marmaduke Davenport and hold elections on Monday, July 5, 1833, at the place of John Barrel in Farnhamsburg, the old trading house of Davenport and Farnham.[22] The legal voters of the county would elect three County Commissioners, one Sheriff, one Coroner, three Justices of the Peace, and three Constables. Sixty-five votes were cast and George Davenport was elected one of the three County Commissioners. The following story of the first county election provides some insight into the times and the man as well.

At the election there were two tickets: one for the community surrounding Rocky Island, and the other made up of those settled in the upper part of the county around present-day Hampton. There was some contention between the groups, each suspecting the other of trying to rig the election. An arrangement was made for Davenport, who represented the Island party, to signal those on the island should extra votes be needed for their side. Believing that it was in fact necessary, Davenport waved a handkerchief making the signal, but he was discovered. The Hampton party, thinking that he was signalling for help from the soldiers at the fort, seized the poll books, mounted their horses, and rode off. The clerks of the election had anticipated their intentions and substituted a blank poll book for the real one, so when the Island party arrived, their votes elected their candidates.[23] Only the location of the permanent county seat was not yet settled, as no towns had yet developed in the county.

Davenport, along with John Spencer and John Vanatta, began holding court at the Barrel House and making decisions about county development. The commissioners met regularly there and it became the temporary seat of justice. Here they established roads, built bridges, granted licenses for public works, and levied taxes, and in the absence of other legal authorities they performed marriages and other legal services. Davenport himself performed the third marriage in the county, between Adrian Davenport and Harriet Sibley at Fort Armstrong. Adrian was the son of Marmaduke Davenport, the current Sauk and Mesquakie Indian Agent, and no relationship to George Davenport. During his three-year term as County Commissioner Davenport sat on the County Commissioners' court a total of 29 days for which he was allowed forty-five dollars.[24]

With county government taking charge, there was no further need for a standing army at Fort Armstrong, an assessment that Lt. Colonel William Davenport made very quickly upon assuming command in 1833. The Indians came regularly for their annuities, but the money was paid by the Indian Agent without the aid of the garrison. If the troops were withdrawn, Colonel Davenport argued, the Agent could move into the fort buildings where he could have better accommodations and room to store his Indian supplies. Besides, settlers were already crowding onto the island and interfering with garrison duties and the fort was badly in need of repairs if the troops were to stay much longer. Surveying of the lands on the Island was underway, conducted by Charles R. Bennett, in readiness for any sale of Public Lands that might be announced.[25]

Davenport juggled his new county duties with what remained of the Indian Trade. From their villages on the Ioway and Cedar rivers, the Sauk and Mesquakie maintained their trade relations with Davenport whose accounts with Pierre Chouteau and Company show that there was still a demand for his trade goods. The Sauk and Mesquakie still required blankets and yard goods as well as manufactured clothing and traps and other hunting supplies. Davenport also sold them bridles and saddles for their horses, perhaps more than in the past, as well as snuff and cigars and some foodstuffs.   Surprisingly, mustard was included in the goods purchased by Davenport. Had the Sauk and Mesquakie developed a taste for mustard with their pork and beef? Corn was in constant demand by the tribes, as the women had not yet been able to raise enough to feed their people. In all, the invoices of the Chouteau Company show that Davenport owed, with interest, over $ 22,000 for these goods. The debt was due on the first of July 1835, but Davenport did not seem as concerned as he had in the past.

To accommodate the tribes on their hunt, Davenport built a new temporary trading post, a small double log cabin, at present-day Muscatine, Iowa. It was in the same vicinity where he and Farnham had built a post before. It was conveniently located near the new villages on the Ioway and Cedar rivers, but close enough to Rock Island to maintain some trading relations with his old friends for a little longer. A marker stands there today, on Water Street just above Iowa avenue. Called Grindstone Bluff by locals, it operated until 1835.[26]

Davenport's son, George L., took over more and more of the day-to-day responsibilities of the Indian trade, at least when he was home. George L.'s education continued at St. Louis for a time and later at Winchester, Virginia. What had changed drastically since the Black Hawk War, and disturbed Davenport greatly, was the lack of moral integrity of some of his competitors. The "new" traders seemed to be capitalizing on the weakened condition of the tribes, charging exorbitant prices and selling frivolous goods to them. The tribes had not been able to grow enough corn since their move to the interior of Iowa and were becoming more and more dependent upon their charity.[27] It was a situation that Davenport and son only tolerated until the Indians removed to western Iowa.

Le Claire, who was still working as the government interpreter, was among the first to move to the new lands on the west bank of the Mississippi River. At the request of the Sauk and Mesquakie, Le Claire and his wife Marguerite built their house on the very spot where General Winfield Scott had stood during the treaty negotiations. It was a small French-style cottage, one and a half stories high, with a large piazza across the front. Their land in the Lower Reserve, as seen in the painting from Ft. Armstrong, stretched from the riverbank to the bluff in a French long lot manner with an orchard planted near the house.[28]

George L. Davenport, too, built a house in what is now Iowa, in the fall of 1832. As the soldiers vacated the treaty grounds, he made the first "claim" in Iowa territory. He was then fifteen years old. His younger brother, Bailey, then nine years old, helped him break the sod on his claim. Although the claim was premature according to the terms of the treaty, George L. managed to maintain his hold on the land largely because he was an adopted brother of the Mesquakie. He farmed there for many years, experimenting with new varieties of corn that were then coming onto the market.[29]

As mentioned in the previous chapter, Davenport, Le Claire, Governor Reynolds and E.C. March officially formed a partnership to start a town on Le Claire's section at the head of the Rock Island Rapids. Each purchased a forty-acre parcel for $80 from Le Claire. The fourth forty-acre parcel Le Claire reserved for himself. The agreement, signed on the 27th of March 1833, provided for the survey of the resulting quarter section to be done as soon as possible for the purpose of laying out a town and surveying it into lots, which was to be called "Le Claire," Also that year, George bought from Le Claire a parcel of his reserve land at the lower end of the Rapids.[30]

On June 1, 1833, the lands on the western bank of the Mississippi were officially opened to settlement. People had been coming for months, anticipating the opening of the new lands. Many families lined up at the river's edge waiting for the official opening of the western lands beyond the Mississippi. One such family was the Josiah Bradley Chamberlain family. They had watched and waited for opening day from the town of Hampton, Illinois. Mr. Chamberlain had come out from New York State the previous year to scout out a choice spot in the new country, but the Black Hawk War had been in progress and he had to wait. Mr. Chamberlain had chosen a place along the river just above the mouth of Crow Creek, and had cultivated a small field while they waited for the Indians to move. He had even driven his oxen across the river using a

dugout canoe he had made from a walnut log. All during the spring, family
members could see bands of Indians moving up and down the river bank
on a daily basis. According to family stories, it was a difficult time for the
family. Mrs. Chamberlain was expecting their seventh child and the other
children were sick with fever and ague. The family's provisions were in
short supply and the children grew tired of Johnny Cake everyday. The
nearest store, kept by George Davenport, was nearly fifteen miles away.
But moving day finally came and they made their way across the river.
Their oldest daughter later recalled that then they were really isolated,
being the only white family in Scott County.[31]

Even some of the Fort Armstrong soldiers could not resist the call of
the Iowa lands. Pvt. Simon Cragin of Company G, 1st Infantry, resigned
from the army and settled in Pleasant Valley. He taught school there for
a time. Sgt. James Haskill, formerly of Company C, 3rd Infantry, also took
his family to Pleasant Valley where he partnered with Tom Davis in
constructing the first saw and gristmills.[32] Land that had recently seen only
the animals of the forest and an occasional hunter was now beginning to
hum as settlement and the ensuing industrialization began to reform the
landscape into a new way of living.

Underscoring the recent changes in the Upper Mississippi Valley was
the return of Black Hawk. After being released from prison, Black Hawk
and his braves were welcomed back to Rock Island in a formal ceremony.
On the first of August, a welcoming party led by Keokuk returned to Rock
Island from their new villages on the Des Moines River. The warriors,
including Keokuk and Pashepaho, had just returned from a buffalo hunt
when they received the news of Black Hawk's release. A short distance
from Rock Island, the warriors stopped to ready themselves for the
occasion. They dressed in their finest and painted themselves in red. A
day of feasting was held to honor the returning members of the tribe and
Black Hawk was welcomed back to his people with speeches by the tribal
leaders. The feasting lasted into the night and soldiers and Indians danced
together in celebration. But there was no home to which Black Hawk
could return. Saukenuk was gone, the bones of their ancestors scattered,
and the land now belonged to others, the biggest part to Farnham and

Davenport. The ceremony stirred the memories of those who had participated in the war and caused them to reflect on how it was just a few short years ago.[33] The Davenports must have been living in their new home by this time, but Black Hawk did not mention visiting his old friend or the new home.

Near Black Hawk's old home of Saukenuk, Davenport entered into a partnership with Joshua Vandruff to operate a ferry for settlers coming overland from the south across Rock River. It was located at the most favorable crossing place between Vandruff's Island and Davenport's land at Saukenuk. It was a small business operated by Vandruff and his sons with a single flat boat that he pushed across the river with poles. Two skiffs were also on hand for use during high water when it was dangerous to cross. For the fee of $8 plus clerk's fees the two men received a license from the county for one year, renewable upon application to the county commissioners. Davenport was also granted a one-year license to operate a ferry across the slough, now called Sylvan Slough. Ferry rates set by the Rock Island County Commissioners were a little higher than those set by the Jo Daviess county commissioners a few years before.[34] It must have been a profitable business as he renewed his licenses for several years.

Davenport was still serving as postmaster, a position he had held since 1825, but the residents of the county were not pleased with that appointment, because they had to use Davenport's ferry to cross the Slough, and pay the established ferry rates to get their letters or papers from him. The residents petitioned for a post office on the mainland and Joseph Conway was appointed postmaster with an office in the courthouse.[35] This ended Davenport's term of postmaster.

In June, Davenport built another store near his house on the island, most likely for the trade of the general public rather than exclusively for the Indians. This one was brick, and located nearer to his house than the trading posts. He was granted a license to "vend, sell, or retail at public auction or private sale any goods, wares, or merchandize upon the paying in the County Treasury ten dollars tax."[36]

Sometime that summer the Reverend Cutting Marsh and his Stockbridge Indians paid a visit to Davenport. Marsh and his Indians were missionaries who hoped to establish mission schools among the Sauk and Mesquakie, convert them to Christianity, and bring civilization to them. Marsh wanted to break the tribes into small family groups and change their life style to permanent village life, from hunting and gathering to farming and domestic arts.

Rev. Marsh first approached the commanding officer at Fort Armstrong, Colonel William Davenport, and the Indian Agent, Marmaduke Davenport. While the Indian Agent received him kindly and had no objections to a mission, he suggested that the trader, George Davenport, had more influence among the Sauk and Mesquakie and should be approached on the subject. Davenport, according to Marsh, was not overly enthusiastic about converting the Sauk and Mesquakie and were more concerned with illustrating how happy they were with their traditional lifestyle. Antoine Le Claire was not much use to Marsh either. Marsh did not trust him, primarily because Le Claire was a Catholic and not inclined to promote any other religion. There seemed to be no other interpreter who could converse in spiritual language and Marsh eventually concluded, reluctantly, that he had no way to infiltrate the camps. These people were, in his words, "strongly attached to their superstitions ... and they guard with jealous care against any change. Their great object is war and hunting, so as to rank among the braves, wear the polecat's tail upon the calves of their legs, and the shau-no-e-hun (small bells), and strike the post in the war-dance and tell the number they have killed in battle." Despite his failure to establish any school or mission among these people, Marsh was able to interview many of the tribal leaders and recorded his observations about the Sauk and Fox, their beliefs, and their culture at that time.[87]

Davenport's discouragement of Marsh has been viewed as an anti-Christian movement on Davenport's part, but Reverend Marsh acknowledged that Davenport was a Universalist who believed that everyone would be saved, regardless of their beliefs, and worked energetically against all changes in the tribes. Indian Agent Joseph M. Street said that Davenport was relentless in his campaign for temperance among the Indians and other changes that others wanted to make in the tribal lifestyle. Davenport's lack of enthusiasm for missionary interference was more likely motivated by self-interest coupled with an interest in keeping whatever relationship he still had with Black Hawk's people intact. Black Hawk's band had fought hard to maintain their traditional lifestyle and the traders understood that the Sauk and Mesquakie were happy in their ways. Attempts to Christianize them would only ruin them as many Eastern tribes had been.[38]

Marsh represented a large body of people who saw the Indians as savages and felt it their duty to either convert them or exterminate them. Converting the tribes to farmers would, of course, eliminate the need to hunt and that, in turn, would eliminate the Indian Trade. The best that traders and friends of the Indians could do was to prevent open conflict or warfare - a nearly impossible task. Davenport and Farnham's proposed solution had been to sell the Indian land and remove the Indians far enough from settlement so that they could live as they always had. Selling would not only settle debts, but also they reasoned, provide a safer environment for the Indians. Once, the Indians had been able to pay off their debts within one season. Now they were unable to repay the traders for debts accumulated over the past seven years. Those debts, in 1831, amounted to $53,000.[39] Compounding the problem of a dwindling fur trade was the whiskey influence and conflict with the Sioux over hunting grounds. In the past, hunting was serious enough to suspend fighting between tribes for the duration of the hunt, but now, Sauk and Mesquakie braves frequently interrupted their hunting time to wage war with their enemies. Without provisions from the hunt, the Indians were totally dependent on the traders to supply their barest necessities. And, as a rule, new settlers had little interest in or understanding of the native lifestyle, despite Davenport's efforts to convince them otherwise.

The Mesquakie now numbered about 3600 souls in their villages on the Red Cedar and Ioway Rivers. The Sauk, estimated at 1200, were in three locations: at Keokuk's village on the Des Moines about fifty-five miles from Fort Des Moines, at Appanoose's village about seventy-five miles from Fort Des Moines, and on the reservation on the Iowa River.[40] Despite Marsh's observations about their uncivilized nature and unwillingness to change, there had been changes in the Indian lifestyle. Even in their villages beyond the ceded lands there were far too many distractions for them to maintain their traditional ways: too many settlers, not enough hunting grounds, too much whiskey, not enough animals to hunt. Clearly the days of the old Indian hunts were over, but the trading business continued.

The Indian trade had clearly changed. Some fur-bearing animals were nearly exterminated and the Indians were less interested in hunting and trapping, as it required too much effort. Beaver, once the driving force in the demand for furs, was now out-of-fashion, and silk was the material of choice for the manufacture of hats. John Jacob Astor had retired from the American Fur Company, and the Western Department of the American Fur Company was sold to Pratte, Chouteau, and Company. This caused a stir in St. Louis as the emphasis shifted away from the Upper Mississippi to the western reaches of the Missouri and the Rocky mountains. Altogether they signalled the end of an era. With so many new settlers and other demands on George's time and energy, one would have thought that the Davenports would retire from the business. But they had developed friendships with these tribes and so they held on for another eight years.[41]

With the death of Farnham in 1832, Davenport took his place as middle management for Pratte, Chouteau and Company. Supplies came to them and they supplied their traders with goods and were content to remain on Rock Island. Their Des Moines Outfit was under the direction of Wharton McPherson, but what profits there were must have been minimal. Other traders, like John Gilbert, Wheaton Chase, and Chase's brother-in-law, Sumner Phelps, had also established posts near the Sauk and Mesquakie villages on the Ioway River. They did a fair business, as the Indians could no longer support themselves by hunting and their gardens had not yet had time to produce the quantities of corn they once enjoyed at Saukenuk, but the debts were paid from their government annuities until they had to sell more land.[42]

While Davenport was preoccupied with a variety of new enterprises in 1834, his family was away from Rock Island. Son George L. was in the east with his mother, perhaps finishing his schooling in Winchester,

Virginia, where he had cousins.[43] His studies at Jacksonville had been interrupted by the Black Hawk War and he was of an age when he needed to complete them. Because his family would be gone nearly a year, Davenport hired Catherine Pouit to run the household. Little is known about Catherine, but her descendants believe that she had been a laundress at the fort before her employment with the Davenports. It is more likely, however, that Davenport had hired her through his contacts in St. Louis to keep house for him while his family was gone. Catherine added a new dimension to the family, a story that will be discussed later.

Surprisingly, Rock Island County had no towns at this time, nor had the county seat been located. All that changed when the Illinois Legislature passed an act for establishing a permanent seat of justice (winter term of 1834-35). The name of the town as designated in the official act was to be Stephenson, in honor of the Black Hawk War hero, James Stephenson. Three commissioners, one each from Jo Daviess, Knox, and Warren counties, were selected to decide upon a site: William Bennet, Peter Butler, and John G. Sanborn were appointed. Contention between the Island and Hampton, or Upper County, parties proved to make the selection process politically interesting. Although the original act selected the house of Indian Agent Marmaduke Davenport for the commissioners' stay, Miles Conway, who was living with his family in a log house near the Farnhamsburg trading post at that time, hosted the commissioners at his house. Because Conway was in favor of the present location, he exerted as much influence as he could for that place.[44] Arguments from the Hampton faction could not overcome the reality that there was only one place free from the annual floods with a good steamboat with a point for the transhipment of goods to the Rock River. Accordingly, the three county commissioners, Davenport, Spencer and Vanatta, purchased from the U.S. Government sixty-one and ninety-five hundredths acres in the northwest fractional quarter of section 35. They paid the going government rate of a dollar and a quarter an acre and prepared to establish the county seat. In time it became known as Stephenson. The champions of Hampton, however, fought for the county seat for years.

Despite the designation of the name in the official act, there is a legend about how the county seat got its name. The first name proposal was, according to the story, "Davenport," but the name was not approved by the State Legislature. According to the legend, George Davenport had publicly criticized, and humiliated, a lawyer by the name of Colonel James Strode (often mistakenly spelled Stroud) for his disgraceful conduct at Stillman's Run during the Black Hawk War. Strode was then practicing law in Galena in partnership with Thomas Ford and influential in state politics. In retaliation for this alleged ill treatment at the hands of George Davenport, Strode persuaded his friends in the legislature to reject the name of Davenport for this town, and after much debate the name of Stephenson, in honor of James W. Stephenson of the Galena Mounted Volunteers in the Black Hawk War, was given to the new town instead.[45] Despite any difficulties in naming the site, the town was an instant success. Lying in one of the most beautiful places on the Mississippi river, it had all the features for success: clean water, a natural port for steamboat landings, coal, iron, hardwood timber, and water power suitable for harnessing for manufacturing purposes.

Davenport, with Antoine Le Claire, immediately applied for and was granted a license to operate a ferry from the new townsite for one year. The partners paid the seven dollar tax and entered their bond. They were allowed to charge the same rates as other ferrymen across the Mississippi River in the Rock Island County.[46]

The platting of Stephenson followed the rules set down by the 4th Illinois General Assembly. A true and correct plat was first prepared to show the public grounds and streets and alleys properly marked with their sizes. All lots were numbered in numerical order and the size of the lots marked. Any donations or grants were noted and the plat was certified and recorded in the public record. Non-compliance of the rules could have resulted in a stiff fine and any monies collected were to be used for building schools.[47] The Rock Island County Commissioners followed the rules exactly.

Advertisements of the auction appeared in the Northwestern Advertiser and Galena Gazette. It was a promotional advertisement touting the best features of the site: healthy country, rich soil, good timber, building stone nearby as well as opportunities for the mechanic, tradesman, and farmers. Terms were standard for the time: one third cash, and two thirds on credit of 12 and 18 months, with a mortgage on the lots for security. But the most interesting part of the ad was the statement that several unnamed gentlemen from Zanesville, Ohio, had purchased a part of the rapids on Rock River and were about to build mills.[48] Speculation was in full swing.

Rock Island County had entered the boom years – years when speculation was high in the Upper Mississippi Valley. Between the years 1835 and 1837 hundreds of towns were planned. Some were even platted. A few developed into towns. What Rock Island County needed to be viable were housing and the amenities that would attract settlers. Being a county seat would help to make this town a success.

Davenport and his fellow commissioners used a standard plan for their town and hired a surveyor to lay it out. Using a gridiron system for laying of the town into blocks and lots, Charles Bennett and his assistants prepared the town for public sale, surveying each lot and marking it with stakes driven into the ground. Eighty-five lots in all were auctioned on the 11th of July 1835. Michael Bartlett cried the sale (as the auctioneer) with Benjamin Pike serving as his assistant. Donations of lots were given to Louden and Charles Case and to William Brashar, but the county commissioners' records do not give reasons for the donations. Often a donation was given men who had agreed to settle permanently and operate certain businesses that would attract others. Donations were, therefore, promotions for the town. The auction was considered a success and Clerk Joseph Conway recorded the deeds.[49]

The auction was well-attended by men and women from far away, so the commissioners must have been quite pleased that their town had sold so well. Records show that lots sold for an average of about $155. The highest priced lot went to G.C. R. Mitchell, at $300, a lawyer born in Tennessee, and the least paid lot was for a mere $25. The total sales would bring over $14,000 to the new county. Deed records indicated that the buyers were from the following places: New York, Pennsylvania, Ohio, other counties in Illinois and, of course, St. Louis, Missouri. Only two women purchased lots at the sale, but surely there were many more there that day. Davenport himself bought four lots and George L. bought one. Antoine Le Claire bought two connected lots in Block One, right on the river. He quickly established a ferry from this spot. His first license, in partnership with George Davenport, had already been granted the month before, and the ferry rates established by the County Commissioners. Le Claire was in business in no time at all.[50]

One woman who bought lots was Davenport's stepdaughter, Susan Lewis. She and her son, George L., had returned from Winchester and Cincinnati earlier in the summer and what Susan discovered at home might have prompted her to buy lots for herself. The servant Catherine, hired to help with the domestic duties during her absence, was pregnant and she claimed that George Davenport was the father. How this affected the harmony within the Davenport house can very well be imagined and may have been the reason that Susan Lewis bought two lots on the western edge of the town plat not far from the present Rock Island county courthouse. It was an area that would become an up-and-coming residential area where many prominent Rock Island families settled. Susan Lewis herself never talked about this situation, only hinting once that she wished things had been different. How they resolved the family issue is not known, but she remained on the island. She retained ownership of her lots in Stephenson until after Davenport's death, but did not develop them. Catherine gave birth to a daughter, whom she named Elizabeth, in November 1835, and they remained in the house until the baby was about six months old when mother and daughter moved to southern Illinois.[51]

A second child was born into the Davenport household that year, Mathilda Barrett. Persistent rumors claim that George Davenport was her father and that her mother was the Davenport's cook. There is no conclusive evidence. Mathilda was mulatto and grew up in the house. She remained with Susan Lewis in the island house as a paid servant until 1860 when she married Henry Hilbring, a German immigrant. The Hilbrings bought one of Susan Lewis' farms in Henry County where they lived until their deaths.

It has been alleged or presumed that George Davenport fathered a number of Indian children as well. This may or may not be true. There are no claims to substantiate this, nor are there any family stories that suggest it. The official Sauk and Mesquakie claims for support of mixed blood or half-breed children show no such claims for any children of George Davenport. There are, however, annuity claims for the children of both Davenport sons. Perhaps this is the source for the claim that the elder George Davenport had fathered Indian children. These children of both George L. and Bailey Davenport visited the island frequently and were playmates of some of the local pioneers.

With their town lots sold, the commissioners focused on improvements, laying out roads, letting contracts for bridges, and building a jail. Stephenson grew quickly. Others, seeing a chance to capitalize on Stephenson's position as county seat, began to lay out additions to the town. The Thompson and Wells addition was the first in April 1836; then Spencer and Case's addition in May. By fall the Chicago or lower addition had been platted by Jones, Garnsey, and Beardsley. Within a year of the auction, Stephenson had more than doubled in size and was thriving.

Other than his service as county commissioner, Davenport's involvement in the development of the town of Stephenson appears to have been as broker for lots. After his term of county commissioner expired, he had little involvement with town government and, in fact, was already involved with projects elsewhere. The new settlers had needs and he had means. They needed ferries to cross the river, well-stocked stores from which to buy supplies, places to live while they found land and built their homes, and other goods and services that organized local governments could supply. According to pioneer reminiscences, Davenport was more than just helpful to the new settlers. There were many times when he carried them through financial hardships.

One area where Davenport had some vested interest was in the county land surveys recently completed in 1834. There were serious questions about conflicting boundary lines, which affected many settlers' claims.

Settlers looked to Davenport for help in navigating the government red tape. Davenport wrote to government officials seeking answers to questions on the surveys, even offering to pay for private surveys to settle disputes among his new neighbors. Of course it was beneficial to him if the land claims were settled amicably, but it also fit his personality of being fair and honest with his neighbors and going a step beyond the expected. It was all good for business.[52]

After his return from the east, son George L. took more responsibility in the Indian business, while his father concentrated on government and land development. The country was rapidly building up and, with the Indians safely removed and government in place, there was no longer a real need for military protection. During the fall of 1835 there had been another outbreak of cholera at the fort. Dr. John Emerson, the medical officer assigned there, apprised the Surgeon General of the situation, and his letter revealed some serious problems with the fort structure, which helped the Secretary of War to make his decision on the future of the fort.

Cholera had come this time with a detachment of recruits from Newport, Kentucky. In all 61 men had been infected and the fort's hospital, which consisted of a single room, was unable to handle the epidemic. The room was only large enough for three beds, very filthy, and whenever it rained the old rotten logs had kept the room damp and nasty with no air. In addition, wrote Emerson, it had been a particularly wet spring and all the medicines, instruments, and medical stores had been damaged by the rotten, damp conditions. Emerson concluded that the conditions were aggravating the disease. He not only sent the soldiers across the river, but also hired a private doctor to help with the treatment of the sick. His recommendation: either build new quarters or close the fort altogether.[53]

The orders to abandon Fort Armstrong came the following January, and the fort was officially abandoned on May 4, 1836. While the Indian Agency would remain on the island for another two years, the Indians, whose presence had caused the fort to be built in the first place, were sufficiently removed so as to cause no harm to the settlers who were rapidly taking over the land.

Some of the fort's buildings were sold at public auction under the direction of Lt. Beach and advertised in the Northwestern Gazette and Galena Advertiser, and took place at nine o'clock in the morning of September 19th. All kinds of goods were to be sold, including out-of-date soldiers' clothing, 560 pairs of shoes, great coats and mittens. Also included were building materials and window sashes, glazed doors and window shutters. Because settlers needing good building material eventually would have cannibalized the buildings, it was considered good government to sell these items while they still had some value. Pioneer Tom Bollman remembered that George Davenport purchased some of the building materials to use in repairing his own buildings, spending as much as three or four hundred dollars for them; what was not needed, he would sell. Two years later, Captain Bell reported "Soon after the sale of the old buildings of Fort Armstrong, all that were of use were pulled down, and carried to the neighboring town of Davenport ... They consist of 70 connected log huts, about 20 feet square, rotten, and in ruins and one old frame building, 28 by 18 feet, nearly gone."[54] By November the soldiers under Lt. Beach's command were ordered to Fort Des Moines and the Island was free of the military.

The Island, however, was still a Government military reserve. Its protection from predators and squatters was left to appointed agents with no real authority. George Davenport was one such agent. His appointment from the Secretary of War made his responsibilities and authority clear. " ... without compensation for the purpose of protecting the military reservation on Rock Island from depredations and settlement upon it by any and all persons."[55] The appointment had little teeth in it. When necessary, Davenport was instructed to instigate legal proceedings against any offenders through the Federal Marshall, a slow and time-consuming process that had little practical affect against timber clearing and building activities of squatters and other persons. Damage to the timber and fuel supplies came quickly as squatters moved into the just vacated fort. The abandoned buildings, which were still standing, were conveniently appropriated as ready-made homes. There were three such offenders that affected the Island and the Davenports directly, Charles and Absolom Baxter and Donnoh Williams.

The Baxter brothers immediately took up residence in the Indian Agent's house. Absolom Baxter was a government surveyor and working for Rock Island County. His brother, Charles had a son with him. John was just a boy, but he was impressionable. Indian Agent Street noted that the Baxters had done the most damage to the timber, almost denuding the land. They had broken into the Agent's house and were using it as part of their preemption claim. The Agency papers and furniture, including a desk, were still in the house. Street had the keys to the house, having received them from Col. William Davenport before closing the fort, but he had not yet moved his family to Rock Island and was unable to secure the house for his own living quarters. The Baxters were well-armed and prepared to defend their claim.[56] Some compromise must have been affected because Street did live in the house for a time, but the Baxters were persistent and living there again in 1845, a part of the story which would haunt the Davenports forever and will be told later.

On the far end of the Island from the Davenports, the east end, was Donnoh Williams. He had cleared a little timber and planted trees and herbs. He had also built a two-room frame house in preparation for moving onto the island.[57] The natural condition of the island was a matter of concern, not only because it was government property, but also because timber was a valuable commodity. It was a pervasive problem and even Davenport had an encounter with timber thieves among his new neighbors.

When Davenport found several trees missing from his own property, he accused Asahel Case of entering his land and removing, without permission, forty white oak trees. They were valued at $320 and Davenport sued for damages. The courts ruled in Davenport's favor, but Asahel's brother filed a countersuit against Davenport, claiming the original suit was without cause. This second case was settled out of court, upon the condition that payment be forthcoming. This incident probably made more enemies for Davenport than friends, but it made the point.

Neither the island, nor the Davenport land, was open for free firewood or building material.[58]

Davenport must have felt some relief when the Indian Agent, Joseph Street, finally moved to the Island. Street had resisted the move from his comfortable home in Prairie du Chien, but finally accepted the position, in large measure because of the wishes of the Sauk and Mesquakie chiefs. How Street was able to evict the Baxters from his house is not clear, but he did take possession and set to work, evaluating Island conditions. There were several preemption claims to the island by persons who had already settled. Of those he deemed George Davenport's the only valid claim. This was excellent news for the Davenports. It would strengthen their petition in Congress to buy their island property.[59]

With the status of the island still in limbo, Davenport again pressed his claim to the island property, this time with Secretary of War Joel R. Poinsett. On Davenport's behalf, Poinsett inquired of the General Land Office whether Davenport's claim would soon be acted upon. Eight days later Secretary Poinsett informed Davenport that the War Department had determined to sell the Rock Island Military reservation, but reassured him that he would be given sufficient time to buy his property before the rest of the island was sold. This was some consolation to Davenport since his Congressional petition was still under consideration by the House Committee on Public Lands. Although the bill progressed to the Whole House on April 11, 1838, no decision was made.[60]

It wasn't long after when the Indian Agency was moved nearer to the Indian lands on the Des Moines River. No longer would the Indians need to visit Rock Island. Street dismissed the blacksmith at Fort Armstrong who promptly seized the smith's house and shop and claimed it as his preemption. Antoine Le Claire, faced with the decision to move or resign, retired from his interpreter's job for the Sauk and Mesquakie.[61] Once again, without the presence of government officials, the Island was at risk for predation.

One final message of change came to the Davenports that summer. Black Hawk, who had never accepted the white man's treaties, was dead. His final words spoken at the Fourth of July celebration in Ft. Madison were poignant: "Rock river was a beautiful country. I liked my towns, my cornfields, and the house of my people. I fought for it. It is now yours. Keep it, as we did. It will produce you good crops."[62] That same summer, Robert Lucas was appointed Governor of Iowa Territory. Statehood was thought to be imminent.

CHAPTER FOURTEEN:

THE DWINDLING TRADE AFTER
THE BLACK HAWK WAR

DESPITE THE DISTANCE from their new villages on the Ioway and
Cedar Rivers, the Mesquakie and Sauk still came to Davenport's post on
the Island. They followed along the old deeply cut Indian trails that were
fast becoming symbols of a lifestyle quickly passing. In a changing world,
trust in old friends was more important than convenience.

The Des Moines River Valley still provided good hunting and so
Davenport maintained the contract with the Phelps Brothers who had
been his biggest competitors in the past. The brothers had built posts on
the Skunk and Des Moines Rivers and were poised to intercept many of
his credits coming in from the interior of Iowa. Farnham had once
contracted with them in an effort to minimize the damage the brothers

could do his business, but it may also have been a tactic to draw the brothers into the fold of the Company.[1] Davenport kept his posts on the Cedar and Ioway Rivers, which he had established in 1831, because it served the villages of Poweshiek, Wapello, and Keokuk, three of his biggest customers. He engaged the help of Antoine Le Claire for this trade.[2]

His accounting system illustrates some of the changes the Indians were facing after 1832 as well. No longer did Davenport identify individuals in his credit books, as he had in the past. Instead, all accounting was attributed to the chief of each village he served. Keokuk, Poweshiek, and Wapello were the moneymen to whom the annuities were paid and who had the final say on whose debts should be paid at those times.

The Sauk and Mesquakie tried to maintain their traditional way of life in their new villages, but hunting was increasingly less profitable and more time-consuming. The hunters were travelling as much as two hundred miles to find game and were barely able to supply their people with enough meat to eat. The further west the Sauk and Mesquakie went, the closer they came to Sioux territory. Frequently, the hunt was interrupted by warfare, a problem that only increased after the Black Hawk War. Davenport's son George L'Oste, who was taking charge of the day-to-day trading business, encouraged the tribes to remain focused on the hunt rather than their enemies. Letters to Henry Sibley, the American Fur Company agent for the Sioux, acknowledged the difficulty in keeping the tribes separated and offered information that could keep the tribes apart during the hunt. "We shall do all we can to prevent our Indians from striking upon the Siouxs. We will advise them that you are with this and that you will do all you can to restrain the Sioux from interfering with the foxes. Mr. Wm Phelps has gone out with the foxes on a hunting excursion up the desmoines near the line their intention is pacific towards the Sioux will you please inform the Siouxs that they may not strike upon them."[3]

The women began to recreate their traditional gardens near their lodges, as they once had done at Rock Island. The soil was fertile and eventually would produce enough corn and vegetables, but this prairie had never been cultivated and breaking sod was difficult and time-consuming. Corn yields were not yet sufficient to feed the tribes through the winter.

Between 1834 and 1839, Davenport purchased about $25 - 30,000 worth of goods each year for the Sauk Outfit, and distributed them to the villages through his various clerks. When they were hungry, Davenport also supplied them corn. By early 1834, he estimated that he had already advanced $20,000 against the tribal annuities and provided 300 bags of corn.[4] By the summer of 1834, Davenport was concerned about Congress' ratification of the Treaty of 1832. He had not yet received the $40,000 allocated to Farnham and him for the tribal debts leading up to the Black Hawk War. He had learned that there were some amendments to the Indian appropriation and worried about how the final outcome would affect him. Keokuk was more optimistic. He assured Davenport that he would never lose because Davenport and Farnham had treated him so generously. In St. Louis, Chouteau was also anxious about his company getting the money. As the executor of Farnham's estate he inquired of the Commissioner of Indian Affairs in Washington whether he could be paid directly or if he had to go through the Superintendent of Indian Affairs. It was a large sum of money and everyone wanted to be paid.[5]

Davenport was still collecting furs, but it is unclear whether they were coming more from Indians or settlers. In early April 1834, he sent to St. Louis ten packs of muskrat skins, two packs of raccoon and two packs of deer, and one bundle of deer, plus a box of miscellaneous furs and one box of merchandize. It is also unclear whether this was the total amount of furs collected that year. What is clear is that the Sauk and Mesquakie debts continued to mount. The Sac Outfit 1834 owed a total of $25,273.96 from his three posts (Ft. Edwards, Rock Island, and on the Ioway). The Sac Outfit 1835 owed $27, 582.70, and the Sac Outfit 1836 owed $44,338.28. In 1837, the Sac Outfit was $17,897.63 in arrears.[6]

Ledgers recording Davenport's returns during this time period are sparse, so it not certain how much of those debts the Sauk were able to pay off with their hunt, if any, for these year, but it is plain to see that the returns were a far cry from earlier years' hunts. Where once there were hundreds of pounds of furs collected in the spring, in the year 1835 there were only 845 muskrats, 34 mink, 63 raccoons, 26 otter, 1 bear skin and 6 and a half pounds of beaver. As Indian Agent Joseph Street indicated to Henry Dodge, Governor of Wisconsin Territory and Superintendent of Indian Affairs, the fur business was nil. "Young Davenport," he wrote to Henry Dodge, "says no furs are coming in."[7]

Distractions increased from the Sioux, the Menominee, and the Ho Chunk as well as the increasing numbers of settlers, and the Sauk and Mesquakie spent less and less time in the pursuit of game. They could often be found hanging around the groceries in both Stephenson and Davenport, especially in the winter months. In the summers they engaged again and again in revenge attacks. Davenport spent a considerable amount of time attending councils designed to convince the tribes to give up murderers.[8]

Davenport's relationship with the Phelps Brothers was contentious. Their post at Yellow Banks, in Illinois, was a source of temptation to Sauk and Mesquakie hunters, and Phelps undercut Davenport's business by lowering his prices. Davenport had authorized his men to counter. "Mr. Phelps is making great fuss amongst the Indians taking four Musk Rat Skins for a dollar and to Sell the three point Blankets for Six dollars or keep them and to imploy (sic) Indians and Send Skins to purchase his Blankets. I have authorized my Men to give five dollars for good otter." It was not the only problem between them. A formal complaint had been lodged against Phelps, charging him with inducing the Indians to hunt and trade in Illinois contrary to the provisions of the Treaty of 1832. Phelps believed that Davenport had instigated the "lie" as he called it as a reason to revoke Phelps' license.[9]

Indian Agent Joseph Street, who was a friend of Davenport, consulted with Black Hawk. Street saw the situation differently. He believed that the source of the problem was the location of Phelps trading post where the Indians brought their furs to exchange for merchandize. Phelps had probably not asked the Indians to hunt in Illinois, said Street, but the location of Phelps' post was enough inducement for the hunters to go into Illinois, close to settlers' communities. To his credit, Black Hawk and some of his band had sought permission to hunt in Illinois the previous year, but had been denied permission. Although he continued to work with William Phelps until 1840 or so, Davenport also engaged Wharton McPherson for the Des Moines River post. He outfitted Josiah Smart and Gilbert on the Ioway River.[10]

There were inter-tribal problems that affected Davenport's business as well, internal problems revolving around their annuities and how they were paid to the tribes. Without successful hunts, the Indians were dependent on their annuities as their biggest source of income. There were rumors in the villages, however, that Keokuk was hoarding the annuities for himself and spending it frivolously. Some of the village chiefs were concerned that their people, the ones who needed money most, were not getting their fair share of the annuities. Davenport was of the opinion that this was a malicious rumour against Keokuk, without any basis in fact, and that the truth would come out in the end. Nevertheless, Poweshiek and a small group of his followers requested a council with Indian Agent Street, the Commander of Fort Armstrong, and their trader George Davenport to discuss changing the way the tribes were paid. They met for three days at Rock Island in early June 1835. After much discussion, Lt. Colonel William Davenport reminded Poweshiek that his people owed the trader George Davenport for debts accumulated the past year, debts they had promised to pay from their annuities. Colonel Davenport also suggested that the tribes should decide what they wanted to do in the future, so that everyone would be clear and know how to handle next year's payment. After conferring among themselves overnight, Poweshiek and his people agreed that they should keep things as they were and payments should go to the Chief, Keokuk.[11]

This was an important decision for Davenport as it meant that some of the tribal debts could be repaid. The returns for 1835 are incomplete with only the returns at Rock Island noted in Davenport's Account Book for May 20 - July 27, 1835, but those records show a fair return for that one post: 882 muskrat skins, 83 raccoons, 28 otter. There were no notations of the returns from McPherson's Outfit on the Des Moines, or from Smart and Gilbert's Outfit on the Ioway, although lists of goods sent to these outfits were noted. If the returns from those posts were as good as Davenport's at Rock Island, then the hunt was acceptable.[12]

By late fall of 1835, Indian Agent Street reported that the Sauk were, for the most part, settled on the Des Moines River and the Mesquakie on the Cedar and Ioway Rivers. Although uncertain about their numbers, Street estimated that there were about 3,600 Mesquakie and 1,200 Sauk, out of which there were about 800 warriors. Their villages were well situated on the border of the prairie with fresh water and timber areas nearby. Street was unsure how productive the little garden plots around their houses were for producing all the corn that the villages needed, and indicated that some of the people were in danger of starving.

Keokuk, Street reported, seemed interested in farming in the white man's manner and had even requested assistance in learning how to split rails for fencing, but the hired men had not been able to teach him and Keokuk dismissed them. Keokuk did not understand the principles of splitting wood and had become so frustrated that he quit. Street warned William Clark, Superintendent of Indian Affairs, that providing the Indians with a few plows and hoes was not enough. What Keokuk needed was oxen, men to help break the prairie, and men to show his people how farming is done. Keokuk wanted large common fields like the French settlers had for each village, fenced in the American manner, on which to raise cattle and hogs. The Indians had no knowledge about such ventures. Keokuk's horses were unable to break the prairie, and the ploughs and hoes sent by the Quartermaster at St. Louis came too late in the season to be of use. Unfortunately, the Sauk and Mesquakie villages were situated too close to the border established by the 1832 Treaty and white settlement was already infringing on Indian lands.[13]

Accustomed to hunting along the major waterways and in the forests, many hunters returned from the prairie to their old hunting grounds now occupied by settlers. Those who knew the tribal ways observed that they were less and less successful as hunters and becoming nuisances among settlers. Unless they turned to farming they would become shiftless wanderers who had nothing but time on their hands, susceptible to alcohol and to those who had no interest in their welfare. Davenport could see that eventually they would become dependent on the government for their very subsistence. The hunters often came to visit the trading posts of George Davenport, both on the island and near the present-day site of Muscatine, partly out of habit, partly out of having no where else to go. There they were viewed with suspicion and fear by settlers who did not understand the ways or needs of these people.[14]

Mrs. Davenport's nieces told of their own encounters with roving bands of Indians. It was a familiar tale to those who lived on the prairies at that time. One day when her nephew James Bowling was away, a group of Indians came to their cabin and tried to get in. Fortunately, the women had secured the door by pulling the gimlet over the latch. They remained silent as the Indians tried to force their way into the house, but eventually the Indians pushed out the chinking and were able to reach the gimlet. The three women then braced the door with all their strength and the Indians finally tired of the effort and left.[15]

Now that the Sauk and Mesquakie had been removed to the interior of Iowa, the Adjutant General's Office determined that the threat of Indian attacks was over and Fort Armstrong was no longer needed. The fort was closed on 10th of May 1836 and the soldiers re-assigned to Fort Snelling. One officer and ten soldiers remained until the public property of the fort was sold later that summer. The Indian Agency, however, remained open on Rock Island under the direction of Indian Agent Joseph M. Street.[16] Periodically the Sauk and Mesquakie would come to Rock Island in great numbers to discuss selling their lands in order that they might move further away from both white men and the Sioux. George L. Davenport, who was beginning to take greater responsibility in the trade, and his cousin James Bowling were often present at these talks. George Davenport, too, was often present.

One such council house meeting at Ft. Armstrong was described by Cyrus Dickson, who observed the council with his father William on the 30th of May 1836. About four hundred to five hundred braves of both tribes were encamped on the island and there were about 30 chiefs in council.

"I have never seen a more agust(sic) and awful band of men. Keokuk sat on the front bench at the extreme right. He opened the council by rising and shaking hands with Genl Street, and A. LeClaire I. interpreter and Gen Davenport I. Trade. He then made a short but impressive speech, his gestures nay his whole demeanor was very graceful. He is a tall portly dignified looking Indian and has perfect phisogognomy(sic) of wisdom and cunning in a word greatness in all its meanings ... He finished by [unknown word] ceremony and a unanimous grunt or 'ugh' from the chiefs manifested their complete approbation ...Then Wapello or the 'Stabbing Chief' the war chief arose and shook hands with the same gentlemen. He began dignified and calm but soon burst forth in all the storm and tempest of furious eloquence ... Eight chiefs spoke the calumet was passed the council ended and the warriors retired with slow and solemn pace from the fort to their encampment a short distance up the island. It was a solemn thought to reflect that every man in that council had slain a fellow being before he was entitled to a seat in council or to the appellation of a Brave "[17]

Keokuk was particularly anxious to sell his reserve land and had had a letter written to Governor Reynolds to lay the proposition before the President. He and other chiefs wanted to visit Washington City to arrange a sale, even offering to pay for the trip themselves out of the proceeds of the sale. In support of this, Davenport reminded his Congressman, George W. Jones, that the lands were valuable, especially Keokuk's Reserve near Flint Hills, and "verrey much wanted by the Settlers."[18] The trip to Washington City, however, was denied and the Indians came to Rock Island instead.

The treaty was held on the west bank of the Mississippi in September 1836 with Governor Dodge acting as commissioner for the U.S. Government. About a thousand chiefs and warriors attended, camping along the river. Black Hawk, Neapope, and the Prophet attended but had no voice in the matter. The traders presented their claims against the tribes, and the numbers were astounding. The tribal leaders admitted a debt of $48,458.87 to various trading companies and acknowledged that the traders, especially George Davenport, had served a helpful role to them. Keokuk particularly recognized this role of Davenport when he said of Davenport: "He furnishes clothing, powder and lead, and if game is scarce he furnishes us food."[19] It was a simple statement, but one which carried much meaning. Although still respected for his friendship with the tribal leaders and trusted to speak on their behalf, there was little Davenport could do. The Indian Trade had changed from a profitable business relationship to charity for the tribes. The exchange of furs was now an exchange for land.

Pratte, Chouteau and Co. submitted the largest claim of $20,362.42 and a half-cent, which included some of George Davenport's trade to the Sauk Outfits through his various traders. The Davenports' personal claim was only $2,563.50, a significant sum but a far cry from the business they once had with the Sauk and Mesquakie. Le Claire's claim was about equal to Davenport's. By contrast, John Campbell claimed a debt of $10,000, an indication of how much Davenport had reduced his business with the tribes.

To settle their debts and provide for future support, the Sauk and Mesquakie sold Keokuk's Reserve along the Ioway River, 256,000 acres of land for $192,000 or about seventy-five cents per acre. The treaties were signed on the 27th and 28th of September 1836 and the tribes agreed to move from the ceded lands by the first of November 1837.[20]

The Sauk and Mesquakie, however, did not find peace in their new homes on the Iowa and Cedar rivers and wanted to sell more of their lands. The Government was agreeable. In May of 1837, another council was held at the Davenport house to consider an invitation by Washington City authorities for chiefs of the Sauk and Mesquakie nations to visit that city. Present at the council were large numbers of chiefs and braves, including Keokuk, Pashepaho, Wapello, and Poweshiek.[21] In September, George Davenport and his son, as well as Antoine Le Claire as Interpreter, and Joseph Street as Indian Agent, accompanied Keokuk, Wapello, Poweshiek, Black Hawk and about forty other chiefs and prominent braves to Washington City. On the surface, the invitation was a peace settlement between the Sauk and Mesquakie and the Sioux, but the underlying object of the visit was to impress upon the Sauk and Mesquakie how numerous the white men were, and why it was necessary for the Indians to move even further West.

In late August, before heading to Washington City, the Mesquakie again attacked the Sioux. Davenport reported the Mesquakie side of the story in a letter to the Galena Advertiser. The Mesquakie hunting party was starving and found Sioux encroaching on their hunting grounds. Several Chiefs were mortally wounded, the band scattered, and no annuities had been forthcoming according to their Treaty agreements. If, said the editor, the government is serious about taking care of these people, the Indian Agents should be so informed and see that they are properly taken care of. It was clear to the newspaper editor that the Indian situation was a government problem and that residents wanted nothing to do with the Indian situation.[22]

The delegation of Sauk and Mesquakie, headed by Keokuk, left for Washington City on the 12th of September. It was a large delegation including Chauncey Bush, the current Secretary of War, Joshua Pilcher who had been at Rock Island during the Black Hawk War, Antoine Le Claire who served as interpreter, S.C. Stambaugh from Fort Snelling and P.G. Hambaugh, sutler's assistant at Fort Armstrong. George and George L. Davenport were both with them. On the 29th of September Cyrus Dickson wrote that he had seen Mr. Davenport and his son on the road, and that they remembered him and would he please tell Mrs. Davenport that he was well?[23] One month later the Sauk and Mesquakie ceded one and a quarter million acres of land west of the lands ceded in 1832. With the exception of Keokuk's village, which was allowed to remain for two more years, the Sauk and Mesquakie agreed to move within eight months of the ratification of this treaty.[24] That was not much time to cultivate their present fields into production and the Indians were learning that their old ways were not as useful as those of the white settlers.

The summer hunts were becoming more and more dangerous for all tribes, especially the Sauk and Mesquakie. The chances of coming upon a party of enemies increased as the hunting grounds decreased. In August of 1837, Street reported that a hunting party of about 200 men, women, and children was led by Wacoshasee to look for buffalo. They encountered some Sioux hunters and attacked them. They were outnumbered and suffered a loss of eleven warriors and thirteen wounded.[25]

Negotiating peace among the tribes who had long considered each other enemies was not easy and the peace negotiations that were taking place that summer in Washington City were not successful. The Sauk and Mesquakie sat down with a party of the Sioux, but the two tribes were unable to settle their differences. Cary Harris, Commissioner of Indian Affairs, however, managed to convince the Sauk and Mesquakie to cede another sizable parcel of land, one and one quarter million acres of their Iowa holdings. In exchange the U.S. Government agreed to allow $100,000 to pay their debts to the traders, and provide gristmills and other agricultural benefits to the tribes.[26]

George Davenport continued to make public appeals for the Indians' assistance through the newspapers, calling for justice and humanity to do something to make their condition better. "They are truly friendly to the whites," he argued, "and no danger need be apprehended by our frontier settlements ... if the frontier settlers would enter into an association to prevent whiskey being sold or given to Indians, they would find them orderly people and good neighbors."[27] Frontier settlers, however, did not believe that. Despite the pleas of George Davenport and Indian Agent Joseph Street, most settlers were not concerned where the tribes should go, only that they go far away. They had no time or use for them as neighbors.

To help find a new village site after this latest treaty, a small party of men connected with Indian affairs traveled west, beyond the lands recently sold by the Sauk and Mesquakie, in order to establish a new Indian village. This was in May of 1838. George L. Davenport along with Indian Agent Joseph Street, James MacIntosh, Louis Hebert as interpreter, Indian Blacksmith H. Sturdevant, and Surveyor W. Russel journeyed with 30 to 40 chiefs and braves commanded by Poweshiek as the official search party. The newly ceded lands stretched to a point about 76 miles from Rock Island and the search party sought to establish a village beyond that point. Near the Cedar River, south of what is now Iowa City, a village site was selected. The site was not perfectly situated, being too close to Sioux hunting grounds and thus subject to attack. Some recent campfires were spotted, but with constant lookout, it would serve for a time. The site was surveyed and made official. George L. Davenport's presence on this search is another indication that he was taking a more dominant role in what remained with the Davenport's Indian trade.[28]

At age 55, the elder Davenport was looking forward to devoting his time to improving his property, which was considerable at that time. It may be that the years of Indian trade had taken their toll on him. It was, after all, a physically challenging profession, full of dangers, exposure to the elements, and often led to premature exhaustion and disability. Few traders, according to Secretary of War Lewis Cass, reached "an advanced stage of life, and still fewer preserve[d] an unbroken constitution" as Davenport had done.[29] He and his son began to withdraw from the business.

There were more than personal reasons for the Davenports' decision, including the United States Removal Policy on Indians, and strained Indian-White relationships. George alluded to these changes in his letter to Cary Harris, Commissioner of Indian Affairs. The problem of the Sauk and Mesquakie, according to the letter, lay in the unlicensed trader who stooped to unscrupulous practices such as selling whiskey, high-priced horses, and unnecessary goods to the Indians as soon as the annuities were paid. Under such a practice the annuity lasted only ten days before it was squandered. This left the Indians destitute for the remainder of the year, leaving only their land as a marketable commodity.

Davenport had always advocated a morally responsible system whereby licensed or authorized traders exercised careful control over the annuities, and he called attention to that with a plan to the current Indian Affairs Representative. The trader would safeguard the funds for the entire year by selling only necessary goods. The restricted goods would be blankets, strouds, and calico to clothe their families and hunting items such as gunpowder, lead, knives, axes, hoes, traps, rifles, and flint. These items, he suggested, should be sold on credit, with the settlement of debts to be authorized by the chiefs at annuity time the following year. Without this credit system which he had practiced for twenty years, Davenport felt the Sauk and Fox would be "compelled ... to kill the cattle of the settlers or starve as their is little game in the country."[30]

President Jackson's Removal Act had turned the Indian trade into a governmental means for acquiring Indian lands. The traders were encouraged to facilitate removal of the tribes, by promoting huge debts among the Indian tribes. Then, as a means to settle these debts, they encouraged the tribes to sell their lands. Removal of Indians to reservations was becoming a profit-making business for some traders. In anticipation of a treaty negotiation, several of the tribe's traders provided particularly attractive, but unnecessary, goods on credit and inflated the tribal debt which would be paid by the government. Traders could bid for the right to outfit and remove tribes to their designated reservation lands on a per capita basis. The Ewing brothers of Indiana were prime examples of this new big money business. Although George Davenport had publicly expressed his support of the president's policy, the Davenports had no desire to be a part of such business. He insisted on the trader's job security and was no longer willing to take the risks he had taken in his younger years. He and his son officially resigned from the Indian Trade in 1842.

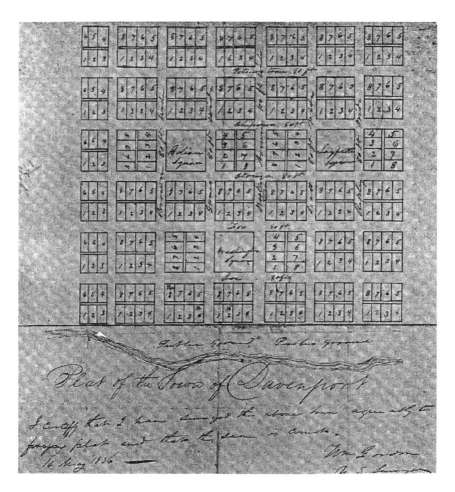

William Gordon, U.S. Surveyor, submitted this Plat of the Town of Davenport on 12th of May 1836.

CHAPTER FIFTEEN:

A NEW TOWN IN IOWA

SOMETIMES IT HAPPENED that large acres of land were unknowingly claimed by two different men who had no knowledge of one another. This happened in the winter of 1833 when John W. Spencer of Rock Island county and Solomon McCloud claimed the same parcel. The dispute had become ugly, so Le Claire stepped in as peacemaker. He first convinced McCloud to sell to Spencer, and then talked Spencer into selling the claim to Le Claire, all 111 acres of the disputed land (in March 1834). Le Claire then erected a log house on the site and rented the land to Stephen Burtis until Le Claire could take up residence on the land himself.[1]

The site seemed like an ideal place for a town. It was located directly across the river from Stephenson and had once been the site of the Mesquakie village of Oshkosh. It was situated on high ground and blessed with waterpower, stone, coal, and timber in the near vicinity.[2] Additionally, it had a good landing place for steamboats and was an ideal place for boats to take on fuel, lighten their loads, and engage knowledgeable pilots before tackling the difficult rapids. Between the riverbank and the bluffs, there was enough room for a good-size town. It was also adjacent to Le Claire's grant of land from the Treaty of 1832 where he was already living.

Le Claire had built his home on the site of the treaty talks, satisfying the requirements of the land grant, but he had more than enough land to farm, perhaps too much and he did not need this additional 111 acres. To turn this site into a viable town would take money, money that Le Claire did not have. As interpreter he had earned a mere $400 each year, a good living, but hardly enough money for financing development. Trading with the Indians was perhaps a little more profitable, but that business would soon move beyond the Mississippi River, and Le Claire did not seem inclined to move with them. He could sell the land as large parcels of farmland, but a more profitable option was to build a town. By dividing a parcel of land into town lots a landowner could sell the same land for many times more than the $1.25 an acre that government land was selling for. Le Claire had no experience in such an undertaking, but his friend George Davenport had both money and experience.

Town founding was big business in the mid 1830s. The rapid increase in the populations of Indiana, Ohio, Michigan, Illinois, Missouri was phenomenal, credit was easily obtainable, and speculating reached feverish levels. Sales of the public lands were brisk and the numbers confirmed what everyone thought. People weren't just moving west, but actually settling. In Illinois, between 1830 and 1835, the population nearly doubled, from 157,445 to 269,974.[3] The new county seat of Rock Island County, just across the river from Le Claire's most recent purchase, was almost an overnight success in attracting settlers. The rapid growth was evident in the number of both private and governmental buildings. Iowa lands, too, were attracting huge numbers of immigrants and Le Claire was eager to take advantage of that.

Sometime in late fall of 1835, seven men met at Davenport's house to discuss Le Claire's town proposition and work out some details of the venture. By the time Davenport requested a copy of the plat of Le Claire's claim the following February the plan was probably well underway because the official agreement was signed a few days later on 23rd of February (1836). In all, there were eight investors in the venture: Antoine Le Claire, George Davenport, Major William Gordon, Major Thomas Smith, Alexander McGregor, Levi S. Colton, and Philip Hambaugh. Captain James May was in Pittsburgh at the signing but was included as the eighth proprietor. Each man agreed to pay Le Claire $ 250 and all eight would share the expenses of laying out and improving the town. McGregor soon sold his share to Captain Stanton Sholes, who became the eighth proprietor. They agreed to act as proprietors until the last lot was sold.[4] Unlike Stephenson, which was laid out and organized by the county commissioners, this town was a totally private enterprise, funded by the proprietors themselves. It was, in some ways, a stock company in which all profits would be divided equally.

They called this town Davenport. Why and for whom has been the subject of much debate. Some thought it should have been named after Le Claire, but Le Claire, Iowa, had already been platted at the upper end of the Rapids. Others believed it was named after Colonel William Davenport, the last commander of Fort Armstrong, but this Colonel Davenport had no association with Le Claire or with the town founding. Others attribute the name to Marmaduke Davenport whose son Adrian was one of the founders of Rockingham, a town now absorbed into the Davenport city limits. But the definitive answer came from Antoine Le Claire, who acknowledged that he himself suggested the name in honor of his friend, George Davenport.

It was a brilliant marketing strategy. George Davenport's name and reputation were well known in the Mississippi Valley. He was long established in the area, and his name was known to most. Furthermore, he was considered honest and forthright in his business dealings. Anything that carried his name would also be, by association, honest and trustworthy. Le Claire must have known that with his name and reputation at stake, George Davenport would surely do all that he could to make this project a success. And he was right. It was an honor for which George Davenport would work very hard to be worthy.

The proprietors were a mix of old and young men whose reasons for engaging in this venture were as varied as their ages and their backgrounds. Each brought a variety of skills, ideas, and expectations to this venture, but success depended on their cooperation and collective efforts as well as good financial backing. Only Davenport had any experience in town planning and developing.

Smith, Gordon, and Hambaugh were attached to the Fort Armstrong. William Gordon was a government surveyor who had designed many area town plats. He was probably about 42, unattached, and considered quite a ladies' man. Philip Hambaugh was young, also unmarried, and working as the assistant sutler at Fort Armstrong. He had come to Brown County, Illinois, with his family in 1824 and had previously worked as a clerk in the Quartermaster Department at Fort Winnebago. He and Gordon had partnered before, buying Rock Island County land together. Major Thomas Floyd Smith was 51 and married to Emilie Chouteau, the youngest daughter of Auguste Chouteau of the famous Chouteau family of St. Louis. Smith was a family man with five living children. While in the Army, Smith had opened the Yellow River sawmill, which had provided wood for the construction of Fort Crawford and he had taken command of Fort Armstrong between December 1832 and June 1833. He was well aware of the water potential of the area and since 1832, Smith had been investing in land while he served out his time in the army.[5]

Captain James May was a Pittsburgh businessman and riverboat captain. He owned and operated the steamboat Dove on the Mississippi River. May was 39 years of age and his interest was primarily as an investor. He had already invested in other towns on the river. Levi Colton had been a sergeant in the Fifth infantry and stationed at Fort Armstrong. He was newly married and his wife Harriet was expecting their first child. He had engaged in some Indian trading and worked for Le Claire as his ferry operator. Although Alexander McGregor had sold his share in the town plan before the town materialized, he served as the town's prosecuting attorney and established the law firm of McGregor, Lewis, and Blakemore. He lived on Fifth Street (near Western Avenue) until his death in 1857. McGregor's substitute, Captain Stanton Sholes, was originally from Connecticut and had served in the War of 1812. Sholes was about 63 years of age and had come to the Mississippi Valley with his adopted daughter and her spouse, the Reverend Elnathan Gavitt.[6]

The burden of developing the town was essentially left to Le Claire and Davenport who remained on the ground. They were no dreamers with visions of a golden metropolis rising magically up on the banks of the Mississippi, but practical, pragmatic men who understood the risks and the hard work that it would take to make this vision a reality. Gordon began immediately to lay out the town into city lots, following the same general guidelines of the town of Stephenson the year before. Because this land was in Michigan Territory, whose capital was hundreds of miles away, the proprietors had virtual autonomy in the execution of their plans. References in the Le Claire Papers suggest that the original plat was officially recorded in the Territorial Deed Book.[7]

The town was designed in a grid pattern, six blocks by six and a half square blocks, with ten lots on each block. Three squares reserved for the development of public buildings suggest that the proprietors had big plans for the site. Professor John Reps, in The Making of Urban America, suggests that the plat of Davenport was a little more creative than the standard plat since lots surrounding each public square faced the square. Indeed, the proprietors were thinking big for this town. It was also, Repp says, " a realization that some degree of municipal control over land development was not incompatible with a democratic society."[8] One square was reserved for the city hall, one for a fine county seat courthouse, and the third for the Territorial capital building. It was ambitious indeed.

Sometime in the spring of 1836, Major Gordon completed the plat and by May the proprietors were ready to hold a public auction. Advertisements appeared two months prior to the sale in a number of newspapers including the Northwestern Gazette and Galena Advertiser.

The advertisement took a little different tactic than many town sale ads of that time. It began, "Aware of the ridiculous custom of newspaper puffing," and then proceeded to lay out the advantages of the site with a minimum of exaggeration. The town had all the usual advantages, with a singular creative perk -- it was suitable as a resort for those living in the South, a cool location from which one could escape the summer heat of St. Louis, Memphis, and other cities in the lower Mississippi. It was an appeal to St. Louis investors and others from the south who were expected to attend the auction.[9]

A steamboat from St. Louis brought prospective investors and served as a floating base as there were no hotels or visitor accommodations yet available. Wilkie says that the steamboat remained at the levee during the two-day sale, providing lodging, food, and drink for the prospective buyers.[10] Sales, however, were disappointing. Only fifty to sixty lots were sold, mostly to St. Louis speculators. The lots, according to Wilkie, brought only a total of $500 to $600, a smaller sum than hoped for.

Who attended the sale is not certain, but three men with French backgrounds and connections to St. Louis appear in the deeds. One was John La Mont, who bought two lots but died before the transaction was completed. His estate was handled by George Collier and Pierre Chouteau Jr., an indication that La Mont was a member of the French community in St. Louis. Lambert La Pierre was another buyer with French St. Louis connections to the fur trade. He was originally from the St. Louis area but more recently employed on the Island as a blacksmith with the Indian Agency. La Pierre was married to the widow of Davenport's former partner John Connelly and living on the Island. Before the town was built, however, La Pierre and his wife were drowned in a boating accident on the Slough one day when the ice was breaking up.

The third French name, that of John Macklot, is particularly noteworthy because he bought a total of eighteen lots in the original town plat of Davenport. Jean Nicholas Macklot was a St. Louis merchant with connections to the Chouteaus and other influential French families there. He had been born in France and married Marie Therese Gratiot, daughter of Charles Gratiot known for his involvement in the Indian

Trade.[11] Monsieur Macklot settled in Davenport with his wife and young children, operated a general store, and belonged to St. Anthony's Catholic Church until his death in 1850.

The terms of sale were reasonable and standard for the time and similar to those given at the Stephenson sales the previous year: one third paid at the time of the purchase, the balance to be paid in two equal instalments, one payable in twelve months, the second payable when a good and sufficient title could be issued.[12] Clear title, however, was an issue, because Le Claire had not yet received his title for this land. He had claimed it as a pre emption claim and buyers were leery, especially speculators who wanted to make quick profits on their lots. To allay the fears of buyers, Le Claire issued a title bond at the time of each purchase, but even this did not stimulate sales.

The problem lay not with Le Claire, but with the Government Land Office. With the large amount of Public Land sales in the preceding years, the Land Office had been overwhelmed with administrative problems. Certificates had been issued slowly. In an effort to push the process, the citizens of Davenport petitioned Congress, explaining their situation and requesting that Le Claire's pre-emption claim be granted quickly. It was referred on the 14th of February 1838 to the Committee on Public Lands, but not until the 20th of September 1839 did they receive official title to the town.[13]

While they waited for clear title, Davenport and Le Claire began the work of attracting permanent residents by constructing public buildings, hiring men to operate them, and starting new businesses in partnership. After a short time, they divided their interests with each taking on new partners and then each moving on to new ventures. It was a slow, but effective, way to build a town.

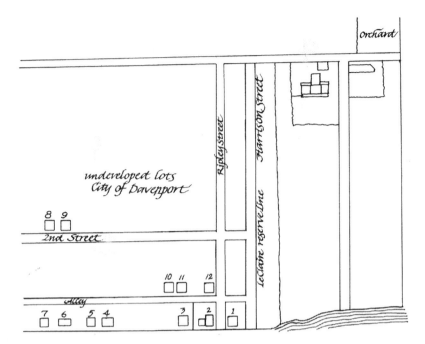

The town of Davenport grew slowly. This map, originally hand drawn by George Parker, illustrates the earliest inhabitants and the buildings that had been built by February 1837. The existing buildings all lay west of Ripley Street, along Front and 2nd streets. The Le Claire house and orchard, not numbered, are outlined east of the town on land now lying near the intersection of River Drive and 3rd. Used with permission of Putnam Museum and Archives.

1. Davenport Hotel frame built by G. Davenport and Antoine Le Claire, Edward Powers Landlord
2. Davenport Hotel frame building built by Davenport and Le Claire,
3. Log cabin occupied by Mr. Allen, wife and two children
4. Large two-story frame, enclosed but not finished inside, occupied by J. Forrest
5. Hewed log house, Levi Coltons occupied by himself
6. Double log building first building in the old town and used by Mr. Colton as a ferry house
7. Captain Litch's grocery and saloon
8. Indian gun shop log building Harvey Sturdevant, gun smith
9. Indian Blacksmith's shop, LaPerche, Blacksmith, and Cooper Shop
10. Log house, J, McIntosh Store
11. Log house, James Kelly, Irishman Tailor by trade
12. Frame Stable for the hotel

At first there was just one main street through town, lying parallel with the river. The first buildings appeared there on what was called Front Street. Captain Litch, an old seafaring man from Newburyport, New

Hampshire, opened a whiskey shop in a single-room, shingled log cabin that measured 16' x 20'. Litch was said to have been a jovial man, "full of anecdotes, and ever ready to toss off a glass of grog with anyone who desired to join him."[14] It may not have been the kind of respectable shop that attracted permanent settlers, but it served a need, and it was a start.

The birth of the first child in Davenport that year to Proprietor Levi Colton and his wife must have seemed like an omen of good things to come. By the end of 1836, Pioneer Willard Barrows recalled that there were only six or seven houses in town and the population had reached 60 souls. George Parker, who arrived in the spring of 1837, remembered those structures and sketched a rough drawing of the fledgling settlement.[15]

Levi Colton built a hewed log cabin for his family with a double log cabin next door to serve as the base for his ferry business. Mr. Sholes erected a two-story frame house next to them and the Reverend Gavitt and his family moved in. Further on was the house of Mr. and Mrs. Allen and their two children. Then came the Davenport Hotel and the house and store of D.C. Eldridge. Across from the hotel were three structures: the house of James McIntosh, the tailor house of James Kelly, and a stable for the hotel. Further from the river, and away from the main part of town, were two businesses designed to serve the Indians' needs: Harvey Sturdevant's gun shop and the Indian blacksmith operated by La Perche. Parker, who drew his map of the fledgling town from memory, may have mis-remembered the blacksmith's name which was actually La Pierre, a blacksmith and a purchaser of a lot in the original town.[16]

According to a number of pioneer reminiscences, Davenport and Le Claire did everything in their power to help these new arrivals. George Davenport offered his home and other assistance to people interested in settling. One story is about William L. Cook whose family stayed with the Davenports on the island while they selected land and built a log cabin. Later William Cook would build a much finer home of native stone.[17]

Another story involved Capt. Stanton Sholes, his wife, and the family of Rev. E.C. Gavitt. When their party arrived at the eastern shore of the river they found a temporary home for which they agreed to pay a dollar per day. The house had been used as Litch's whiskey establishment and the Indians, thinking the newcomers had whiskey for sale, made the first night for these people a night to remember. When George Davenport heard of the predicament, he sent two sail boats to take the families to the island, where he gave them more comfortable living quarters, a cow, and other necessities until a new house in town could be built for them. Mr. Stanton Sholes witnessed the signing of the Articles of Agreement to the town of Davenport, and later bought McGregor's share. Sholes built one of the first public houses, later called the Dillon House, near the river. Reverend Gavitt preached the first sermon in Davenport.[18]

Another story came from D. C. Eldridge who with his family was heading downriver to St. Louis late one fall when winter came early and their flatboat was stranded by ice in the river. Several settlers came to their rescue and they built a cabin with wood salvaged from their boat. The family decided to stay. Mr. Eldridge began to sell groceries while his wife made bread and dried apple pies to sell.[19]

In yet another example, Davenport provided Indian guides across the prairies for settlers when there were no trails to follow. One time when a flock of sheep was being driven north, the sharp prairie grasses cut into the sheep' flesh and, instead of letting them die on the trail, Davenport bought them all. Old Pioneers remembered Davenport as a good and accommodating man who helped others and kept them from bankruptcy.[20]

Le Claire was also known as a generous man whose payrolls show that he, too, supported a number of pioneer families. Serving as a bank in those early days, Le Claire loaned money, sometimes accepting household goods and other possessions as collateral. The terms were often short in duration, but that was standard for the day. Most loans were to be repaid within a year or two and interest rates were sometimes as high as 8%. These were the ways that Davenport and Le Claire encouraged people to stay.

Davenport and Le Claire also discouraged people whom they thought were not the right sorts of people for their town. One well-known story was told by the Clark family, who had settled too close to Davenport's property in Illinois. Davenport used a number of what the Clark's called dirty tricks to discourage the Clark family from settling. He did not tolerate the Clarks' competition and eventually convinced the family to move several miles downriver. They never forgave Davenport for the grief he caused them and were rather vocal about their unfair treatment. Davenport was indeed possessive of his claims, especially where he had built his home.

In order to accommodate the growing number of immigrants Davenport and Le Claire began building the Davenport Tavern House together in 1836. They paid the Incorporation $457 for Lots 4 and 5 in Block 6 (now the southwest corner of River Drive and Ripley Streets) and contracted with Zadoc Kalbough and Mr. Casteel of Rock Island County to build the house and all the structures associated with it -- the bell tower, the necessary house, and the adjoining stable.[21] The Tavern house was a two-story structure that contained an office, a bar room, kitchen, and cellar or vault, plus an undetermined number of sleeping rooms. It was framed with logs hewn on the site, but much of the millwork was obtained from Philadelphia, since there were no locally produced pine planks, window sashes, doors, etc. The construction was completed by early December and was managed by Edward Powers, who lived in Rock Island and was a brother of the well-known riverboat captain.

The grand opening of the Davenport Tavern House was commemorated with a ball. Thirty couples, plus a number of men who came stag, attended. Every room except the bar room was used for dancing. A traveling minstrel provided the violin music. The whole place was lit by candlelight and sperm oil lamps and gaily decorated for the occasion. Refreshments were served buffet style since there were not enough tables for all to be seated at one time. For a few years the Davenport Tavern House, also known as the Davenport Hotel, was in the centre of town. It was the place where the Iowa volunteers rendezvoused when the call to arms came in the Iowa-Missouri boundary dispute, and was at center stage in the bitter county seat battle between Davenport and Rockingham. It was later enlarged and operated by Samuel Barkley who had emigrated from Pennsylvania.[22]

Having an inn was important to a fledgling town, but a well-stocked store was essential. Under the name of Davenport and Le Claire, the partners established a general merchandize store in 1838 on the Northeast corner of Front and Main streets. It was reputed to be the best-stocked store for miles around, specializing in dry goods -- men's and women's ready-made clothing and yard goods -- but also a large variety of other supplies for the new settlers: spades, scythes, sickles and stone hammers; riding equipment such as bridles, saddles, saddle bags, and whips; and household items such as canisters and cooking pots, Epsom salts for sore muscles, and window panes for the new structures. Groceries, provisions and liquor were also available. Levi C. Turner was their agent in procuring goods and merchandize from New York merchants along the Erie Canal. George L. Davenport managed the store for both partners from its inception.[23]

The Davenport-Le Claire partnership was dissolved after eight months when Le Claire took George L. Davenport as a full partner, and George Davenport Senior started a grocery business with Le Claire's nephew, William B. Watts. In this way they integrated their families into the businesses, provided for their futures, and expanded businesses for the new town. It all worked to create a sense of prosperity in town.[24]

These businesses weathered the financially challenging years of the depression and served as magnets, attracting other businesses to the area. They are illustrative of how Davenport and Le Claire worked together as well as in friendly competition to stimulate the economy in their newly founded town. They acted as banking institutions, investing their private money in both public and private enterprise and then selling them as established businesses when buyers became available.

It was not long before two of the proprietors, Gordon and Colton, planned an addition to the west side of the new town. They had speculated before in Stephenson with some success. Within a short time they sold a parcel of land to Anson Morey, a partner of Captain Litch, for $800. Although Morey sold a number of lots in his "addition," he later went bankrupt before his addition could develop, which effectively stifled development on the west side of town for many years.[25]

The entire Davenport family was involved in promoting the new town. Both of Mrs. Davenport's brothers had large families and the young people soon found their way to the Island where they found encouragement, support, and a home with the Davenports until they could establish themselves. One was James Copp. The other was James Bowling.

James Copp was a young Englishman from Devonshire. He was a butcher by trade and, with the help of Davenport, established a meat house in Stephenson (on the corner of Madison and Illinois Streets). He lived with the Davenports when he first arrived and was introduced to Margaret's nieces who had arrived in October of 1836. It wasn't long before he was an official member of the family. He and Sophia Bowling were married in March, 1838, in the Davenport House and raised a family of seven children in Rock Island.[26]

Nephew James Madison Bowling was the son of Margaret's brother Jeremiah who lived in Winchester, Virginia. James also lived at the Davenport house while hunting for land. The Davenports had pre-selected a number of interesting sites for him to consider, and he staked a claim south of town, between what is today Rockingham and Buffalo. Bowling then returned to Virginia to marry Margaret Pelletier. The newlyweds returned to Davenport the following October (1837) accompanied by Bowling's sisters, Sophia and Julia. Sophia married James Copp, as has been discussed, and Julia married William B. Watts. The re-establishing of family ties gradually grew into a strong kinship network around their Island home, something the Davenports had long been missing.

Since buyers had been leery of title difficulties in the original Davenport town site, Le Claire platted a piece of his reserve land as an addition to the town. Davenport purchased a half interest in the addition and together they offered seventy lots at public auction (June 1837). Buyers were more confident in the title to this addition and the lots sold quickly.

Several new businesses responded immediately. Harvey Leonard opened a brickyard on Sixth Street (between Main and Harrison) and

D.C. Eldridge built the first brick house and post office on the corner of 3rd and Main. Eldridge also started a carriage and blacksmith shop. The availability of brick materials, as well as stone from Le Claire's quarry upriver, influenced the cosmetic appearance of Davenport, which had, by the end of 1837, fifteen or sixteen houses.[27]

But then came the Panic of 1837. Almost as quickly as it started, the speculating boom was over. All those investors who had recently been snapping up land with an eye to quick sales and huge profits were suddenly caught, unable to make their first mortgage payments. Surprisingly, even more migrants from eastern cities began to head west. They were looking for cheap land and work.

When Michigan achieved statehood, jurisdiction of the Iowa lands was shifted to Wisconsin Territory and with it came the first real organization of government west of the Mississippi river. Two counties that had been established by Michigan Territory were divided into several smaller counties, one of which was Scott County. That set up a contentious fight between its two principal towns for its county seat, Rockingham and Davenport.

Election Day was set for the 6th of August 1838. Each town's proprietors were anxious to attract energetic and ambitious settlers who would add to the diverse nature of their town. Both set about recruiting people to swell their populations, even bringing in voters just for the occasion, because survival of the town rested on the election outcome.

Arriving in the middle of the controversy was the newspaper editor, Andrew Logan. Logan had had offers and promises of subscriptions for his newspaper in both Rockingham and Davenport, but he was enticed to Davenport with the promise of 500 subscribers. The town even suspended the Fourth of July celebrations until Logan and his wife, and their printing press, arrived from St. Louis. How a village with barely fifty or sixty persons could produce so many subscribers was a mystery until Le Claire admitted to signing up for fifty subscriptions for himself. Davenport and others had followed suit, so Logan was assured of a modest income for his paper. The first edition of the Iowa Sun was issued on the 15ᵗʰ of August 1838, and Logan supported his new hometown in its fight for the county seat.[28]

On Election Day, there were seven designated voting precincts. Rockingham citizens alleged that the Davenport proprietors had imported persons from Muscatine, Cedar, Clinton, and Jackson counties as well as miners from Dubuque to vote illegally. Because there was not enough housing in Davenport, it was alleged that the proprietors paid for their lodging in the town of Stephenson across the river. It was also alleged that Antoine Le Claire had tried to cast more than one vote and that his nephew, a minor, had also voted.[29]

Both sides were certain that they had won as the votes were sent to Territorial Governor Henry Dodge. Davenporters celebrated with bonfires and other expressions of joy and triumph, but Rockingham submitted charges of fraud to the Governor. The celebrations were put on hold until he could decide. Before a decision could be made, however, Wisconsin Territory was divided and Iowa Territory formed. Again, the election of the county seat was postponed for new rules.

Under provisions of the Iowa Organic Act, the Territorial Governor and other officers were appointed rather than elected and were political favors. President Martin Van Buren appointed Robert Lucas of Ohio as Governor and the territorial seat of government was Lucas' choice. All up and down the river, every little community began a campaign to be selected as the Territorial capital, including Rockingham and Davenport, which had already allocated a block of lots for the purpose.

It took some time before all the new officers could reach Iowa Territory. The first was the Territorial Secretary, William B. Conway of Pittsburgh. Conway had been a newspaper publisher who had supported Andrew Jackson and Martin Van Buren in their presidential campaigns. He had no prior experience in government. When Conway arrived in Davenport, he met George Davenport and Antoine Le Claire who wasted no time in promoting their town and convincing the young Conway that Davenport was THE Greatest Town in the territory, the coming city in the West, and the only proper place for the capital of Iowa Territory. Furthermore, they convinced Conway that, having arrived before the

Governor, he had the responsibilities of Acting Governor. Conway bought into their arguments and duly appointed Davenport as the capital of Iowa Territory. He also divided the Territory into three judicial districts and ordered an election for electing members to the legislature.

When Governor Robert Lucas arrived in Burlington a few weeks later he was far from pleased with these proclamations. He was not an easy man to get along with and was said to have a fiery temper and mean disposition when crossed. He immediately declared Conway's decisions null and void and rejected any and all input from Conway. Lucas and Conway never had time to resolve their differences, because Conway died suddenly of typhoid fever four months later, on the 6th of November 1839.[30]

Lucas temporarily settled in Bloomington, now Muscatine, Iowa, and purchased land there for a farm. Then he began to visit all the principal towns of the territory that lie along the bank of the Mississippi in order to get to know the people and the resources of the territory. He was wined and dined all along the way, and every town he visited thought it had the best chance of becoming the capital. When his trip was over, however, Lucas surprised everyone by appointing Burlington as the temporary capital of Iowa Territory. At the first session of the Territorial Legislature he appointed a commission of three to select a suitable site in the interior of Iowa for the permanent seat of government. This must have been disappointing to Davenport and Le Claire, but they still had a chance for their town to become the county seat.

At the second session of the legislature, an act providing for a second election for Scott County's seat was passed and the county seat fight was renewed. One new stipulation was made for this election: voters had to prove residency in the county for sixty days. The date set was the first Monday of August 1839.

Having lost in their bid for the territorial capital and with the new date set for the county seat election, the Davenport proprietors stepped up their recruiting. Again, both towns campaigned heavily. Building lots were offered in exchange for votes in Davenport. In Rockingham John H. Sullivan hired extra men to work in his flourmill. The newspaper became a useful advertising tool in Davenport. Passed along the river highways and exchanged with newspapers in far-flung cities and towns, the paper announced every little growth spurt in the town of Davenport. More businesses came: a sawmill, a millinery shop, and a watch and jewellery repair store. Not only was having a newspaper an important signal to the world that this town was growing, but it also said that Davenport was prosperous enough to support such endeavours.

On the day of the election the ballot box was again stuffed with more votes than residents. This time, Rockingham was declared the winner, but before the election results could be finalized, the ballot box was purged of illegal votes and Davenport was said to have won. Rockingham appealed and was again declared the winner, but before Rockingham could celebrate its victory, the Territorial Legislature called for a third election. This time, two more potential sites for the county seat were added. One was the geographical centre of the county, but this was dropped before the election. The second was a place called Winfield, a town at the mouth of Duck Creek that had not yet been platted. Once again, the proprietors of both towns ramped up the competition, offering lots and money for building a county courthouse in the winning city. Eventually a truce was called between the two towns. John H. Sullivan conceded on the condition that the town of Davenport would actually build the courthouse and jail and let him supervise the construction. A ball, attended by all the principal players in the contest, was held in the Rockingham Hotel to celebrate.

The town of Davenport capitalized on their victory and soon was beginning to look like a real town. In 1839, the Iowa Territorial Legislature incorporated Davenport as a town. The proprietorship of Le Claire, Davenport, and the six others was dissolved and a city government was created. The first city elections were held in April and city services, like the fire department, were organized. Steamboats kept the riverbanks full of goods for shipment to the interior of Iowa. Travellers and emigrants filled the town, seeking housing and business sites. Carpenters were hard pressed to keep up with the demand. Already there was a school run by the Reverend Michael Hummer where Davenport's younger son, Bailey, was attending. Bailey had had some schooling from a retired army man, Captain Stubbs, but Hummer's school, located on the corner of the alley east of Ripley Street between 1st and 2nd streets, was more formal in its organization. It operated from the fall of 1838 through the fall of 1839, when a common school, started by a Mr. Blood, began and the Misses O'Hara started a female seminary.[31] A steam-operated ferry between Rock Island and Davenport was introduced and a paint shop, wagon shop, and drug store were also opened.

Davenport and Le Claire recruited medical doctors and professionals to settle in town, too. Dr. John Emerson, a surgeon stationed at Fort Armstrong, was interested in settling in Davenport when his career in the army was over. From Fort Snelling where he was stationed, he corresponded with his friends Le Claire and Davenport, relying on their judgment to select land for him, to open a farm, and to secure a caretaker to hold his claim until the land sales were held. Le Claire oversaw Emerson's investments and rented the farm to Thomas Lyndsey, a former blacksmith at Fort Armstrong. Emerson's slave, the famous Dred Scott, was sent to work the farm. Le Claire also supervised the building of Emerson's house in town where he hoped to practice medicine and took care of Emerson's business during his absence. Unfortunately, Emerson died in Davenport in 1843, a year after resigning from the Army.[32]

Davenport and Le Claire also recruited churches. Churches were not only benevolent institutions, but also good business -- another viable marketing strategy they employed. Churches attracted members, who also bought land, built houses, and furthered the interests of the new town. About a quarter of the first 100 inhabitants in Davenport was Catholic, as reflected by the first church built in town, St. Anthony's Catholic Church. Construction started in 1838 with donated land and generous cash gifts from Mr and Mrs. Le Claire. G. C. R. Mitchell and George L. Davenport contributed cash gifts for construction. The men of the Noel family provided the labour. The Catholic community was primarily French and Irish. Many were relatives, friends from Portage des Sioux, or former associates in the Indian Trade who found work with Le Claire in the building trades. Early Davenport had a distinctly French flavour, at least for a time.

Another Frenchman was La Perche or La Pierre, the blacksmith at the Fort Armstrong Indian Agency, who established a blacksmith shop on Second Street next to the gunsmith shop of Harvey Sturdevant prior to 1837. Neither man stayed for long. La Pierre died in a drowning accident and Sturdevant moved to the new Indian Agency in Iowa. Louis Hebert had spent many summers on Rock Island with his uncle who had been employed by the Indian Agency. He and George L. Davenport had been childhood playmates and remained great friends through out their lifetimes. Herbert apprenticed to Harvey Leonard, the brick maker, and became Leonard's partner. Hebert's brother-in-law, Joseph Motie, also worked for Leonard in the brick business. Joseph Mallette, originally from French Canada, was in the construction business. He built his house next door to the Hebert's across from the present Sacred Heart Cathedral. George Davenport's old friend and employee, Antoine Gautier or Gokey, remained on the Island with his Indian wife and family.

Antoine Le Claire recruited his family, too, and provided both work and living quarters for them. His elder brother Francois was never a permanent settler, but he worked in Davenport from time to time and some of his children lived with Antoine and Marguerite Le Claire. Le Claire's youngest half brother David was married to Sarah Hall in Davenport and worked in the steamboat industry. Mrs. Le Claire's niece, Catherine Blondeau, came to Davenport and was married to William B. Watts, the first marriage in the new town. Le Claire's sister, Felicite, also came to Davenport. She died there in 1847.

First among the Irish settlers was James O'Kelley, an Irish tailor from Detroit. Many others Irish families followed after first working in the lead mines of northwestern Illinois before settling in Davenport. The Irish district was centered on the Cork Hill neighborhood, near the present Sacred Heart Cathedral.

St. Anthony's Church had significance for the Davenports as well. The first marriage performed there was George L. Davenport to Sarah Grace Clarke in 1839. Sarah and George L. had met in Stephenson when

Sarah was attending her sister's marriage to Stephenson merchant George Meyers. Wedding guests were treated to wedding cake and George Davenport's own currant wine. It must have been a proud moment for the whole Davenport family as they watched their first-born take his place in the community. At the same time George Davenport must have had some fatherly concern about the young couple starting out in such financially troubled times. The newlyweds settled in town on a lot near the corner of Main Street and what is now River Drive. It was conveniently located next door to the Davenport and Le Claire store where George L. was a partner.[33]

With his son managing the store and trading business, George Davenport was free to concentrate on his real estate ventures. Between February and July of 1839, he bought sixty undivided lots in the town of Le Claire and, in partnership with Antoine Le Claire, laid out a second addition to the town of Davenport. This addition added 16 blocks of 10 lots each plus 32 four-acre lots, or out lots, adjacent to the town. The Iowa Sun announced that 57 lots were sold in just a matter of days. Because of the condition of the sales, the appearance of the town transformed almost immediately.[34] Davenport and Le Claire required that all structures erected on these lots within eighteen months of the contract be made of brick, stone, or wood. This supported the local industries of brick making, the stone quarries in Le Claire, and the new lumber mills, as well as steering the town away from a log-cabin image. It was another important marketing strategy that would not be wasted on visitors who daily passed on the river and saw signs of a thriving community.

Both men built working class houses as rental units. Le Claire's row of houses, built like eastern townhouses, was answered by George Davenport's "Son of Row," which he built on eight adjoining lots in Block 29.[35] Davenport improved many of his own personal town lots, either with frame or brick buildings. Some buildings were intended for dwelling, others for business. Improved lots were fenced and had wells dug on them, making them more marketable and valuable. The rents from these were intended to provide income for him and his family in the years to come.

With the success of the additions to Davenport, the town's center shifted to the east side of the original town and here, Davenport and Le Claire built two public houses. Davenport started a modest-sized hotel near the corner of Main and Third. The framework was built of native oak by Nathaniel Squire, but lumber, sashes, doors and blinds were manufactured at Olean, on the Alleghany River above Pittsburgh. They were delivered to Davenport by boat. The hotel was opened as a boarding house but then changed two or three months later to a hotel called White Hall. Under the management of D.C. Eldridge, who later purchased the building and its entire inventory in 1840, the hotel was turned it into a Temperance Hall, which catered to the dry trade.[36]

Le Claire's plan called for a much larger and grander hotel. Located in the heart of town along Second Street between Main and Brady streets, Le Claire's hotel would be three stories high and use 100,000 bricks made by Harvey Leonard. It promised to be bigger, better, and offer more services than either the Davenport Hotel or White Hall. It would also cater to a different clientele, as Le Claire hoped to attract people looking for hunting and other rural experiences, as well as those who wished to escape the heat and diseases of the southern cities in summer. To help beautify the fledgling town, Le Claire also planted trees. George Davenport, perhaps to help finance Le Claire's efforts, bought $3,000 worth of lots in the original town plat from Le Claire.[37] Anticipating that the Iowa lands would soon be opened, the two men continued to expand the services they offered.

In the fall of 1839, the geologic survey expedition, under the direction of David Dale Owen, arrived by steamboat from St. Louis. Their mission as outlined by Congress was to identify the valuable mineral lands of northeastern Iowa, northwestern Illinois, and Wisconsin. After Owen's surveys, it was expected that the mineral lands would be opened to public sale. Owen was a recognized authority in geology mineral lands, and his survey party was a large one, with around 139 participants. Accompanying the expedition was Professor John Locke of Cincinnati, a recognized geologist. Owen divided his crew into twenty-four surveying parties who spread out over the nearly 11,000 square acres that needed to be surveyed.

Owen's base camp was just west of Davenport from mid-September until early December. Surely Owen talked with Davenport and Le Claire about their the knowledge of the mines and purchased supplies from Davenport and Le Claire's well-stocked store.[38]

The two partners had strategized well and had anticipated the needs of western immigrants to their town. They had provided hotels and stores and used the newspapers as well as their own personal connections to market the town's prospects. Their friendly competition had stimulated growth and the town, although hardly more than a village by 1840, seemed assured of continued growth. Residents had government, essential services, and enough mercantile and light industry to sustain town growth and agricultural lands surrounding the town were developing into productive farms.

Visitors to the area noted the many changes that had occurred in just a few short years. Although the old fort still stood abandoned on the island, its flagstaff stood as a reminder of the early days when the only dwellings beyond the fort walls were the longhouses of the Sauk and Mesquakie. From the promontory at the western tip of the Island visitors could see the courthouse spire in Stephenson and the white houses of six hundred inhabitants gleaming in the sun. To the north was Iowa Territory where the neatly laid out village of Davenport stretched along the riverbank with about 150 inhabitants. Three miles down the river was the newest town of Rock Island City at the confluence of the Rock and Mississippi rivers where the tentacles of industry were hoping to take root. But, there was no guarantee of continued success. Looming over the dreams of town founders were two very big issues: transportation and waterpower. What was needed was money, but the State of Illinois was financially bankrupt, unable to provide the necessary Internal Improvements that the fledgling towns along the rivers needed. So businessmen and investors alike began to look to the Unites States Government for financial help.

Speaker of the House, Henry Clay, had long understood that developing western states like his own state of Kentucky needed roads, canals, bridges, as well as tariffs and subsidies, and that they needed federal assistance in these matters, especially in these depressed times. What was called his American System, proposed as early as 1816, called for federally funded internal improvements for the western states. It had become a popular concept west of the Appalachians, but had never been implemented as a federal policy, mainly because Jacksonian Democrats opposed such policies.

With the approaching presidential election, eighteen men of the Rock Island region formed a branch of the Whig party to oppose the re-election of Andrew Jackson and the Democratic policies of his administration, policies they saw detrimental to the country as a whole. George Davenport was among those organizing members. Held in September of 1839, they were all involved with local development -- merchants, government officials, land developers, and river navigators – all of whom would benefit from policies espoused in Clay's American System ideas. The country was still feeling the effects of the depression and needed better access to federal money. The local Whigs chapter sought to select candidates who would support chartered banks, the distribution of banknotes, and subsidized internal improvements that required the issue of state bonds – all of which would help to spur growth in their area. Seeking change, they threw their support behind the Whig party.[39] This is the only time Davenport's party affiliation had been publicized.

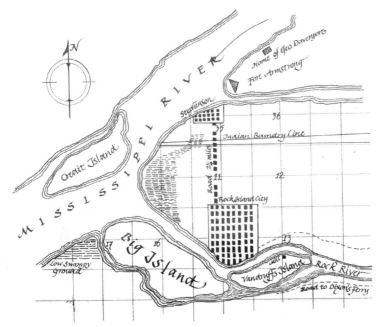

The plan for Rock Island City was ambitious and reflects the expectations of the investors in the plan. Several events conspired to defeat the city plan: the Panic of 1837, which pushed many of the investors to bankruptcy, the failure of the Rock River itself to support river traffic, and the lack of co operation among the mill owners on the

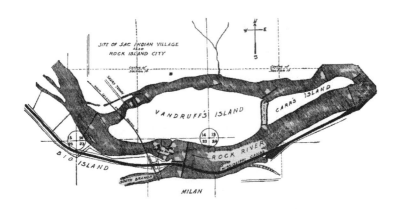

river.

Potential for the use of waterpower on the Rock River centered on Joshua Vandruff's successful use of wing dams for his mill. But the Rock River never lived up to its expectations.

CHAPTER SIXTEEN:

OUT ON THE ROCK AND ROCK ISLAND CITY

THE 1880'S WAS a time of rapid expansion and wild speculation. Promoters and speculators spoke of western lands in superlatives and vied for investor dollars to accomplish their development dreams. The population of the areas surrounding Rock Island increased noticeably and the demand for lots and houses was on the rise. Already, in 1835, there were 35 houses in Stephenson and 15 in Davenport, and the increase in value of lots was an indication of the demand. River lots that had originally sold for $220 in 1835 sold for $500 in 1836 and in 1837 the asking price was $2,000. Courthouse lots that Davenport had purchased for $150 were sold in 1836 for $350 and in 1837 were commanding $1,500. In Iowa, Davenport city lots were increasing in value in much the same way. Lots that originally sold for $100 had risen to $200 and $325. It is no wonder that Davenport bought six more lots in Stephenson and looked for new ways to profit.[1]

Most important to prospective development was waterpower. Consequently, the land all along the Rock River began to attract national attention as perfect for manufacturing. George Davenport owned a prime piece of the real estate on the north shore of the Rock River in Rock Island County. By 1835, Davenport had been approached by a number of speculators interested in buying the old village site where Black Hawk once lived. Where once were Indian wiki-ups and long houses, speculators and developers envisioned a great industrial city rising up from the shores of the rivers. With the Rock River on the east side and the Mississippi on the west, lead mines to the north, coal mines to the east, and an agricultural back country to support a large population, men with manufacturing in their blood began to plan great things for Black Hawk's former home

By 1837, land agents representing some of the wealthiest families in the United States such as Murray, Russell, Warren, and Stephenson, had already snatched up most of the available land along the river's edges. Land Companies such as the Rock River Land Company had purchased land south of the Rock River for agricultural purposes. Other land companies organized as colonies brought groups of people to create instant communities, particularly in Henry County. But it was manufacturing and milling that made the Rock River lands most valuable.

Davenport had purchased some of the Sauk and Mesquakie land in 1829, a small portion of which was in partnership with Russel Farnham. Davenport and Farnham had hoped that the Government would allow the Sauk and Mesquakie to continue living there and hunting as they had always done, but on private land. But, Jackson's Removal Policy pressured the Indians to move and opened the western lands to settlement. Now, only the bones of the Sauk and Fox ancestors, scattered over the landscape and gleaming in the sunlight were left as reminders of the people who had lived there for a hundred years. The old Indian village was just a part of what many developers hoped for -- an entire peninsula bounded by the rivers, perfect for industry. The land around the mouth of the Rock River was a place where the river, railroad, manufacturing and agriculture could all come together. But, by 1837, there had not yet been an official partition, or division, of the Davenport-Farnham partnership lands in Rock Island County, and Davenport was eager to sell the land.

Davenport submitted a formal petition for partition of the partnership lands to the Rock Island County Circuit Court on 1ˢᵗ of March1837. Later that summer the county Commissioners presented a formal division of the land, awarding Davenport just under one hundred acres on the bank of the Rock River.[2] Manufacturing and milling efforts on the Rock River had already started, aided by Joshua Vandruff who built wing dams to supply his gristmill with waterpower.

Vandruff was a Pennsylvanian who had claimed the island in the middle of the river, which now bears his name. The Reverend Peter Cartwright, the famous Methodist Circuit Rider, described Vandruff as a cantankerous man, and " a very mean man, (who) charged high, and imposed very much on travelers." His meanness was probably a result of the fact that he had a large family and was heavily in debt when he arrived in Rock Island, and trying to repay his debts.[3]

The Vandruff-Davenport ferry had been a successful operation. Over the years the demand for the ferry had increased, but now there was competition. Rinnah Wells, a newly arrived Vermonter, began a ferry a short distance down the river and provided a somewhat gentler competition. Benjamin Carr also had started a ferry operation, just above Vandruff's.[4]

It was Vandruff's gristmill, though, that had caught the attention of a Michigan investment group, which was then negotiating with Vandruff to buy his mill before it was even operational, hoping to engage in various kinds of manufacturing with lead, lumber, paper, and wool. Rafts of lumber floated down from Wisconsin had already arrived at Galena for building purposes and visionaries saw the Rock River being used in this way, too.[5] The agricultural lands surrounding the mouth of the Rock River had also been snapped up, mainly by a number of enterprising men who dreamed of producing wool. Already sheep were grazing in the meadows along the riverbanks.

Benjamin Carr also had a mill in operation on Mill Creek (present-day Milan) on the southern or slough side of the Rock, and the Sullivan brothers, John Hamm and David from Zanesville, Ohio, also intended to start milling on the Rock. The Sullivan brothers had purchased several parcels on the Rock in 1835, including two parcels on Carr's Island for a flourmill, and expected to capitalize on the wheat produced by farmers south of the Rock. They purchased another parcel of 27 acres from George Davenport. This land wasn't cheap, nearly fifteen dollars an acre, and well above government prices, but it had potential to make money.[6]

Davenport bought several more parcels of land further up the Rock from its mouth where there were good boat landings close to the coalfields. Like others, he seems to have caught the speculating fever. His interest lay in lands with good transportation possibilities. In the three years between 1835 and 1838, nearly all the land along the river banks was claimed, much of it by absentee investors who shared Davenport's interest in creating grain storage and shipping facilities. The story of William Dickson, one of the earliest settlers in the region, is illustrative of the way some speculators worked at the time.

William Dickson had fallen in love with the Rock River Valley from the first moment he saw it in 1834. He was an old canal man from northwestern Pennsylvania and, had his wife approved, he would have moved to the Rock River Valley after his first visit there, but she did not. When Mrs. Dickson died unexpectedly a year later, Dickson wasted no time in returning to Rock Island. After paying his respects to the commander at the fort, and sitting in on a Sauk and Mesquakie council, Dickson sought out George Davenport to talk business. He negotiated an option to buy Davenport's property, agreeing to the price of $15,000 for an undivided half of six hundred and eight acres. Davenport gave him three weeks to find financing to seal the deal. Then Dickson, along with his son Cyrus and cousin William C., went to Chicago to seek financing.[7]

Chicago that summer was swarming with speculators attending the Chicago Land Sales. The State of Illinois was offering some of its lands prior to building the Illinois-Michigan canal works in order to encourage development along the proposed canal routes. Advertising in many eastern newspapers had caused a frenzy among speculators in the East and regular steamboat passage across the Lakes had made Chicago, and Illinois in general, accessible for the Public Land Sales. Speculators and their agents of every Eastern land company worth its stock descended on Chicago in anticipation of buying land, which they could turn around at high profits in a short time. So, Chicago was teeming with high-pitched fever of speculation. Sales were expected to last for several days and the local newspaper reported that they were more successful than anyone had predicted. Many Illinois landowners with land or townsites to develop also went to Chicago and attempted to attract buyers to their own projects. Some speculators, looking for better land deals than they were finding in Chicago that week, fanned out into the Illinois countryside to look for better deals. Many found their way to the Rock River.

The Chicago American observed: "the whole West seems to be literally in commotion -- and towns are carving out of every practicable point with a restlessness of enterprise that defies all calculation ... houses are born in a night -- cities in a day, and the smaller towns in proportion!" Anthony Cooley wrote that the country was completely inundated with land pirates ... they are surging on everything that is above water in the shape of land. The land officers are compelled to keep the office closed at least one half the time in order to fetch up the arrears of the time it is open. Not less than from $10,000 to $20,000 per day has been received for the last month."[8]

During these sales, Dickson met Hiram Cross, an old friend related by marriage, and a young lawyer and distant cousin from Cherry Valley, New York, named Levi C. Turner. In late June, Dickson returned to Rock Island to purchase what Dickson called, "Black Hawk's ancient city" with a small contingency that had originated in Cooperstown, New York. In that group were Levi C. Turner, his wife Julia, her brother William

Campbell, E.B. Morehouse and his wife, and Richard Fenimore Cooper, the nephew of James Fenimore Cooper.

The Turner party came in a two-horse wagon with a cotton cloth covering, and two saddle horses. The journey was difficult at best. They "crossed prairies, forded rivers, mired in swamps, were frightened by Indians and thunder-gusts, slept in log-huts" and came to Galena. From there they took a steamer to Rock Island. Whether they stayed on the Island or in one of Davenport's buildings is not certain, but they remained a week during which time George Davenport and the Dickson-Turner party explored Iowa Territory and discussed Turner's interest in the site of Black Hawk's city. Finally, on the first of July, George Davenport and Levi C. Turner shook hands and concluded a deal on the former Sauk and Mesquakie lands.

Davenport and his wife, Margaret, sold Turner three quarters interest in the soon-to-be laid out town. Turner paid them $20,000 in cash. The Davenports also gave Turner their power of attorney to sell their remaining quarter interest and $1,000 in cash to survey and lay out a townsite, which they named Rock Island City (RIC). Turner's job was to sell shares in this city and, once the town was off and running, to sell Davenport's remaining one-quarter interest. It was to be an industrial city and expectations were high.[9]

By the terms of the agreement, George Davenport's role in Rock Island City was fairly straightforward. He retained a quarter interest, but only until such a time as a buyer could be found. He seems to have had no other obligation in the venture and, unlike his leadership role in the town of Davenport, there is little evidence that he took an active part in the planning or development of the prospective town. Turner represented a partnership, which may have included silent partners whose only objective was making money. As agent for these investors, Turner's job was to find others to develop the site into an industrial city.

Before returning to New York, Turner bought other land in the area. With William C. Dickson (cousin to William Dickson) he bought land a little further from the mouth of the Rock River in Henry County. And, in partnership with Lewis Moss of Wisconsin Territory, Turner bought a one-half interest in the town of Buffalo, Iowa. Located on the Iowa bank of the Mississippi River at the point where the Rock and Mississippi came together, the Buffalo townsite was small, just 64 blocks in all, but its location was ideal should the Rock River prove to be navigable. There was already a ferry business there, operated by William Clark, across the Mississippi. Turner also bought land from Benjamin Carr on the northern edge of RIC.[10]

Within days of the signing, the Northwestern Gazette and Galena Advertiser ran a feature story about the new town. George Davenport, revealed the editor, would reserve a public square in the center of town where the scattered bones of the Sauk would be buried and memorialized with a monument. The editor was enthusiastically supportive: "in this age of city making and speculating, we know of no place more peculiar and interesting in its history, or commanding and desirable in its location." A similar article appeared in the Cooperstown newspaper where Turner's in-laws lived in New York State. There is no doubt that the connection to Black Hawk was an important advertising feature of Rock Island City. Everyone in the East would recognize Black Hawk's name. It was a fact that George Davenport was willing to use in order to help the site stand out above all others.[11]

Having name recognition was important in the town-founding business. George Davenport was keenly aware of fierce competition among town founders. New towns were popping up almost overnight on both sides of the Mississippi and its tributaries. Developers vied for the choicest lands and promoted their own dreams and expectations. Town advertisements, glowing with exaggerated descriptions of prospective sites, were calculated to attract settlers and developers. Most were actual towns, the *Advertiser* noted, with real settlers and improvements, giving testament to the rapidly increasing population of the Mississippi river valley. The population of Illinois had nearly doubled since the 1830 Census, and people were still coming. By 1835 there were already 269,974 residents and George Davenport hoped to attract some of them to his towns.[12]

Besides the association with Black Hawk, Davenport recognized that Rock Island City had other features that helped it stand out above the other speculative towns. From his years of visiting the Sauk village, he knew it was the first and only good landing area on the Rock River from the Mississippi River, making it an ideal location for a port city that could control the flow of agricultural and manufactured goods to and from the interior of Illinois, as well as to St. Louis and New Orleans. Nearby there was coal, called stone coal or anthracite, which the Fort Armstrong soldiers had mined for the post blacksmith. This coal burned with a lot of heat and little smoke, a characteristic that made it useful in industry such as smelting lead brought down river from the Galena mines.[13] There was also a good supply of limestone that could be used as cut stone as well as in the production of lime. Iron had also been discovered in the vicinity, as well as copper and zinc, by-products of the lead mining in northwestern Illinois. Pine timber in the North Country could be rafted down the Rock River to sawmills near Rock Island City. And, most importantly of all, the rapids of the river could provide unlimited amounts of power for all manner of mills and manufacturing operations. These were qualities that Davenport knew well from his years of traipsing the prairies as he traded with the Sauk and Mesquakie.

On the day after Turner's agreement with Davenport, William Dickson and his cousin William C. began surveying and platting the site. The finished plat was mailed to Turner in New York, where it was lithographed. The resulting map was to be the principal tool for selling the lots or parcels of land in his three-quarters of this town. The map of Rock Island City filed with the Rock Island County Recorder reveal a large city and suggests a grand vision of the city as a manufacturing and transportation hub.[14]

The first impression of the plat is the shear magnitude of the city. The proposal called for 114 city blocks and 62 waterfront lots. By comparison, Stephenson's original 20 blocks seem quite small. Perhaps the size of Rock Island City reflected the size of Saukenuk, which lay directly under its plat. Waterfront lots were reserved for the proprietors, who promised no alterations to the city plan except for improvements of waterpower on the Rock. Some kind of canal or dam on the Rock River had been in discussion for years, but as of 1836, no location for one had been designated. The city planners expected, or maybe hoped is a better word, that the canal or dam would be located somewhere in the vicinity of Rock Island City's riverfront.

Not everyone, however, saw the vision behind all the speculating. George Featherstonehaugh, a geologic surveyor employed by the U.S. Topographical Engineers to investigate the lead and minerals between St. Louis and Galena, was highly disapproving of such "drunkenness," as he called the speculation. He had seen enough to convince himself that: "This part of the world has been regularly drunk since I was here in 1835 ... I have either seen or landed at twenty sites of pretended cities with swaggering names, all of them having engraved plats got up in a showy way, ... having building lots sufficient for a population of 250,000 people, a public square, etc. ... Scarce one has more than one house upon it ..."[15] Featherstonehaugh could only see these infant towns as pipedreams and a foolish waste of effort and money. What he did not see were the hundreds of immigrants moving westward and the determination of those men to take on the challenge of finding new lives and livelihood.

George Davenport understood first-hand the role towns played in attracting settlers when they offered amenities like food, tools and equipment, places to stay until more permanent homes could be found or built, and most of all, business opportunity. This is what the Rock Island City needed in order to attract settlers. It was up to Levi C. Turner to find those investors who would develop the city plat to attract settlers.

Davenport also knew first hand the challenges of the land, the vagrancies of the rivers and hindrances to transportation. Despite all the minerals upriver, the pineries, and wheat fields, success for industry in the west hinged on making the rivers navigable throughout the year in order to get supplies to communities and products to market. The Rock River was subject to floods in the spring and low water in the summer. Newspaper reports of the time illustrate how dangerous the river conditions could be. At Galena, the river fell three inches in one night and as a result, several of the small steamboats on the river at the time were in danger of being grounded, caught in too shallow water without warning.[16] In addition, the rapids were a constant hazard to transportation and dangerous in any conditions.

How to control the water flow for year-round waterpower was a problem not easily solved. It was costly and beyond the capability of engineering technology of the time. Anxious for solutions, entrepreneurs put forth a number of ideas. One was to build a water reservoir in Wisconsin at the head of the river; another was to build canals to bypass rapids in the river. Both involved government action. Another solution was to use small boats that could navigate in shallow waters and between and around the rapids. Davenport had solved this problem by using keelboats, but keelboats were bulky and slow. Light water steamboats, like the Frontier, were thought to be a better solution for the smaller rivers such as the Rock, Wisconsin, and Pecatonica Rivers. The light water steamboats were smaller than the steamboats used on the Mississippi, which generally ranged in size from 63 tons to 121 tons. Unfortunately, they did not live up to their expectations.

Captain Daniel Smith Harris was able to pilot the *Frontier* as far up the river as Dixon, Illinois, largely because of the spring floods of 1836, but the high water levels could not be maintained without improvements and the Frontier was never able to repeat this accomplishment. The Gipsy, captained by John Mason of Sterling, was able to go as far as Janesville, Wisconsin, in 1840. These were hardly the regular visits that were needed.[17]

Harnessing the Rock River without hindering transportation was a challenge. Vandruff's wing dams were acceptable as they helped to channel the flow of the water into his mill without hindering navigation in the main channel, but a dam stretching the full width of the river would not only be expensive, it would also be illegal. A state-sanctioned dam was the only viable solution and that would take money. The State of Illinois was reluctant to approve such a venture.[18]

Although there was plenty of local support for Rock Island City, there was no one person or group to finance such an undertaking. Perhaps this is the reason why Davenport accepted the offer of Dickson and Turner.

Perhaps he thought that Dickson had enough experience in canal building and that Turner had the financial backing to make it all work.

Turner turned to New York City merchants for investors and was successful in finding men willing to invest in Rock Island City. It was a logical place to start. Lower Manhattan had undergone a devastating fire in December of 1835 and the city was only then beginning to recover. Millions of dollars worth of property had been lost, including the Market Exchange and over six hundred businesses. Insurance companies had been ruined. Property values escalated in the rebuilding phase. Even businesses that had not been directly touched by the fire were affected. With credit readily available and land schemes booming, businessmen were eager to invest in Western lands as a way of recouping their losses and beginning again.

Turner's first sale was a forty-thousand-dollar interest to a group of merchants on Pearl Street, in the heart of what is today Manhattan: J.P. Coffin, Cyrus Carlton, Edwards W. Fiske, and Leander Allen. Coffin was a hardware merchant on Maiden Lane. Carleton was originally from Maine but had been associated with the house of C. Carleton & Co. of Montreal. Leander Allen was one of Carleton's accountants and brokers who specialized in the sale of American cotton to mills in Sheffield, England. Fiske was a lawyer and close friend of Robert Campbell, Turner's father-in-law. They paid Turner $10,000 and mortgaged the rest for a one-sixteenth share.[19]

The following month Turner sold shares to Charles A. Spring, also of New York City, for $10,000. Spring promptly sold his interest for $7,000 to Hugh T. Dickey, a young New York City lawyer. A short time later, Spring purchased a thirty-second interest from Turner for $5,500, which he kept for himself. Finally there was Nathaniel Norton. Like Coffin and Carleton, Norton purchased a one-sixteenth interest for $10,000. All designated Turner their power of attorney to sell their shares in the future to other investors.[20]

The investors in Rock River lands were not typical speculators of the era who never set foot in the county in which they invested. Most of these men had spent some time in Rock Island County, an indication of the seriousness of their interest and of the plan itself, but none of them appear to have been builders or industrialists. Charles Spring and his family lived along the Rock for a number of years, investing in other lands over time and eventually working as agricultural agents for Cyrus McCormick. Leander Allen moved his family to Stephenson sometime in the summer or fall of 1837. He was listed as an accountant in the 1840 census and appears to have been a part of the new community, even serving on jury duty when called. His daughter, Caroline, was born there and both of his sisters, Phebe and Adeline, settled in Rock Island County. Phebe was married to John Bully and they lived in south Rock Island until their deaths. Adeline was married to Joseph Gerrard who was involved in an unfortunate incident where a man was killed.[21]

Nathaniel Norton moved to Whiteside County where he bought an established farm along the Rock River and started a nursery with an orchard of two thousand apple trees. By 1840 his trees were available for sale at twelve and a half cents. Norton also operated a store in the town of Camden, now called Milan. Hugh Dickey settled in Chicago where he became a distinguished lawyer. Turner and his father-in-law, Robert Campbell were evidently feeling confident in their choice of Rock Island City as they bought another thousand acres just to the north of the proposed city, between the northern boundary of Rock Island City and the town of Stephenson. This may have been the first step to join Rock Island City with the town of Stephenson[22]

One final investor was the famous orator, Daniel Webster. Webster was interested in western lands, and his son Fletcher had opened a farm near Peru, Illinois. Webster's friend and agent, Henry L. Kinney, kept him informed of other possible investment lands between Peru, Illinois, and Rock Island. Webster had already bought canal lands along the Illinois-Michigan route and was urged by two other agents, Henry Moore and Fisher Ames Harding, to cash in on the deal at Rock Island City quickly. In January (1837) Davenport was in Washington City, petitioning Congress regarding the purchase of his Island property. At the same time, Turner was also in Washington City negotiating with Daniel Webster to invest in Rock Island City, but whether Davenport and Turner met at that time is not known. It is hard to imagine that they didn't. When it looked as though the State of Illinois would pass the Internal Improvement Act, which it did officially on 27 February 1837, Webster bought into Rock Island City. His investment was listed as $60,000 and he was credited with a one-eighth share in Rock Island City.[23]

The importance of the Internal Improvement Act to Rock Island County cannot be underestimated, because it provided for public works throughout the State, works that included canals, rail roads, dams and bridges. These public works were important to the local economies, providing money for infrastructure that counties could not otherwise provide. Rock Island County desperately needed to develop and improve the power of the river, waterpower to operate mills as well as to support transportation in the form of steamboat navigation. Talk of a state-operated dam near Rock Island City was an important element to the founding of Rock Island City as well as the improvement of the navigation capabilities of the river. Improvement included canals to by-pass the rapids as well as controlling the water level of the Rock throughout the year.

Linked to this proposed dam were based a number of privately funded projects chartered and regulated by the State of Illinois. One of the earliest charters important to the development of Rock Island City was a grant to the Rock Island City Bridge Company.

The Rock Island City Bridge Company was a capital stock company with stock divided into one thousand three hundred shares of one hundred dollars each. Its purpose was to construct a bridge across the Rock River. The Commissioners designated in the charter were George Davenport, Levi C. Turner, William Dickson, Miles W. Conway, John W. Spencer, John S. Miller, and William Carr. All but Turner were residents. The charter stipulated that the bridge would not damage the navigation of the river and that steam or other boats might pass under it without difficulty. The president or directors of the company or their employees were granted the privilege of taking possession of as much land on both ends of the bridge as was necessary for a gate, toll booth and all other works for such a bridge. This would have involved the riverfront lots reserved by the proprietors in Rock Island City. Procedure for purchasing said land was spelled out as well as rules and regulations for crossing, charging tolls, and width of proposed bridge. The bridge would improve trade between Rock Island City and Stephenson and settlers to the south from Henry and Mercer counties, some of whom came from as much as forty miles away to the mills.[24]

The charter and its underlying plan suggest that the entire area encompassed by Rock Island City and Stephenson would draw business from a radius of about fifty miles. It also indicates a cooperation of residents who could be seen as competitors of one another. Conspicuously absent from this venture is Joshua Vandruff, who was not known for neighborly cooperation.

Rock Island City's neighbors were ready to capitalize on the plan of Rock Island City with plans of their own. One was called the Western Addition to Rock Island City. Another was Rockingham, across the Mississippi in Iowa Territory. The Western Addition to Rock Island City was platted on land owned by Rinnah Wells, one of the first settlers in Rock Island County, a farmer, and ferry operator on the Rock River. Just days after Turner and Davenport concluded their deal, Wells concluded a similar deal with agents representing Kalamazoo, Michigan: Anthony Cooley, Hezekiah G. Wells, Pinander and Joseph Pollock, and Edwin G. Munn. Cooley was at that time engaged in milling on the Kalamazoo River and an experienced town developer, having founded the town of Allegan, Michigan, two years before. Anthony Cooley noted the nearby resources as a prime reason for investing here. He wrote to fellow investor, E.G. Munn, that if he got the land it would be a "grand speculation and will be more important than Chicago."[25]

The Western Addition, while smaller and designed differently than Rock Island City, had its own merits. Mineral springs on the site, variously known as "White Sulphur Springs," "Soda Springs," and "Rinnah Wells Springs," were known to have medicinal properties and had been improved with stone curbs and other accommodations for obtaining the pure water without contaminating it. Expectations were high for developing this area as a health resort around its healing properties, but the plat looked more like a mill town than a resort and further supports the concept of a manufacturing center for the entire area. The lots and blocks are of uneven sizes and configuration, designed not only to fit the shape of the land, but also to afford as much manufacturing as possible.[26] The partnership of Cooley, Wells, and others also arranged to buy Vandruff's mill through their agent Daniel G. Garnsey. Although it is tempting to view these individual town plats as isolated, they were in fact a part of a greater plan that, if successful, would develop the peninsula of Rock Island into a great manufacturing center.[27]

Across the river, John Hamm Sullivan and Adrian H. Davenport were organizing their town of Rockingham. They had first considered building a mill above Vandruff's Island but reconsidered that site because of the proposed State dam, which would have rendered that location useless for waterpower. Instead they chose a point on the west side of the Mississippi River below the confluence of the Rock and Mississippi rivers, in what would become Rockingham, Iowa. There they built the first steam-powered flourmill in the area planning to supply southern plantations in exchange for cotton. A ferry license, granted in Rock Island County, provided for the transport of grain to their mill. Sullivan also bought land along a line from his new town towards the interior of Iowa Territory towards Iowa City, the new capitol of Iowa Territory.

One other area worth noting was just west of the Rock River where the town of Andalusia is now. This was the location of Rockport, considered a good crossing point on the Mississippi River. Benjamin Clark's town of Buffalo on the Iowa side, still known as Clark's Ferry, could be reached through a cut in the islands in the middle of the river.

Reports of Rock Island City and its prospects for growth and development appeared in New York papers. The writer, identified only by initials, G.W.L., was enamored of Rock Island, calling it "a bright spot in this rude world." He supported the connection of the mouth of the Rock to the Illinois River at the termination point of the Illinois & Michigan canal as an impetus to trade. The only impediment to growth was the lack of mechanics, lumber, and venders of staple necessaries.[28]

Altogether, the area surrounding George Davenport's property on the Rock was on the verge of major development. Expectations were indeed high, but actual building was slow to develop and what no one anticipated was a crash on Wall Street. The financial bubble burst in early spring when overextended eastern banks closed their doors and called in their credits. Panic was felt immediately in New York and other eastern cities, and by the middle of April (1837), Wall Street was very black indeed. Factories shut down. Men were forced out of work. Speculators in western lands felt the effects rather quickly.[29]

Levi C. Turner optimistically continued his land dealings near Rock Island City, traveling back and forth between New York and Illinois. On return trips from New York, he brought merchandize for Davenport and Le Claire's mercantile business, perhaps as a way to pay his debts. In October of 1837, Turner became a partner with Davenport and Le Claire in developing the town of Le Claire, Iowa, and was given power of attorney to sell shares in that town.[30]

Like many speculators of the 1830s, Rock Island City investors had been confident that the favorable economics conditions would hold long enough for them to make a return on their investment. Those who had invested on borrowed capital, according to frontier economics historian Paul W. Gates, were unprepared for the continual management costs of their western investments, such as taxes and building costs, and unable to meet their obligations.[31] Thus began a scramble of trading shares for shares, revoking powers of attorney, and eventually a series of lawsuits between and against partners with bankruptcy for some. Since no buildings had yet been started in Rock Island City, the whole speculative project seemed gloomy indeed.

Only William Dickson and his family were actually living in Rock Island City in the spring of 1837. Spring and Norton had visited the city recently but had not yet settled. Others had yet to arrive. Dickson was living in the lower level of a stone house on the bank of the river, which his son, William B. Dickson, had built. He was strapped for cash and he had a family to support. Sons Cyrus and George were away at college with expenses and there were four adult children living at home who had to make sacrifices to pay for that education. Another son was running the family farm back in Erie County, Pa. Despite Dickson's financial situation, he had bought out his late cousin's interests in RIC [32] and with Levi C. Turner as partner, had begun building a sawmill on Mill Creek with Edmund Hollister and Alfred Gilman. He needed lumber and this was the only way he could get it. He knew others would need lumber, too.

Dickson's mill was located three miles south of the Rock River and he calculated that he could pay for the mill in twenty days. He had put his sons to work. Thomas was producing bricks. William B. was building a brick building in RIC (on Lots 10 and 11 in Block 36). This brick building, which Dickson had contracted to build for Davenport, Turner, and Webster, was intended to be a public house or tavern for Rock Island City – the first official building for the City. In addition, Dickson was building an office on Lot 10 and a dwelling on Lot 11, both in Block 46 for himself. It was hoped that these buildings would show that Rock Island City was viable and would attract others. [33]

Because local businessmen continually petitioned government for help, a new round of surveys began about this time to address the transportation problem. James Seymour studied the Rock River from its mouth at the Mississippi one hundred and fifty miles to the state line. He found that the average depth of the Rock was between five and six feet, a depth considered sufficient for transportation of small steamboats and flatboats. Commissioner John Dixon agreed that the Rock River was, in fact, navigable in most places for boats of three or four foot draft, except at two particular places, which could be easily remedied with dams and locks. Two proposals were put forth. Since Rock Island City had the deepest channel and the riverbanks were high enough for a dam to back the water beyond the head of the rapids, Dixon proposed that a small dam be stretched across the slough between Vandruff's Island and Carr's Island. A canal, 1,900 feet in length would be cut across Vandruff's Island. A second proposal, to cut a canal three quarters of a mile long across the entire length of Vandruff's Island, dispensed with a dam. Although the canal would have no advantage to the State without a dam, this plan was nevertheless accepted. Expectations were that the Pecatonica River could also be made navigable and used to boat the lead from the mines down to the Mississippi.[34]

The state plan was not alone in looking for ways to solve the transportation problems. A private group headed by Charles Oakley, Henry Ogden, John Whipple and Charles C. Wilcox saw a way that might skirt the dangerous rapids of the Mississippi and bypass the Rock Island Rapids on the Mississippi by cutting a canal between present-day Hampton, across the wetlands to a place on the Rock River called Sugar Grove. In times of high water this area had been used by steamboats in the past and seemed to be a natural cut between the two rivers. If built, this canal would allow steamboats to cut across the northern part of Rock Island County on what geologists believe was an ancient river bed, enter the Rock River, and then proceed back to the Mississippi below the rapids. Coinciding with this canal plan, the town of Milan, formerly known as McNeal's Landing and presently known as Hampton, Illinois, was laid out (June of 1837). Located just upriver from Stephenson, its proprietors advertised it as having a "fine steamboat landing, two stores, two taverns, a new one building, and a good schoolhouse in progress." In addition there were four sawmills within a short distance and twelve within ten miles. The proposed canal between Hampton and Sugar Grove would allow mineral and agricultural products from the Rock River and the Pecatonica River in Northern Illinois to land here, boosting the importance of Hampton's landing point.[35]

This plan was called the Mississippi and Rock River Canal Company and the charter located the canal close to the town of Milan (now Hampton) and ran across swampland to the Rock River. The corporation planned to raise capital stock and open their books not only at Milan, Illinois, but also in Providence, Rhode Island, New York City, and any other places deemed expedient. They were given two years in which to start their canal and four years to finish.[36] While not publicly involved in this project, George Davenport owned land that would be served by this second canal and he would stand to profit from it as well as the one at Rock Island City.

The first of the public works began to materialize in the summer of 1837 when a surveyor party arrived on the Rock River. Eight to ten men including a leveler, surveyor, chainman, axe man, teamster, and cook began surveying at Dixon's ferry. Their mission was to survey to 150 miles of the Rock. Amadie Blanc, considered to be one of the best draftsmen at the time, was in charge. Blanc concluded that there were no important obstacles to either of the rapids and that improvement of the Rock River for steamboat navigation would have few difficulties in comparison to its advantages.[37]

The public works put some much-needed cash in the local economy.

One hundred thousand dollars were allocated for the Rock River Improvements. Sealed proposals for constructing a stone lock and a three-quarter mile long canal on Vandruff's Island were received at Dixon, Illinois, on 12th of May, as well as proposals for grading, masonry, and bridges for 20 miles of the Central Railroad near Galena. The work was scheduled to begin in 30 days and be completed in 18 months. In preparation for the workers, local settler Rinnah Wells built a large two-story frame building, later used as the county Poor-House, to house the engineers and others involved with the canal project. The canal engineers paid board and lodging, $6.00 per day for seven men, a figure set by the State. The Dicksons started a taxi service to carry the engineers between the work site and their office in Stephenson, which was rented from Shannon Gregory, son-in-law of the county surveyor Absolom Baxter. Other locals hired out to haul goods to the work site. Limestone for making of lime for the construction of the lock and dam was produced in a kiln built on Vandruff's Island. Dickson's sawmill on Mill Creek cut all the oak in the vicinity for the canal works.[38]

It was Joshua Vandruff, however, who negotiated one of the sweetest deals of the time, selling a portion of his land for the mile long canal for $13,000. In addition, he obtained a ferry license from the state, rather than from Rock Island County.[39] But because the State of Illinois was in financial difficulty at that time, it is doubtful that he actually received the money.

With the canal under construction, the land escalated in value, especially on Vandruff's Island. Land that had been sold at $1.25 per acre just a year before was now sold for more than $60.00 per acre. Land Agent Thomas Harris of Madison County, Illinois, bought two parcels of land on Vandruff's Island and sold them immediately to John Dement and H.B. Truett of Jo Daviess County, Illinois, for $6,000. Vandruff sold an acre near his house to James Craig and Daniel H. Whitney for $3,800. Craig, who was a founder of Hanover, Illinois, had been involved in the Galena lead industry and had established a number of mills and a chair manufactory in that area. His partnership with Whitney, whose family was involved in lead refinery, suggests that they might have been planning to use this small parcel of land for a shot tower for the production of lead shot. It was cheaper to ship lead from Galena to the Rock River for smelting and processing before being shipped to St. Louis or to the east than to ship coal to the mines.[40]

George Davenport also thought land on Vandruff's Island had potential. He remained a partner with Vandruff in the ferry business and when he had a chance buy land on the Island, he took advantage. He had won a judgment against Dement and Stone, a mercantile business in Galena that had defaulted on a debt to him. The judge ordered a sale of the businessmen's land in Rock Island County to settle the debt. When the property came up for bid at public auction, Davenport was the highest bidder—a strategy Davenport sometimes employed to recoup his losses. Davenport's son, Bailey, later operated a sand and gravel business on the site.[41]

Soon after the canal work began, trouble set in. The cut stone on which the contracts were based was not suitable for building the lock and no suitable substitute could be found within the prescribed three-mile radius of the canal. Fearing that delay would jeopardize the project for the year, the Internal Improvement Commission agreed to re-let the contract, calling for a reduction in the original cost and a composite stone lock.

Then, there was an accident on the river. Three men, workers at the limekilns on Vandruff's Island, were drowned. One of the men was Thomas Dickson, William B. Dickson's brother. William B. himself was rescued by Joshua Vandruff in his canoe. Two brothers by the name of Drury were able to swim to shore. Another man, who had been a neighbor of the Dickson family in Pennsylvania, also drowned.[42] It was a reminder to everyone just how powerful the Rock River could be.

After a year of work on the canal the project was over budget, and in the winter of 1838-1839, the Illinois General Assembly appropriated $50,000 more to complete the Rock River Improvements. But then, Chief Engineer Amadie Blanc died. Ice and winter weather conditions in late November halted construction and work never resumed. The State of Illinois was out of money, bonds had not been invested wisely, and with the financial situation across the country worsening, workers could be paid only in script.[43]

Without the dam that everyone had anticipated, the bridge that was supposed to have been built by the Rock Island Bridge Company was never started. Consequently, the charter was allowed to lapse.

The Rock Island City investors were also feeling the pinch of the financial crisis. Edwards W. Fiske, anticipating a hefty loss in other investments, sold his interest in RIC to partners Carleton and Allen. (5 April 1837). When the international cotton market collapsed, the price of cotton, which had been as high as sixteen cents per pound, fell as low as five cents in the summer of 1839. That was especially devastating for Cyrus Carleton who dealt in raw cotton. In September (1839) Carleton assigned over $8,000 in debts to a financial backer in the east, but the debts took a toll on his health. Less than two years later, he died in Jamaica where he had gone to recover. Charles Spring sold much of his land outside of the city for some much-needed cash. Daniel Webster was also feeling the pinch of overinvesting in Illinois. He instructed his agent, Nathaniel Ray Thomas, to sell all of his real estate in Ohio, Indiana, Illinois, Michigan, and the Territory of Wisconsin, excepting his farm called Salisbury near LaSalle, Illinois.[44]

Turner began to fail financially. He was involved in a lawsuit with Gurdon Hubbard who claimed to be an investor in Rock Island City by giving Turner a letter of credit for the sum of twenty thousand dollars to purchase Rock Island City land. In return, Hubbard claimed, Turner had promised to split the profits of the investment of that land to Hubbard and convey to him half of the land. That was never done. When Turner failed to appear in court, Judge Dan Stone took that as an admission of guilt and ordered Turner to pay Hubbard one half of all sales. Turner requested the case be transferred to the U.S. Federal Court, which caused a delay of judgment. He expressed his frustration and fear of his reputation being ruined to Webster, but there were no transfers of title to Hubbard in Rock Island County. Both Turner and Hubbard were on the brink of financial ruin and Hubbard in particular may have used the courts as a last ditch effort to save himself at the expense of Turner. [45]

Turner then turned to Samuel Blackwell for a mortgage on Rock Island City. Blackwell (1791 - 1857) was a wealthy New York City merchant, descended from a long line of iron merchants. His brothers were involved in lumber, shipping, and naval store. He himself had been engaged in manufacturing turpentine, steam ferry and railroad. Turner assigned the mortgages of the Fiske group to Blackwell for $32,000. Others would come to Blackwell in the future. Blackwell retained his interest in Rock Island City until his death in 1857. [46]

At least three of the Rock Island City investors (Charles Spring, Leander Allen, and Nathaniel Norton) had come to Illinois, but by 1840 there were only five or six structures in the whole of Rock Island City, primarily those built by Dickson and his sons. This was hardly enough to make the appearance of a viable city. In the Western Addition there had been some building, too, a store and three or four other buildings, enough to give some encouragement to its investors, but the mill agreement with Vandruff had fallen through and the mill deeded back to Vandruff. It is doubtful that it was ever in full operation. Anthony Cooley's expectations of profit in that venture became more and more elusive. [47]

The Mississippi and Rock River Canal Company, backed by Oakley and others, had also run into delays. Their petition for public lands for their proposed canal had been tabled again, lost in committee. It had become Senate Bill # 96 and sent to the Committee on Roads and Canals of the 25th Congress, but no action seemed forthcoming and the investors sold out. As George Davenport knew very well, the process of pushing a bill through Congress could be time-consuming, and there were no guaranteed results.

Desperate to get something going, yet another group implemented still another plan to get something done on the river. The Rock River and Mississippi Steam Navigation Company formed as a stock company to improve the Rock River. The duly elected officers were all local businessmen: Daniel G. Garnsey, G.C.R. Mitchell, Sylvester Talcott, Antoine Le Claire, and George Myers. George Davenport's name is not on the charter, probably because he was still in St. Louis by the time of the elections. The company purchased the steamboat Pike, built specifically for the Rock River trade with the hope that she would carry passengers from Stephenson and Davenport on regular tours up the river. Unfortunately, the Pike failed. She was unable to pass the lower rapids as the water level was only 12 inches deep, and then was relocated to the Wisconsin River where she was grounded later in the summer.[48]

By 1840, the effects of the Panic of 1837 and ensuing depression were being felt throughout the Mississippi Valley. So many plans, once filled with high expectation and hope, had failed to materialize. Hopes were fading fast for Rock Island City, which remained largely unimproved and property taxes on the city lots remained unpaid. Without a dam to provide waterpower for operating mills and no viable means of river transportation, there was no incentive for the investors to build there. George Davenport filed for partition of his one-fourth interest in the Rock Island City property from the three-quarter interest held by Turner and Company. The vacation was approved by the Legislature of the State of Illinois in 1841 and signed by George Davenport in 1842.[49] The Turner and Company lots came up for public auction in the June tax sales of 1841-1845. Davenport must have thought that the land still had some prospective use, because he attended the sales and purchased many of the choicer lots for pennies on the dollar.

Despite all the dreams and elaborate plans, the Rock River never became navigable for commercial purposes. In the end, the interest shifted away from the Rock River to the Mississippi River when a milldam across the backwaters of the Mississippi River was built. The new dam generated a great deal of excitement and financial opportunity. George Davenport, too, was looking at the potential there.

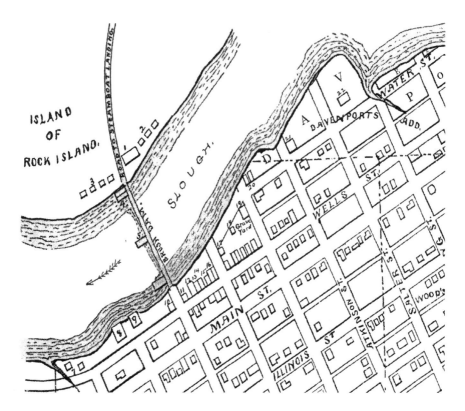

The brush dam created first by David Sears attracted mill owners and other industry along the Slough or Mississippi backwaters. By the early 1850s Moline was thriving with a mix of industry, stores, and houses. On the Island is the Dimock & Gould pail shop and related buildings (1,2,3). Sawmills lay along the dam itself, namely White's (4), Chamberlin's (5), and Pits, Gilbert, and Pitts (6). Among the industries on the bank of Moline are the plow shop of John Deere (8), Wheelock's paper mill (9), and the carriage shop of Darling & Edwards (20). In Davenport's Addition are the sash factory of Ruggles and Nourse (21) and the sawmill of Stephens, Gault & Hartzell.

CHAPTER SEVENTEEN:

HARNESSING THE WATERPOWER

DESPITE THE HARD TIMES, there was no shortage of hopes, dreams, and visions for the lands surrounding Rock Island. Progress came with such dreams and visions. In the 1830s, when little had actually been built, the plans were endless. All of them built on the waterpower. George Davenport seemed not to take sides. He could work with whatever developed, because he had positioned himself in so many places around Rock Island that he could take advantage of any and all development. There were two main concepts of the kind of development being promoted at the time. George Davenport owned land in both.

First is the Rock Island concept as envisioned by Dr. Silas Reed, a St. Louis man living in Stephenson in the 1840s. Reed saw the entire area now known as Rock Island as the Cincinnati of the West, a comparison based on location on the river, expected population growth, and natural advantages of the region. His vision depended on the Government improving the Lower Rapids. Reed sang the praises of the minerals found in the region: coal, stone for building, pine forests to the north, lead, and iron ore. Reed pointed to the fertile river valleys around Rock Island where grains would thrive and sheep would graze. He predicted that Rock Island would become as famous for pork packing as Cincinnati with boats shipping pork to the south and returning with cotton for manufacturing here. The Rock River waterpower would provide a cheaper place for smelting the lead from Galena and attract other industries.[1]

A competing and more involved idea went beyond manufacturing and commercial interests and referred to the area as "Hesperia." It was envisioned by Professor William Jenks of Boston, who visited the region in 1838, and was a friend of the Davenports. Like Reed, Jenks predicted a large unified city with commercial and manufacturing interests, but with an added feature of a literary center. Jenks predicted that in twenty years of his visit, there would be east- and westbound railroads emanating from Hesperia in addition to traffic on the "grand Mississippi thoroughfare." He envisioned the city extending to the Rock River where Rock Island City flourished as the tenth ward of the current city of Stephenson. Bridges, he predicted, would cross the Rock River to points south, a causeway would allow access to the island of Rock Island, and from the island, a bridge to Iowa for both private and railroad travel.

In addition, Jenks envisioned a Federal Government Arsenal on the Island of Rock Island, with a foundry and arms depot, common schools for all children, and a variety of churches. Also on the Island, would be a great center of learning, a University with schools of law, science, health and medicine, and literature and a great library. The whole area would be a beautiful, even idyllic, place to live with a long grassy promenade connecting the Rock River Bridge with the Rock Island Bridge, lined with shade trees and houses set on two-acre lots and the residents, whom he called Hesperians, would have public baths and be brought together in annual games much like the Sauk and Mesquakie once held. It was a beautiful dream.[2]

The name of this future city was important. Already there was a call for changing the name of Stephenson, but "Hesperia" did not sit well with some, as it sounded too high-handed and poetical, and it's meaning, "City of the West," was too easily associated with the Mormon's "City of the Far West" on the Missouri River. Stephenson was not suggestive of the region either, or to anyone associated with it. Even though there was already an island called Rock Island and Rock Island City on the Rock River, the citizens chose "Rock Island." Long associated with Black Hawk and the Rock Island Rapids, it was familiar to those who had followed Black Hawk's story and the Black Hawk War. It was designed to attract more attention to their beleaguered city as the financial situation worsened in the entire Upper Mississippi Valley.[3]

In the early 1840s, the financial depression had finally affected the west and many settlers were unable to pay their mortgages or taxes and lost their land through foreclosures. The Davenports were also affected by the cash shortage, although not as much as others. By working with government and establishing services like ferries and inns, they were able to generate enough cash to pay their taxes, to buy back some lands that they had previously sold, and even to build new structures. Despite the hard times, the towns surrounding Rock Island were making marginal progress in attracting new settlers and small industry.

Anxious to publish every little bit of good news in their weekly editions, the newspaper editors grabbed onto the latest stories of promising development. In the fall of 1839 the Rock Island Banner announced that two unnamed capitalists were planning to establish a pork packing plant at Stephenson. The availability of hogs in the vicinity and the location, just two days from St. Louis, had led the two capitalists to choose this place. Another new business was involved in refining salt. Both would use the rivers to transport their products. In Davenport, the Upper Mississippian reported that a large contingency of settlers from Cincinnati had arrived there to settle permanently. With more and more families arriving, prominent citizens petitioned for and obtained a charter to start a seminary. George Davenport was one of the appointed trustees.[4]

Small mills began to appear on every little creek and stream up and down the Mississippi. By 1840, there were 12 mills employing 59 men just in Rock Island County alone: 3 flouring, 3 grist, and 6 sawmills. Wind power had proven ineffective in one experiment on Duck Creek. Horsepower had been employed in another, but the waterpower had proven to be the easiest and cheapest power to harness in these early years. With the exception of Sullivan's steam flouring mill in Rockingham, these early mills were geared for local consumption rather than large-scale business. Hopes for a boost in the local economy focused on harnessing the waterpower for large-scale industry was still in the future.[5]

Transportation on the rivers remained difficult, especially for the lead industry. Already over thirty million pounds of lead were being sent down river from the mines each year, but it was too heavy to be economically portaged across the Mississippi River rapids in such large quantities. Shipping was expensive and costs, calculated as losses had been estimated to be at $90,000 annually. Copper, iron, and zinc deposits had not been tapped for the most part, because of lack of capital, but these minerals held potential for future development if the shipping problems could be solved.[6]

In the Upper Mississippi Valley, some citizens looked to Government for help. Talk of building a Western Armory on the Mississippi River raised new hopes that government money would build a dam, perhaps on the Rock River. Several other government facilities had also been proposed for the region. One was a Marine Hospital on the Island of Rock Island. Congress wanted to establish seven inland hospitals in the Mississippi Valley with views of the river or the Great Lakes. Always a healthy location, with the exception of the cholera outbreak after the Black Hawk War, Rock Island had all the benefits for ailing boatmen for whom these facilities were to be built.[7] It seemed a perfect location, but because the island had never been relinquished by the War Department, another site was chosen.

Another proposal was to build an armory in the west. Congress had appropriated $75,000 for a new facility to furnish arms from the West. With trouble brewing with the Seminole in Florida, conflicts with the Mexicans in Texas, and the potential for trouble with Western Indians, there were fears that the country could not be armed quickly and efficiently. The closest armories were in the east at Harper's Ferry, Virginia, and Springfield, Massachusetts, so Congress was looking at sites in the western states. Two local sites were deemed worthy of consideration: Vandruff's Island on the Rock River, and Rock Island on the Mississippi River.

Captain William H. Bell of Jefferson Barracks was charged with preliminary assessments of both sites. Bell's opinion was that the best source of waterpower was on Vandruff's Island, at the Rock River rapids opposite Rock Island City. The fall of the water was greater there than on the Mississippi and a dam could provide almost unlimited waterpower. There were, however, two drawbacks to the Rock. It was subject to severe fluctuations in water level and could not reliably power machinery on a year-round basis. In addition, the land on Vandruff's Island was prone to flooding and not suitable for building. Still, Bell considered it the better location in Rock Island County for the waterpower.

Unfortunately, the State canal on Vandruff's Island had never been completed. Optimistic local supporters estimated that only $15,000 to $20,000 would be needed to finish the project. When completed, they argued, there would be superior waterpower as well as steamboat transportation for sixty miles up the Rock. With coal and iron in the vicinity, it had many of the requirements for an armory.

In spite of his preference for Vandruff's Island, Bell expected that the Government would prefer the island of Rock Island on the Mississippi because it had proven, since the early 1800s, to be a good location for the security of the nation and could continue to do so with ease. Its position on the Mississippi River made it a central supply point with guaranteed access to eleven states without transshipment[8] Additionally, it was already owned by the Government and had only two occupants, only one of which had a legitimate claim to his property. This was George Davenport whom

Bell noted had been petitioning Congress for many years in regards to his property. The island had a solid rock foundation, was near to all the natural resources required in building such a facility, and had a long history of healthy conditions for inhabitation.

Most important of all, Bell noted that the island had good waterpower and that a recent charter had been granted to two local citizens to build a milldam from the south side of the island to the mainland. The dam, which had been completed and was operational, was 600 feet long. A sawmill had recently been put into operation. The waterpower there was good, but Bell noted that it would fluctuate during periods of low water and ice. What the national armory would need was constant, uninterrupted power. To this end, Bell suggested the construction of a river wall, which would channel a portion of the river into the slough where the dam was located. Bell also noted that the Mississippi River would require improvement because the Rock Island Rapids were a hindrance to transportation at predictable times during the year. This was a reference to the increased steamboat traffic on the river, which almost doubled in the two years between 1841 and 1843. Still, the river was closed for four, sometimes five, months out of the year.[9] Aside from ice and low water levels, the biggest detriment was still the rapids.

Hardly a week went by that some steamboat incident on the Mississippi wasn't reported. Accidents were expensive and financially ruinous to the developing economy of the Upper Mississippi Valley. The lower rapids around Keokuk were all but impassable except during the highest waters and the Rock Island rapids had claimed its share of disasters. There was a particular section in the upper rapids, called the Rock Island Chain, where the channel was so narrow that passing steamboats had difficulty in maneuvering past one another. In 1841 the S. B. Brazil had moved to one side to let the S.B Empire pass when she struck a rock and sank within thirty minutes. The 3500 pigs of lead on board were saved, but the boat was a total loss.[10] Despite repeated visits from civil engineers and numerous proposals for solutions, the river remained unimproved and was the biggest drawback to landing an armory or similar government facility in the area.

Before hopes could be raised too high, the Burlington Hawk-eye cautioned: "In the present financial state of the Government, it cannot be expected that it should immediately construct such a building as will eventually be needed; but it can lay a foundation ... " The caution was warranted. The site of Fort Massac was selected instead, but Congress failed to appropriate any money for the facility and the armory was never built there either.[11] Years later, a citizens' group spearheaded by Bailey Davenport finally got their wish when an arsenal was located on Rock Island.

Still looking for ways to attract a government contract, a group of citizens interested in the improvement of Rock River, petitioned the State Legislature to complete the improvements started by the State on Vandruff's Island, or authorize either a corporation or individuals who could. Citizens began to meet in Rock Island to discuss how to improve the Rock River not only in Rock Island County, but also at the upper rapids in Whiteside County and at the rapids at Rockford in Winnebago County. Called the Rock River Navigation, the corporation opened their books in June 1841. But, again, nothing happened. Men like Joshua Vandruff, who had been firmly established on the Rock, were taking a harder look at the waterpower on the Mississippi River rather than the Rock River. What was generating the most excitement for the Mississippi was the new dam built by David Sears. The dam gave new life to the land in what is Moline today. Even Vandruff purchased a number of tracts just above where now are the towns of East Moline and Silvis. George Davenport began to look at the potential there as well.[12]

Using information from John Buford, whose son N.B. Buford had surveyed the Mississippi rapids in 1829, David Sears applied his knowledge of harnessing waterpower to the backwater slough between Stephenson and Rock Island,. The area became known as Rock Island Mills. Along with John Spencer, Sears was granted a charter to build a dam across the backwaters of the Mississippi with the customary water privileges. Lacking funding, Sears built the dam in the most economical way possible, with brush and rocks and locally available material. The remarkable aspect of the project was not so much the dam, but the way

Sears and Spencer managed the waterpower rights, using John Buford's suggestion.[13]

Buford had proposed that a joint stock company be formed to build a mile and a half long canal with a depth of nine feet. Along this canal he proposed that a gristmill, three stories high, and a saw mill be built. These, he suggested, would build up Stephenson and additions to the town could be added as the need arose. In ten years, he predicted, it would pay for itself.[14] Unable to build such a wall with limited funds, Sears created a canal-like situation with his dam between the upper end of the island of Rock Island and the mainland. Although the details of the original agreement have been lost, the waterpower was sold as some form of cooperative venture. Buford's predictions were right on target. By 1840, the Sears and Spencer dam across Mississippi Slough, now called Sylvan Slough, was successfully supplying power for grain mills and for turning machinery to produce lumber and other products needed in the housing construction.

The local newspapers noted that the new industries were drawing business from forty miles away. In 1842 it was proudly announce that an iron foundry was in the works and that Zadoc Kalbough (Vandruff's son-in-law) had been given the contract for the building or buildings. Ainsworth and Lynde had built a large warehouse there, one of the biggest at that time on the Mississippi. In addition a huge flourmill, to be called the Merchant Flour Mill, was also in the plan by Spencer, Sears & Co.[15]

The waterpower at Rock Island Mills put the island of Rock Island on the map again. In just one year the increased production there had enabled local industrialists to obtain pine lumber at such a good price that everyone was taking advantage of it and this, in turn, was promoting more development. The sawmills were also using locally cut oak in the production of keelboats and steamboats and the steamboat *Clarion* was nearly ready for launch. All in all, it was exciting for town developers and citizens alike to hear the mills running almost nonstop and in such bad times to see how much progress had been made in so short a time.

Surprisingly, instead of continuing as Rock Island Mills and incorporating as an addition to the already established county seat, the founders of the mills pronounced their area a separate townsite and called it Moline, City of Mills. It was a significant change, and a complete rejection of the all-encompassing concept of Rock Island or Hesperia. The Moline town founders added something more. They injected a new vision into their community based on the Congregational Church and the anti-slavery and temperance movements. To many community leaders in Rock Island, this was a totally unexpected move of independence for Moline's founders and they hoped the founders of Moline would change their minds. Even into the 1850s, Rock Islanders hoped that the Moliners would come back into the fold of Rock Island. But the founders of Moline had found a way to share the waterpower without the kind of litigation found out on the Rock River and they began to attract other like-minded persons.

The development was important to George Davenport, too. Although he was no miller or dam-builder, he did own land along the south bank of the river, on both sides of the new developments where the founders were planning to plat the area as a town.   Nor did Davenport subscribe to many of the tenants espoused by the founders of Moline. He was neither pro temperance, nor a church-going Congregationalist. As a former slave owner, he was not an anti-slavery advocate either. But he was a practical man. Despite his ideological differences with the founders, Davenport supported the Moline founders and their development. From its very beginning, the town was characterized as an industrious, work-oriented community destined for success. This appealed to Davenport's own personal aspirations. On either side of the plat of Moline, he laid out two new additions.

On the riverbank directly west of his former trading post at Farnhamsburg, Davenport hired the county surveyor, P.A. Ogilvie, to lay out a parcel of land into lots in May (1842). Ogilvie divided the northwest quartersection of Section 36 into five lots, which he marked "A","B","C","D", and "E" on his survey map. Each lot was 79 1/3 yards in width and the five lots varied in size from 4 to 6 acres.[16] Exactly what Davenport had in mind for this land is hard to determine. It was not recorded as a town, nor was it an addition to either Rock Island or to

Moline. And, since it was located on the backwaters of the main channel of the river, the lots were hidden from view and accessible only by small craft. Perhaps it was simply laid out to capitalize on Moline's industry.

The Slough was beginning to look a lot like the Riverhead that George remembered from his boyhood and the inspiration for this particular project may have come to him when he visited England in 1827. Davenport had seen how it had revitalized his hometown of Louth and remembered how the area had almost been a little village of its own, functioning as both housing and work areas along the canal. It was a simple and workable idea that could easily be implemented on the bank of the slough. The eastern boundary of Moline was closer to the open river and more suitable for industry like sawmills that needed direct contact with the river.

The following year, and within days of the platting of Moline, George Davenport again hired county surveyor, P.H. Ogilvie, to lay out his land on the east side of Moline into an addition to the town. His streets followed the original Moline plan. Blocks were divided into lots the same size as lots in the Moline plat. This addition was bounded on the east by Bass Street (now 17th Street) and on the west by Edwards Street (now 22 Street) and by Water (1st Avenue) and Wells (2nd Avenue) and called Davenport's Addition to Moline. In all there were approximately 40 lots in this addition, but because of the odd shape of the tract, many of the lots were not full-sized. By today's standards these lots, 80 feet wide by 150 feet deep, were small for industry, but the location near the river was desirable. The first person to buy a lot in this addition was industrialist Charles Atkinson, who chose Lot three in Block four and paid George Davenport twelve dollars for the land.[17]

Davenport also began ferry operations at this Moline site, operating between the Illinois shore and the Iowa side of the river. A good ferry could attract business to a town, and particularly to his town of Davenport across the river. In September (1843) he applied for and was granted by the Rock Island county commissioners a license to operate a ferry from the east end of his Moline addition across the Mississippi River. David Sears remembered that the ferry was a flatboat propelled by big long sweeps or oars. It went to the Iowa shore and to Benham's Island where Sear's large flouring mill was. According to Sears, Davenport's Moline ferry landing was situated at the easternmost boundary of Davenport's Addition, on 22nd Street where the street strikes the Mississippi.[18]

This ferry, however, was short-lived. For one thing, the river was wide at this place and the Mississippi river looked particularly formidable, especially to those who had never experienced the "father of waters" before. The crossing was dangerous and took a longer time than at other locations. Pioneers usually sought out the shortest and easiest crossings. But the biggest reason for removing the ferry landing in Moline was that Keator and Skinner had purchased land to the west of the landing and built their sawmill at the common boundary between Moline and Davenport's Addition. Rafts of logs were floated past the ferry landing and held against the shore outside the mill entrance. This was no place for a ferry and so Davenport petitioned the county commissioners to withdraw his bond. The five-dollar tax was rescinded, and his ferry operations ended at that place.[19] Although it may have been a poor choice for crossing the river at that time, he was, in fact, way ahead of his time. Today the site is the location of I-74 Bridge between Illinois and Iowa and a major link between the East and West coasts.

In addition to Keater and Skinner's Steam Saw Mill, other manufacturing businesses as well as the residence of Charles Atkinson began to appear along the bank of the river. By 1843 the entire shore of Moline was in production with the manufacturers and mills for which it would be known as the City of Mills.[20] Sears planned to expand the milling facilities of Moline to the island side of the Rock Island where he laid out a townsite that would include workers' housing as well as more factories and mills.

Seeing the success that Moline was enjoying with their waterfront development, the residents of Davenport were anxious not to be left behind in developing waterpower. Petitions had been circulating there for some time, calling for an organized effort to develop waterpower similar to that in Moline. Since there were no backwater or slough areas near the town, the Davenport residents would have to create their own. At a public meeting in 1843, Davenport citizens agreed on a plan to cut a canal from Duck Creek to the town limits and to petition the Territorial Government to form a hydraulic company for that purpose. Unfortunately, the bill introduced by the Territorial Legislature was badly written with a fatal flaw that ultimately destroyed the company before it even got off the ground. Section 11 of the bill provided that "any future Legislature could alter or repeal the act." Efforts to repeal Section 11 were unsuccessful. The Scott County Hydraulic Company's plan was too expensive and uncertain for financial backers to take such a chance on it and, although the project was kept in the public eye for a couple of years, it was never enacted.[21]

Out on the Rock River, the businessmen of the Rock River Navigation Company continued to dream of finishing the State works on the Rock River, despite Governor Ford's order to sell the remains of the State Canal on Vandruff's Island. After several town meetings, however, it became clear that this was a much bigger project than they previously believed. A similar lock and dam at Sterling, Illinois, required more money than they could hope to raise in the current financial climate. Having only $300, they decided to remove the "loose and prominent rocks" at the lower rapids, but the results were disappointing as even that work proved more difficult than anticipated.[22]

Improvement on the Mississippi also proved more difficult than predicted by experts. In the winter of 1828 - 1829, N.B. Buford had first surveyed and mapped the Des Moines or Lower Rapids as well as the Upper or Rock River rapids " with a view to overcoming the obstacles to navigation." Buford noted the commercial advantages of improving the rapids and considered several options to improve the river: removing the obstacles or large boulders in the rapids, the feasibility of cutting canals on either side of the rapids, or deepening the channels. Buford's suggestions were too general to be of use, but a few years later, in 1836, Government Surveyor Henry Shreve identified seven specific places in the Mississippi River where improvement was needed. Buford had suggested that buoys could be used to mark the channel, but Shreve had tested this method and thought it unreliable. Few practical suggestions, however, were made for removing the rapids or for solving the problem of the low water flow during the summer months. Technology of the time was not advanced enough to offer workable solutions. As an alternative, Shreve recommended that experienced steamboat pilots be licensed specifically to run the rapids. Each steamboat would pick up a licensed pilot at either Davenport or Le Claire for the express purpose of guiding the boat through the rapids.[23]

Lt. Robert E. Lee later concurred with the findings of Henry Shreve, again testing Buford's buoy idea, but because the rapids were so dangerous he agreed that something must be done. Clearing the Upper Rapids would be difficult as the rocks were under water and would have to be blasted. In addition, the work season was short because of the duration of the summer levels when water was lowest. Until the upper rapids could be cleared, the licensed pilot idea would help make navigating the rapids safer. The towns of Le Claire and Port Byron became the homes of many of those specialized riverboat pilots.[24]

This recommendation may have been one of the reasons Davenport and Le Claire revived their plans for Le Claire, Iowa, and also why Davenport invested in Port Byron at this time. Plans for the town of Le Claire had been on the shelf for the past four or five years, and it had never been formally platted. When the Le Claire townsite was formally surveyed and laid out in city blocks and lots, George Davenport bought an additional sixty lots from Le Claire. To promote the town, Davenport and Le Claire hired Levi C. Turner. The deal he struck with George Davenport and Antoine Le Claire looked much like his earlier deal with Davenport in Rock Island City. For the sum of $10,000, he bought a share in the Le Claire townsite and, in return, was given the power of attorney to sell shares in this town to outside investors.[25]

Shreve's suggestions may have stimulated Davenport to turn his attention to Port Byron, too. Situated directly across the river from Le Claire, the site had recently been surveyed and laid out by Walter Phillips and four other local men: Samuel Allen, Moses Bailey, Dr. Patrick Gregg, and Nathaniel Belcher. Phillips had retained a quarter interest but sold an eighth interest in the town to Davenport just three days after the surveying. C.R. Bennett, the surveyor, also bought an eighth interest. By comparison with other proposed town sites of the time the town plat was small, only three blocks wide along the river and three blocks deep.[26] Because the town was so small and there was so much interest in the town, the sale of lots was advertised but there was no public auction.

Port Byron was the smallest speculating venture for Davenport, but the site held several potentials. It was a proven steamboat landing, having already been used for several years. Positioned at the upper end of the Rock Island Rapids, it was considered a prime location for warehousing and businesses associated with river transportation. Both Port Byron and Le Claire were poised to serve the many steamboats that navigated up and down the river, but they had another feature that made them desirable in terms of investment. The upper end of the Rapids between Le Claire and Port Byron was also the narrowest point in the river and some thought it the best place for a railroad bridge across the Mississippi River.

Davenport's investment in Port Byron paid off quickly. Le Claire, Iowa, however, had not prospered as much as its developers had imagined it would, but its next-door neighbor upriver, the town of Parkhurst, had. Some of the problems may have been related to Turner who was essentially bankrupt and preoccupied with his own money problems and lawsuits. Davenport and Le Claire eventually decided to promote the town of Le Claire on their own. They sold portions of Le Claire to a number of out-of-state investors, but industry was slow to develop. Davenport and Le Claire's focus was more on the town of Davenport, especially with the push to greatness across the river in Stephenson, now called Rock Island.[27]

In the winter of 1842, John H. Sullivan turned his attention back to the Rock River. After closing his steam flouring mill in Rockingham, he and a new partner Albert Moyer purchased the small island south of Vandruff's for the purpose of building a private dam there and starting another flour mill. Dickson, Vandruff and Co. had already started building a dam of their own on the slough side of the Rock between Vandruff's Island and present-day Milan. They were concerned that the proposed mill would interfere with their water supply. Sullivan and Moyer petitioned the State to build a second dam lower down the river, but Dickson and Vandruff vehemently opposed this plan. The controversy between the two companies over water rights escalated into litigation and divided Rock Island County. The courts were pelted with writs and injunctions, petitions for both sides, and bitter feelings. Dickson and Vandruff Company were issued an injunction to halt their building, but ignored it. Eventually the Rock Island County Commissioners forced a compromise between the two companies, allowing Sullivan and Co. to share the waterpower. Sullivan & Company proceeded to lay out Big Island in the Rock River for industrial purposes, but before Sullllivan could build, his wife became ill. He dissolved his partnership with Moyer, sold many of his land holdings, and returned to Ohio where his wife died soon after.[28] Although Sullivan's brother David remained on Big Island, their plans for Big Island never developed.

On Vandruff's Island Davenport remained in partnership in Vandruff's ferry. It was a busy crossing place and eventually required a bridge. The "free bridge," as it was called, was chartered by the Illinois State Legislature in the winter of 1843. Unlike the Rock Island City Bridge charter that had sanctioned a toll bridge, this bridge was to be free to all persons and vehicles and built with draws so as not to hinder any navigation on the Rock, although steamboats had never been able to establish a regular route up the river.[29] The steam Steamboat Lighter, guided by Captain Hight, eventually navigated as far as Madison, Wisconsin, a distance of 300 miles, but that was in exceptionally high water. Still, some people held onto the hope that the Rock could still be navigable. It was a vain hope.

After all the litigation, the Dickson-Vandruff mill was finally put into operation by 1844, but it was heavily mortgaged to a wealthy New Yorker investor, James E. Cooley. Two towns were laid out nearby the mill -- one on Vandruff's Island, called Lowell, and the other on the south bank of the slough, called Camden, which is today called Milan. A sawmill, too, was put into operation there. It was hoped that the free bridge leading from Henry, Knox, and Mercer counties on the south would direct business to the town of Rock Island.

George Davenport retained his interests and land holdings in the Rock River lands, but he never developed them. His expectations for those lands lay far into the future.

By the early 1840s, George Davenport had invested in all of the major towns in what was to become the Quad Cities of Iowa and Illinois: Davenport and Le Claire in Iowa; Stephenson/Rock Island, Moline, and Port Byron on the Illinois side of Mississippi; and along the Rock in what is today south Moline and south Rock Island. He had parlayed his trading skills into real estate becoming an agent and developer. In 1842, his trading days with the Sauk and Mesquakie officially ended.

CHAPTER EIGHTEEN:

DIGGING OUT and DIGGING IN

"THESE ARE HARD TIMES" was the message of many newspaper editors in the early 1840s. It was, in some ways, a gross understatement. Although speculators had been affected quickly by the financial situation in the Mississippi Valley, the settlers did not feel the pinch quite so soon. The hardest years for them were between 1840 and 1844. The Upper Mississippian reported that money market was tight in New York and getting tighter. Money could " not be obtained on the best and most ample securities."[1]

Desperate men mortgaged everything they had for a little cash. Money, always scarce on the frontier, was so tight that cash was almost non-existent in the Mississippi Valley through the early 1840s. Those looking for cash squirreled away by immigrants coming into the Mississippi Valley were disappointed. Exchanging goods on the barter system was all that kept many people from starving. One man even mortgaged his horse together with saddle and bridle and carriage and harness for $300. He was one of the lucky ones who could repay the loan.[2]

Foreclosure and bankruptcy were on many minds. Bankruptcy notices appeared frequently in the local newspapers and Scott County Sheriff Adrian Davenport was kept busy securing property and holding public auctions at the direction of the circuit courts. Taking a case to court was time-consuming and rarely profitable, but the law was designed to settle such disputes and sometimes the only recourse a man had when he had his family to provide for. It is noteworthy that of the sixty-some land transactions Davenport made in the 1840s, only four resulted in foreclosures. Still, it might have been more than he might have wished. There was often a heart-breaking story with each one.

Among the settlers, George Davenport stood out as an assertive, even powerful, man of money and property in the 1840s. He had had years of experience in the geography and geology of the land between Galena and St. Louis and was frequently consulted about locating valuable land that might be available. He had kept himself in good financial health throughout hard times in the past by diversifying his interests. Where once it was government that provided him cash in times of need, now it was real estate that kept him afloat. He managed to make thirteen land sales in Scott county during the depression years, excluding sales to his son and Antoine Le Claire with whom he bought and sold many parcels of land between 1841 and 1845. Twelve additional transactions took place across the river in Rock Island County. Davenport's terms were fairly straightforward and standard for the times, despite the depression: one third down with the balance to be paid in two equal installments, at twelve months and eighteen months. Davenport was dependent on buyers making their payments to keep the cash flowing, but buyers did not always come through and then Davenport found himself strapped for cash as well.

Since cash was scarce in those years, Davenport was often forced to manage on what he could collect on debts owed him. Although his credit was good with Pierre Chouteau Jr. & Co., he advised his son to sell anything that would bring cash, as there was no money to borrow in St. Louis. Even from the American Fur Company on which he had relied for so many years, there was nothing to borrow. The company had failed. Le Claire, too, was strapped for cash and Davenport helped him as best he could, using his own credit.[3]

News of the ratification of the Sauk and Fox Treaty on 16 February 1843 was great news to everyone. It would pay Davenport's past debts to the American Fur Company and put the family in "cosey circumstance." But the strain of not being able to acquire cash to support his family showed in his vow "never to ow to the amount of one dollar as long as I live." While in St. Louis, Davenport had seen too many men of property selling land at a quarter of its value just for the sake of cash. "I See Dailey men of large property forrist to raise a Small Sum of money to meet demands, and property Sold for one fourth of Its Value." Clearly, Davenport was afraid of losing all that he had ever worked for.[4]

In the summer of 1842 tax collectors were pounding on Davenport's doors as well as the doors of half of Rock Island County. Davenport owed $138.38 for his 1842 State and County taxes in Illinois and some in Scott County as well. He advised his son to sell any of the cattle that he could and take in exchange plank or any other local produce that they could make money on in. Somehow the Davenports managed to scrape together enough cash to pay the taxes. But there were other debts to pay.[5]

There was a judgment against Davenport filed by Daniel C. Doty. Doty had come to Rock Island in 1837 and invested in building a steamboat there. The steamboat sank before any of the building debts had been paid. Doty's partners declared bankruptcy, but Doty did not. Instead he engaged with George Davenport to build a brick storehouse, but he and Davenport argued over the quality of the bricks Doty bought and construction details. Unable to resolve their differences, they sought arbitration in the courts and in April 1841 the arbiters awarded Doty six hundred and forty-four dollars and sixty-six cents. In return, Doty agreed to remove all material from Davenport's property. Although Davenport repeatedly agreed to pay Doty, he did not. Nor was the material removed. Doty filed suit against Davenport again at the October term of 1841.

Finally, in summer of 1842, Doty got his money. He returned to his home state of Ohio and took up farming.[6] Davenport might have been buying time until he could pay Doty, but he was also stubbornly holding onto the notion that he had a gentleman's agreement with Doty, something that Doty could or would not fulfil.

The case with Doty was just one example of Davenport's stubbornness and inability to come to an agreement. There are many more examples of how he helped many settlers that attest to his generosity while maintaining the dignity of those in need. One old settler recalled, "lots of old settlers would have gone up if it hadn't been for Davenport."[7] Cynics might see this as nothing more than good business, and he knew very well how to do business.

In family matters there was a softer side to George Davenport. His first priority was to his sons and their welfare. While his earlier letters reveal only a man of business, the few surviving letters written to son George L. Davenport show an affectionate man connected to his family in spirit, anxious to get home to them while away, and relying on them to carry on without him. He was especially fond of his grand babies. Son George L. and wife Sarah had presented him with his first grandson in 1840 and named him George Alphonse, who was soon followed by Joseph in 1841, Naomi in 1842, and Catherine, called Kitty, in 1844. It is clear in these letters that they were dear to him. "Kiss our little boys for me," he wrote "and tell George I am coming with his drum." When they were a bit older, he would bring little George a toy gun and a drum for Joseph. He enjoyed the role of grandfather and was satisfied, perhaps even relieved, to know that there was a next generation to carry on the family name in America. What Davenport did best was to provide his sons a foothold on the future. Land was the most valuable asset he could acquire for them.[8]

Davenport spent the early years of the 1840s tending to his land and acquiring more. In tune with the development of the land surrounding his island home, he bought and sold when the prospects were favorable to him. He bought more land, more than he sold, which he either developed for rental or for future sale to the many immigrants arriving daily around

Rock Island. His final will written in the fall of 1844 is especially revealing about how he expected the land to provide an income for the years to come and will be discussed in the Epilogue.

Immigration to the Upper Mississippi Valley only escalated during these hard times. The Mississippian noted that many emigrants from the eastern states were attracted by the "cheapness and fertility of the soil." They had hopes for a chance to regain what they had lost in the recent downturn of the economy. Iowa Territory was one destination for these emigrants. The newly formed territory attracted wagonloads of people heading to settle on the prairies. The Burlington Hawkeye noted that in just a single week fifty-one wagons, all from the same neighborhood in Ohio, had crossed the river there. The lure of easily cultivated, highly productive land with plenty of water and timber and land for grazing, all at a low price, was hard to resist.[9]

The Gazette predicted that, based on the number of ferries crossing the river at Burlington, Iowa's population would soon double. A traveller from Kentucky reported 500 wagons heading for Iowa in just one day. At Keokuk fifteen wagons per day had been crossing for the past two months. Wilson's steam ferry between Davenport and Rock Island had carried more than a hundred wagons in just one week. Many travellers camped on the outskirts of Davenport while they searched for their own land.[10]

By 1840 the prime lands along the rivers and streams were all claimed, resulting in a rise in open market value. The men who were already settled were focused on expanding agriculture, developing industry, and improving transportation. For Davenport it was his own home overlooking the Mississippi River that became his primary focus. The Davenport's house was in the center of a beautiful and well laid out farm complex of gardens, orchards, and outbuildings. Over the years Davenport had continuously improved the home site by investing some $20,000 in the buildings, an impressive amount that was not wasted on the surrounding community. Some called it a romantic setting, others idyllic. It enthralled all who visited.

Shade trees surrounded the house and in the orchard were Catawba and Isabella grapes grown on arbors, as well as Morello cherry trees.

There were nearly fifty peach trees planted in 1827, pear planted as early as 1820, and numerous apple trees as well. The grape vines had produced enough grapes for winemaking and some of Davenport's own wine was served to guests at the wedding of his son George L Davenport and Sarah Grace Clark. In later years Susan Lewis Goldsmith showed how they preserved some of the grapes by wrapping them tightly in cotton. She presented them to the editor of the Daily Union on New Year's Day.[11]

Bailey Davenport was charged with the care of the gardens, both vegetable and flower. His mother was particularly proud of her flowers. The Davenports kept livestock, both cattle and hogs, primarily for their own use and, although they occasionally sold them for profit, it was nothing on the scale of the army days. Some of the land they owned was used for grazing and for hay to feed the livestock, as well for raising corn. At least one cow and calf were kept for milk and butter and the usual chickens and other wild fowl ran freely. It is no wonder that Davenport was particularly anxious about his claim to his island property. After months of anticipation, the Government had finally opened the Iowa lands to public sale, but still there was no decision about the Island's military reserve status, and George Davenport's claim was still in limbo.

The Iowa Land Sales on June 6, 1840, attracted hundreds of persons to Dubuque from all over eastern Iowa. It was the first opportunity they had had to plunk down their hard cash and make a formal claim. Every hotel and boarding house in town was filled and it was estimated that about a hundred men camped on an island opposite Dubuque until they could formally buy their land. The Iowa Sun reported that no speculators had even been in evidence.[12] The land clubs had done their job keeping them out, and the transfer of land was orderly. But Davenport's land was not in the Public Domain and he was still waiting to secure his home on Rock Island.

For many years George Davenport had persisted in his petitions to Congress, but Congress still had not acted on his request to buy his island quarter section. The unresolved question, which continued to delay the process, was whether or not the island, or any part of it, was still a "Military Reserve." There had been several setbacks over the years and more than once Davenport had had to start the petition process over again. Once there was even a ruling that a Special Act of Congress was needed, but then the Attorney General overruled the Act. Discouraged, but not defeated, Davenport pursued his preemption claim with help from his state representatives.

While waiting for his answers, Davenport continued his real estate business. Le Claire's additions to the town of Davenport had proven to be good investments for both men. They sold well. The first addition had none of the title concerns of the original town and sold so quickly that a second addition was platted almost immediately. Rather than partnering with Le Claire on successive additions, George bought half of the additions outright, and the two friends began to separate their interests as the town grew. Davenport also began to develop some of his town lots into rental property. He owned a variety of houses, or hotels, both frame and brick with offices, stables, and apartments as well as two stores. He developed eight lots in Block 29 (at the corner of Fifth and Gaines) into a complex, which he called "Son of Row." This was in response to Le Claire's building of a similar row house. In the town of Stephenson (now called Rock Island), he still owned two blocks with houses, one of which had a log cabin and stable attached, but his heart and most of his attention was in the town of Davenport, where his elder son was taking charge of the family businesses.

Since his marriage in 1839, son George L. Davenport had been more than just his father's clerk in the Indian Trade. He had begun to take a more public role in community affairs while his father began to play a more supportive role. George L. and Sarah had lived for a time in an apartment above one of his buildings on Front Street, but in 1842 moved their growing family to a house on the corner of Third and Brady Street. He was also becoming more involved in the town affairs. Like his father, he had moved from the Indian trade to settler merchandizing and assumed many of the daily aspects of running the Davenport family businesses, especially the mercantile business which his father had started with Antoine Le Claire, at the corner of Front and Main Streets. When Le Claire retired from that business sometime in early 1841, George L.

continued it in partnership with his cousin, James M. Bowling. They advertised themselves as General Commission Merchants and dealers in dry goods, groceries, liquors, stores, castings, iron, nails, glass, etc. -- just as his father and Le Claire had in previous years. In the same entrepreneurial spirit that characterized his father, he used the newspapers to promote his business, announcing the arrival of the latest goods and specialties in the local Gazette. He had also become an authorized dealer of patented medicines, a marketing ploy worthy of his father. He was elected as one of the town Trustees and was active in the business of land and development. He also advertised his available rental lands, as shown in this example.

> *FOR RENT - two story frame store house on*
> *corner of Main and Brady streets containing*
> *four rooms. Also two dwelling houses in*
> *complete order, for very low rent.*

> *VALUABLE LOTS, FOR SALE*
> *Several good building lots situated in the*
> *central and improved parts of Davenport, are*
> *offered for sale at very low prices.*[13]

One improved piece of land that George L. retained was his original land claim east of town where he continued to farm. Like other farmers he experimented with new strains of corn and was concerned with higher yields, insects, and other problems associated with farming. He used gifts of produce to the editor as a cheap way to advertise his success and to promote the richness of the agricultural lands surrounding Davenport. The enormity of the produce - fourteen-inch apples weighing seventeen ounces - attested to rich prairie soil of the Midwest.[14]

The elder Davenport was less visible in the public eye. He spent his time with real estate issues, building new storefronts and houses, and improving some of the lots with fencing, wells, etc. He, too, used the local newspapers to publicize his property and merchandize for sale. Most of his property was improved, which meant that there was a good dwelling house on the property and, most importantly, a never-fail spring of water.[15]

The elder Davenport was also spending time in court. His relationship with settlers was different from the way he interacted with the Indians. In a trading relationship with the Indians, traders followed the law of the land. If a Sauk or Mesquakie hunter had a bad season one year and unable to repay his credits, the debt was written off as a loss and forgotten. The trade had built in security for the trader with a high mark up on the trade goods and the trader always had the option of not giving out credit to hunters deemed a bad risk. But with settlers, transactions between two people were governed by laws and courts designed to enforce them. If a settler or speculator reneged on a promise or failed to make a payment or honor a debt, the creditor could get some satisfaction through the courts to recoup his losses. It was not unusual for disputes over land and debts to be decided by the courts and, in fact, the majority of cases heard in Territorial Iowa were over land disputes.

Davenport resorted to the courts many times in the 1840s. It was not a matter of being disagreeable or difficult to please. Davenport could be quite generous and had demonstrated that over and over again, but he had a deep sense of principle and a clearly defined sense of fairness. When crossed, he could be stubborn and retaliatory. That the settlers called him Colonel shows that they recognised this and treated him with respect, and perhaps with a little awe.

Now that clear title to the city lots had been received, Davenport and the other proprietors expected the monies owed them for city lots would be paid promptly. That was the agreement at the time of purchase. For the most part, the proprietors had been fortunate in their sales, but two years after clear title to the property had been conveyed, there were still three outstanding debts. Le Claire and Davenport, as representatives of the Proprietors, took these three cases to Chancery court.

The court process was cumbersome and time consuming but similar to the process followed today. Charges were filed with the Clerk of the District Court in Scott County and publicly announced in the newspapers in 1842. The Proprietors as Complainants requested payment plus interest and costs of the suit or, in lieu of payment, that the defendants surrender all claim, rights, and equity to the property, and that it be sold at public auction. All proceeds of such auction would be applied to the payment of the principal, interest, and costs of the proprietors. The amounts of the suit were far from frivolous.

The first case involved all seven living proprietors of Davenport, Iowa, vs. Neil Cameron. Cameron had purchased four lots for a total of $770 from proprietor Philip Hambaugh in 1836. One third of the purchase price had been paid at the time of purchase and Cameron had been issued a title bond. Since that time, a clear title had been available for Cameron whenever he paid his note in full, but in the interim, Hambaugh had died and no payments had been received from Cameron. Cameron was a non-resident and not represented in court, so the case continued at each term of court until September 1844. No record of the case can be found after this time. It is possible that the suit was allowed to lie dormant and the property finally sold for back taxes.[16]

The second case involved James Goodwin who had purchased from Davenport and Le Claire a parcel of land containing 336.11 acres in 1840. Soon after, Goodwin mortgaged the land to Alexander Donaldson. Neither Davenport and Le Claire nor Donaldson had received any payment by the fall of 1841 and a suit for foreclosure was begun. The Court determined that $600 was due on the principal plus $78 interest and that Goodwin had until the first of June 1842 to pay the total. Since the court received no notice of payment, this parcel of land was sold at public auction on October 8, 1842. Davenport and Le Claire were the highest bidders. They were then free to resell the property to someone else.[17]

In the third case, William McLellan was delinquent on his payments to the proprietors. He had purchased a lot in the summer of 1839 for $200 with the usual agreement to pay the balance. McLellan had further agreed to erect on the property a house of brick, stone, or frame construction within twelve months. Fifty dollars had been paid at the time of purchase, but since then no payments had been paid and no construction had taken place. At the April term of Court, both parties agreed to dismiss the case and McLellan paid the court costs. The sale was put on hold until the 18th of September when payment was promised. Since there was no further mention in court records, McLellan must have satisfied the terms of his agreement with Davenport and Le Claire.[18]

Davenport and Le Claire were represented in the courts by two old friends, G. C. R. Mitchell and Ebenezer Cook. Mitchell would eventually be a brother-in-law to son George L. Davenport. Ebenezer Cook later became a judge in the Scott County Circuit Court. Both Mitchell and Cook represented the proprietors in their Scott county cases. Mitchell represented Davenport in his Rock Island County cases. The client-lawyer relationship was an important one in town founding and Davenport found himself in need of a lawyer's services on several occasions. With the population of the towns so small, the business and personal relations often overlapped.

Another troublesome case was with Elizabeth Nichols, a case that illustrates the difficulty of the time as well as the uncertainty of life, especially on the frontier. The case also reveals something about George Davenport. The situation began in July 1838 when Mrs. Nichols' husband William together with Gershom Biddle purchased Lots 3, 4, 5, and 6 in Block 7 in the new town of Davenport from George Davenport. They paid him with a promissory note for $553.34. The first installment was payable in twelve months and the second at the time when clear title could be conveyed. William Nichols immediately took a leadership position in the new town, becoming active in the struggle for county seat, and participating in town government. He was appointed Street Commissioner in 1838 and two years later elected as one of the town trustees. He was also a subscriber to the Public Buildings Fund and, by all accounts, a good credit risk, ambitious, and community-oriented. But, on the 25 September 1840, William Nichols suddenly died after a short, but painful illness. He left a widow, three small children, and debts. His widow, Elizabeth, was forced to sell most of their personal property at public auction to settle those debts, but she retained the lots. At the sale, held in November of 1840, she sold livestock, tools, and many of her household goods including the cook stove, bedsteads, and bedding for the sum of $587.57.

The terms of the auction reflect the hard times: cash for amounts under five dollars and nine-months credit for amounts over five dollars.[19]

Elizabeth Nichols, however, did not immediately pay off her debts. Her court appointed securities, Harvey Leonard and William Axford, notified the court that she was uncooperative in filing the required inventory and appraisal of the estate. By this non-action, she put them in danger of liability for the mismanagement of the estate. By April of 1842, the Nichols debt was four years overdue and Mrs. Nichols still owed George Davenport $480. Davenport filed suit against her.[20]

After appointing Mrs. Nichols as guardian for her children, the court attempted to locate Nichols' original partner, Gershom Biddle, and the case was continued for ninety days. Biddle was a resident of Lycoming County, Pennsylvania, and by affidavit admitted to the court (on first of March 1843) that the debt was a true debt and that he had not in fact paid any of his share. There was also no hint that he expected to pay his share. Not until June 1843 did the judge take the case under advisement. Finally, on 6 October 1843, the judge ruled that Elizabeth Nichols could have 75 days to make the payment of $480. Failure would result in sale of the property at public auction.

The Nichols' lots were, in fact, sold at public auction on the 16 March 1844, and Elizabeth bought her own lots back, being the highest bidder at $526.46. At three o'clock on 4th of May she received the deed to all four lots, and one hour later sold them to Antoine Le Claire for three hundred dollars. Finally, after six years, two of which were spent in court, the situation was concluded. How much it cost George Davenport in time away from his work and in lawyer's fees were all elements that had to be calculated when one was involved in the land business.[21]

Davenport also used the courts to settle personal claims. Some were attempts to get payment for debts, but there were three cases in which he had signed as legal security for others and was drug into court, not by his own failure to act, but because others had reneged and the creditors were looking to him for satisfaction. Being someone's security had its risks.

The first case took place in Rock Island County, Illinois. Davenport had agreed to be one of three securities for Joel Wells Sr., the County Treasurer. When Reverend John Brich(sic) was found frozen to death in March 1837, a large sum of cash and notes amounting to just over $3,000 was found on his body and in his saddlebags. The money was turned over to Wells as County Treasurer. When Joel Wells Sr. left office, the Rock Island County Commissioners sued him for not turning over to them that sum of money, a fact that he denied. But Wells died before the suit could be resolved. The County Commissioners pressed charges against his three securities, including Davenport. After several years the case was ruled in favor of the County Commissioners. The three defendants then hired the Springfield firm of Logan and Lincoln to appeal the decision to the Illinois State Supreme Court. The issue was finally resolved in December 1843 when Joel Wells Jr. paid $3,500 to the County Commissioners and the suit was dismissed after six years of court appearances.[22]

Another case involved John D. Ansley, a dry-goods storeowner and copper mine operator in the Mineral Point region north of Galena. Ansley sought financial backers when his mining operations became too expensive, but there was some controversy over the prospects of Ainsley's mine. Samuel C. Stambaugh wrote a highly encouraging article about the prospects of this mine, but an English geologist by the name of George W. Featherstonhaugh disagreed. He wrote a disparaging report on Ansley's mine. Ansley's backers in the east had him jailed on fraud charges based on Featherstonhaugh's opinion. Davenport, Stambaugh, and John P. Sheldon paid his bail, which allowed Ansley to go to England to search for other financing, but as Ansley's securities, the three were liable for his $1,208 debt. Featherstonhaugh's opinion prevented Ansley's finding financial backing. Unable to collect from Ansley, his creditors sued in Jo Daviess County in 1837, but was later transferred to the District of Columbia and continued in the courts through 1843. During this time Davenport and the other securities stalled on paying Ansley's debts, hoping that Ansley would be able to make the payment. The rush on copper had begun by this time, and copper prices had risen. Fortunately,

Ansley's mine produced good quality copper. His mine was finally incorporated as the Iowa Copper Mine in 1844 and when the case was returned to Scott County, Iowa, it was dismissed.[23]

A more complicated suit involved the ferryman John Wilson who sued the owners of the Steamboat Ariel, all of whom were associated with the American Fur Company and business associates of George Davenport. A judgment of $1,837.50 plus costs was awarded to Wilson for debts claimed by Wilson against the company. The plaintiffs challenged the judgment and appealed to the Iowa Territorial Supreme Court. While that suit was under advisement, Wilson brought a writ of attachment against the steamboat Ariel, her tackle, apparel, and furniture. In order to release the steamboat, Davenport executed a bond of security to John Wilson in the amount of $10,000. Wilson then filed suit against Davenport on that bond to recover his damages. Davenport countersued with an injunction, asking that Wilson's suit be postponed until the Territorial suit on the original damage suit could be heard. But Wilson ignored that injunction and filed a suit against Davenport across the river in Illinois. Davenport then filed contempt charges against Wilson. In the meantime, based on the suit on the bond in Iowa, Sheriff Adrian Davenport seized George Davenport's property for the purpose of selling it to satisfy the debt to Wilson. As a result, Davenport could do nothing with his own property. An injunction to stop the whole proceeding failed, but when George Davenport was murdered a few months later, the whole case was dismissed.[24]

A final series of lawsuits against Davenport was instigated by Sophia Farrar, the widow of his former trading partner, Amos Farrar. It will be remembered that Farrar was Davenport and Farnham's partner in Galena until 1829 when the partnership was dissolved. Farrar married schoolteacher Sophia Gear in 1830 and died in 1832. Farrar's estate was penniless and his daughter by his first wife was a minor. Mrs. Farrar sued Davenport in an attempt to get an income for herself and Farrar's daughter Elizabeth.

As in the case of Elizabeth Nichols, widowhood on the frontier was difficult and women were forced to be resourceful in order to survive.

How different women coped with their individual circumstances was in part based on their own personality and situation. Sophia' Farrar was a former schoolteacher, an educated and independent woman. Although she had two brothers in Galena who could well afford to support her, she believed that she had a dower right to the land and profits of the business her husband had held in partnership before their marriage. Court documents reveal how little she understood the nature of her husband's business, and her persistence in suing Davenport managed only to waste time and what little money she had. Although the local courts took pity on her condition and awarded her sums of money, the higher courts to which Davenport appealed, did not.

In the first suit, filed in 1835, Sophia attempted to claim a portion of the lands Farnham and Davenport held in partnership. The commissioners charged with dividing the land, however, were aware of the circumstances of the land ownership, which did not included Farrar. They had been unable to divide the land in such a way that would not prejudice the proprietorship of Farnham and Davenport. So the case was dismissed.

Mrs. Farrar then petitioned the courts for her dower rights in the sale of those lands and a jury awarded her an annual sum of money carefully calculated on the size and value of the property held in partnership. Davenport appealed the award and in 1836 the judgment was reversed, based on the fact that the partnership with Farrar had been dissolved prior to her marriage to him. Mrs. Farrar, therefore, had no inheritance, or dower, claim to the property. She, however, was not satisfied with this reversal and again filed suit against Davenport, as well as the heir of Russell Farnham, and others.

This time Farrar claimed $10,000 of the $40,000 which Davenport and Farnham had been awarded in the Treaty of 1832 as settlement of the trading debts of the Sauk and Mesquakie. Since the debts dated back to the seven years prior to the Treaty, she reasoned that she should be awarded that amount, which she calculated should have been her husband's share. The case was tried at the October term, 1839, in the Jo Daviess Circuit Court, and Mrs. Farrar was awarded $9, 233.33 damages plus the cost of the suit. Again, Davenport appealed. Again, the judgment was reversed, on the basis that the Farnham-Davenport partnership had been dissolved and settled fully with no statement of debt to Farrar at the time of the final settlement.

Farrar filed suit yet again against Davenport, this time in May of 1845. Again, she demanded $10,000, which she calculated as her third of the money received by Farnham and Davenport in the Treaty of 1832. Further, she asked to see all the books, papers and letters pertaining to the business that would account for the way the treaty award was divided and spent. She claimed that she had repeatedly asked Davenport to see such accounts and papers, but that he had ignored her requests. Nor had Davenport ever paid her any money, despite asking him in the kindest of manners. The suit was dropped on account of the untimely death of Davenport two months later, but it should be noted that Davenport's books were the property of the American Fur Company, which claimed the entire $40,000. Furthermore, the books were not in Davenport's possession.[25]

The 1840s were desperate times indeed, and George Davenport helped more settlers than he sued in court. Court suits took time, but they were sometimes necessary to settled disputes in orderly and civilized ways. It was not the way of the Sauk and Mesquakie, but George Davenport learned to use American law to his benefit. He was stubborn, but patient, and he showed himself to be fair. As a man of principle, he stood up for his rights under the law. In many instances, it might have been less time-consuming and perhaps nicer to give in, especially in the cases of Nichols and Farrar, but these were tough times and George Davenport had his family's future to consider.

CHAPTER NINETEEN:

WRAPPING UP THE INDIAN TRADE

IN 1840 GEORGE DAVENPORT formally contracted with the American Fur Company for his son to work as a paid agent, although George L. had been taking a more authoritative role for some time. The $400 per year salary that Davenport negotiated for his son was a far cry from the sum he had earned in his early years in the business and speaks to the greatly diminished role that the Indian Trade was playing in their lives. The distance between the Sauk and Mesquakie and their home on the Rock River was about to grow even farther.

The Sauk and Mesquakie had again moved their villages, this time to the Skunk and Des Moines rivers in central Iowa. The one exception was Poweshiek, who had moved further north on the Ioway River. The tribes were almost totally dependent on government annuities since their hunts were not sufficient to feed them and their cornfields too new to be productive. The traders supplied food to feed the tribes, but their annuities were not enough to sustain them and also pay off their accumulating debts to the traders.

The Davenports were still agents of the American Fur Company, now owned by Pierre Chouteau Jr., and managing the company's trading posts with the Sauk and Mesquakie. Some things had changed in the nature of the business. Accounts were now identified by village chief rather than by Outfit and Year as in years past, and the traders manned year-round posts near each village, rather than on a seasonal or temporary basis.

The nature of the trade since the Black Hawk War had changed as well. Trading agreements were made solely through the chiefs and there was more dependence on goods for daily needs rather than just for the hunt. Where other traders were said to have supplied luxury items, the Davenport inventories suggest that they were less willing to provide more than basic necessities to them. Corn and flour, as well as meat, were more noticeable in the accounts than previously, and the traders were also providing horses, which the tribes had always bred themselves in the past. There were also more clothing products such as shirts and coats than yard goods to produce those articles. The Davenports did not sell luxury items such as silver studded saddles to the chiefs, nor did they sell spirituous beverages to the Indians. There were plenty of other traders who did.

Davenport was concerned about the number of whiskey merchants who demanded their pay when the annuities were handed out. The whiskey merchants were aggressive and "determined to have their money" despite the warning of the Agent to the Indians not to pay them. The trading house debts took priority because those traders furnished necessities in the way of corn and meat to the tribes. But, Davenport had had trouble getting paid and was considering reducing the amount of credit he was willing to extend if something couldn't be done.[1] Tribal debts had been paid through 1836, but since that time, over twenty thousand dollars worth of goods had been furnished by the Davenports to the various chiefs. Interest was accruing on top of that, interest that Davenport owed to the Company.

Invoices from Pierre Chouteau Jr. & Co. are far from complete after 1835, but there was a distinct reduction in the amount of trade done by the Davenports after 1838. Farnham's Des Moines River trade was closed at that time and the hunts were producing fewer furs at all the posts. On the other side of the ledger, however, Davenport was supplying blankets, cloth, and ready-made clothing, and hunting supplies for the tribes without any assurance of being paid. It was the credit that he gave, Davenport maintained, that had kept the Sauk and Mesquakie in better circumstances than other tribes.[2]

Davenport continued to buy his merchandize from St. Louis merchants, but he was also able to offer goods from many eastern merchants who were now supplying the western stores. In the absence of complete records, it is difficult to distinguish the Indian Trade goods from goods intended for the settlers, although some assumptions can be made based on living styles. Sperm candles and carpet binding, for instance, were used more by settlers. Beads and blankets were generally intended for the Sauk and Mesquakie.

One big change in the business was how the annual payment (annuities) was made to the tribes by the U.S. Government. The tribes were almost completely dependent on their annuities to settle their debts with their traders as well as for provisions of flour and corn. The government, however, was slow in making payments. By early summer of 1837, the Sauk and Mesquakie were desperate for their annuity payments, which were usually paid to them in June. They travelled to St. Louis to see if they could get their payment, and when they could not, determined to go on a summer hunt. About 200 Mesquakie men, women, and children led by Waucoshausee, went into central Iowa where they hoped to get enough meat to feed their people, but they encountered the Sioux hunting on the same land. After a deadly encounter, the Mesquakie reported eleven men killed and thirteen wounded. Their chief, Waucoshasee, was severely wounded. Not finding their Indian Agent at Rock Island, they told their story to their trader, George Davenport, who then recorded their story. Waucoshasee's account was later published in the newspapers. By late August the government had neither paid them in money nor in bank notes with which to pay their traders, nor had they delivered any food provisions to the tribes as promised by treaty. Davenport's letter to the Galena newspaper explained that the Indians were asking the government to plough and fence a couple sections of land for their women so they could grow corn. It was difficult to break up the prairie sod with only hoes, and giving them assistance in agriculture, Davenport said, "would better their condition." Not selling them whiskey would also help. Davenport's was a lone voice calling for fair treatment for the Indian tribes who were seen by the general public as being as nuisance, more interested in whiskey than planting corn.[3]

Late in the summer, George Davenport and his son accompanied Keokuk and a contingency of Sauk and Mesquakie to negotiate a peace treaty with the Sioux and to sell more of their lands. Black Hawk and his son were among them. They left Rock Island on the 12th of September and arrived back home on the 24th of November. At this treaty the Sauk and Mesquakie agreed to sell Keokuk's reserve, a tract of 1,250,000 acres in exchange for payment of their traders' debts, $28,000 worth of good, two gristmills and the support of two millers, as well as help in agriculture, horses, and an investment that would guarantee the tribes an annual income.[4]

The annuities were still causing problems within the tribe and there were disagreements among the various villages as to how the payments should be made. After the 1839 payments, some tribal members had complained that the fur companies got all the money and the people got nothing. In the fall of 1840 a delegation led by Hardfish and a son of Black Hawk rode seventy-five miles to Burlington to present their grievances to Governor Lucas. Like Poweshiek several years before, Hardfish's followers complained that paying the annuities to the headmen was unfair and allowed for abuse of the funds. They also complained about their Indian Agent who had not been willing to take a side on this matter. Lucas intervened, but only served to make the problem worse by attacking the Indian Agent and dividing the tribes further.

The annuities were to be paid to the Indians at the new Indian Agency on the Des Moines River. All the Sauk and Mesquakie gathered there to receive their payments as well as the traders who hoped to collect the money owed to them by the tribes. Governor Robert Lucas, who was also Superintendent of Indian Affairs in Iowa, had nothing but contempt for the traders, considering them a bad influence on the Indians. He banished them from the negotiations. Davenport, his son George L., and Antoine Le Claire were among them. They were kept away from the Indians under guard in the American Fur Company Trading Post, about a mile from the agency. When time came for the annuity payments to be distributed in October of 1840, the tribal factions could not agree how the money should be distributed. The situation between the factions was so contentious that Lt. Beach, the Indian Agent, sent the annuity money back to St. Louis for safekeeping.

By February, the tribes offered to sell more land. The offer, presented by Lt. Beach to Territorial Governor John Chambers was accepted, but the question of where the tribes should go was still unanswered, so there was no treaty. Anticipating that the Indians would be leaving soon, squatters moved into their lands and when removed, retaliated by burning the mills the government had built for the Indians.[5]

In a vain attempt to maintain their traditional lifestyle, the Sauk and Mesquakie continued to go on summer hunts. They attempted these through the early 1840s, although the risks of infringing on other tribes hunting grounds were great. Life had been especially hard since their first removal from Rock River and getting harder with each removal. They had never had time to adapt to any new environment. Game was scarce in central Iowa, as was timber for their houses and fires. The soil was too poor for their gardens. The Sauk and Mesquakie population, which had numbered nearly 6,000 in 1833, had been reduced to 2,488 in 1845. Malaria, resulting from the many lakes and swamps of central Iowa, was a large cause of illness and death in the two tribes.[6]

In June 1841, the tribes again gathered at Agency, Iowa, for their annuity payments. By this time, the tribes were poverty-stricken and ready to come to a consensus. Robert Lucas had also been replaced as

Territorial Governor, and the new Territorial Governor, John Chambers of Kentucky, was a very different man from Robert Lucas, easy going in temperament and more willing to listen to the Indians. Chambers agreed to let the Chiefs consult with any of their white friends, including George Davenport and Antoine Le Claire, to help them make their decision. In this way Chambers was able to bring the factions together and they were able to make a unified decision.

The consensus was that the overdue 1840 annuities should be paid to Keokuk and the other chiefs as usual. The 1841 annuities, however, were proportionately divided between Hardfish's followers and Keokuk's and distributed among their followers as they saw fit. The two groups agreed, that in the following year, the 1842 annuities would be paid to heads of families.[7]

That summer (1841), the Sauk and Mesquakie attempted another buffalo hunt. This time they took with them about three hundred warriors in anticipation of meeting the Sioux on the hunting grounds. The hunt was successful and they cured enough meat to get the tribe through the winter, but the Federal Government wanted to start new treaty discussions for the remaining Iowa lands held by the Sauk and Mesquakie.

The 1840 and 1841 annuity payments had been delayed so that the land cession discussions could be held at the same time. Contrary to administration hopes, the Sauk and Mesquakie were not then agreeable to selling any more of their land. Negotiations resumed the following October 1842 and, largely through the efforts of Antoine Le Claire, the Sauk and Mesquakie reluctantly agreed to sell their remaining Iowa lands and remove to a tract of land on the west side of the Missouri river. This cession was between twelve and fourteen million acres for which they would be paid $800,000 plus $40,000 annually. At $1.25 per acre, this meant a revenue of $15 to $17.5 million for the United States. Settlers and speculators alike were ecstatic. The land, according to the Davenport Gazette, was the best purchase made by the U.S. Government as it had been purchased for the low price of about eight cents an acre and contained "five lead mines, one copper mine, a salt lake, and exhaustive mines of bituminous coal" in addition to fertile agricultural land.[8]

By agreement the tribal debts, which amounted to the staggering sum of $258, 566.34, were to be paid. The largest amount, $112,109.00, was paid to Pierre Chouteau Jr. & Co. and included the debts of Davenport's Sauk Outfit for the years dating back to 1837. In all there were 44 debts approved for reimbursement by the treaty commissioners who examined and adjusted all claims.

The Davenports were present at the negotiations. Their debts were among the smaller claims. George L. Davenport's personal claim was for $320 and Le Claire's claim for $1,375, which he owed to Pierre Chouteau Jr.

The Sauk and Mesquakie were allowed to stay in Iowa for the winter and agreed to remove themselves by the following May 1843. That winter, though, was one of the worst winters on record. Many ponies died and the meat they had cured in the summer was barely enough to get them by.[9]

Thousands of settlers wanting their land gave little thought to the miserable conditions of the Sauk and Mesquakie who continued trying to maintain their old lifestyle against incredible obstacles. As news of the government's successful treaty and imminent removal of the Indians from Iowa spread, the soon-to-be settlers packed up their belongings, ready to move onto the vacated land. The Gazette predicted how quickly the land would be claimed. In addition to those who had already migrated westward "thousands of our hardy and enterprising citizens, as soon as the Indians depart west of the Missouri to their future homes, will emigrate and permanently locate ... " on the prairies. Moving westward was hardest for the more traditional Indians and their ties to the Mississippi Valley were difficult to break. The Fox, now wishing to be called by their traditional name, Mesquakie, were particularly unsettled. They often returned to eastern Iowa, sometimes camping out on the outskirts of Davenport, as the Gazette noted: "A remnant of Musquawka tribe has bivouacked amongst us this winter. Their tents are pitched in the outskirts of our town, while their dingy occupants daily saunter listlessly through our street or lounge about the stores ... "[10]

Collecting his credits from the Sauk and Mesquakie could not have been the only thoughts that dominated Davenport's mind. There had been many political changes among the Sauk and Mesquakie since the Black Hawk War, changes that affected the Indian Trade and Davenport's relationship with the surviving elders. In many ways, the tribe's pending move to western Iowa helped Davenport to make the break from the Indian Trading business. As Poweshiek and his band of Mesquakie prepared to move even further west, Davenport and his son officially withdrew from the Indian trade.

In a timely sequence of events, the American Fur Company announced it had failed. It was the right moment for the Davenports to resign from the Indian Trade. Their friendship with the tribes, forged over many years, would continue since both boys had grown up with them and George L. was an officially adopted son of the Mesquakie. George L. Davenport also had a daughter, Jennie, who remained with the tribe. For many years after this, Jennie returned each summer to Rock Island to live with her father. Ledger accounts with Pierre Chouteau Jr. & Co. show that Davenport began to withdraw his money from the company in cash payments.[11]

The Indian issue was less and less prominent in the newspapers, although explanations of the various treaty agreements were of interest to settlers who impatiently waited for the Indians to move off their land. Only on occasion was there any public reflection on the Indian issue as the Indians were no longer a part of life around Rock Island. As noted by the Davenport Gazette, the Indians "were truly passing away." Their numbers were rapidly decreasing and soon, the editor predicted, they "will only be known in history."[12] There was no concern for what was truly happening to the Indians.

28th CONGRESS,
1st Session.

S. 44.

[Private.]

IN SENATE OF THE UNITED STATES.

JANUARY 11, 1844.

Mr. WOODBRIDGE, from the Committee on Public Lands, submitted a report, (No. 40,) accompanied by the following bill; which was read, and passed to a second reading.

A BILL

For the relief of George Davenport, of Rock island, in the State of Illinois.

1   Be it enacted by the Senate and House of Representatives

2   of the United States of America in Congress assembled, That

3   George Davenport be, and he is hereby, authorized to enter

4   the fractional quarter section of land upon which he resides,

5   on Rock island, in the State of Illinois, it being the southeast

6   fractional quarter of section twenty-five, in township numbered

7   eighteen north, range numbered two west of the fourth prin-

8   cipal meridian, upon his paying to the receiver of public

9   moneys of the United States land office at Dixon the mini-

10   mum price of one dollar and twenty-five cents for the same,

11   upon which usual certificate and patent shall issue, as in

12   other cases.

This Bill has passed both Houses of Congress and is now a law. March 25th 1844 —

After years of petitioning Congress for the right to purchase his property on Rock Island, Bill S. 44 finally passed on the 25th of March 1844.

CHAPTER TWENTY:

FRONTIER IS PASSING
1840 – 1844

NOW THAT DAVENPORT was in his late fifties and his sons were taking some of the family businesses, it was time for him to enjoy his family as a grandfather, time for reflection and the benefits of old age. His years of hard work and investments had paid off and by frontier standards he was wealthy, a pillar of the communities surrounding Rock Island. His legacy was assured.

George L'Oste Davenport was established in Davenport, and Bailey was experienced in the agriculture, overseeing the family garden as well as their rental farms. As a child Bailey had been attracted to the horses at Fort Armstrong, and the soldiers had taught him much about horse breeding and horse racing. For his twenty-first birthday Davenport transferred to Bailey some of the Rock Island County land, farmland east of present-day Coal Valley, as well as town lots in Davenport's Addition to Moline and in Rock Island.[1]

Some of the Bowling relatives had joined the kinship circle. James, Julia and Sophia Bowling, Mrs. Davenport's nephew and nieces, had married and settled in the area. Mrs. Davenport's brother Ambrose Green Bowling and his family had also settled in Rock Island County. Ambrose had been slowly moving westward in the years following the War of 1812, farming first in Ohio and then in Indiana. With his wife Margaret and six children, Ambrose bought one of Davenport's farms south of the Rock River and settled in Rock Island County. Present-day Bowling Township is named for him. Now, for the first time in their lives, the Davenports had their own kinship network around them.

George Davenport was concerned most with taking care of his property and helping his sons and Bowling relatives. Winters found him in St. Louis on buying trips for the mercantile business. He usually stayed at the Planter House, a popular landmark on the corner of Randolph and Wells where lodging was modestly priced at $16 per month. Financial matters, as well as personal matters, filled his letters home. He sought out buyers for his land. At the Planter House, he found proprietor, Benjamin Stickney, a willing listener. Stickney bought two of Davenport's five lots east of Moline. The price of the property, seven hundred dollars, was high for anything except manufacturing, especially if a new dam could be built a little further west of the original one.[2]

The question of whether the island would still be a military reserve was still unresolved. While reading the newspaper one day in St. Louis, Davenport was thrown into a panic when he noticed a sale ad for the entire island of Rock Island. The St. Louis Republican reported that all 895 acres were to be sold in four tracts or parcels. Even Davenport's own quartersection was to be sold. Considering that there might be a scam to take his possessions from him, he headed directly to Washington City on the first available boat. "I have a long Jorney before me but am willing to incounter it to Secure my home," he wrote to his son with instructions on business he wanted finished at home. Benjamin Clapp reported to Pierre Chouteau Sr. in New York: "Our friend Davenport is now in quite a quandary in consequence of the government having advertised for sale on the 1st -- next, the entire Rock Island - Capt. Ball of the Arsenal advertises it by direction - Davenport will go home as soon as Boat sails (?) for some Papers and then be off to Washington for the purpose of securing the preemption right claimed by him." Davenport planned to take the next departing steamboat up the Illinois and to home by an overland trail from Dixon's Ferry, but ice was not yet out of the river. Without his papers, Davenport headed directly to Washington City from St. Louis to defend his petition to buy the land where he had lived for twenty-seven years. He prepared his arguments along the way.[3]

The potential sale of Rock Island puzzled him. An arms depot had been established on the island two years before. Arms and ammunition had come by the steamboat *Agnes* and William R. Shoemaker had been appointed superintendent. Having a government official on the island had been a relief to Davenport. Shoemaker was considered a good choice, a Whig, as well as "a man of science and literary information ... "[4] It appeared from this appointment that the War Department would continue using the Island. All Davenport wanted was to have the Government relinquish a small portion of the island for him.

Again, Davenport wrote to the Commissioners of the General Land Office explaining his claim to the island property. " ... I obtained a certificate from the commanding officer (Col. Willoughby Morgan) that my possessions on the Island were located So far from the garrison that thay did not in any manner interfere with the military command. I forward this Certificate to the Secretary of War [J.C. Calhoun] and imeadeally received a written premption from him to remain on the Island and keep possession of my Improvements."[5] Davenport arrived in Washington City a few weeks later. The sale was cancelled, but his preemption petition continued.

Pre emption was an important issue in the 1840s as Congress debated whether the pre emption clause passed during the Jefferson administration should be modified. Jefferson's law prohibited persons from settling on unsurveyed lands, but that law was rarely enforced. It had become customary for persons to settle on unsurveyed lands and make an official claim after the survey had been conducted. The modification sought in Congress would allow those who had settled on public lands after June 1810 to make a formal claim and be given preference when the land came into the market.[6]

The modification was approved by Congress on 3rd March 1843. To comply with the new law, a settler had to notify the appropriate land office in writing, designating the tract and the time of his settlement. Davenport had done that. He believed that he had been the first permanent settler north of the Illinois River. He offered, as additional testimony, his ten years of military service through the War of 1812, for which he was not awarded military land compensation.[7] But, the question remained, did the law apply to Rock Island?

Congress finally acted upon his petition the following year. On the sixteenth of May 1844, the Davenport Gazette announced that a bill had been passed. Davenport was allowed to purchase the quarter section of land on which he had lived for so long at the minimum government price of $1.25 per acre. It had taken twelve long years of persistent petitioning and personal trips to Washington to get what George Davenport considered his right. "This is as it should be, " pronounced the Gazette.[8]

Buoyed by Davenport's success, other men sought to claim land on the island, too. When Davenport returned from Washington City, after having been absent from home for four or five months, he learned that David Sears was planning to expand the townsite called Rock Island Mills across the dam onto the upper end of the Island. Business was so good on the mainland side of Moline that he was planning a town and more mills on the island. Davenport could see, and hear, the changes in the rapidly developing countryside, except out on the Rock River.

In stark contrast to Moline, the Rock River area lagged behind in "the gloom of obscurity," according to the Upper Mississippian[9] It was an appropriate description. With the exception of five or six scattered dwellings the north shore of the Rock River, particularly Rock Island City, remained undeveloped. Turner and his investors were struggling to keep afloat financially. They had not abandoned their investments, but neither were they able to develop the townsite. Davenport formally petitioned the state legislature to have the "city" withdrawn and legally vacate his share of the town plat. It was a move to free him of city obligations and to use the land for his own purposes again. Davenport retained his interest in the general area and bought large numbers of lots at the annual tax sales held by the county on lands on which the taxes had not been paid for the past two years.[10]

Next door, in the Western Addition to RIC, the investors were in a similar situation, waiting for something to happen. Anthony Cooley, who had been so enthusiastic about the addition, remained in Bronson, Michigan, where he served as a trustee and was involved in local politics.[11] None of the other investors in the Western Addition had involved themselves with actual building either. All attention had shifted to the Mississippi Slough where industrial development was thriving.

By 1840 Rock Island County had grown so that now there were some two hundred buildings and seven hundred plus inhabitants.[12] Between 1840 and 1845 the population of the county nearly doubled, mainly because of the growing industries. Local newspapers reported the friendly competition between the mill owners in Moline and Rock Island. New businesses had been recruited. In Rock Island's Lower Addition or "Town of Rock Island," Lemuel Andrews and Joseph Knox brought William Zimmerman of Pittsburgh to build a steam sawmill near the foot of Fourth Avenue (where the Weyerhaeuser and Denkmann sawmill would later be built). The boatyards of Mr. Holt were engaged in building a new steamboat, the Clarion, which promised to be the biggest steamboat above St. Louis. The steam ferry of John Wilson was busy operating daily between Rock Island and Davenport and transporting goods between the two cities and the many people heading west. The Davenport Gazette prodded the citizens of Davenport to get building or be left behind.[13]

The New Purchase as western Iowa was called, had opened on May 1, 1843, and the four to six millions of acres of land were attracting great numbers of settlers. This was good for Iowa Territory and good for the town of Davenport. Thousands of immigrants had congregated around the town for months prior to the opening of the land. They pitched their tents on the outskirts of towns like Davenport, Burlington and Dubuque, and from those places scouted for claims.[14] Some decided to stay; others moved on westward to the vacated Indian lands. The Sauk and Mesquakie had just two years to vacate the land and move to Kansas.

The symbols of the frontier-- the Indians and their canoes, the bison, the unbroken prairie -- were nearly extinct. Already, the log cabin, once the most common structure on the frontier, was becoming a thing of the past. The Iowa Sun called the log cabin erected for the Harrison presidential election in 1841 a shrine to which all immigrants should pay homage.[15]

Another symbol of the frontier - the wolf that Farrar had so proudly hunted - was nearly gone. It was the bane of all pioneer farmers, preying on livestock, destroying the farmer's growing herds, and putting fear into children's heads as they lay in the beds at night. In 1843 Scott County placed a fifty-cent bounty on each scalp. Scott county residents turned in ninety-four scalps to authorities that year as settlers began to domesticate the prairies. In Mercer and Rock Island counties in Illinois, there were organized wolf-hunts as late as 1845. By the yardsticks of the frontier, only when the wolf was gone was the land truly civilized.[16]

In Davenport, most of the founding proprietors were gone as well. P.G. Hambaugh was dead. He had gone to Florida to operate a government store for the soldiers fighting in the Seminole War and died there. William Gordon, the surveyor of the original town, had declared insolvency, moved on, and literally disappeared. He was never heard from again. Levi Colton, who had been involved in the Indian Trade, had also moved, first to Iowa City where his wife died in March 1841, and then to Dubuque. His whereabouts after that were unknown. Captain James May owned a farm along Duck Creek, although he had not settled there. He retained unsold lots in the original plat, but was unsatisfied with his profits in land sales. He had become a whiny, bitter old man who complained until his dying day of being cheated by Davenport and Le Claire. May's lawsuit against them far outlived both men. Major Thomas F. Smith retired from the army in 1837 and with his wife and their six children returned to St. Louis where they were involved in family business. Major Smith died in 1843. Stanton Sholes returned to Ohio where he lived until

1865. Alexander McGregor, who had sold his share to Sholes, was a successful lawyer in Davenport, having founded a law firm that specialized in real estate. He lived on Fifth Street with his family until his death.

The proprietors' vision, however, was becoming a reality. The strategies they employed had worked. Recruiting desirable businessmen had brought new industries to town. Offering easy payments for their lots had been accepted. Improving their lots with move-in ready structures had made settlement quick and easy. The little town on the west bank of the Mississippi was beginning to look like a prosperous place to live and the surrounding fertile farmland had made it a productive agricultural center. The Iowa Sun regularly featured articles on the latest techniques for farming the prairies, ads for purebred stud service like Le Claire's Durham Bull's (named Veto), and stories about new varieties of corn, like Chinatree, that promised increased yields over the old varieties. Most newly arrived settlers were more concerned with opening their farms and getting seed planted than they were about waterpower or mills, but they needed mills to grind their grain.

When John Sullivan conceded Rockingham's county seat fight to Davenport, he officially vacated the town, sold his land, and closed his steam flourmill. Area farmers really needed a mill, so George Davenport and Le Claire went to Cincinnati to recruit mill operators. Cincinnati had been especially hard hit by the depression, for mill operators, and they were able to recruit Isaac Straub who had been the proprietor of flour and saw mills in Pennsylvania before settling in Cincinnati. Straub arrived in Davenport with a steam engine and fixtures enough to power several runs of burrs.[17]

By the standards of the time, Davenport was thriving. The arrival of the Messrs. Webb and Seaman with families and furniture, both men of enterprise and capital according to the Upper Mississippian, was much heralded as a sign of even better things to come.[18] The symbolism of both men building homes on the bluff overlooking the city and high above the annual flooding of the town was recognized as a sign that Davenport would soon be lifted out of the depression. Another hotel, the Worden House, was constructed on Third Street. A new newspaper, the Weekly Gazette, began publication when Andrew Logan, editor of the Iowa Sun, decided to try his own hand at farming. Gazette editor Alfred Sanders brought a new voice and his own interests in promoting the West that went beyond Logan's farming interests.

The county seat was now permanently located in Davenport and this designation boosted the town's importance. Construction on the courthouse and county buildings began with a public auction of 44 lots and 4 out lots for the purpose of funding those public buildings. Advertisements for the sale were published across the Midwest in the Iowa Sun, the Burlington Hawkeye and Patriot, the Chicago Democrat, and the Cincinnati Gazette as well as others who picked up the news. The sale terms were easy by frontier standards with credit offered for 6, 12, 18, and 24 months and designed to appeal to a large audience. People from far and wide came.[19]

The first town elections were held and the elected officials took over the responsibilities of the original proprietors: passing city ordinances, building roads, and generally promoting continued development. George L. Davenport kept the Davenport name associated with town government when he was elected as one of the Trustees.[20]

The town took on the appearance of permanency with buildings made of locally produced brick, which replaced many of the original log houses. Harvey Leonard's brick works were located on the hillside just above the original town plat. A clause in deeds in Le Claire's 2nd Addition required buildings at least one and a half stories high and of brick, stone, or frame. Some forty or fifty houses had already been built. The Le Claire House, too, was built of Leonard's brick. The hotel was one of the largest and most lavish hotels north of St. Louis. George Davenport was also building brick houses and office buildings in addition to his frame structures. John Shay's new Pork House, which was taking advantage of the cheap pork prices, featured a brick smokehouse adjoining his establishment. And finally, there was the brick building that housed the cabinet manufacturing business of Geyer and Schoolfield, who featured showrooms that displayed their products such as rush-bottomed chairs. A distillery, operated by Gibbon and Wood, was acquired by George L. Davenport and his cousin James Bowling when Wood and Gibbon defaulted on their debt to them. The distillery was a new venture for the family and noted by Gazette editor Alfred Sanders in an article describing one of his strolls about town. Unfortunately, Sanders was pro-temperance and chose not to describe the business any further.[21] For the two cousins it was a short-lived venture, one that was perhaps ahead of its time, since corn was not being raised around Davenport in large enough quantities at that time.

As Le Claire's many additions to the town prospered and developed, the town center shifted to the east, where Le Claire controlled the riverbanks. Recognizing the town's need for more access to the river, Le Claire began to offer some of his river lots for sale. Le Claire's Third Addition to Davenport (1842) was a small triangular piece of land containing just two blocks of lots (#63 and 64) between Front and Second Streets, now near the Government Bridge. They were perfect for operating a ferry or other businesses needing access to the river. Le Claire's ferryman, John Wilson, replaced his horse-driven ferry, with the first steam-operated ferry from that location, but the river was still a hindrance to the economy of the Upper Mississippi Valley.[22]

Transportation issues came to the forefront when Ambrose C. Fulton arrived in town. Fulton was a distant cousin of Robert Fulton who turned the steamboat into a commercial success, and he was interested in transportation. He arrived one day after tiring of his situation in New Orleans. He sold his business there, and with cash from the sale, bought a load of goods that he thought would be in demand on the frontier. He arranged to move it by steamboat up the Mississippi river. While the boat was refuelling at Rockingham, Fulton walked to Davenport, arranged for living quarters, and rented a two-story brick store with a basement and a warehouse. He had drays on hand to haul his goods from the steamer when the boat arrived and opened his store the next morning. As he had expected, he "had a big rush of customers."[23]

With growing industries in all the towns surrounding Rock Island and no improvements in the rivers, the businessmen of the Upper Mississippi Valley were looking for alternative transportation solutions. Since 1839 the summer river levels had been so low that the river closed down completely. Local advocates of the railroad began to be more vocal about the advantages of this technology. Although the State of Illinois had once been interested in developing railroads, it was not financially stable enough to fund such ventures. Despairing of government assistance, businessmen sought solutions of their own. A.C. Fulton would be a prime mover in this quest.

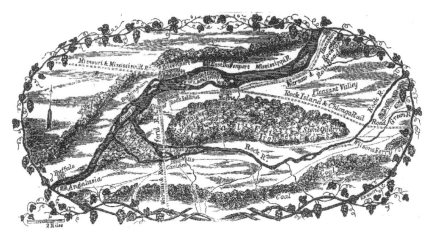

By the end of 1853, local developers envisioned the Quad Cities as a railroad hub, connecting the area with both the east and the west with many separate rail road companies. The Rock Island Advertiser promoted the concept by printing this map on the front page throughout the month of November 1853.

CHAPTER TWENTY-ONE:

THE IRON HORSE

IT IS HARD to pinpoint just when George Davenport began to think seriously about bringing the railroad to Rock Island, or even when the first idea of such national importance became common talk in the Rock Island region. Americans had embraced the idea of railroad with the first race in England between the horse and the iron horse in 1827 and the interest had crossed the Atlantic immediately.

Practically speaking, travelling was difficult across the United States, and this new technology promised to be faster and easier than anything available at the time. Although there was regular steamboat service on the Great Lakes, the journey between the eastern seacoast and the Mississippi River was long and arduous -- no matter what route one took. Rail would make travel easier and quicker than overland or water routes could provide. Davenport was well aware of the difficulty. He had made the long journey to Washington City a number of times in his lifetime. From Fort Armstrong on Rock Island, it was 1,932 miles by river. By land it was 830 miles. It usually took Davenport three weeks by using a route over prairie, through forests, and across rivers. By 1838 the National Road ran from Vandalia, Illinois, to Baltimore, but it was a mix of rutted mud roads -- hardly more than animal tracks -- sometimes covered with logs or planks, and macadamized surfaces through swamps, over hills, across rivers and streams. There were no direct routes, but a series of routes by stagecoach, canal boat, and horseback. In the winter the journey was almost impossible to make. Rail was the transportation mode of the future and, perhaps, the answer to all their transportation woes.[1]

Within a short time after the introduction of rail in England, several eastern railroad companies formed in the United States. By 1830 some tracks had been laid and the manufacture of steam locomotives begun. Illinois had been in the forefront of those adopting this new technology when Illinois Governor John Reynolds announced his plan for six railroads, all connecting the Illinois lead mines with better ports. Although financially strapped, the State had allocated money to begin the Illinois Central Railroad. The Galena Advertiser took up the cause of the railroad, publishing nineteen arguments on the benefits of the railroad in an open letter to the people of Illinois. There were essentially three main benefits of rail. The first was that railroads were so much faster than canal boats, 15-36 mph compared to 3 mph. Secondly, the cost of building railroads was considerably cheaper than cutting canals. And thirdly, railroads were usable year-round whereas canals were useable for only five months of the year. The editor correctly predicted that the I & M Canal would be constructed, but that in ten years time it would be abandoned for the railroad.[2]

Between 1830 and the mid 1840s, a number of chartered railroads were directed towards the rich mineral and agricultural lands of the Mississippi River Valley. The many plans called for a Great Railway, or a nation wide link of all the canals and navigable waters with railroads across

New York, Pennsylvania, Ohio, Indiana, Illinois, Michigan, Missouri, and adjacent states and territories. The plan also identified the head of the Rock Island Rapids, between Le Claire, Iowa, and Port Byron, Illinois, as the ideal place to bridge the river.[3] There was even talk of linking the East with the Mississippi River in the West and beyond. Because there were immigrants heading to Oregon, the concept of a transcontinental railroad was appealing.

One early plan that involved the Rock Island area was the Buffalo and Mississippi Railroad out of New York State. Its intended route would follow the Maumee Bay along the Great Lakes to the rapids of the Illinois River and then generally to the Mississippi River. A specific destination was not yet determined. Residents in Adams County, Illinois, had petitioned U.S. Representative Joseph Duncan for the route to reach their county seat of Quincy.[4] Investors along the Rock River hoped to extend the Maumee Road along the south bank of the Rock River to the Mississippi River by going through present-day Milan, across Big Island, through Rock Island City, and through Rock Island. Driving speculative interests were lead and waterpower because the lead mines of northwestern Illinois had already shipped some 14 million pounds of lead to New York alone. The present route, however, was long and expensive: down the Mississippi to New Orleans, through the Gulf of Mexico and up the Atlantic coast to New York Harbor. It was the familiar problem of transportation: finding a cheaper, faster route to the markets. Agents of these many canal and railroad companies were already camped in Stephenson, buying land for their eastern investors. Hence, nearly all the public lands along the Rock River had been sold by 1837 or so. George Davenport was among those interested in travel by rail.

But by 1840, when the editor of the Iowa Sun called for a railroad to be built to the Mississippi from Chicago, railroads had been discussed to go to the Mississippi River, but no railroad was actually planned to go to Rock Island or Davenport. Alfred Sanders regularly published notices of advancing roads and called for town meetings to see what might be done locally to attract a road to this area.[5] Having lost out on getting a government arsenal in the area had revealed just how serious the problem of the rapids was and how difficult it would be to clear their hazards. A railroad might solve the problem of the rapids, but bridging the river between Moline and Rock Island and Davenport was crucial to local access to any rail system.

A. C. Fulton was of the same mind as Sanders, and singularly interested in a route to Chicago. His argument, made to anyone not convinced of the need for such an expensive venture as the rail road, was to think of railroads as rivers: "each and every railroad," he said, "is equal to a river that never freezes or is affected by a dry season." In the winter of 1842-43, he took soundings and measurements of the river at the old Indian crossing below the water works in Davenport for the purpose of determining the best place for such a bridge. He noted, "the depth of the water, the nature of the bottom and the shore banks, made an examination of the land east to Chicago and west to Cedar River." That place, he concluded, was the best place to build a bridge. Fulton published his findings in the Philadelphia Sun and invited the local communities up and down the river from Davenport to meetings "to talk bridge and railroad." The farmers in the surrounding communities were not so certain. It was a new and expensive venture. Looking back on it later in his life, Fulton thought that time had proven his timing right for action.[6]

Fulton had a personal reason for wanting a route to Chicago.

His onions and other produce were worth more in the city. He knew first hand the problems of getting fresh produce to market, of unloading at some distant port only to find the flour full of weevils or vegetables rotted. He was tired, he said, of sending his onions to St. Louis in the fall and having them arrive the next spring. There were, however, no easy routes to the city at that time. An east-west route independent of rivers and canals he thought would be faster and more efficient than following meandering rivers and cheaper than man-made canals. After campaigning for a year and holding public debate meetings up and down the river in order to get subscriptions for a new railroad to service this area, local merchants and even farmers were beginning to see that railroads could reach larger markets and save time, increase efficiency, eliminate handling, and be free of weather and river conditions. They were not, however, convinced enough to help pay for the privilege by funding the railroad.[7]

When Sanders and Fulton began their campaign, there were hardly any rails actually laid between the Alleghenies and the Mississippi River. It was not a question of if, but when railroads would reach the Mississippi River. By 1845 railroads were servicing the state of Ohio, the Great Lakes, and the Ohio River valley, and they were under construction in Indiana. The six Illinois railroad projects abandoned in 1839 were renewed in the 1840s. In all, there were about 3,000 miles of projected railroad in the works and the Illinois communities surrounding Rock Island began to think of tying into these roads.[8]

The mill owners of Moline were especially receptive to Fulton's ideas. They had a thriving milling business, but no steamboat landing. There was a new five-story flourmill of D.B. Sears, a new foundry, and factories whose products were being sent all over the nation. A railroad could reduce the costs of getting products to market, but they needed a plan to come to them.[9]

Some visionaries, like John Plumbe of Dubuque and Asa Whitney of New York, saw the railroad as a Pacific or Transcontinental Road and the Mississippi River no longer a destination, but a way station between east and west. Largely inspired by the colonization of Oregon, the focus changed from routes destined for the Mississippi River to bridging the great river to get further west. Their plans sought routes that could easily cross the Mississippi and the prairies of Iowa, but they did not consider Rock Island.[10]

In 1845, Asa Whitney promoted his ideas about how to fund such a transcontinental enterprise. His published work, Railroad Connecting the Pacific, got people talking about the best way to do this. His proposed route was similar to Plumbe's, crossing Wisconsin Territory from Lake Michigan at Milwaukee, running to Dubuque, and then proceeding across Iowa to Council Bluffs and the Missouri. This route, however, would totally by-pass Rock Island, and leave businesses there without access to rail. On the 19th of June 1845, Asa Whitney left Milwaukee on an exploration trip to determine a feasible route from the Great Lakes to the

Missouri River at Council Bluffs. In an open letter to James Bowling of St. Louis, he affirmed that he could build his railroad if he could get a Government grant of land for funding.[11]

Whitney's plan required a bridge somewhere across the Mississippi River. Whitney believed that there was nothing below Prairie du Chien that was feasible. Fulton wanted to prove Whitney wrong. He had concluded that the best place for bridging the Mississippi was at a place just two miles from the town of Davenport.[12] That site would put the crossing very near to George Davenport's home. Local leaders, armed with the notes and soundings of A.C. Fulton, moved quickly. They could not afford to wait and see if Whitney would get his funding or what crossing he might choose.

Whoever built the bridge controlled the route: all roads would funnel into it in order to cross the river. Whoever controlled the crossing, also controlled the markets. If Rock Island and Davenport were by-passed, all hopes and dreams for developing this area would suffer, maybe even die. However expensive they were to build and to operate, community leaders around Rock Island understood that their economic livelihood was dependent on this new technology. Building a bridge here would assure them of an economical future. It would require heavy lobbying of the Illinois Legislature and some serious wheeling and dealing with Chicago, because every community up and down the river would be vying for the same privilege.

Fulton called for an early July meeting and invited all interested men to meet at the home of George Davenport. Although son George L. Davenport recalled taking notes at this important meeting, the details have been lost. Who was there is uncertain, but some leaders can be surmised. In addition to Davenport and his sons, Antoine Le Claire, A.C. Fulton, and Judge James Grant must have been there, as well as Charles Atkinson from Moline and perhaps representatives from Henry County. The task at hand was a three-pronged discussion. First, they had to have a railroad leading from the manufacturing areas of Rock Island and Moline to Chicago. This was a backwards plan, west to east, but a pro-active plan that guaranteed railroad service to the manufacturing interests already developing in the area.

Secondly, they would need a railroad on the Iowa side to serve the town of Davenport. A route from Davenport through the new State Capital at Iowa City and on to Council Bluffs was proposed. It would later be chartered as the M & M Railroad (Mississippi and Missouri). And most importantly, they had to connect their two railroads with a bridge across the Mississippi. Fulton's soundings had located a particular spot in the middle of Rock Island where there was solid rock for foundations and at one of the narrowest places in the river. It was within a mile of George Davenport's home on Rock Island.

Time and secrecy were essential to the plan's success. Within the week, Judge Grant and Hiram Price travelled to Chicago to discuss their plan with Charles Butler Ogden.[13] Ogden must have supported the idea, and perhaps tutored Price and Grant on the logistics of bringing a bridge into being. Crossing rivers, especially one as big and important as the Mississippi, was a daunting venture, which would take time and money, money they did not have. Although they might have wished for state support, the State of Illinois was in no position to give financial support, and these men had no experience in railroad building. Regardless, they were determined to forge ahead as a private venture.

This meeting hosted by Davenport indicates that he had an interest in rail to an extent that is not revealed in public records. It might also explain some of his land purchases in the 1830s and why he seemed so determined to hold onto some and not to others, particularly along the Sylvan Slough with his addition to Moline, as well as his repurchasing the land in the former Rock Island City and other lands. In the town of Davenport, Le Claire and Davenport divided the unsold lots in the original plat, particularly along Fifth Street, the projected railroad route for the M & M railroad. Davenport also bought lots along Brady Street, which is today a main artery between downtown and the bluff development.

Davenport sold most of his land adjoining Le Claire's in Parkhurst to James Eads. The town, known as the town of Berlin, was gaining a reputation for its skilled rapids pilots who, as Shreve had suggested, steered steamboats through the dangerous rapids. Across the river in Port Byron, Davenport divested himself of his remaining unsold lots.[14] Hopes of a bridge at this point in the river, so promising just a few years before, had now vaporized. At least it appears that Davenport thought the prospects diminishing.

Out on the Rock River, dreams of using the Rock River as a transportation route were now dormant, and plans for using the river for waterpower were in jeopardy. A court judgment against Joshua Vandruff put any hopes of a cooperative venture on the Rock River out of reach because a wealthy New Yorker now controlled much of the waterpower. The flourmills of Dickson and Sullivan were in limbo as well. Davenport kept his bottomlands along the south shore of the Rock River in the general vicinity of Mill Creek. They were close to, but not on, coal and iron deposits. But in his 1844 will, he directed his family to sell these lands, in Townships 16N and 17N, for cash and were offered for sale in September 1845.[15]

On the north shore of the Rock, Rock Island City lay dormant, and perhaps dead as a town, but it still held some interest for Davenport, perhaps as a railroad route. He had officially vacated his portion of the town plat in 1842, but regularly attended the tax sales and purchased lots along the waterfront for pennies per lot. He also bought blocks in the center of the town.[16] Should a railroad be built coming from the south, or the center of Illinois, a good crossing could be made at Vandruff's Island and cut through the center of his purchases towards the town of Rock Island. One such plan, the Peoria and Warsaw charted in 1838, had just such a plan.

Another potential railroad route lay along the Slough and touched land where George Davenport and Russel Farnham had built a trading post in 1825. Davenport and Farnham had purchased the part of the section south of the Indian Boundary land when it was offered for sale in 1829, but the land north of the Indian Boundary line, which lay on the bank of the Slough, had not yet been declared public land. It was therefore not available for purchase at the Land Office. Davenport had been farming that section for many years, growing corn and hay and had rented the trading post building to John Barrel, who operated it as a public house. It also served the county as a courthouse. But Davenport had not yet made a formal claim to the land at the Land Office and Henry McNeal took advantage of that. It was an act of revenge.

Henry McNeal was a young man in his twenties, who had settled in the upper part of Rock Island County in the late 1820s. There he built a log cabin for his family, farmed and operated a woodlot for the steamboat trade. He and Joel Thompson had invested in land that is now the village of Hampton. He was devastated when Hampton was not designated the county seat and of the opinion that Davenport had been to blame for their loss. With the help of Sheriff Lemuel Andrews, who was said to have been shrewd and quick to pounce on defective land titles for his own profit, McNeal entered the land on which the old trading post stood and claimed it for his own.

So determined was McNeal to have the land that he said he was willing to fight George Davenport. Evidently, Davenport resisted the challenge. Sometime later, McNeal made a formal pre emption claim to 38.65 acres. His claim stated that he had fenced in fifteen acres on which he grew oats, corn, potatoes, and other vegetables, and was actually living on the property in 1834. To pay for the claim, McNeal either sold or mortgaged his claim with William Hempstead, who was a long-time friend of George Davenport. Three months later Mr. Hempstead sold the land to Davenport for $800, a price well above the government price of $1.25 per acre. Davenport then proceeded to rent the farm, first to John Barrel and then to Henry and Moses Powars. To make public his ownership of the land, Davenport published a warning in the newspaper: He had purchased the property in 1836 and cautioned anyone who had a desire to purchase land from Henry McNeal.[17] Renting the land provided some security for Davenport.

The rental agreement with Henry and Moses Powars is particularly useful in illustrating how determined Davenport was to retain ownership of that parcel. The agreement stipulated that the Powars brothers would rent Davenport's Rock Island farm for five years. During that time the brothers would improve the farm with five hundred dollars worth of material provided by Davenport and they would maintain the buildings in good order for the duration of their tenancy. No rent would be required of the brothers for the first three years and the brothers would vacate the premises at the end of five years, which would be 1842.[18]

McNeal was not yet finished exacting revenge on Davenport. In 1844, he finally received a patent for that land from the Land Office. At that time, there was already talk of a railroad route along the slough and through Davenport's land. Ignoring Hempstead's sale to Davenport eight years before, McNeal divided the parcel into three equal parts and sold each part for $250. The buyers were all Rock Island County residents who knew Davenport very well and willing participants in McNeal's scheme: Nathaniel Belcher, Martha Andrews, the wife of the county sheriff, and Francis Babcock, a miller. Rather than taking them all to court, Davenport negotiated with all the three parties who had purchased the land from McNeal. It cost him dearly, but in the end, the high price was worth it. Davenport paid $300 to Belcher, $800 to Mrs. Andrews, and $500 to Babcock.[19]

The story illustrates the sharp divide that remained in the county between the upper and lower parts and the lengths to which some men would go to seek revenge. While Stephenson thrived, the towns where McNeal and others had invested had not. Nathaniel Belcher had led a movement to have the county divided and the lower part, where the county seat lay, be added to Mercer County. The movement failed but George Davenport was seen as responsible for the failures of the upper part of the county. His participation in the county seat fight, and perhaps instigator of the scheme which led to the winning of the Stephenson as the county seat, had not been forgotten or forgiven.

The story also illustrates just how hard headed and stubborn George Davenport could be and how he strategized to get what he wanted. After twenty-five years of living with new settlers, providing them with goods and services, and developing towns for them, George Davenport was still an Indian trader at heart: highly competitive, fiercely independent, and trying to dominate every market he could. The land along the Slough was potentially a valuable piece of land for the railroad.

The railroad route along the Slough through Moline and into Stephenson, now called Rock Island, led to a bridge crossing identified by A.C. Fulton. Local businessmen from Rock Island and Henry counties in Illinois and Scott County in Iowa were hard at work in their planning of such an enormous venture. Should the railroad be built across Illinois to a bridge near his home, Davenport's Moline and Rock Island lands along the river would become even more valuable, and the high price he paid for it would prove a wise investment. Roadbeds and railroad rights-of-way were potentially lucrative business propositions.

By the end of 1845 the Gazette announced that the local citizens were in fact organized to build a railroad. The single most important consideration was not which path it should take before it reached the Mississippi river, but where it should cross. By Fulton's calculations and soundings, the place most advantageous was near Davenport's house on the island, where the river was only 75 to 100 yards in width and the high rocky banks were well suited for the bridge foundation. The land on both sides of the river was ideal for a railroad, being without many streams or ravines, which would have required additional bridging. Armed with Fulton's observations, the argument for bridging the river at Rock Island was made.[20]

Out of the 1845 meeting grew the Rock Island and LaSalle Railroad Co. The General Assembly of the State of Illinois approved the charter on February 27, 1847, with Judge James Grant of Davenport as president. The capital stock was fixed at $300,000. The commissioners named were from Rock Island, Henry, Bureau, and LaSalle counties. Those from Rock Island county included George Davenport's good friends and associates: Joseph Knox, N.B. Buford, William Vandever, Nathaniel Belcher, and F.R. Brunot.[21]

In 1851, the railroad was re-christened the Chicago and Rock Island. Construction began in 1852 and the first train reached Davenport two years later. A second railroad company in Iowa, the Mississippi and Missouri, was under the same management and would essentially be a

continuation of the Chicago and Rock Island Line across Iowa to Council
Bluffs, connecting the Mississippi and Missouri rivers. Approval for the
bridge came in 1853 when the Illinois legislature granted a charter to Rock
Island to construct a bridge at or near Rock Island. The selection process
was highly contested by other communities that also wished the privilege
of being the first to bridge the river.[22]

Davenport's lands were eventually sold to various railroad companies.
In 1853, Bailey sold the first of many of the fifty-five foot wide tracts
through the Davenport lands. Not only did the railroad come along the
Mississippi through Moline, but eventually a railroad also came through
Rock Island City. George Davenport had indeed chosen wisely.

Davenport's obituary mistakenly identified his hometown as "South" instead of "Louth" Lincolnshire. The $1500 reward was also posted at various locations throughout Rock Island County as the search for Davenport's murderers began.

1,500 DOLLARS REWARD.

STOP THE MURDERERS!

ON FRIDAY, (4th of July,) GEORGE DAVENPORT, Esq., was shot at his residence on Rock-Island, by a gang of robbers. They forcibly entered the house and shot Mr. D., which terminated his existence a few hours afterwards; he was dragged by the robbers up stairs and laid on a bed and was there told if he did not tell them where his money was they would burn him; he told them, whilst they took from him about 600 dollars, mostly Missouri money, of tens and twenties, and a valuable gold watch, chain and seal.

The watch was an old fashioned double case, plain French Watch, No. 104.

The following is a description of a portion of the Bank Notes taken.

No.	Letter			
No. 169.	Letter A,	Missouri Bank,	$20.
" 1733.	"	A,	"	"	10.
" 280.	"	B,	"	"	10.
" 1366.	"	N,	"	"	10.
" 7218.	"	A,	"	"	10.
" 7013.	"	A,	"	"	10.
" 3866.	"	A,	"	"	20.
" 309.	"	A,	"	"	20.
" 1947.	"	A,	"	"	20.
" 147.	"	A,	"	"	20.
" 153.	"	B,	"	"	20.

The above horrid transaction took place between one and two o'clock P. M. in the absence of his family attending the Celebration.

One of the robbers was a small, close set man, had on a blue coat, white pantaloons, a cloth cap, and it is thought is the person who shot him. Another was a tall spare man, another was a short thick square built man, and there were two or three others in company. They have been traced to the river or slough, and suspicious persons were seen on the main shore soon after. Whoever will take and deliver up the offenders, to the proper legal authorities, will be entitled to the above reward, or $500 for either one of them.

GEORGE L. DAVENPORT.

Rock-Island, Ill., July 5, 1845.

CHAPTER TWENTY-TWO:

SEDUCED BY THE DEVIL

"ENTICING" IS HOW the local newspaper editor described the town of Davenport in early 1845. There were larger towns and towns that had more business, he wrote, but this town was enticing. What made it so were its beautiful scenery, healthful location, and good society. The town could use, he suggested, a good hatter, and a tanner considering all the furs they shipped to eastern cities, and also a steam flourmill, since Sullivan's had closed. Now there was enough wheat in the area. One farmer alone had shipped 800 or 900 bushels of wheat to markets in St. Louis and Cincinnati just the previous season since there was no local market for the wheat.[1] The implication was that the town should be self-sufficient without having to rely on other markets. Not everyone was so provincial in his thinking. Fulton's dream of a transportation link to Chicago had infected many others, and after the June meeting at the Davenport house, a

contingency of representatives went directly to Chicago to pitch their idea to Chicago financier William B. Ogden.

Ironically, George Davenport never saw the results of that vision because a gang of river thieves, often called banditti, broke into his home and murdered him. The outrageous attack was a jolt that shook the surrounding communities. Whether they liked him or not, the pioneers and settlers never dreamed that he, of all people, would be murdered.

The spring of 1845 had been a quiet one. Steamboats came and went, as did strangers on their way to other places. The farmers of Rock Island and Scott counties had been hard at work in their fields all season and had been too busy to come into town. Gazette editor Alfred Sanders complained about how quiet and monotonous it was, so monotonous that he could find only two complaints: the arrival of the annual invasion of gnats, and a minor fire that had occurred in the blacksmith shop of S. Sargent that was contained quickly. The removal of the last of the arms and ammunition stored at the old fort was duly noted as a final gesture to the terrors of the Indian days.[2]

Sanders filled his paper with idle chitchat and musings about how Rock Island and Davenport could be "the theatre of considerable business" if they had just a little more manufacturing. A steam-powered flourmill, he thought, would keep the market closer to home and cheaper to operate than water power. Building material and grain were abundant and locally available, but a railroad could add to the quality of life here.[3]

Following the tradition of the former editor in town, Sanders continued to report on agriculture. The winter wheat crop looked remarkably well and, if the weather held, would be harvested by most farmers by the end of the week. George Davenport's own wheat was already cut and he planned on spending a relaxing Fourth of July holiday, and his family planned to go to the Sabbath School Scholars picnic in Rock Island. Sanders offered a bit of advice for the revellers, an eerie warning that would soon haunt all his readers. "Tomorrow will be the 4th of July," he wrote, "the anniversary of American Independence. There are no doubt those living today enjoying health and rejoicing in the prospect of a temporary happiness on the morrow, who on the eve of that day will slumber in death, violently caused by an improper mode of celebrating it. "⁴

Sears recalled past Fourth of July celebrations with fondness. They were, he recalled, "never-to-be-forgotten affairs," where long tables were set with all kinds of things to eat, including roasted pigs with their mouths filled with fruit or even grain. The minister usually offered a prayer and someone else read the Declaration of Independence. Everyone feasted and frolicked.⁵

For some unknown reason, George Davenport did not accompany his family to the day's festivities. There had been strangers lurking about the towns lately and a law office had been broken into. That was troubling enough to Davenport, but he had also had a strange dream that bothered him. Two or three days before, he had confided to Ezekial Steinhilber, an ice merchant in Davenport, that he had dreamed of dying and going to meet his Maker. It was an unsettling dream.⁶

Between one and two o'clock in the afternoon, Davenport was alone in the house, sitting in his armchair and smoking a cigar, when he heard a poker fall from one of the kitchen windows. As he rose to investigate, several men rushed toward him. A gun discharged, hitting Davenport in the thigh. He rushed to his chair for his cane and was in the act of striking when he was hurled to the floor, his hands tied with bark strips, and his eyes blindfolded.

His assailants demanded his money, about $170 in his pocket, and his gold pocket watch. Davenport indicated that there was more money in a safe in the little room at the top of the stairs. The robbers, however, were unable to unlock the safe with the key, so they dragged Mr. Davenport up the stairs by his stock and collar. Not finding as much money as they expected, the assailants choked him, beat him, and stamped upon him. Twice he fainted. They revived him by throwing water in Davenport's face. Again they demanded money and threatened to burn down the house. They beat him, and burned him with hot coals. Then, they put him on his bed and left him. They took his gold watch, chain, and seal, about 600 dollars, a gun and a pistol.

Benjamin Cole heard Davenport's cries for help while fishing nearby on the river. At first Cole hesitated to enter the house, but when he followed the sounds and the trail of blood to the second floor, he found Mr. Davenport bound, gagged, and bleeding on his bed. He went for Dr. Brown, who was picnicking on the island. Across the river, Antoine Le Claire heard Davenport's cries and came to help. Later the family and Drs. Gregg, Barrows, and Witherwax arrived.[7]

Several women went to the house to scrape linen and prepare bandages for Mr. Davenport. They had been told that Davenport was suffering from loss of blood and the summer heat. What they saw in the house was horrifying. Evidence of the struggle was everywhere. Furniture was overturned. Davenport's newspaper and cane were lying on the floor. There was blood on the floor, on the walls, and in all five rooms of the house.

The search for clues to the culprits' identity began almost immediately. Authorities confiscated the hickory bark and handkerchief that had bound Davenport. They found footprints underneath the kitchen window. They listened as Davenport gave his account of the assault, being lucid enough to give a detailed description of his assailants, but he was in great pain and complained about being cold. He had lost a lot of blood from an eleven inch wound just above his knee, and he lapsed in and out of consciousness. Four medical doctors stood at his bedside, but there was nothing medical science could do. George Davenport died about 8 o'clock that night, just a few months short of his sixty-second birthday.[8]

In some ways, Davenport's violent end is a reminder of lingering frontier conditions, but it also illustrates the state of law and order in the emerging social landscape of the region. As word of Davenport's murder spread, the residents in all the surrounding communities organized posses to search for the culprits. Many were on horseback; some on foot. Some were spurred to action by outrage and fear for their own safety and that of their family; some by a sense of justice and the need to do something; others by promises of monetary reward. Their action was, by the yardsticks of the time, swift and effective.

Dr. Gregg examined the footprints found under the windows. Bailey Davenport and others followed the prints across the island to the slough. One company discovered a trail across the Rock River at Wilson's ferry and scoured the swamps, but the attackers made their escape. Some men searched all day; others for several days without compensation or regard for their own businesses. There was one exception.

John Wilson, the old ferryman who operated the crossing between Davenport and Rock Island, and whose court suit against George Davenport was still pending, did not seem so community-spirited, at least to someone calling himself "Decency." Wilson had appeared to offer free crossing to anyone wishing to go to Davenport's funeral or to those searching for the murderers. But once crossed, according to "Decency," Wilson demanded payment from them, and actually collected some. He attempted to justify his self-serving actions with a rebuttal, but he had transgressed the common idea of decency and community-spirit that others were exhibiting at the time.[9]

Davenport's death plunged the surrounding communities into deep mourning. The shock and horror of such brutality sent waves of fear and panic throughout the community. Years later many pioneers, who had been young at the time, vividly recalled their own fears of the murder. They remembered the precautions that their parents took to protect their families, how husbands and fathers slept in the doorways of their cabins to prevent similar invasions, or slept with loaded shotguns by their bed. They recalled how frightened they were for months after the murder and the outrage.[10]

Such a bold attack, perpetrated in broad daylight, cut deeply into the sense of security of the local communities. For the first time, the communities were forced to examine their own security measures and take action for public safety. No longer could they remain preoccupied with their own needs and day-to-day struggles. The murder had jolted them out of their own private thoughts and concerns, to look beyond themselves and into their community. They began to see their connection to one another and to question how they, as God-fearing people who shared a common work ethic and similar goals, could have allowed such a deed to happen.

As they looked deeply in their communities, they found pests breeding in places like the grog shops and gambling rooms. These n'er-do-wells lounged and gamed their days away. They rejected the commonly held Protestant work ethic that the general community held in high regard. They preferred to get their justly rewards the easy way, by preying on those who worked for a living. The Gazette called for vigorous, collective action to put an end to these "enemies of the public" and aroused the public to discussions about taking matters into their own hands. With the mood of the community at that time and the state of government in such a newly settled region, it is almost certain that, had the suspects been caught immediately, they would have been lynched without trial.

Weekly updates in the newspapers kept settlers apprised of the search. The lone exception in the Mississippi Valley was in Nauvoo where the Mormons were preoccupied with their own business of removing themselves from Illinois. Family members remained publicly silent on their grief and outrage, but surviving news clippings show that they followed the progress of the murderers' pursuit along with everyone else. Susan Lewis pasted them in her Bible.[11]

One man, by the name of Charles Budd, was arrested as an accomplice. Some thought his description matched one of the suspects, and Budd's alibi was shaky enough to arouse distrust. He was thrown into the Rock Island County jail for safekeeping. The Gazette pronounced Budd "indirectly concerned in the foul outrage." His arrest temporarily satisfied the public demand for immediate action.

Within the Davenport house the body of George Davenport was prepared for burial. The women scrubbed the walls and the floors with marginal success. Old Settlers recalled that a carpet was placed over the bloodstains on the bedroom floor because no amount of scrubbing could remove them. Davenport was buried at noon on Sunday from his house. Hundreds of people from both sides of the river attended. Some came out of respect. Many came in disbelief. Others were curious about the house, about the family, about the murder. The Reverend Zachariah

Goldsmith, an Episcopalian missionary from Maryland, conducted the service. The sermon he chose seemed particularly appropriate. From Luke XII: 39 Reverend Goldsmith read: "And this know, that if the good man of the house had known what hour the thief would come, he would have watched and not suffered his house to be broken through." George Davenport was buried under an oak tree about 250 yards from his home.[12]

The family's only public statement was issued through George L., who announced that they would offer a reward of $1500 for the legal apprehension of the perpetrators of this hideous crime. A broadside, offering the family's $1500 reward and a complete description of the murderers, appeared throughout the countryside. It gave all the pertinent details of the murder, especially a description of the attackers, serial numbers of the Missouri notes, and a description of Davenport's gold watch. Later, the State of Illinois offered an additional $200 reward for each of the five suspects. The broadsides were likely posted at the most public places in Rock Island County: on the door to the courthouse, on a tree on the Rock River Bottom Road at the south end of the Bluff Road, on the road at Abraham Frisk's place, at Sears' Mill, and at the Rosborough Store on the Moline Bluff.

Friends and family of George Davenport reached out to other counties for help in solving the crime, asking for information on similar attacks committed in recent months. One reply by Dixon resident Sam Fisher provided a description of suspects in his area. Among those he described was that of Robert Burch, age 28, five feet ten inches tall and called Captain. He had light complexion, blue eyes, long features, a trim build but broad in the shoulders. This seemed to match Davenport's attackers, and they had not yet been apprehended.

The summer of 1845 was unusually hot and dry and the leads on the murderers evaporated. Rumors ran rife that they had been apprehended in such places as Hannibal, Quincy, and Peoria. But the truth was, the murderers were still at large. The Gazette served as the official clearinghouse for information, repeatedly reporting that it was a duty to correct the rumors and wrong reports.

In mid-July a group of Mesquakie Indians encamped on the bluffs above Davenport heard of the murder of their friend. After confirming the details at the Gazette offices, they performed a funeral service of their own at the gravesite with the same ceremony used to bury their own tribal members. Addison H. Sanders, who was himself present at this ceremony, remarked that the Indians " who had known him in life ... perhaps loved him more or esteemed him higher than any real soldier on the island."

The ceremony was a rare, if not unique, honor to a white man and an acknowledgement of the long friendship the Mesquakie had with George Davenport. The braves asked the Great Spirit to make Davenport happy in the Spirit Land and to make their Sioux enemies, whom they had slain in battle, Davenport's servants in the Spirit Land. As part of the ceremony, a cedar post was painted with headless figures and two warriors. Waucoshaushe and Pautaucoto, told the story of their heroic feats against the Sioux. The cedar grave post is a very rare example of tribute paid by Indians to a white man and is housed at Hauberg Museum, Black Hawk State Park. A stone tree stump stands on his Chippiannock gravesite, where Davenport now rests, as a reminder of this Indian tribute. After this time the Sauk and Mesquakie annually returned to Rock Island, even after they were removed to Kansas in 1846. Each year they would make a special visit to Susan Lewis, Bailey, and George L. Davenport whom they knew as Musquakie.[13]

Tragedy struck the Davenport family a second time that summer when George A., the eldest child of George L. and Sarah, suffered a paralytic stroke. It was the first of three seizures that left him mentally and physically arrested. His condition that summer was tentative as the family had little medical treatment to offer him. For weeks no one knew if he would live or die.

Sometime in the middle of July, Lee County Sheriff Estes notified Rock Island County Sheriff Lemuel Andrews that a man by the name of Edward Bonney had knowledge of the gang in Nauvoo. He recommended Bonney as a suitable man to track down the Davenport murderers, calling him a man of skill, ingenuity, and perseverance in ferreting out rogues. In the previous spring he had aided in capturing two murderers in a well-publicized case in Lee County, Iowa. Upon request from George L. Davenport, Joseph Knox, G.C.R. Mitchell, and Sheriff Andrews, Bonney came to Rock Island and agreed to work for them as a private detective. Joseph Knox later justified their actions: "Our anxiety for the speed(sic) arrest of these wretches is so great, that we feel inclined to sacrifice time, comfort, money, anything and everything to affect the Object."[14]

Through the remainder of August and into September there was no public news concerning Bonney's search. Privately, Davenport, Mitchell, Knox, and Andrews were kept abreast of his progress. Bonney had met a man on board the War Eagle while travelling between Galena and St. Louis. The man, whose name was Granville Young, admitted that he knew all about the murder of Col. Davenport, and the information he shared provided the details Bonney needed. The trail to the murderers led across Illinois and Indiana and into Ohio as Bonney interviewed families and friends of the men he pursued. Finally, on the 30th of September, three men were arrested. Robert Burch and John Long were arrested in Sandusky County, Ohio. William Fox was arrested at Centreville, Wayne County, Indiana. Aaron Long was arrested at his father's home in Jo Daviess County, Illinois. On Friday, the 3rd of October, Dr. Gregg captured John Baxter, at the home of Baxter's brother-in-law near Madison, Wisconsin.

The Chicago Democrat called them the most abandoned set of ruffians ever beheld. All were familiar with Rock Island and aware of George Davenport as an immensely wealthy man. They had expected to get thirty thousand dollars from him. They were young, said the paper, and deeply entrenched in lives of crime. The Galena Gazette provided some physical descriptions of those arrested.

Robert Burch was probably the oldest member. He was 27. Physically he was tall, spare and good-looking, and said to be intelligent, cunning, and circumspect. He did not believe that Davenport had any money in the house, but the thought of thirty thousand dollars was enough to convince him that the job was worth the risk. When captured, he was wearing the watch and seal of George Davenport. During the transport across Lake Michigan, Burch threw overboard a suitcase belonging to Edward Bonney thinking he could get rid of the evidence against him. Fortunately, the evidence Bonney had collected was not in this bag.

William Fox was short and very strong, hence, the nickname Chunky. He was always ready for action and his description matched the man Davenport identified as having fired the gun.

John Long was not yet 22 years old, but considered by the Galena Gazette to be the evil spirit of the band. He was described as short and sinister-looking with sharp, restless eyes and a quick mind. He claimed to be an "honorable" tradesman. His trade was murder and robbery. He had had an active career in crime, particularly in Mississippi and in Arkansas, and knew no fear.

Aaron Long was John Long's twenty-year old brother. Although characterized as being slow and stupid, he was always ready for action. He spoke very little and seemed unconcerned about his fate. When arrested, he remarked that he didn't know what they could be arresting him for, unless it was the murder of Col. Davenport.

The fifth suspect was John Baxter, who had lived in Davenport for a time. His family was known and respected in this area, a fact that gave him some community sympathy. Of the five, he was the only one who was not a hardened criminal, but lazy and willing to make a fast, easy buck, even if the means of it was a little shady. He had once taken money to give a false affidavit professing a cure for bronchitis that had rendered him unable to work for eighteen months. He frequented drinking and gambling houses, but was not known to have been involved in any criminal activity.[15]

About the time of the five arrests, Davenport's gun and pistol were recovered in Lee County, Iowa. That led to the arrest of Granville Young, whom Bonney had met earlier in the summer on board the War Eagle, as well as William H. and Grant R. Redding. Granville Young was a nineteen-year-old orphan from Virginia who had drifted west. He had fallen in with this gang and made his home with the Reddings. He was not part of the original plan, but bought into the deal for fifty dollars, which he got by selling a couple horses for his share of the thirty thousand dollars. He was characterized as weak, both physically and morally.

The Reddings were a father and son team whose house on Devil Creek near Nauvoo was known throughout the Mississippi Valley as a rendezvous point for gang members. Edward Bonney later called the gang "the Banditti of the Prairie," which became the name of his book. The gang was a loose confederation of as many as 100 outlaws who preyed on residents in the Mississippi Valley by robbing, stealing, counterfeiting, assaulting and murdering. Old Man Redding was considered the genius behind all the crimes committed by this gang.

The Nauvoo connection was particularly troublesome to Rock Island and Davenport residents. Rumors circulated that the "confederates" of the four jailed suspects would attempt a rescue "even if it should cost the destruction of the town in which they were confined." A Night Watch was established under the captaincy of Nathaniel Belcher for added security during the overnight hours. Rock Island was divided into three wards for the Night Watch - Upper, Middle, and Lower -- and the watchmen were compensated for their services. Trustees of the town requested 200 stands of arms from Governor Ford of Illinois: muskets with bayonets and ball cartridges for any emergency revolving around the trial and execution of the murderers.[16] The town of Davenport, too, organized a Night Watch of its residents.

Once arrests were made, the wheels of justice moved quickly. The Grand Jury had already been scheduled for the first week in October and, on the first Monday, all five plus Fox - Burch, Baxter, the two Longs, and Young – were indicted for murder. Although Fox had escaped in Indiana, he was included in the indictment. In light of these other arrests, Charles Budd, who had been the first to be arrested, was released from jail and never again considered to be part of the murder conspiracy.

The indictment read: "not having the fear of God before their eyes but being served and seduced by the instigation of the Devil ... with force and arms ... feloniously, wilfully, and of malice aforethought ... did strike, penetrate and wound ... George Davenport ... "[17] Space was limited at the trial itself, and Judge Browne had placed a gag order on the newspapers until the trial was over, so the pubs and meeting places of both towns hummed with news that came from those who could attend the court proceedings.

On Tuesday the two Longs, Young, and Baxter were arraigned in court. All entered pleas of not guilty. They were ordered to be tried together and assigned public defenders. The two Longs and Young requested a change of venue, but the request was denied. Baxter, who had a different lawyer, obtained a continuance. The process of seating the jury began.

On Wednesday the court swore in the remaining jurymen and proceeded with the case against John and Aaron Long and Granville Young. Burch, who had not yet been arraigned, testified against both Longs and Young. His testimony revealed the entire plan and strengthened the case against everyone but himself.

The trial concluded on Friday, the tenth of October. Closing arguments were completed at 9 o'clock in the evening and the jury deliberated just two hours. John Long, Aaron Long, and Granville Young were all pronounced guilty of murder in the first degree. They were sentenced to be hanged on the 29th of October. Burch and Baxter were expected to apply for a change of venue.[18]

Both George L. and Bailey Davenport attended the court proceedings and provided testimony for the prosecution. George L. had been the last one to see his father on the day of the murder. He testified that he had offered to stay with his father that day instead of attending the picnic with the others, but the elder Davenport had insisted he would be fine by himself. Both men were concerned with recent break-ins in Stephenson and reports of strangers hanging about town. There was no mention of Mrs. Davenport or her daughter Susan as having attended the trial.

Thousands of people came from miles around to watch the hangings - men, women, even children. Estimates ran as high as 4,000 people, more than the populations of Stephenson and Davenport combined. They came to see what these banditti looked like, not so much out of ghoulish curiosity, but more because they could not picture in their minds what these monsters looked like. How would they recognize one if they should pass one in the streets? They were driven by a need to identify anyone who threatened their values so much in order to protect themselves, their families, and their property from them. In the days before photography and visual technology, the only way to see these men, whose values were so different from everyone else, and to see what they looked like, was to come and see for themselves.

Excitement ran high on the day of execution. A scaffold for the occasion had been built at the intersection of Illinois and Deer streets, the present day intersection of 14th street and 2nd avenue. It was built about 10 to 12 feet from the ground and could accommodate 15 to 20 persons. Seated on the platform were some of the members of the jury as well as two of the condemned men's counsel.

At one o'clock the prisoners were marched from the jail to the scaffold, each with a personal bodyguard, several selected ministers, and a contingency guard of 150 men under the leadership of Captain Belcher. The Green Mountain Boys played a slow and solemn dirge composed for the occasion by George P. Abel, manager of the musicians. Rumors ran through the crowds that a rescue attempt would be made as the procession neared the scaffolding. After a second piece played by the band, the sheriff read the writ of execution and the prisoners were offered an opportunity to speak. John Long addressed the crowd first, speaking for some time. Then his bother Aaron spoke, and finally Granville Young. After a Hymn and a reading from scripture by Rev. Mr. Haney, they were hanged; Aaron Long twice since the rope broke on the first attempt.[19] The entire event had taken two and a half hours, but the message was clear. This community was ready and able to enforce law and order. It was willing to shed the last vestiges of the frontier.

Baxter and Burch remained in the Rock Island county jail for several months, despite several escape attempts. In December, Baxter's irons were off and Burch was ready to shed his, when they were discovered. A bar on the window grating had been filed so that it could be pushed out. Despite double irons and more care in guarding these men, another near escape occurred the following month when they broke through the stone wall of the jail, dug through the earth, and were just about to break out when the jailer's dog aroused the jailer.[20] Burch and Baxter both won changes of venue after this.

In the spring, John Baxter was re-tried in Warren County. By this time he had lost all public sympathy. His role in the attack was seen as a betrayal because he was the man who had "gotten up the site." About two weeks before the robbery he had gone to the Davenport house under pretext of a friendly call, taken tea with the family, and sized up the situation. Baxter had determined that there were four men in the house, all well armed, and that the money was kept on the second floor. It was he who had given the all-clear signal on the day of the robbery. He was also sentenced to be hanged, but managed a lesser sentence of life imprisonment for the information he provided.

Robert Burch was never tried. He was granted a change of venue from Rock Island County to Knox county and obtained continuances of his trial. While in the Knoxville jail, he made several attempts to escape and was finally successful in escaping on 22nd of February 1847.

The case of the Reddings was continued on the fourth Monday of May 1846. William Redding, the father, was acquitted for lack of witnesses, and Grant Redding, the son, found guilty as an accessory before the fact. Grant Redding was sentenced to one year in prison, two weeks of which were to be served in solitary confinement.

Neither Burch nor Fox was recaptured. As late as 1860, Edward Bonney was still following leads on their whereabouts. There are stories that they had fled to Texas where Fox later died. Burch, however, did not stay in Texas long. He was lured by the rumors of gold in California and died there that same year in a pistol duel over a game of cards.

Edward Bonney was at first lauded to the skies, then condemned as a crook. He was indicted for counterfeiting, but it was later revealed that the charges against him were brought by other members of the gang to which Burch, Fox, and Long had belonged. Bonney acknowledged that his methods in capturing the murderers had been so successful that it had stricken terror into the very heart of the banditti, and that their very livelihood of crime was threatened.[21] His personal account of the capture, called Banditti of the Prairie, was first published in 1850, and is still in print today. He continued to pursue William Fox as late as 1860 and was rumoured to have been associated with the Pinkerton Detective Agency in its formative years. He died in Chicago in 1864.[22]

There were lingering debates in the community concerning the conviction and whether the hanging had been justified. The issue of trying all men as one rather than offering them separate trials was raised, as well as the influence of newspaper coverage on the outcome of trials and impartiality in a highly-publicized case. For months editorials in the newspapers discussed whether the Rock Island community had been able to provide a fair and impartial jury because everyone knew the victim. The Mississippian supported the jurors as God-fearing men who would not perjure themselves when they took the oath. But the Gazette maintained that there could be no impartiality when all the jurors had known the victim and the gruesome details of the murderer. The issue of capital punishment was also raised, and it should be noted that never before had there been such a public hanging in Rock Island county, nor has there been one since that time.

George Davenport's death, as shocking and horrible as it was, was his final contribution to the towns he had worked so hard to build. His murder had drawn the people together and made them think of themselves as a community. They had acted together, in an organized and law-abiding manner, and ridded themselves of the banditti. No longer could they be called frontiersmen, but urban citizens.

Davenport's dreams of transplanting his roots in a new land had taken hold and born fruit. He had established his name in this new country, created his family and secured for them a future. He could rest now, with the spirit slaves of his Mesquakie friends as his servants. Davenport's sons would carry on.

EPILOGUE

THE TRIAL AND HANGING were expensive for the young county government. Sheriff Lemuel Andrews was paid four hundred dollars to hang the three criminals. The gallows, built by Jacob Starr, cost fifty dollars. There were jury expenses of twenty-five dollars paid to Robert Early for rooms and fees and the county lawyers, Knox and Drury, were paid twenty-five dollars for defending the accused. Aaron Long was the only one buried at the time. Jacob Millirow was paid five dollars for that task.[1]

The rest of the bodies were dissected for medical study. In the name of science, Judge Browne had given all three bodies to Dr. Patrick Gregg, but the weather was warm and Dr. Gregg could not handle all three bodies. He personally dissected John Long's body for study purposes and kept his skeleton in the post hospital on the island during his lifetime. Later the skeleton hung around for years in various county locations until it was buried in the 1970s. Granville Young's body was sent down to a doctor for study in the St. Louis area. Dr. Gregg's story of the adventure of the body in the whiskey cask is worthy of repeating, though it was a familiar one well into the 1870s.

A doctor in the St. Louis area had requested one of the bodies to study and sent a barrel of rum upriver in which to transport the body. When the cask arrived in Rock Island Dr. Gregg had it unheaded and the body placed in it. It was then sent downriver on the deck of a steamer. When the cask arrived in St. Louis, it was delivered to the doctor's office. During the course of that day the doctor went to the dock and said to the captain that Dr. Gregg had sent a barrel of rum to him but that the rum was nearly all gone. The captain made his excuses saying that the roustabouts could smell liquor a mile away and go for it, but that he would pay for any damages. "Oh, never mind, Captain," said the doctor, "the body came through just fine." "Body!" exclaimed the captain, "what body?" "Oh!" said the doctor, the body of one of Colonel Davenport's murderers was in that cask." The captain raced for the side of the boat and the doctor dropped the subject. That was the end of the matter.[2]

George L. and Sarah's family continued to grow and, not long after Davenport's murder, the family moved into a new home on the corner of Brady and Third Street in Davenport. With the birth of William A. in August 1846, they now had five children. Bailey, too, had a child that year: Harry Davenport, born to Hianope, a Mesquakie woman. Harry and his mother Hianope lived with Susan and Mrs. Davenport in the Davenport house for several years.[3]

On the 5th of February 1847, Naomi King L'Oste, George Davenport's sister whom he had visited in 1827, died in Louth, Lincolnshire. Although she had probably never met her brother's sons, she left most of her estate to her nephews, George L. and Bailey. In August of the same year, Margaret Davenport died quietly in her Island home and was buried beside her husband on the Island. The Davenport property then passed to Susan Lewis in accordance with the provisions of George's will.[4] Suddenly, at the age of 46, Susan was a very wealthy and eligible woman. She was also, for the first time in her life, alone.

A year after her mother died, Susan Lewis took a big step towards exercising her independence. She bought a large portion of the lands that George Davenport's will had designated for sale. These properties had not yet been sold or mortgaged. Had they been sold George L., Bailey, and Susan would have divided the profits equally, but this purchase gave her complete control over the disposition of her own land. Bailey Davenport also bought some of these estate lands at the same time.

Susan Lewis was then almost entirely in charge of her own fortune, and two years after her mother died, she married the Rev. Zachariah Goldsmith. The marriage took place in the Davenport's home on the island. It was a small, private affair officiated by the Rev. Mr. Hall of Rock Island.[5] Goldsmith and Susan Lewis had some things in common: religion, a love for books and reading, and ties to King George County, Virginia. But the feelings they had for one another were not able to compensate for the difficulties in Goldsmith's life. Whatever hopes and dreams they may have had for their marriage never were realized.

Early settlers remembered Mr. Goldsmith as a proud and arrogant man, who professed to be a widower and aristocrat, coarse in speech and unsociable with church people and others. He had come to Davenport as an Episcopalian missionary from Maryland after some personal difficulties with the Church in Virginia and in Maryland. He was, instead, divorced from his wife, Elizabeth, who remained in the East. After leaving his two children with a trusted relative in Maryland, Goldsmith accepted the call to Davenport and came to Iowa looking for a fresh start in life. He arrived in October 1841. As rector of Trinity parish, his duties included travelling to outlying communities such as Muscatine, Blue Grass and Pleasant Prairie, to perform religious services as well as to help with the fundraising for a new church facility for his Davenport parish. He called upon many of his acquaintances in Virginia and Maryland to support the building fund in Iowa. The parishioners in Davenport, however, could not see that Rev. Goldsmith was making much progress. The Church was no further along in 1848 than it had been three years earlier and the parishioners complained that Rev. Goldsmith's expenses were extravagant. In April 1849, Rev. Goldsmith resigned from his position of

Rector over a question of irregularities in the fundraising expenditures.[6] This was three months before his intended marriage to Susan Lewis.

Considering that Zachariah might be liable for any missing church funds, or that he might have some private designs on her legal assets, George L. Davenport, as executor of his father's estate, instigated a prenuptial agreement with Goldsmith, his mother, and himself in June 1849. All real and personal property provided his mother by the will of George Davenport as well as the properties she had purchased from the estate were placed in the legal trust of George L. Davenport until the death of either his mother or Goldsmith. In accordance with the trust agreement, Goldsmith relinquished any right or claim to any and all of his wife's property.

For her part, Mrs. Goldsmith refrained from any or all claim to her husband's property. Although the agreement left Goldsmith without any control of land or means of support from his wife's estate, the agreement effectively protected all parties from any future claims against Goldsmith, particularly from Trinity parish that might attempt to recover their missing church funds. It also protected Mrs. Goldsmith from losing the independence that she had so recently achieved. In late fall of 1849, Trinity parish formally requested that Mr. Goldsmith's "papers, correspondence and documents" pertaining to an earlier donation be turned over to the parish, but there was no legal action taken to recover the lost funds.[7]

It was about the time of the Goldsmith marriage that the house was "remodeled," according to the Minneapolis architectural firm of MacDonald and Mack. The front porch was enlarged in a Greek revival style by the addition of four large walnut pillars. Windows were added on the end walls of the upper story, and extensive remodelling was done to the interior woodwork.[8] Dating the remodelling has been based on stylistic designs of the woodwork and on the only significant event known to have taken place in the house after George's murder, the Goldsmith marriage. Such a remodelling is in keeping with the life style to which pioneers thought Reverend Goldsmith aspired before his marriage to Miss Lewis, and this gives plausibility to MacDonald and Mack's conjecture.

The marriage did not last long. Goldsmith began to drink heavily again. His assignment to Iowa had been a last chance for Goldsmith to get his life together and he must have felt humiliation, anger, and frustration that he had not been able to prove himself worthy of the chance given him by Bishop Kemper of Wisconsin.[9] Resorting to alcohol only served to ferment inside him and, according to family stories, he erupted into a violent, unpredictable maniac that served to isolate the couple from their friends and her relatives. Many who were closest to them remembered that the entire household was in fear of Reverend Goldsmith.

Mrs. Goldsmith did not tolerate this behavior for long. Within the year the reverend was no longer welcomed on the island. It is uncertain whether or not she obtained an official divorce, but Goldsmith is not listed as a resident on the island in the 1850 Federal Census, the summer after their marriage. Legal transactions recorded in August of that year suggest that some kind of financial agreement had been reached between them rather than a messy and public divorce. In Scott county, Iowa, Mrs. Goldsmith "requested and directed " her son, George L. Davenport to convey several lots of Davenport city property to Zachariah Goldsmith for the sum of $1,000. Goldsmith, then, relinquished all right, title, and claim to property in both Scott and Rock Island counties -- land which any other husband might have claimed by virtue of his marriage -- to George L. Davenport in exchange for $3,000 cash. Essentially the Davenports bought him out of the family. Goldsmith re-established himself in Davenport. In 1851 he was officially removed from the ministry of the Episcopal Church by Bishop Kemper. Details of his removal remain sealed today. Three years later in September 1854 he died of the Delirium Tremens in a Davenport hotel.[10]

Mrs. Goldsmith continued living in the island house with her servants, Katherine (sic), age 30, Mathilda Barrett, age 16, and Henry Smith, age 13, as well as Harry and his mother, Hianope. Jennie Davenport also lived there during the summer months. The identity of Katherine who was listed in the Federal Census as a Swiss immigrant has never been established, but her service continued a tradition of hiring help for the house. Henry was the son of Scottish immigrants who later became a familiar figure and carriage maker in Moline. At that time Bailey had moved out of the island home and was living in a Rock Island hotel run by B.F. Barrett. He was involved in a number of Rock Island county enterprises.[11]

Elizabeth Davenport, who had been living in southern Illinois, eloped in 1852 with Nicholas Ferkle. On her eighteenth birthday they returned to Rock Island to claim Elizabeth's inheritance of a thousand dollars promised to her in George Davenport's will. After a few years they returned to Monroe County until 1871-72 when they again returned to Rock Island County. This time they set up housekeeping on a farm owned by Bailey Davenport near Illinois City. Their relationship with the Davenport family at this time is unclear, although it seems that Bailey took them under his wing and helped them financially. Bailey, although said to have been furious with Elizabeth's extravagant spending at his expense, did pay her bills. Some pioneers remembered that Bailey had promised to give her the deed to the farm they lived on. He never did, however, and the Ferkles were evicted from the farm after Bailey's estate was settled around 1893. Elizabeth's mother Catherine, probably now in her mid-thirties, married a Mr. Hehmann in southern Illinois where she lived the rest of her life.[12]

In 1853 Harry and his mother Hianope joined the Mesquakie who were moving to Kansas. Jennie Davenport and her mother also moved with the tribe at the same time. Their absence must have been painful to Susan Goldsmith who was now alone with two servants to help her care for the house.

Susan Goldsmith lived simply on the island. The only hints that give us any idea of how the Davenports lived comes from the one surviving account book she kept from August 1850, to December 1853.[13] The accounts reveal a rather modest life-style that must have been similar to the style the family had always lived on the island. Her main income was from the rents she received from several buildings among them the U.S. Hotel (formerly built as the Davenport Hotel by Le Claire and Davenport), White Hall, and at least two brick houses in Davenport including one on Brady Street rented by A. C Billon, a jeweller, clockmaker, and engraver. These buildings generated around $50 each month. The income from the rents was augmented by the occasional sale of bacon, some of her hogs, and bushels of apples from her orchard. From time to time, in accordance with the terms of Davenport's will, she sold some of her lots in Le Claire, Iowa, and in the town of Davenport.

Mrs. Goldsmith's expenses were primarily household expenses including foodstuffs, the care of her servants, and the feeding of her livestock, but there were also expenses in the upkeep and improvement of her rental properties. In the time she kept this account book, she purchased a number of foodstuffs on a regular basis: Sugar, tea, flour, syrup, molasses, nutmeg and potatoes. She sometimes bought candles, starch, and rice. Less frequently she bought mackerel for herself and corn and oats, presumably for her horses. She paid Katherine and Mathilda wages and also bought yard goods such as calico, Marino wool, gingham, and flannel. She bought only a few manufactured clothing items such as shoes, boots, and kid gloves. She also bought suspenders for Henry. Clothing was made at home either by herself or Katherine or Mathilda since there are no entries that indicate a seamstress was regularly hired. Occasionally she bought skeins of silk and oil prints for the house and once she bought a quart of brandy. There were tools to replace, scythe stones, rakes and hoes, and she bought a dozen plates in 1853 and a new molasses pitcher. Since there are no purchases of vegetables or eggs and butter, it seems likely that Mrs. Goldsmith was maintaining her garden and raising a few chickens in addition to her hogs and horses. She might also be milking a cow each day for milk and butter and probably still had a few cattle for butchering.

During the period 1850 - 1853 her rental property was undergoing some improvements and repair. She bought pounds of nails, shingles, and glass. She paid for walling a well and cellar windows at the Billon House and two stone crocks for the U.S. Hotel and one for White Hall. She had both brick houses painted, presumably on the inside. In addition to these everyday kinds of expenses, there were taxes to pay: State and county, as well as school and corporation taxes.

Beginning in 1854, however, several things happened which must have caused Mrs. Goldsmith to reconsider whether she should continue living on the Island. For one, there were maintenance problems with the old house. According to visitors in the area, the house was beginning to look a bit neglected. George Davenport had always attended to the building and rebuilding and now there was no need to keep the outbuildings. Nor was there anyone to help with the upkeep of the house and outbuildings. Although Bailey moved back into the island house from time to time, his own businesses were expanding and demanding his full attention. Her older son, George L., had a growing family and businesses that kept him from becoming more involved with the island estate. Another incentive for moving to the mainland was that she now had relatives nearby.

First of all, her uncle Jeremiah Bowling, his wife Sarah, their two unmarried daughters, Lucinda and Adelaide, and their married daughter, Barbara Swann and her husband, Eli, finally migrated to Rock Island County. They joined Jeremiah's other children, now with children of their own, who had been settled here nearly twenty years: Julia Watts, Sophia Copp, and James M. Bowling. Although Jeremiah and Sarah died soon after their arrival, the family had been, at least for a brief time, reunited. For Susan Goldsmith, her mother's people remained very important to her and she kept in close touch with them with Sunday dinners to which all were invited.

Susan was also beginning to become active in the newly organized Episcopalian community. For about a year, the parish had been holding services in a storefront in Stephenson and were now beginning to plan for the construction of a church building. Mrs. Goldsmith took comfort in the Church and Pastor Holcombe became a close friend. She and Bailey were part of those early planning sessions and large contributors to the new building. The church was completed in 1857.[14]

Travelling to and from the Island was also changing. On January 17, 1853, an act was passed by the General Assembly of Illinois to incorporate a bridge company for the sole purpose of constructing a railroad bridge across the river. The plan to connect the Chicago and Rock Island railroad at Rock Island with the Mississippi and Missouri railroad at Davenport was completed in February, 1856, when the first railroad bridge to span the Mississippi River was completed. For Susan Lewis Goldsmith, the bridge may have been an intrusion on the peace and quiet she had grown accustomed to over the years.[15]

The railroads crossed the island on an hourly basis. The rates were reasonable - ten cents each way, considerably less than the dollar Davenport used to charge for the ferry crossing. But railroads were also noisy. They rumbled across the island, blowing big puffs of steam and sounding their shrill whistles. What Susan Goldsmith thought or felt when she heard those rumbles on the tracks and the steam whistles echoing down the valley can only be imagined.

The railroad had come with a heavy price to the Island's idyllic environment. The western tip of the island had been totally devastated and reconfigured. The ground had been levelled, and great mounds formed to make the railroad bed. A report by Brevet Major E.S. Sibley read: "... several acres of land ... have been scalped, and the earth to the depth of from two to three feet has been taken for its construction, thus disfiguring and injuring to some extent the appearance of the Island."[16] Even the river was changing. Work was begun in 1854 to remove rock from the channel at Campbell's Island. It was an attempt to deepen the river and eliminate the hazards to river transportation, one that never materialized.

With all these improvements, there was a growing interest in the island for development. The island had always attracted developers and squatters and several commercial interests were taking a good look at the possibilities Rock Island offered. Some envisioned a university on the island; others a great manufacturing center, but squatters had settled on the island and some were engaged in questionable activities. One night in October of 1855, fire destroyed the abandoned barracks and one blockhouse of Fort Armstrong. The fire may have been deliberately set to a keg of gunpowder still stored at the fort. Bucket brigades were formed, but they were unable to put out the flames that were enhanced by the exploding gunpowder. All remaining damaged buildings were ordered razed. Only one building that was occupied by a squatter remained standing to give any remembrance to historic Fort Armstrong.[17] It was an unsettling situation to an old woman living alone nearby, but that was not the only unsettling news for Mrs. Goldsmith.

In May 1856 Judge McLean ruled that the War Department had no title to the island and therefore 703 acres, including the Davenport property, were thrown back into the public lands and subject to homestead. It was a renewal of the old question of whether the island was a military reserve.[18]

About this same time, Bailey was engaged to marry to Mary Grace Lynde, a Rock Island schoolteacher and sister to Cornelius Lynde, a prominent banker and business partner of Bailey. With his anticipated marriage, the uncertainty of a court battle over property rights, and the expectation that some kind of government facility would in fact be established on the island, Mrs. Goldsmith's thoughts must have turned to the problem that George Davenport had faced so long, removal from the island.

On the day before Bailey's wedding in July of 1856, the local newspaper announced that Mrs. Goldsmith had purchased the Brackett home in the town of Stephenson (later Rock Island, Il) and the following spring, the island property was sold. The house on the island was already boarded up and abandoned.[19] No longer was the house a cultural and economic center, nor was it the grandest home north of St. Louis. It was only a house that had witnessed and been participant in a great transformation during the past forty years. It would, from time to time, be rented out to others, but no Davenport would ever live there again.

The changes were evident everywhere as note by a contributor to the Port Byron Messenger:

Now we have all sorts of those who call themselves white folks. Our prairies, and prairie posies, have nearly all been annihilated by the plow of the white man. The tall blue joint-grass, that grew all through the woods from one to ten feet high, and the thousands of large fine strawberries and blackberries, are nearly all crowded out by the young and thrifty undergrowth of timber. The thousands of deer and other wild animals have retired from our sight, and we now behold the cattle, hogs, sheep, and other domestic animals. But I can find nothing that can compensate us for our honey-bees.

Now we have apples, plums, pears, cherries, currants, and all manner of tame fruits, and roses and posies and also rabbits, fleas and bedbugs: timothy, clover, thistles, burrs, mayweed, burdock, pennyroyal, sorrel, gimsen(sic), dandelion, and a thousand different kinds of weeds: which are all of recent origin. And last, though not least, three bull-frogs have made their debut in this country, viz: two in the vicinity of Port Byron, and one in the vicinity of LeClaire; such an animal never honored the inhabitants with its melodious music till about the middle of June, 1858.[20]

Then came the official announcement that the island would be continued as a military reserve. On 12th June 1858, Congress passed an act that forbade the sale of island property.[21] But Mrs. Goldsmith had made her decision too. It was time for her to move on, both physically and emotionally, to put the past in perspective. By 1858, Rock Island was no longer the frontier outpost of Indians, military men, and fur traders. It was an urban center of industrialization. And the pioneers who had contributed to the changes were beginning to recognize the success of their efforts. Accordingly, the Pioneers and Old Settlers formed an organization designed to celebrate the accomplishments of those who had paved the way for others. Susan Lewis Goldsmith willingly took her place among them.

DAVENPORT'S WILL

THE WILL OF GEORGE is probably the most important document to offer insight into Davenport's motives for his lifelong land accumulation and business enterprises. Rather than a simple accumulation of wealth, Davenport's motives appear to have been centred on care for his family. As such, the will was a roadmap for his family to follow after his death. In it he mapped out their financial future, suggesting that he intended that they continue the life they had already known. George L. Davenport, as the eldest, was named executor of his father's estate, settled the business affairs, and continued to run the mercantile business. Son Bailey Davenport oversaw the extensive farming operations and attended the tax sales buying up property for little or nothing, just as his father always had. Mrs. Davenport was granted a life estate, which was essentially the dower right provided for widows under the prescriptive laws of the time. By this arrangement, she could stay in the house on the island for her lifetime, managed by her grandson, George L'Oste Davenport, with certain income-producing properties set aside for her care and maintenance. The same provision was made for Susan Lewis who would inherit her mother's life estate after her mother's death.

Susan Lewis was treated the same as her mother, a married woman. As a single, unmarried woman or *femme sole* under the law, she was eligible to own property in her own name, but Davenport's will treated her as a widow, the same as her mother. Whether this was an attempt on Davenport's part to compensate her for the service she had given him in lieu of marriage, as in the case of his wife, or whether it was simply the easiest way to be fair to both women in this unusual relationship can not be known. It must be noted, however, that the estate Davenport left was a sizable one and presumably neither Susan nor her mother had experience in making the decisions needed to run it. On the other hand, son George L. Davenport had been his father's right hand man in business for many years and was well prepared to assume the responsibility.

Several parcels of land were set aside for the exclusive use of Mrs. Davenport and her daughter Susan. The income from these lands, their rentals, leases, etc., was designated as their primary means of support although other land could be sold when cash was needed. They two women were allowed to live in the house on the island with all the furnishings and outbuildings, farm equipment and livestock, but they had no power to sell anything. That decision was left to George L. Davenport who alone could make any decision concerning the sale of property and to divide the profits equally among Margaret, Susan, Bailey, and himself. Upon the deaths of Mrs. Davenport and Susan Lewis, the property was to be transferred to sons Bailey and George L. and to Davenport's four grandchildren: George A., Joseph, Catherine, and Naomi Davenport. Each and every parcel of land was conveyed specifically to the sons and grandchildren. Nothing was unaccounted for.

The Grantor-Grantee Indexes of Rock Island County Deed Records show that few of the Davenport properties were sold following Davenport's murder -- mainly those sales that had been agreed upon by

Davenport himself before his death. Evidently, the family had enough cash to live on. The rents of buildings are harder to discern, but they evidently provided enough income for the family for a number of years. After 1855 when Susan Lewis Goldsmith left the Island, until 1875, three years before her death, sales of land increased in frequency. Those land sales provided her with a steady income that supplemented the income generated by the rental properties.

Davenport's will also provided a settlement for Elizabeth Davenport, for Julie Watts, and for his old friend and loyal employee, Antoine Gokey. Elizabeth Davenport, who was living in southern Illinois with her mother at the time of her father's death, was provided a settlement of one thousand dollars payable at the time she turned eighteen. George L. Davenport was appointed her guardian and instructed to pay her five per cent interest on the total sum each year.

Julie Bowling Watts was willed a lot in Davenport, Iowa, containing a frame house and improvements. This was probably the house in which she and her two children were living. Julie was Margaret Davenport's niece and had been married to Davenport's business partner, William B. Watts. At the time of Davenport's murder, Julie Watts and her two daughters had been abandoned by Watts and she soon filed for divorce.

Davenport directed his son George L. Davenport to set aside one thousand dollars for the support and maintenance of Antoine Gokey Senior from which Gokey was to receive seventy dollars each year in provisions and clothing during his lifetime. After the Davenports had retired from the Indian Trade, Gokey had taken up farming in Henry County, Illinois, along the Rock River, and was living there as late as 1852. He probably remained there until his death sometime before 1855 when the family disappeared from Henry county records. David Sears recalled that after Antoine Gokey's death, Rosa Gokey and two of her daughters joined her tribe on the Des Moines River. Some of the family removed to Wisconsin and others to the Chippewa and Muncie Reserve in Franklin Co., Kansas.[22]

*I George Davenport of Rock Island Rock
Island County State of Illinois being in perfect
helth(sic) and understanding consithering the
certainty of death and the uncertainiy of the time
thereof and being desirous to settle my worldle
affairs Do therefore make and publish this my last
will and testament in manner and form following
that is to say: I give and bequeath to Margaret
Davenport and Susan Lewis hir daughter the
following described property to have and to hold
and to receive the rents and amoluments jointly for
their mantanance and benefit and the Surviver to be
continued in the occupation and benefits of the
property during their life time and then disposed of
as further provided in this will. The property given
and bequeathd to Margaret Davenport and Susan
Lewis her daughter for the purpose above stated is as
follows The South East frac. Qr Section 25
Eighteen North two west containing one hundred
and fifty seven acres & 81/100 with all the buildings
and aparances thereunto belonging. All my
household furniture Books Cattle horses hogs
wagons carriages and farming implements and every
thing appartaning to my establishment as it know
stands Also the rent and proceeds of the following
property in block Six lots four and five frame house
and stable and other improvements in Block forty
one lot five Store and other improvements in Block
forty two Part of lots Six Seven and Eight frame
Building called White Hall and the Part of Lots as
now fenced in in(sic) Block forty three Part of Lots
Six & Seven Brick house and other improvements in*

*Block forty two lot four Frame house. I again repeat
that their may be no mistake of my intention I give
to Margaret Davenport and Susan Lewis hir
daughter the above described property to have the
sole management and benefit during their Lifetimes.*

*I give and bequeath to my son George Loste
Davenport the following property viz: In Block forty
one lot one Brick Store and other Improvements
Also in Block forty two lot three Frame house and
Improvements Also out Lot No Seventeen
containing four acres and Forty acres of Land South
East corner of An Le Claires reserve in Block fifty
five lots four five six & seven in Block fifty Seven lots
Six Seven and Eight lots called Son of Row Block
twenty three Brick house Eight lots in the town of
Davenport Also my gould watch chins & seals all
my guns & Pistols*

*I also give and bequeath to my son George
LOste Davenport to have and to hold possion of at
the death of his Grand Mother Margaret Davenport
or after the death of his mother Susan Louis the last
that may be the survivor of the two the South East
fracnal of Section twenty five Eighteen North two
west on Rock Island with all the buildings and
appurtenances thereunto belongin*

*I give and bequeath to my son Bailey
Davenport as follows viz my part of lot four in Block
two Hous log cabbin & Stable also sixty feet lot Six
Block twelve also lot one & half lot Eight in Block
Sixteen Also lot six Block twenty the above lots in
the town of Rock Island Also South half North
West quarter Section One Seventeen North two
west also South half North East quarter Section two*

*Seventeen North two west Also Lot number two
containing fiftey acres of land. The above lots and
land lay on the bank of the Mississippi above the
town of Moline Also five qr Sections of Bounty
lands will be found in Book describing all my
property. I also give and bequeath to my son Bailey
Davenport Lot Nine containing two Hundred acres
in the same tract of land as the above mentioned
named lots two and three they will be found on
Record in the Clerk's Office being the land assigned
to me in division of land with Charles Farnham in
Rock Island County. I also give and bequest to
Elizabeth Davenport daughter of Catherine Pouit
the Sum of One Thousand dollars the money to be
placed in the hands of my son George L Davenport
who I hereby appoint hir guardian to pay in trust at
the rate of five per cent to Elizabeth Davenport
yearly until she arrives at the age of Eighteen and at
that time to han hir the one thousand dollars*

*I give and bequeath to my Grand Son George
Alfonse Davenport the whole square Number fifty
nine containing ten lots fenced round with a board
fence also after the death of Margaret Davenport
and Susana Lewis to have inn Block number forty
three part of Lot six & seven a Brick house and
other Improvements in the Town of Davenport
Scott County Iowa Territory I give and bequeath to
Joseph Davenport (my Grand Son) at the death of
Margret Davenport and Susan Lewis the property
they hold for life in Block forty one lot five frame
house and other improvements in Town of
Davenport Scott County Iowa Territory. I give and
bequeath to my Grand daughter Naomi Davenport
at the death of Margret Davenport and Susan Lewis*

the property they hold for life in Block forty three
lot one Brick house and other improvements in
Town of Davenport Scott County I. T. I give and
bequeath to my grand daughter Catherine
Davenport at the death of Margret Davenport and
Susan Lewis the property they hold for life in Block
forty two lot or parts of lots as before described part
of lots six seven and Eight frame house and other
improvements in the Town of Davenport

I give and bequeath to Mrs. July Watts in Block
forty four lot one, frame house and other
improvements in the Town of Davenport Scott
County Iowa Territory I do hereby further give and
bequeath to my son Bailey Davenport at the death of
Margret Davenport and his mother Susana Lewis the
property they hold for life in Block Six lots four &
five frame house and other improvements alts in
block forty-two lot four frame house and
improvements in the town of Davenport Scott
County Iowa Territory I further Will and decree
that all the remainder of my property of every kind
not otherwise disposed of in this will shall be sold to
the best advantage and at such time and or on such
terms as my son George L Davenport may direct but
if sold on credit bond and mortgage must be taken
on the land to secure the payment and the sale not
to be put off for a longer period than three years the
money arising from the sale of my property and the
money collected that is due me to be disposed of as
follows

1st to pay my debts 2nd One thousand Dollars to
be placed in the hands of Geo L Davenport to pay

*the legese as directed in this will to Elizabeth
Davenport 3ᵈ One thousand dollars to be placed in
the hands of Geo L Davenport for the support of
Ant Gokey, Senr to pay him yearly Seventy Dollars
in provisions and Clothing during his life at the
death of Ant Gokey Senr the money left for his
metanance to go to Geo L Davenport and shall be in
full for his services as Executor of this my will the
balance of all the money arising from the sale of my
estate to be equally divided between Margret
Davenport Susan Lewis hir daughter & George
LOste Davenport & Bailey Davenport Share &
Share alike and to be divided from time to time as
the money is Received and I hereby make and
ordain and appoint my son George Loste Davenport
my sole executor of this my last will and Testament
and further declare that the share given to my wife
Margret Davenport to be in lieu of dower and I do
hereby revoke all former wills by me made In
witness whereof I have hereunto set my hand and
Seal at my place of residence Indian Lodge Rock
Island October the twenty fifth day One thousand
and Eight hundred and forty four*

George Davenport

Seal

*Signed Sealed published and declared by the
above named George Davenport to be his last will
and testament in the presence of us at his request
and in his presence have subscribed our names as
witnesses thereto*

A H Miller

G B M Klower

G C R Mitchell

State of Illinois   Act – we G C R Mitchell and
A H Miller having been

Rock Island County   first duly sworn on
our oaths depose and say that we

Were present and heard
George Davenport whose signature appears to the
foregoing will and testament acknowledged the said
Last will and testament to be his free act and deed
and we believe him to have been of sound mind and
memory at the time of said acknowledgement.

Sworn and Subscribed to before
G. C. R. Mitchell

Me on this 28th day of July AD 1845
A H Miller

Harman G. Reynolds PJP

This close up of the images on the gravepost tell the story of the slain Sioux warriors given to Davenport for his use in the afterlife. The post is part of the Hauberg Collection and is currently in storage.

An Indian Ceremony:

Davenport Gazette, July 31, 1845

ON THE LAST FRIDAY afternoon we were witness to a strange and interesting ceremony performed by the Indians over the remains of Mr. Davenport, who was murdered at his residence on Rock Island on the 4th inst. Upon proceeding to the beautiful spot selected as his last resting place, in the rear of his mansion on Rock Island, we found the War Chief and braves of the band of Fox Indians, then encamped in the vicinity of this place, reclining on the grass around his grave at the head of which was planted a white cedar post some seven or eight feet in height.

The ceremony began by two of the braves rising and walking to the post, upon which with paint they began to inscribe certain characters, while a third brave armed with an emblematic war club, after drinking to the health of the deceased from a cup placed at the base of the post, walked three times around the grave, in an opposite direction to the course of the sun, at each revolution delivering a speech with sundry gestures and emphatic motions in the direction of the north-east. When he had ceased he passed the club to another brave who went through the same ceremony passing but once round the grave, and so in succession with each one of the braves. This ceremony, doubtless, would appear pantomimic to one unacquainted with the habits or language of the Indians, but after a full interpretation of their proceedings they would be found in character with this traditionary people.

In walking around the grave in a contrary direction to the course of the sun, they wished to convey the idea that the ceremony was an original one. In their speeches they informed the Great Spirit that Mr. Davenport was their friend and they wished the Great Spirit to open the door to him and to take charge of him. The enemies whom they had slain they called upon to act in capacity of waiters to Mr. Davenport in the spirit land. They believing that they have unlimited power over the spirits of those whom they have slain in battle. Their gestures towards the north-east were made in allusion to their great enemies, the Sioux, who live in that direction. They recounted their deeds of battle, with the number of the enemy that they had slain and taken prisoners. Upon the post were painted in hieroglyphics, the number of enemy that they had slain, those taken prisoners, together with the tribe and station of the brave. For instance, the feats of Wau-co-shaw-she, the Chief, were thus portrayed. Ten headless figures were painted, which signified that he had killed ten men. Four others were then added, one of them smaller than the others, signifying that he had taken four prisoners, one of whom was a child. A line was then run from one figure to another, terminating in a plume, signifying that all had been accomplished by a chief. A fox was then painted over the plume, which plainly told that the chief was of the Fox tribe of Indians. These characters are so expressive that if an Indian of any tribe whatsoever were to see them, he would at once understand them.

Following the sign of Pau-tau-co-to, who thus proved himself a warrior of high degree, were placed *twenty* headless figures, being the number of the Sioux that *he* had slain.

The ceremony of painting the post was followed by a feast, prepared for the occasion, which by them was certainly deemed the most agreeable part of the proceedings. Meats, vegetables and pies were served up in such profusion that many armful of the fragments were carried off – it being a part of the ceremony, which is religiously observed, that all the victuals left upon such an occasion are to be taken to their homes. At a dog feast, which are frequently given by themselves and to which white men are occasionally invited, the guest is either obliges to eat all that is placed before him, or hire some other person to do so, else it is considered a great breach of hospitality.

With the feast terminated the exercises of the afternoon, which were not only interesting, but highly instructive to those who witnessed them.

NOTES

Prologue

1. Gillum Ferguson, *Illinois in the War of 1812*, University of Illinois, 2012; Davis, James E. *Frontier Illinois*. Bloomington, IN: University of Illinois Press, 1998, 173.

2. Myers, Jacob W. "History of the Gallatin Salines, "*Journal of the Illinois State Historical Society*, October 1921 – January 1922, 14: 3-4 (347 – 349).

3. For a good discussion of the Indian tribes during the War of 1812, see Ferguson's *Illinois in the War of 1812*, University of Illinois, 2012.

4. "An Act to Promote Retaliation Upon Hostile Indians, December 24, 1814." "The Laws of Illinois Territory, 1809 – 1818", edited by Francis S. Philbrick, *Collections of the Illinois State Historical Library, Vol. XXV, Law Series Vol. V*. Springfield: Illinois State Historical Society, 1950.

5. Article IX, of the "Treaty With Great Britiain, 1814." Ratified February 17, 1815. online, A Century of Lawmaking for a New Nation: U.S. Congressional Documents and Debates, 1774 – 1875.
URL: https://memory.loc.gov/ammem/amlaw/

6. "Treaty with Sauk, May 13, 1816, "Kappler, ed. *Indian Affairs: Laws and Treaties, 126, 127, 128*. Produced by the Oklahoma State University Library
URL: http://digital.library.okstate.edu/kappler/

7. "Treaty With the Ottawa, Etc. August 24, 1816." Kappler, ed. *Indian Affairs: Laws and Treaties*. Volume 2. Online: Oklahoma State University Library http://digital.library.okstate.edu/kappler/pp126, 127, 128; Letter: George Graham to Ninian Edwards, November1, 1817, quoted in "The Indian Boundary Line Under the Treaty of August 24, 1816," by Charles G. Davis, *Journal of the Illinois State Historical Society*, Vol. 28, April 1935: 26–48 and 36-37; NOTE: The line was actually surveyed by John C. Sullivan in 1819, but surveyed by Flack and Bean in 1821.

8. Letter: NInian Edwards to Secretary of War William H. Crawford, September 24, 1816. Carter, ed. *Territorial Papers of the U.S., Illinois Territory 1814 – 1818*, Volume XVII, 398 – 399.

9. *Missouri Gazette*, December 23, 1815.

10. Letter: Graham to the Secretary of War, July 8, 1816. Carter, ed. *Territorial Papers, of the United States, Illinois Territory*, Vol. XVII, 359.

11. Letter: Richard Graham to George Graham, April 29th, 1816. Carter, ed. *Territorial Papers of the United States, Illinois Territory.* Vol. XVII, 328-329.

12. Davis, James. *Frontier Illinois.* Bloomington: Indiana University Press, 1998, 160-161, 204.

13. Rohrbough, Malcolm J. *The Land Office Business; The Settlement and Administration of American Public Lands, 1789 -1837.* Belmont,California: Wadsworth Publishing Company, 1990, 50; Letter: Graham to Graham, April 29th, 1816. In Carter, ed. *Territorial Papers,* Vol. XVII, 328-329.

14. Act of Congress, (May 6, 1812, 2 Stat.729); Rezah, Gordon, "Land Speculation in Fulton County, 1817 – 1832," *Western Illinois Regional Studies,* Vol 3, No. 1, Spring 1980, 22–35; Davis, p. 156; Park, Siyoung "Land Speculation in Western Illinois Pike County, 1821 – 1835," *Journal of the Illinois State Historical Society,* Vol. LXXVII (Summer 1984), No.2,115.

15. Letter: Gershom Flagg to Artemas Flag, September 12, 1818, in Buck, Solon J. ed.. "Pioneer Letters of Gershom Flagg." *Transactions of the Illinois State Historical Society,* Vol.15. Illinois State Historical Library: Phillips Bros, State Printers, 1912.

Chapter 1 – To America By Accident

1.Wilke, Franc B. *Davenport Past and Present,* Davenport: Luse, Lane & Co., 1858: 145.

2. Robinson, David, N. *The Book of Louth: The Story of a Market Town,* Buckingham, England: Barracuda Books Limited, 1979: 23.

3. Olney, R.J. *Rural Society and County Government in Nineteenth Century Lincolnshire,* Volume X, History of Lincolnshire Committee, 1979. What is known about John King and the King family has been gleaned from Church records of St. James of Louth and St. Margaret's of Keddington, the histories of Louth, and from correspondence with Miss Dorothy King of Spilsby, a descendent of the King family. Miss Pauline Franklin of Birmingham provided important information about the related L'Oste family. Both women contributed greatly to my understanding of what life was like in Louth in George Davenport's childhood, why he left Louth, and why he changed his name.

4. Christening record, August 5, 1794, St. James Church Records, Louth.; St. Margaret's church was closed in 2000, but Dorothy King plans to be buried there, as she said, "at the end of a long row of Kings."

5. Robinson, David N. *Book of Louth,* 63.

6. Olney, 21; Painter, Bill. *Upon the Poor Rate: The Story of Louth Workhouse and the Paupers of East Lindsey.* Louth Naturalist's, Antiquarian and Literary Society, 2000: 16,18.

7. Marriage record, St. James Church, Louth, on microfilm, LDS reel #1541999.

8. Interview with Dorothy King, March 2001.

9. Billy-boy is a trading vessel, of river-barge type with a single sail, used until the beginning of the 20th century: *Oxford Companion to Ships and the Sea,* 2006. http://www.encyclopedia.com; Franklin, Pauline. *The L'Oste Family of Lincolnshire. Birmingham, England: Keyway Communications, 1994*; Robinson, *Book of Louth*,136-137.

10. Wilkie, 145; Robinson, David. *Book of Louth*, 136-137.

11. Davis, Ralph. *The Rise of the Shipping Industry in the 17th and 18th Centuries.* Chapter VI: The Merchant Seaman, New York: St. Martin's Press, 1962.

12. Wilkie, 145: Although some records from the port of Liverpool do exist from this time period, Davenport's voyages have not been found.

13. Letter: Stephen Shairp to Right Honorable Lord Newbury, His Majesty's Principal Secretary of State, St, Petersburg, November 1, 1802. And also, Alexander Shairp to W. Shairp & Co., 26 October 1800. And also, "Claims Not Yet Accepted by the Russian Government, but Settled by the Commissioners to be Recommended." October 31, 1802. Class FO65/51. Public Record Office, Kew, London; Correspondence of Alexander and Stephen Shairp from St. Petersburg, Russia, to London, England, October23 and 30, 1800, November18 and 21, 1800, December 13 and 15, 1800. Class FO65/47 - 48. Public Record Office, Kew, London.
14. *Stamford Mercury*, three articles, dated December 4, 1800, December 5, 1800, and January 2, 1801. Microfilm, Lincoln Central Library, Lincolnshire, England.

Chapter 2 – Into the Army

1. Wilkie, Franc B. Davenport Past and Present. 1852, 145.

2. Coffman, Edward M. The Old Army: A Portrait of the American Army in Peacetime, 1784 – 1898. New York: Oxford University Press, 1988, 17, 180.

3. Captain John Armstrong's advertisement in a Philadelphia newspaper in Spring of 1791 as quoted in Coffman, 16.

4. Cunliffe, Soldiers and Civilians: The Martial Spirit in America, 1775-1865, 117; Coffman, 16.

5. Companies in the Old Army were known by their officers' names rather than by a letter of the alphabet.

6. Wilkie, 146.

7. "Dr. Erich Bollman," Concise Dictionary of American Biography, New York: Scribners, 1964: 421.

8. Wilkinson, James. General Order Book, RG 98 Records of U.S. Army Continental Commands, 1784 – 1821, M654, Reel 3, National Archives and Records Administration, Washington, D.C.; Wilkinson, James. General Order Book, 4 March 1807, M654, Reel 3, 726.

9. Gillson, Gordon E. The Development of a Military Frontier: The Story of Fort Adams and its Hinterland. M.A. Thesis, Louisiana State University, 1954: 790 Gillson, 97-98.

10. A gill measures one-fourth of a pint.

11. "Garrison Orders, Nov. 24, 1807. Fort Adams, November 1807 - October 1808," RG 98, Records of U.S. Army Commands, 1789 – 1821, Company Books, National Archives and Records Administration, Washington, D.C.

12. "Garrison Orders," Fort Adams.

13. Quarles, Garland R. and Lewis N. Barton, editors. What I Know About Winchester: Recollections of William Greenway Russell, 1800 - 1891. no date: 33.

14. Jones to Major Alexander Macomb, 22 August 1836, Adjutant General Letters Relative to Recruiting, RG 94, Entry 647, quoted in Silton, Graham Stanley. Life of the Enlisted Soldier on the Western Frontier, 1815-1845. Unpublished Dissertation. North Texas State University, 1972: 64.

15. "New Rules for Recruiting the Army." Adjutant and Inspector General's Office. Washington. 10 February 1814. Richard Graham papers. Missouri Historical Society, St. Louis, Mo.; Company Book of Captain Simon Owens of the First Infantry, 1810 - 1814, RG 98, Records of U.S. Army Commands, 1789 – 1821, Company Books, National Archives and Records Administration, Washington, D.C.

16. Norton, W.T. "Old Fort Bellefontaine." Journal of the Illinois State Historical Society 4: 336; Hansman, John. Everyday Life at Old Fort Madison. no publishing co., 1990: 17-20.

17. Company Book of Captain Simon Owens.

18. Prucha, Francis Paul. The Sword of the Republic. New York: MacMillan, 1969: 10119Emerson, Thomas E. and Floyd Mansberger. "The Search for French Peoria." French Colonial Archaeology: The Illinois Country and the Western Great Lakes, edited by John A. Walthall. Urbana: Univ of Il Press, 1991: 156.

20. Wilkie, 150.

21. Company Book of Captain Simon Owens; also, Executive Document 331, 25th Congress, 2nd Session, Volume X: 5; NOTE: General Bissell was court-martialed a short time after the war on a variety of charges including gambling, and a false claim of a loss of public property. Davenport was called as one of the witnesses. This may have been the incident that caused Davenport's reduction in rank, see "General Bissell." The National Register, Vol. 2, No. 10, November 2, 1816.

22. Tevebaugh, J.L. Merchant on the Western Frontier: William Morrison of Kaskaskia, 1790 - 1837. unpublished dissertation, University of Illinois, 1962: 99-100.

Chapter 3 – Frontier Outpost

1. Wesley, Edgar Bruce. *Guarding the Frontier: A Study of Frontier Defense, 1815 – 1825*, Minneapolis: University of Minnesota Press, 1935: 133; *Missouri Gazette*, Jan. 21, 1815.

2. The three commissioners were: William Clark, Governor of Missouri Territory and Superintendent of Indian Affairs, Ninian Edwards, Governor of Illinois Territory, and Auguste Chouteau, an Indian Trader noted for his successful dealings with Indians. "From St. Charles County." *Missouri Gazette*, 9 Set 1815.

3. "Extract from a letter from Portage des Sioux, dated 7 July 1815", *Missouri Gazette*, 15 July 1815; Fisher, Robert L., "The Treaty of Portage des Sioux," *Mississippi Valley Historical Review*, 19, 1933: 502-503.

4. Fisher, 504-508; also Brown, Lizzie M. "The Pacification of the Indians After the War of 1812," *Journal of Illinois State Historical Society*, VIII, Oct 1915: 558; Letter: Richard Graham to the Secretary of War, July 8, 1816. Carter, ed. Territorial Papers of the united States, Illinois Territory, Vol XVII: 359 – 360.

5. Letter: Henry Swearingen to unknown, Fort Knox, October 7, 1811. Collection # OM66, W.H. Smith Memorial Library, Indiana Historical Society, Indianapolis, Indiana.

6. Davenport, Bailey. "Reminiscence of Early Days, No.1." *The Daily Argus*, Rock Island, Illinois, January 6, 1876; Tevebaugh, J.L. *Merchant on the Western Frontier: William Morrison of Kaskaskia, 1790 – 1837*, unpublished dissertation, University of Illinois, Urbana, Illinois,1962: 98; Letter: E. Shipp to Wm. Morrison, August 29, 1816, Thomas Adams Smith (1781 – 1844) Papers, Manuscript Collection, State Historical Society of Missouri, Columbia, Missouri .

7. Letter: George Wilson, to James Morrison, St. Louis, September 24, 1815. James Morrison Papers, 1790 – 1849, contained in the Henry Clay Papers, Library of Congress, Washington, D.C.

8. Wesley, Edgar Bruce. *Guarding the Frontier*, 1; Letter: Wilson to Morrison, September 24, 1815, James Morrison Papers, 1790 – 1849, in the Henry Clay Papers, Library of Congress.

9.The cold remained through the summer. It was called "the year without a summer," caused by a volcanic eruption that affected the entire world.

10. Wilkie, 151; Letter: John Cleves Symmes to Marianne Symmes, 13 December 1815, and 28 January 1816. Draper Collection 1WW, Wisconsin Historical Society, Madison, Wisconsin; License to trade issued to John Cleves Symmes : Vol. XV, Territory of Louisiana-Missouri. p. 190; also, License: signed by William Clark. 24 April 1816. William Clark Papers. Chicago Historical Society, Chicago, Illinois.

11. "Extract of letter dated Cantonment Davis, (Upper Mississippi) May 8, 1816." *Missouri Gazette*, 18 May 1816.

12. Colonel Nicholas was arrested on charges of cowardice in battle and returned to St. Louis to face court martial. Ds James T. Dent, Judge Advocate Director of South, and D. Bissell, Brig. General St. Louis, "Specification of Charges." June 3, 1816, in Daniel G. Bissell Papers, Missouri Historical Society, St. Louis, Missouri; Davenport, Bailey; also, Thomas Adams Smith papers.

13. Dunn, Mrs. Julia Mills, "Saukenuk." *Transactions of the Illinois State Historical Society* (1902) VII: 132 -133; Fisher, "The Treaties of Portage des Sioux," Robert L. Fisher. *Mississippi Valley Historical Review*, 1933, 19: 507. Fisher says the Sauk and Mesquakie returned twenty-two horses they had stolen; Flagler, A History of Rock Island Arsenal, Washington: Government Printing Office, 1877: 14.

14. Letter: Smith to unknown, July 8, 1816. Thomas Adams Smith Collection, Letterbook Vol. 4: 114 Western Historical Manuscript. Collection, Univ. of Mo-Columbia, Columbia, Missouri; *Missouri Gazette*, 15 June 1816; Letter: Charles Jouette to the Governor of Michigan Territory, June 26, 1817, Carter, Clarence Alvord, ed. *Territorial Papers of the United States, Territory of Michigan,* Volume XVII: 516 – 517.

15. *Black Hawk: An Autobiography of Black Hawk*, ed. Donald Jackson, Urbana: University of Illinois Press, 1964: 88.

16. There were just 767 soldiers on the entire Mississippi-Missouri frontier. Wesley. *Guarding the Frontier* :137; Parker,D. October 1818 Inspection Report. *American State Papers,1789-1819; Military Affairs*, Vol.1: 821.

17. Francis Paul Prucha, *Sword of the Republic: The United States Army on the Frontier, 1783 – 1846*. Bloomington: Indiana University Press, 1977, pp. 174-1750; Major Morrell Marston, "Extract from Report to Major General Macomb," September 10, 1819, copy in files of Colonel Davenport Historical Foundation; Hayne, A.P. "Report of Inspection of the Ninth Military Dept., 1819." *Mississippi Valley Historical Review*, Vol. 7 (1920 -1921): 268.

18. Tevebaugh, p. 166, ftn #43; Letter: Henry Swearingen to unknown, 7th October 1811, William Henry Smith Memorial Library, Indiana Historical Society, Collection OM – 66.

19. Delo, David M., "The Army Sutler: Regimental Rip-Off Artist Supreme," *Army*, January 1989: 44; also Tevebaugh: 156-157.

20. Trial of Captain Peter Pelham, W15, Court Martial Case Files, 1809 – 1894, RG 153: 95-98. Records of the Office of the Judge Advocate General (Army), National Archives; White, Helen McCann. "Frontier Feud,1819-1820: How Two Officers Quarrelled All the Way to the Site of Fort Snelling." *Minnesota History*, Fall 1970: 103.

21. White, "Frontier Feud: 1819-20." *Minnesota History*, Fall 1970: 103.

22. Davenport, Bailey, January 20, 1876.

23. At times, the troops at the outposts on the Mississippi River were in danger of starving if rations were not delivered on time. See General T.A. Smith letters to various contractors in T.A. Smith Letterbooks; Davenport, Bailey; Tevebaugh, 253; Letter: Mathew Duncan to Governor Edwards, Fort Clark, 31 October 1816 in Carter, Clarence Edwin, ed. *Territorial Papers of the United States*, Vol. XVII, U.S. Government Printing Office, 1934: 440; Tevebaugh, 253.

24. Letter: 8 July 1816, Vol. 4: 114, T.A. Smith Papers; Davenport, Bailey ; William A. Meese. *Early Rock Island*. Moline: Desaulniers & Co., 1905: 82 – 83.

25. Coffman, 150.

26. Wilkie, 155; History of Jo Daviess County, Chicago, IL: H.F. Kett & Co., 1878: 227.; Lippincott, Isaac. "Industrial Influence of Lead in Missouri." *The Journal of Political Economy*, Vol 20, No 7, July 1912, P. 706; also, Henry Rowe Schoolcraft, *Narrative Journal of Travels Through the Northwestern Regions of the United States*. Ann Arbor: University Microforms: 345; Lockwood, James. "Early Times and Events in Wisconsin." *Wisconsin Historical Collections*, 1856. Vol. II: 224.

27. William Morrison's interest in a lease at the northern lead mines in included in Letter: Josiah Meigs to the President, April 2,1816, Edwin Carter, ed. *Territorial Papers of the United States, The Territory of Illinois, 1814 - 1818*, Vol. XVII: 324-325; "Trade with Indians", St. Louis Enquirer, March 22, 1820; Letter: Marston, Major Merrill to Reverend Jedediah Morse, "Report on Indians of the Upper Mississippi Valley, 1820." Wisconsin Historical Society, Madison, Wisconsin.

28. Letter: Thomas A. Smith to Willoughby Morgan, 17 Sept. 1817, T. A. Smith Papers, Letter Book Vol.5:19, 27, 34, and 46.

29. *Missouri Gazette*, 23 December 1815; also, Letter: Nicholas Boilvin to the Secretary of War, Prairie du Chien, 11 Jan 1816 in Carter, *Territorial Papers of Illinois Territory*, Vol. VVII: 281-282; Letter: Richard Graham to the Secretary of War, St. Louis 8 July 1816 in Carter, *Territorial Papers,* Vol. XVII: 359 - 360.

30. Buck, Solon. *Illinois in 1818,* revised edition, Chicago, 1918: 12-15.; Letter: Daniel Parker to Commanding Officers of Divisions and Military Departments, 7 December 1818. in Hemphill, W. Edwin, ed. *The Papers of John C. Calhoun*, Vol. III, Columbus, South Carolina: University of South Carolina Press, 1964: 362.

31. A search for these letters has been made in the National Archives in "Letters to and From the Secretary of War," but no letters have been found to this date. Davenport made reference to these letters in his application for preemption for his island property.

32. Letter: Benjamin O'Fallon to Governor Clark, 10 May 1817, Carter, *Territorial Papers*, Vol. XV, pp. 260 – 266. NOTE: George Davenport used the preemption laws of Illinois as his right to claim land rather than as a veteran of the War of 1812. Western Illinois and Missouri lands were then being distributed as awards to veterans for their service in the late war Distribution of those lands had begun on the first Monday of October, 1817, but *(Western Intelligencer,* Kaskaskia, Illinois Territory, Nov. 6, 1817. printed in Early Kaskaskia, Illinois, Newspapers, 1814 -1832 by Lola Frazer Crowder. Frontier Press, Galveston, Texas, 1994, p. 11) Davenport had been mustered out of the army a few months short of his re enlistment contract, so he was not technically eligible for bounty land. Under the laws of the Illinois Territory, however, he was guaranteed the right of preemption on public land until the land was surveyed and entered as public land. Like other would-be settlers, he expected that the fort would be closed in a few years and the island would become public land, available for purchase by preemption claimants. His consultation with Colonel Morgan suggests that both men thought that only a portion of the island was identified as military reserve and the rest would be part of the public lands and opened to settlement whenever the land had been surveyed.

The Sauk and Mesquakie had several traders already licensed by the Governor of Illinois with Sauk and Fox: John Campbell and his Co. who served as the contractor's agent for Fort Edward, George W. Kennerly, Antoine Laugrain and Jean Beaulieu, Paul Tramble and Russell Farnham and John Hays p.251, ftn.#50, Tevebaugh; Calendar. Official Bond - Indian Traders, Box 71, Ill. State Archives, Springfield, Illinois.

33. Wilkie, 152 - 155; Letter: George Davenport to the Commissioners of the Government Land Office, April 3, 1843, Naomi L. Davenport Collection, State Historical Society of Iowa, Division of History and Archives, Des Moines, Iowa; also, Petition of George Davenport, April 13, 1838, Executive Document No. 331, 25 Congress 2 Session. Vol X: 1; Letter: Forsyth to Clark, St. Louis, June3, 1817, in "Letter-book of Thomas Forsyth." Wisconsin Historical Collections, Vol. XI: 347 - 350. Note: Thomas Forsyth had been subagent to the Sauk and Fox since 1812 and lived at Fort Clark, near present day Peoria, Illinois. He was also a well-known trader in the Illinois country, a half brother to trader John Kinzie at Fort Dearborn. He had been born in Detroit, entered the fur trade around 1790, and established a trading post. During the War of 1812 he operated a trading post in Peoria and met George Davenport there.

34. Temple, Wayne C. *Indian Villages in Illinois Country*, Scientific Papers, Vol 2, Pt 2, Illinois State Museum, 1977: 112 – 113.

35. Letter: Forsyth to Clark, St Louis, 3 June 1817, in Letter-book of Thomas Forsyth, *Collections of* the *State Historical Society of Wisconsin*, Volume VI: 347 – 351; Letter: Charles Jouett to the Governor of Michigan Territory, 26 June 1817, in Carter, *Territorial Papers*, XVII: 516-517.

36. Kane, Lucille M., June D. Holmquist, and Carolyn Gilman, eds. *The Northern Expeditions of Stephen H. Long: The Journals of 1817 and 1823 and Related Documents*. Minneapolis: Minnesota Historical Society Press, 1978: 99.

37. Wade, Richard C. *The Urban Frontier: the Rise of Western Cities, 1790-1830*. Cambridge: Harvard Univ. Press, 1967: 60-63.

38. "Invoice of Trade Goods for the Mississippi River and Rock River Indians by George Kennerly, July 1816." Calendar. Official Bonds – Indian Traders. Box 71, Item # 21b "7S/13A/b5, Illinois State Archives, Springfield.

39. Bryan and Morrison Ledgers, Kaskaskia Ledger D (1805 - 1831) and Daybook # 23, Microfilm Reel # 1, Illinois Historical Survey, Univ. of Illinois, Champaign, Illinois.

40. Thwaites, Rueben Gold ed. "Licenses for Wisconsin Traders," 27 July 1819. Wisconsin Mnss.55B72, WHC, Vol. XX (1911): 118. Lockwood had been licensed in Mackinac to trade on the Upper Mississippi and at or above Prairie du Chien, but his men could easily have ranged as far south as Rock Island; also, Lockwood, James H. "Early Times and Events in Wisconsin." Second Annual Report and Collections of the State Historical Society of Wisconsin, for the Year 1855. Madison: Calkins & Proudfit, 1856. Vol II: 112.

41. Jackson, Donald. "Appendix B, The 1832 Roster." *Voyage of the Yellow Stone.* New York: Ticknor & Fields, 1985: 168.

42. Temple, 190-191.

43. Crooks-Stuart Letterbook, 1816 -1820. AFC Northern Dept. Michilimackinac Vol. 2: 62-63.

44. Letter: Jacques Portier to Pre.Rocheblave, no date. Rueben Gold Thwaites, editor. *Collections of the State Historical Society of Wisconsin, 1910.* 19:445 - 447.

45. Crooks-Stuart Letterbook, 47, 48, 49; Lavender, David. *Fist in Wilderness*, Albuquerque: University of New Mexico Press, 1979: 286.

46. Wesley, 1; Letter: Gov. Ninian Edwards to Richard Graham, 4 August 1818. Richard Graham Papers, Missouri Historical Society, St. Louis, Missouri.

47. Forsyth to Wm. Clark, St. Louis, September 22, 1815. "Letter-Book of Thomas Forsyth" *Collections of the State Historical Society of Wisconsin*, Vol XI: 344-345.

48. Wesley, 21.

49. Letter: Forsyth to Secretary of War, J.C. Calhoun, 2 April 1818, in Carter, *Territorial Papers, Louisiana-Missouri Territory*, Vol.XV, p. 379; Nothstein, Ira O., *History of Rock Island Arsenal From Earliest Times to 1954*, Vol 1 to 1958. Rock Island: U.S. Army, Armament, Munitions, and Chemical Command, 1985: 1.

50. Nothstein, 41; Wesley, *Guarding The Frontier*, p.142; Letter: Smith to Major Morgan, November 1817. T.A. Smith Papers, Letter Book, Vol. 5: 66; Johnston, Oda B. *History of Fort Armstrong, 1816 - 1836.* Unpublished M.A. Thesis. University of Iowa, 1940.

51. "Forty Years Ago." *The Daily Union.* Rock Island, Illinois, July 17,1867; "The Last Will and Testament of Naomi Davenport," 15 September 1915, Rock Island County Probate Records, Rock Island, Illinois.

52. Atwater, Caleb. *Remarks Made on a Tour to Prairie du Chien: thence to Washington City in 1829*, New York: Arno Press, 1975,:64; Black Hawk, 88.

53. "Forty Years Ago."

54. Davenport referred to his place on the Island as Indian Lodge as late as October 1839 and probably always thought of it as Indian Lodge. See: "Married." *Davenport (IA) Gazette*, 16 October 1839.

Chapter 4 -- Domestic Life on Island

1. "Mrs. Davenport." *Rock Island and Moline Daily Union*, July 17, 1867. The story comes from an interview with Susan Lewis Goldsmith, who was often identified as Mrs. Davenport. The existence of a son named William has not been verified. Sources are conflicting and he is never mentioned in family stories; Van Kirk, Sylvia. *Many Tender Ties: Women in Fur-Trade Society in Western Canada, 1607 – 1870*. Winnepeg,, Manitoba: Watson and Dwyer Publishing, Ltd., 1980: 192.

2. Family History of Bowling Family; Tombstone for Susuan Lewis Goldsmith, Chippiannock Cemetery, Rock Island, Illinois.

3. Obituary. *The Rock Island (IL) Argus,* August 5, 1876; "Reminiscences of Early Days – No. 2." *Rock Island Argus*, January 20, 1876; L'Oste is a family name. George Davenport's sister was married to Frederick L'Oste in Louth, Lincolnshire, England.

4. Willa G. Cramton, *Women Beyond The Frontier: A Distaff View Of Life At Fort Wayne*. Historic Fort Wayne, Inc. 1977: 3.

5. Letter: M. Marston, Fort Armstrong, to Capt. James H. Hook, Washington, November 28, 1820. RG 92, Quartermaster General, Consolidated Correspondence File, National Archives and Record Administration.

6. Letter: Amos Farrar to Brother, Fort Armstrong, October 6, 1820. Mnss. Beinicke Rare Books and Manuscripts Library, Yale University, New Haven, Connecticut.

7. Letter: Amos Farrar to Jacob Farrar, Fort Armstrong, October 6, 1820. Beinicke Rare Books and Manuscripts Library. Yale University, New Haven, CT; Spencer, J. W. "Reminiscences of Pioneer Life in the Mississippi Valley." in *The Early Days of Rock Island and Davenport* ,edited by Milo Milton Quaife, The Lakeside Press, Chicago: R.R. Donnelley & Sons Co, 1942: 20.

8. Helen McCann White. "Frontier Feud,: 1819-1820   How Two Officers Quarreled All the Way to the Site of Fort Snelling," *Minnesota History* 42 (3):99-114.

9. Robert Belt was the factor, or government agent, at Ft. Edwards., which was a government-operated trading establishment, called a factory. Belt sold trade goods and collected fur and peltries as payment for those goods from the local native hunters and trappers. The U.S. Government abolished the factory system in 1822.

10. Fort Armstrong Post Returns, photographic copy, Rock Island Arsenal Museum Archives; Orders No. 16, June 20, 1826 and Orders No. 34, September 20, 1826; Garrison Order Book, Company E, Fifth Infantry, 1826 - 1828. Burton Historical Collection, Detroit Public Library, Detroit, Michigan.

11. Interview: John Hauberg with David Sears, November 6, 1917. Hauberg Collection. Tredway Library, Augustana College Archives. Rock Island, Illinois.

12."A Visit to Fort Armstrong." *Rock Island Banner and Stephenson Gazette, January 9, 1840*; Fort Armstrong Post Cemetery records, National Cemetery, Rock Island Arsenal, Rock Island, Illinois; Orrin S. Holt. "Story of the Pioneers Who Blazed the Trail For Us in This Community." *The Moline Dispatch*, April 6, 1916.; Orrin S. Holt. "Story of the Pioneers Who Blazed the Trail For Us in This Community," The Moline (IL) *Dispatch*, April 6, 1916: Chapter VII.

13. Caldwell, Norman W. "The Frontier Army Officer, 1794-1814." *MId-America.* Vol XXXVII (April 1955):104; Emerson, Military Pay Records, RG217, Settled Paymaster Accounts, National Archives and Records Administration, Washington, D.C.

14. Transcript of the Journal of the United States Factory at Fort Edwards for the Quarter Ending Thirty-first day of March, 1821." Entry dated, March 26, 1821, Bureau of Indian Affairs. RG 75. Records Pertaining to Factory at Fort Edwards. National Archives and Records Ad ministration; Cramton, 14; Leucke, Barbara K. Feeding the Frontier Army 1775 – 1865. Eagan, MN: Grenedier Publications, 1990.

15. Phelps, Caroline. "Mrs. Caroline Phelps' Diary." *Journal of the Illinois State Historical Society*, Vol. 23, No. 2, (1930): 202-239.

16. "Ft. Armstrong Weather Diary," entries for 1823, mnss in Rock Island Arsenal Museum Archives, Rock Island, Illinois.

17, Wilkie, 158.

18. Cramton, 14; Farrar, Amos, Letter to his brother, November 20, 1827, in History of Lafayette County, Wisconsin, 407.

Chapter 5 – Entering the Indian Trade

1. Wilkie, 154-155; Letter: Richard Graham to John C. Calhoun, October 31, 1818. *The Papers of John C. Calhoun, Vol. III, 1818-1819,* edited by W. Edwin Hemphill. Columbia: University of South Carolina, 1967.

2. Contract: Samuel C. Muir and George Davenport with Thomas Forsyth. September 22,1822. Draper Mnss 1T66, Wisconsin Historical Society. Madison, Wisconsin.

3. The two sides, Susan Lewis Goldsmith remembered, were the Osh-kosh and the Kish-ko-gay, and painted to identify their membership. First there would be a line drawn across the prairie; then a toss to see which side would start. The ball was large, made of hair, and covered with hide. The object was to keep the ball from crossing the

line. Some players were on foot, some on horseback, and each man carried a net on a pole. Davenport, Bailey, January 20, 1876; also, *Black Hawk*, edited by Donald Jackson. Urbana: University of Illinois, 1964: 94.

4. Jackson, 90-95.

5. Red deer was the trader's way of distinguishing deer hides collected in the summer.

6. Jackson, 94-95.

7. Forsyth, in Blair, Vol II, 234; also, Jackson, 89-99.

8. Wilkie, 157.

9. Forsyth, Thomas. "The French, British and Spanish Methods of Treating Indians &c -" *Ethnohistory*, 4(2) Spring 1957: 213.

10. Licenses and Contract of Joseph Frazier, Pierre Chouteau-Maffitt Collection, Missouri Historical Society, St. Louis, Missouri; Holt, *Moline Dispatch*, Chapter XII, April 16, 1916.

11. Brown, Jennifer S.H. *Strangers in Blood: Fur Trade Company Families in Indian Country*, Norman: University of Oklahoma Press, 1996, 45.

12. Letter: James H. Ballard, Capt R., Rt Comg Post, Fort Edwards I.T., April 3rd 1818, in Carter, Edwin ed., *The Territory of Louisiana - Missouri, 1815 - 1821*, Vol. XV: 381, 382.

13. Letter: James H. Ballard, Capt R.,Rt Comg Post, Fort Edwards I.T., April 3rd 1818, in Carter, Edwin ed., The Territory of Louisiana - Missouri, 1815 - 1821, Vol. XV:381, 382; "Personal Narrative of Col John Shaw of Marquette, Wisconsin." Appendix No. 7,WHC Vol. II (1856): 220; Also, Letter: James H. Ballard, Captain R., Rt. Comg Post, Fort Edwards Indian Territory, 3 April 1818, in Carter, *Territorial Papers, The Territory of Louisiana-Missouri, 1815-1821*, Vol XV: 381-382.

14. Summaries of letters printed in Hemphill, W. Edwin, ed. *The Papers of John C. Calhoun*, Vol. II: 226, 236, 396. Columbus, South Carolina, 1964; Goodrich, James W. "Richard Campbell." *Missouri Historical Review* LXXII October 1977 - July 1978: 29.

15. Letter: O'Fallon, St. Louis, to General Clark, May 20, 1818, in Carter, *Territorial Papers of the U.S. The Territory of Louisiana - Missouri, 1815 -1821*, Vol. XV: 412, 413.

16. Letter: Gov. Ninian Edwards to Richard Graham, 4 August 1818. Graham Papers. Missouri Historical Society, St. Louis, Missouri; Letter: Forsyth to Sec of War. J,C. Calhoun, 2 April 1818, printed in Carter. *Territorial Papers. Louisiana-Missouri Territory,* Vol. XV: 379.

17. Sullivan, John C. "Map of Boundary Line, Plate LXXXV. *"Atlas of Indian Villages of the Illinois Country, 1670-1830*, Springfield, IL: Illinois State Museum; Snyder, Rev. Charles. "Antoine Le Claire, The First Proprietor of Davenport." *Annals of Iowa*.

Vol .XXIII (1941-1942): 85. Also, Graham Papers. Missouri Historical Society; Forsyth, Thomas and Lyman Copeland Draper. ed. "Journal of a Voyage From St. Louis to the Falls of St. Anthony in 1819." *Collections of the State Historical Society of Wisconsin*. Madison: Wisconsin State Historical Society, 1872. Vol VI: 194.

18. Davenport, Bailey, January 26, 1876.

19. Wilkie, 156.

20. Mary Brackett Durham was the daughter of Joseph Brackett with whom the Davenports developed close friendships. According to her sister, Mrs. Schwatka, loved to listen to Susan Lewis' stories about the Indians and based her poems on those stories. Hauberg interview with Ada Brackett Schwatka, October 2, 1921, Hauberg Collection, Thomas Tredway Library, Augustana College, Rock Island, Illinois; Durham, Mary Brackett, "The Lost Winnebgao," Hauberg Collection, Thomas Tredway Library, Augustana College, Rock Island, Illinois.

21. "The First Permanent Settlement in Hancock County, Illinois," by Calvin S. Sifferd, Jr. *Journal of the Illinois State Historical Society*. Vol. XVIII, No 4, Jan 1926: 1031; "Reminiscences of Fountain Green, Illinois." by C.C. Tyler, Fountain Green: Illinois. Vol. 8, No 1, April 1915: 56; "Col. Davenport's House Scene of First Sermon," *Daily Dispatch*, Moline, Illinois, June 19, 1948.

22. Letter: Crooks to Farnham, 28 December 1818. American Fur Company Letterbook, Ramsey Crooks, Missouri Historical Society, 152.

23. Buck, 29-30; Letter: Crooks to Farnham, same as above; Lavender, 339.

24. Lavender, 288; also, License issued to Russel Farnham and Patrick Lee, September 30, 1818, Box 2, Folder 38. St. Charles County, Historical Society, St. Charles, Missouri.

25. Letter: Governor Ninian Edwards to the Secretary of War, September 30, 1816, *Territorial Papers of the U.S., Illinois Territory,1814 -1818*, Vol. XVII, 402; Blondeau was replaced by Forsyth in April 1818. Letter: Acting Secretary of War to Governor Edwards, March 26, 1817. Carter, *Territorial Papers of the United States, Illinois Territory, 1814 – 1818*, Volume XVII, p 495. (Ftn. 59. Senate Executive Journal, III, 139, 140.

26. Letter: Ramsay Crooks to M. Blondeau, 9 August 1818. AMF Letterbook, 121-122.

27. Letter: Crooks to Russel Farnham, 28 December 1818, AMF Letterbook, 152 – 154; Letter: Crooks, Mackinac, to Russell Farnham, St. Louis, 20 August 1819 AMF Letterbook, 226. ; Letter: Crooks, New York, to Farnham, 20 February 1820, AMF Co. Letterbook, Reel #18. Missouri. Historical Society, St. Louis, Missouri.

28. April 1821, Case No. 200, Circuit Ct Case Files, Office of the Circuit Ct, City of St. Louis, Missouri. Available on-line. http:// stlcourtrecords.wustl.edu.

29. Wilkie, 153.

30. Letter: Crooks, to Samuel Abbott, New York, 19 December 1822. Chouteau-Papin Collection, Missouri Historical Society, St. Louis, Missouri.

31. Forsyth, Thomas. "Journal of a Voyage from St. Louis to the Falls of St. Anthony, in 1819." *Collections of the State Historical Society of Wisconsin*, 1872. Vol VI: 194 - 195.

32. Bickel, R.J. "'Rat Row' in Keokuk," *Annals of Iowa*. 3(1956): 450; Powell, William H., comp. *List of Army Officers of the United States from 1790 to 1900*, Philadelphia: L.R. Hamersly & Co., 1900: 497.

33. Draper, ed., *Wisconsin Historical Collection*, Vol. 10, 1888: 492; also, Schoolcraft, Henry. Entry for August 6, 1820. *Narrative Journal of Travels ... American Lakes to Mississippi River in Year 1820*. Albany: E. & E. Hosford, 1821: 342.

34. Letter: Thomas Forsyth to Wm Clark, St. Louis, Sept 23, 1819, *Collections State Historical Society of Wisconsin*, VI: 218.

35. Letter: Major Morrell Marston to Rev Jedediah Morse, November 1820, in Emma Blair, ed., *Indian Tribes of Upper Mississippi Valley and Region* of the Great Lakes, New York: Kraus Reprint Co., 1969; also, Wayne C. Temple, *Indian Village of the Illinois Country*, 112-113.

36. Forsyth, Thomas "Account of the Manners and Customs of the Sauk and Fox Nations of Indians Tradition," in Blair, 192.

37. Letter: Farnham to Samuel Abbott, 30 Jan 1830, Ayer Collection, Newberry Library, Chicago, Illinois.

38. Sanford, J.F.A. "Sale of Lots, Clarksville, May 15, 1819." Richard Graham Papers, Missouri Historical Society, St. Louis, Missouri.

39. Gussow, Zachary, "An Ethnological Report of the Historic Habitat of the Sauk, Fox, and Iowa Indians," *Sac, Fox, and Iowa Indians*, Vol I, New York: Garland Pub. Inc., 1974: 32.

40. St. Louis Enquirer, Wed, 19 April 1820; Thwaites, Rueben Gold, ed. Letter Jno. W. Johnson to Governor Cass, *Fur-Trade in Wisconsin, 1812-1825, Collections of the State Historical Society of Wisconsin, 1911: 167;* Letter: Farrar, Amos, Letters to his brothers, Western Americana Collection, Beinecke Rare Book and Manuscript Library, Yale University.

41. Letter: Belt to McKinney, Supt. of Indian Affairs, 18 June 1820, RG 75, Microfilm T58, Letters Received by the Office of the Supt of Indian Trade, 1806 – 1824, National Archives and Records Administration, Washington, D.C.; Letter: Johnston to McKinney, 28 June 1820, RG 75, Microfilm T58, National Archives and Records Administration; Niles Register, XVIII, July 29, 1820: 400.

42. St. Louis Enquirer, 28 Oct 1820.

43. Morrill Marston Estate Packets, Box 1. Hancock County, Illinois, Microfilm available at IRAD, Western Illinois University Archives, Macomb. reel #1533649;

Draper, ed. Wisconsin Historical Collections, Vol. 10 (1883-85). 1888: 492; "The 1831 Probate Inventories of Daniel Harris and Morrill Marston: Early Documents of Warren and Hancock Counties," by John Lee Allaman, Western Illlinois Regional Studies, Vol. XIV, Spring 1991, No.1: 9-10.

44. Originally from a large family in Hampton, New Hampshire, Marston was the fifth of eight children in the family of Judith Morrill Marston and Elisha Smith Marston. He served in the War of 1812 and attained the rank of Bvt. Major for his action at the siege of Fort Erie. He died in a drowning accident in 1831.

45. In 1818 rapid expansion and too much credit extended after the War of 1812 led to an economic panic followed by a general depression that lasted for several years. As a result the United States as a whole and the frontier in particular experienced little new settlement even though large tracts of land had been set aside for veterans of the war with just that idea in mind. While this may have been disastrous to businessmen and industrialists, for Davenport and other traders in the Illinois country this situation meant that the migration to western lands would slow for a time, leaving the regular Indian life cycle of hunting uninterrupted by encroaching settlers, at least until the country had time to recover. No one believed that this would be a permanent condition, but those in the Indian trade hoped it would last for a few more years.

Chapter 6 – Davenport's Credit Books

1.Davenport Ledgers and Credit Books, SHSI, Des Moines, on microfilm at Davenport Public Library, Davenport, Iowa.

2. 1819 Indian Accounts with Kickapoo, Renard, Fals Avoins, Algonkian, Iowas. In French. On microfilm. Davenport Collection, Special Collections, Davenport Public Library.

3. For an economic discussion of credits and debts, see Kurtz, Royce, Ph.D. dissertation: *Economic and Political History of the Sauk and Mesquakie: 1780s – 1845*, Univ, of Iowa, 1986.

4. Letter: Ramsay Crooks to Russel Farnham, 17 March 1819, Chouteau Collection, Missouri Historical Society, St. Louis, Missouri.

5. Letter: Major Marston to Reverend Doctor Morse, Ft. Armstrong, November 1820, in Blair, Emma, *The Indian Tribes of the upper Mississippi Valley*, Vol. 2: 151.

Chapter 7 – Full Steam Ahead

1. "The First Born." *The Davenport Democrat*, Monday, March 2, 1885.

2. The *Virginia* was a small boat measuring 118 feet in length and 18 feet 10 inches at the beam, not much bigger than George Davenport's keelboats, but much faster. Her capacity, set at 109.32 tons, was hardly noteworthy by comparison. A sternwheeler with a small cabin on deck but no pilot house. She was steered with a tiller at the stern of the boat. built in 1819 in Wheeling, Virginia, owned by a group of nine men. She

left St. Louis on the 21 April carry supplies for Ft. Snelling. See, Beltrami, Giacomo. *A Pilgrimage in America*. Chicago: Quadrangle Books, 1962: 127-128; Petersen, William J. *Steamboating on the Upper Mississippi*. Iowa City: State Historical Society of Iowa, 1968: 90, 105-106; Baldwin, Leland D. *Keelboat Age on Western Waters*, 45..

3. Petersen, 169.

4. Tweet, Roald. *A History of the Rock Island District U.S. Army Corps of Engineers 1866 - 1983*. Rock Island, 1984: 2.

5. William Jones. "Notes on the Fox Indians," Iowa Journal of History and Politics. Vol XII: 87; John Hauberg interview with Mrs. Schwatka, October 2, 1921. Hauberg Collection, Box 55, Notebook #9: 3. Augustana College, Rock Island, Illinois.

6. Treaty of August 4, 1824. Kappler, Charles J. compiler and editor. *Indian Treaties, 1778 – 1883*. New York: Interland Pub., 1972: 207 – 208. In 1824, The Missouri Band of the Sauk ceded northern Missouri to the U.S. Government.

7. Letter: George Davenport to O.N. Bostwick, May 30, 1826, and July 25, 1826. Chouteau-Papin Collection. Missouri Historical Society, St. Louis, Missouri.

8. Letter: George Davenport to Russel Farnham, November 16, 1824. Chouteau Collection, Missouri Historical Society, St. Louis, Missouri.

9. Wilkie, 155; Lytle, Wm. M, editor. *Merchant Steam Vessels of U.S., 1807 - 1868*. Rhode Island: Steamship Historical Society of America, 1952; also, On the Upper Mississippi very short boats, shorter than eighty feet, were sometimes required for the Indian trade, but these were made to order and more expensive than a standard size. Keelboats were built in many river towns along the Ohio River, particularly in the vicinity of Pittsburgh and Louisville. Letter: Jacob Bowman to General John Mason, Superintendent of Indian Trade, March 29, 1815, RG 75, Letters Rec'd by Office of Supt of Indian Trade, 1806 – 1824.

10. Letter: Maurice Blondeau to Russel Farnham, August 15,1823. Chouteau-Papin Collection. Missouri Historical Society.

11. "Deed Record Book A." Jo Daviess County Deed Records, Galena, Illinois, 140 – 141. One of the first places where slaves were found on the frontier was at the military establishments. Slaves had been considered indispensable to life at the army post since colonial days and the army had not taken measures to curb the practice. In fact, slaves were preferred over enlisting the services of servants drawn from the lower ranks because slaves were cheaper. Military pay records preserved at the National Archives show that the army provided additional rations to officers who had slaves. Each servant's name, age, and a general description was included on each pay voucher. While most officers had one slave, high-ranking officials such as Generals often could afford two and these persons followed their masters to every outpost on the frontier. It is theoretically possible, then, to trace the movement of these persons.

12. Sixth Federal Population Census (1840), Rock Island County, Illinois.

13. Willard Barrows, "History of Scott County, Iowa," no date, clipping in Davenport Family Scrapbook, George L. Davenport Collection, State Historical Society of Iowa, Division of History and Archives, Des Moines, Iowa.

14. Letter: Josiah H. Vose, Major 5th Infantry, Commanding Fort Armstrong to Brig. Gen. Thomas S. Jessup, QM Gen, Washington City, July 18, 1823; Letter: C. Burbridge, Lt 5th Infantry, Post Quartermaster, Fort Armstrong to Major Josiah H. Vose, Commanding Fort Armstrong. NARA RG 92, Fort Armstrong Consolidated Correspondence File.

15. Letter: Russel Farnham to Samuel Abbott, November 24, 1823, Ms#278, Ayer Collection, Newberry Library, Chicago, Illinois.

16. Letter: Russel Farnham to Samuel Abbott, January 31, 1824, MS #278, Ayer Collection, Newberry Library, Chicago, Illinois.

17. Letter: Joshua Palen to Russell Farnham, August 24, 1824. Chouteau-Papin Collection, Missouri Historical Society.

18. Letter: George Davenport to O.N. Bostwick, Agent of AMF, September 9,1824, MS# 215, Ayer Collection, Newberry Library, Chicago, Illinois.

19. Kappler, Treaty of 1824 and Treaty of 1825: Treaties with the Sauk and Foxes, Iowa, Sioux, Osage, Kansa, Ponca, Otoe and Missouri tribes.

20. Kappler, Treaty of 1824.

21. Contract: Capt. J.B. Brant, Asst Quartermaster, with O.N. Bostwick, December 27, 1824. 19th Cong. 1 sess. House Doc. 101. Vol 5. No 136. Fiche 6.

22. Senate Document No 58 (19th Cong, 1st Sess): 3; Letter: Thomas Forsyth to Thomas L. McKenney, Office of Indian Affairs, August 28, 1824, Prairie du Chien Indian Agency 1824 - 1842. NARA M234, Reel #696.

23. Letter: John Connolly to Brother Miche, February 2, 1824. John Connolly Papers, Minnesota Historical Society, Minneapolis, Minnesota.

24. Letter: George Davenport to Samuel Abbott Esq., September 20, 1822, Chouteau Collection, Missouri Historical Society.

25. "Statement of Operations at U.S. Lead Mines." American State Papers, 20th Cong. 1st Sess. Military Affairs, Volume 3, 654; Sophia Farrar: Administratrix of Estate of Amos Farrar, Dec'd vs. George Davenport et al. Filed May 5th 1845, Clerk of Circuit Ct. Rock Island County.

26. Letters: George Davenport to O.N. Bostwick, October 3, 1824, June 30, 1825, September 17, 1826, and November 20, 1826, P. Chouteau-Maffitt Collection, Missouri Historical Society, St. Louis, Missouri.

Chapter 8 – New Commander, Different Ideas

1. Letter: Josiah Vose to George Graham, January 8, 1825, NARA RG 107, M221, Reel #102.

2. Estimate of Buildings requisite for the Indian Agency at Rocky Island. December 7, 1824. Forsyth Papers 1824. Tesson Collection, Missouri Historical Society, St. Louis, Missouri.

3. Letter: S. McRee, War Dept., to Commanding Officer, Fort Armstrong, 2 March 2, 1825 . NARA, RG 393, Dept of War Letters Sent, Pt 1, 1825 - 26, 3 of 12, Entry # 5568.

4. Monthly Returns of the Garrison at Fort Armstrong, July 1824. Photocopies at Rock Island Arsenal Museum, Rock Island, Illinois.

5. Hebert as Gunsmith, "A List of Persons Employed at Ft. Armstrong Indian Agency, 1824 – 1825." Draper Manuscript Collections, Thomas Forsyth Papers, State Historical Society of Wisconsin, 3T25; Obituary of Louis Hebert, *Daily Democrat*, October 18, 1867.

6. Using four souls per warrior, this put the Sauk population at just under 5,000.

7. Letter: Thomas Forsyth to William Clark, April 22, 1825, *Wisconsin Historical Collections*, XX: 374.

8. Letter: Julius d'Laynie, AAQM, Fort Armstrong, to Brig. Gen. T.S. Jessup, Q Gen, Washington City, April 1, 1825, NARA RG 92, Fort Armstrong Consolidated Correspondence File.

9. Letter: Thomas Forsyth to William Clark, December 13, 1824. Thomas Forsyth Papers, DraperManuscript Collection, Wisconsin Historical Society 4T 213 -216.

10. Letter: Thomas Forsyth to John C. Calhoun, June 2, 1824, NARA, Letter Received by OIA, Sac & Fox Indian Agency, 1824 – 1880, Reel #728.

11. Tavern License, issued June 6, 1822, *History of Pike County, Illinois*, Chicago: Chas. C. Chapman & Co., 1880: 259.

12. Letter: Josiah Vose to George Graham, 8 January 1825.

13. Extract from post orders now in force. "Garrison Orderly Book, Company E, Fifth Infantry, Major Josiah Vose, Commanding Post." Josiah Snelling Papers, Burton Historical Collection, Detroit Public Library, Detroit, Michigan, Microfilm 231, Reel #1: 75.

14. Letter: John W. Johnston to John C. Calhoun, Sec. of War. February 9, 1819. Papers of John C. Calhoun, Vol III: 558; also Carter, Clarence Edwin ed. Territorial Papers of the United States, Territory of Michigan. Washington: Government Printing Office. 1943. Vol. 10: 812-814.

15. Oda B. Johnson, History of Fort Armstrong, 1816 – 1836. Unpublished Master's Thesis, University of Iowa, 1940: 53; Letter: William Clark to Thomas Forsyth, June 16, 1825. Draper Manuscript Collection, Thomas Forsyth Papers, State Historical Society of Wisconsin, 2T; also, Hauberg, John. "Farnhamsburg", unpublished

manuscript, Hauberg Collection, Notebook 17, Box 58, Augustana College, Rock Island, Illinois.

16. Letter: Josiah Vose to Brig. Gen. H Atkinson, 2 February 2, 1825, NARA, M567, Roll #13.

17. Abstracts of Disbursements for the Fort Armstrong Indian Agency show that Louis Pettle was the Interpreter for the Agency between September 1825 and September 1826. Vol. 24. Indian Agency at Rock Island. Records of the Superintendency of Indian Affairs at St. Louis. William Clark Papers, Kansas State Historical Society. For Forsyth's reply to the duel challenge, see Letter: Thomas Forsyth to Major Josiah Vose, June 1, 1825. Draper Manuscripts, Forsyth Papers. 4T18.

18. Letter: George Davenport to O.N. Bostwick, March 6, 1826, P. Chouteau-Maffitt Collection, Missouri Historical Society, St. Louis, Missouri.

19. "Circular to Registers and Receivers of The United States Land Office," January 6, 1838, *The Peoria Register and North-western Gazetteer.*

20. Siyoung Park, "Land Speculation in Western Illinois Pike County, 1821-1835." *Journal of Illinois State Historical Society*, Summer 1984. Vol. LXXVII: 115-128.

21. Theodore L. Carlson, *The Illinois Military Tract.* New York: Arno Press, 1979: 570; Deed Records of Hancock, Fulton, Adams, Pike, Henderson, Madison, Mercer, and McDonough Counties, Illinois.

22. Schoolcraft. Henry Rowe, *Personal Memoirs of a Residence of Thirty Years with Indian Tribes on the American Frontiers*, New York: Arno Press, 1975: 215-217.

23. Mahan, Bruce E. *Old Fort Crawford and the Frontier*, Iowa City: State Historical Society of Iowa, 1926. Chapter VII.

24. Letter translated from French: Russel Farnham to O.N. Bostwick, Flint Hills, February 1, 1826. MS# 279. Ayer Collection. Newberry Library, Chicago, Illinois; Letter: Russel Farnham to O.N. Bostwick, February 16, 1826. Chouteau-Papin Collection. Missouri Historical Society, St. Louis, Missouri.

25. American Fur Company, Account Book J, Chouteau Collection, Missouri Historical Society, St. Louis, Missouri.

26. Letters: Davenport to O.N. Bostwick, dated 10 Sept 1824 and 19 Sept 1824 and January 29, 1826, Chouteau-Papin Collection, Missouri Historical Society.

27. Keelboat *Missouri* purchase. Letter: George Davenport to O.N. Bostwick, November 20, 1826, P. Chouteau-Maffitt Collection, Missouri Historical Society, St. Louis, Missouri.

28. Letter: George Davenport to O.N. Bostwick, June 27, 1826, Missouri Historical Society, St. Louis, Missouri; Kurtz, Royce D., "Economic and Political History of the Sauk and Mesquakie: 1780s-1845," unpublished dissertation, 1986: 145; American Fur Company Ledger, Book AAA, Chouteau Collection, Missouri Historical Society, St. Louis, Missouri, 88; also, Lavender, 338.

29. Lavender, p. 388.

30. John Hauberg interview with David Sears, Hauberg Papers, Augustana College, Rock Island, Illinois; Letter: George Davenport to O.N. Bostwick, August 26, 1826, P. Chouteau-Maffitt Collection, Missouri Historical Society, St. Louis, Missouri.

31. Letter: George Davenport to Russel Farnham, November 19, 1826, Ayer Collection, Newberry Library, Chicago, Illinois.

32. The Marais d'Ogee or Maredosia Slough was a long marshy channel between the Mississippi and Rock rivers. It was a favorite hunting area, located near Albany in Whiteside County, Illinois.

33. Letter: George Davenport to O.N. Bostwick, May 30, 1826 and October 17, 1826. Chouteau-Papin Collection. Missouri Historical Society; Letter: George Davenport to Russel Farnham, November 19, 1826, MS#216, Ayer Collection, Newberry Library, Chicago, Illinois.

34. Letter: Ramsay Crooks to O.N. Bostwick, August 6, 1826, Chouteau-Papin Collection. Missouri Historical Society, St. Louis, Missouri.

35. Gilman, Rhoda, "How Henry Sibley Took the Road to New Hope," *Minnesota History*, Vol 52, No. 6, 222; Letter: George Davenport to Russel Farnham, November 19, 1826, Ayer Collection, Newberry Library, Chicago, Illinois; Haeger, John D. "A Time of Change: Green Bay, 1815 - 834." *Wisconsin Magazine of History*, Summer 1971. Vol. 54: 294 -295.

36. Letter: George Davenport to O.N.Bostwick, June 27, 1826 and July 25, 1826, Missouri Historical Society, St. Louis, Missouri.

37. Cash payments to George Davenport, June 5, 1827. American Fur Company Journal Book O, March 1826 - November 1829, Chouteau Collection, Missouri Historical Society.

38. Letter: George Davenport to O.N. Bostwick, January 29, 1826, Chouteau-Papin Collection, Missouri Historical Society; Letter: George Davenport to O.N. Bostwick, June 27, 1826, and July 25, 1826, Chouteau-Papin Collection. Mo. Hist. Society.

39. Diary of the Weather, Fort Armstrong, Rock Island. August 27, 1827, Unpublished Manuscript in Rock Island Arsenal Museum, Rock Island, Illinois.

Chapter 9 -- To England

1. Orders # 101 and 102, 30 October 1826, Garrison Order Book, Company E, 5th Infantry, Josiah Snelling Papers, Burton Historical Collection, Detroit Public Library, Detroit, Michigan. Microfilm #231, Reel #1.

2. Orders No. 43, 21 November 1826, Garrison Order Book, Burton Collection, Detroit Public Library, Detroit, Michigan.

3. Mahan, Bruce E. *Old Fort Crawford and the Frontier*. Iowa City, Iowa: State Historical Society of Iowa, 1925: 104.

4. "Fever River Mines." *Missouri Republican*, St. Louis, March 15, 1827.

5. Mahan, 105 -109.

6. Mahan, 109 -111.

7. Newspaper clipping pasted in Susan Lewis Goldsmith's account book, no date, Davenport Manuscripts, Microfilm Reel # 3, Frame #116, Rock Island County Historical Society.

8. "Notice." *Miner's Journal*, Galena, Fever River, Illinois. May 16, 1829.

9. Wilkie, 171.

10. Robinson, David N. *The Book of Louth*. Barracuda Books Ltd. Buckingham, England, 1979: 23.

11. Beckwith, Ian, ed. and comp. *The Louth Riverhead, a case study of the development of an industrial and commercial quarter in a Lincolnshire Market Town in the period 1750 -1850*. Published by Louth WEA Branch, 1976, 26.

12. Robinson, David N. *The Book of Louth*. Barracuda Books Ltd. Buckingham, England, 1979; Beckwith, Ian, ed. and comp. *The Louth Riverhead, a case study of the development of an industrial and commercial quarter in a Lincolnshire Market Town in the period 1750 -1850*. Published by Louth WEA Branch, 1976, p. 17; also Perkins, J.A. "Working-Class Housing in Lindsey, 1780 -1870." Lincolnshire History and Archaeology, Vol. 10, 1975.

13. Stuve, Dr. Bernard. "The State's Internal Improvement Venture of 1837-38." *Transactions of the Illinois State Historical Society*. Springfield, Illinois: Illinois State Historical Society, 1902: 115.

14. New York, 1820 - 1850 Passenger and Immigration Lists. On-line: www.ancestry.com; Letter: Davenport to O.N. Bostwick, November 3,1827, P.Chouteau - Maffitt Collection, Missouri Historical Society, St. Louis, Missouri; Letter: Davenport, George to Pierre Chouteau, Esq., November 3, 1827, P. Chouteau-Maffitt Collection, Missouri Historical Society, St. Louis, Missouri.

15. Letter: Charles D. St. Vrain, 3 Oct 1827. Chouteau-Maffitt Collection, Missouri Historical Society, St. Louis, Missouri.

Chapter 10 – Influx of Settlers

1. Atwater, Caleb. *Remarks Made on a Tour to Prairie du Chien in 1829*. Columbus, Ohio: Isaac Whiting, 1831: 65.

2. Letter: Russel Farnham to P. Chouteau Jr, February 9, 1828. P. Chouteau-Maffitt Collection, Missouri Historical Society, St. Louis, Missouri.

3. Letter: Street, Joseph M. to Dr. Alexander Posey, December 11, 1827, Edgar R. Harlan, ed. *Annals of Iowa*, Vol XII, No. 7, January 1921: 533 - 537; Smith, Marjorie. "The Winnebago War of 1827 Chronology of Events." Available online. www.geocities.com/old lead/winwarchron.htm. Accessed February 26, 2006.

4. Letter: George Davenport to P. Chouteau Jr, July 23, 1828. P. Chouteau-Maffitt Collection, Missouri Historical Society, St. Louis, Missouri.

5. Letters: Davenport to P. Chouteau Esq, Rock Island, August 22, 1828 and Oct. 28, 1828, Dec.1, 1828, and December 23,1828. Chouteau-Maffitt Collection, Missouri Historical Society.

6. Phelps Claim, July 6, 1837, Letters Rec'd, 1824 - 1881. Sac and Fox Agency, 1824 - 1880, Office of Indian Affairs, NARA, M234.

7. William Clark's Diary, Part I. *Kansas Historical Quarterly*, February 1948. Footnote #50.

8. Wm. Clark Papers, Records of the U.S. Superintendent of Indian Affairs, St. Louis, Vol. 4, p.64 Kansas State Historical Society; Mahan, Bruce E.. *Old Fort Crawford and the Frontier*. Iowa City: SHS, 1926, 158.

9. Letter: George Davenport to P. Chouteau Esq., 23 December 23, 1828. P. Chouteau-Maffitt Collection, Missouri Historical Society, St. Louis, Missouri.

10. Document: "Answers of Messrs. Farnham and Davenport, to Inquiries on the subject of the Fur Trade." November 21, 1831. Senate Document 90, 22nd Congress, 1st Session, 64; Black Hawk, 101-102.

11. Gallaher, Ruth A. "The Military-Indian Frontier, 1830-1835." *Iowa Journal of History and Politics*. 15, (July 1917): 398.

12. "Dubuque Mines," *Gazette*, August 3, 1843.

13. Fort Leavenworth had been established across the Missouri River. Jones, Charles T. Jr. *George Champlin Sibley: The Prairie Puritan, 1782-1863*. Jackson County Historical Society, Independence, Mo., 1970; Letter: Russel Farnham to P. Chouteau Jr., February 7, 1828. P. Chouteau-Maffitt Collection. Missouri Historical Society St. Louis, Missouri.

14. Letter: Russel Farnham to Pierre Chouteau Jr, August 1, 1830, P. Chouteau – Maffitt Collection, St. Louis, Missouri; Spencer, J.W. *The Early Day of Rock Island and Davenport*. Chicago: The Lakeside Press, 1942: 15, 17, 23.

15. References to Le Claire can be found in William Clark Papers, Vol. 24, Indian Agency at Rock Island. Records of the St. Louis Superintendency of Indian Affairs. Kansas State Hist. Society; Richard Graham papers, Missouri Historical Society, St. Louis; Richard Graham Accounts. Vol. 20, William Clark Papers. Kansas State Historical Society; also, Portage des Sioux Church records, on microfilm. After his marriage to Marguerite Le Page in November 1820, in Portage des Sioux he and his wife settled in Portage des Sioux where Le Claire had also served as a town trustee,

organized a local militia company, and acted as Justice of the township while working as government interpreter at the same time.

16. *George Davenport Day Book, 1828*, Rock Island County Historical Society, Moline, Illinois.

17. Spencer, 17; "Memorandum," in Davenport's 1828 Day Book; Barrows, Willard. "History of Scott County, Iowa." *Annals of Iowa*, January 1863: 16.

18. Discharged November 23, 1827. Ft. Armstrong Post Returns, Co. E, 5th Infantry, photocopy in Special Collections, Rock Island Public Library, Rock Island, Illinois; also, Mrs. K.T. Anderson, "some Reminiscences of Pioneer Rock Island Women," *Transactions of the Illinois State Historical Society*, 17(1912): 66.

19. Letter: George Davenport to Russel Farnham, August 19, 1828. P. Choutesu-Maffitt Collection, Missouri Historical Society, St. Louis, Missouri; Letter: George Davenport to Pierre Chouteau, October 28, 1828, Chouteau-Papin Collection. Missouri Historical Society, St. Louis; Peake, Ora Brooks. *History Of U.S. Indian Factory System*, Denver: Sage Books, 1954, 239. For a discussion of AMF traders in Green Bay and Chicago, see John Haeger. Chapter II,:"An Era of Exploitation." *Western Town Growth: A Study of the Development of Towns On the Western Shores of Lake Michigan, 1815 – 1843*: 70 – 95. Unpublished dissertation, Chicago: Loyola University, 1969.

20. Wilkie, 171.

21. Letter: George Davenport to P. Chouteau Esq., 16 February 16, 1829. P. Chouteau Collection, Missouri Historical Society, St. Louis, Missouri.

22. John Hauberg, unpublished manuscript, Hauberg Collection, Box 58, Notebook 17. Augustana College, Rock Island, Illinois; Black Hawk,104.

23. Rock Island County Commissioners' Record Book A, 1833-1838, July term, 1833: 4.

24. Wagner, Mark J. and Mary R. McCowie. *The Archaeology of Frontier Taverns on the St. Louis-Vincennes Trace*. Illinois state Museum Popular Science Series, Vol.XI, 1993: 13; John Hauberg interview with Eliza A. Laflin, August 4, 1915, Rock Island County Historical Society Library, Moline, Illinois.

25. Anderson, Mrs. K.T., 70.

26. Holt, *The Moline Dispatch*, Chapter XII; also, entry for "one dozen pieces of glass for store windows, 4 panes of glass for Farnhamsburg." George Davenport, 1829-30 Ledger, Hauberg Papers, Augustana College, Rock Island, Illinois.

27. "Memorandum of a Conversation that took place between myself, Le Claire and the Black Hawk Respecting Their Returning to the Village," in *George Davenport Day Book, 1828*, Rock Island County Historical Society, Moline, Illinois.

28. Depositions of several settlers, Whitney, Ellen ed. *The Black Hawk War*. Vol. II . 174 -188; Black Hawk,101; also, At the heart of their dispute was the Treaty of 1804,

which had been signed by Quashquame and members of the Sauk and Fox tribes in St. Louis. Both tribes maintained that those who had signed the treaty were not chiefs nor had they been appointed representatives of either tribe and, consequently, had no power to make such an agreement. A cession of land was a serious matter, which affected all tribal members and to be valid would have to have had the consent of every chief and counselor of both tribes. Since this had not been done, the treaty to them was invalid. See, Green, Michael. "'We Dance in Opposite Directions': Mesquakie (Fox) Separatism From the Sac and Fox Tribe," *Ethnohistory* 30 (3): 30.

The U.S. Government, however, did not distinguish between chiefs and non-chiefs and maintained not only that the Treaty of 1804 was valid, but also that the terms of that treaty had been reaffirmed by a second pact, signed at Portage des Sioux in 1815. (90) Black Hawk and his followers had refused to attend that treaty session as well, although as noted earlier, Black Hawk had signed a third treaty agreement, at St. Louis on May 13, 1816. See, *Black Hawk*, 87.

Most important to the interpretation of land use was Article 7 of the 1804 Treaty. It read: "As long as the lands which are now ceded to the United States remain their property, the Indians belonging to the said Tribes shall enjoy the privilege of living and hunting upon them." With such an agreement, it was difficult to remove the Indians until more settlers arrived and claimed the land. See, Letter: William.Clark to Secretary of War. August 12, 1831 in Whitney, Vol. II, 1973: 135 -138.

29. Mahan, Old Fort Crawford, 144-145.

30. Mahan, 147.

31. Today this land is east of the I-74 bridge extending into the East Moline. Rock Island; Deed: Antoine Le Claire and Francois Le Claire to George Davenport and Russel Farnham, October 30, 1830, Rock Island County Deed Book T, 174 -177.

32. Mahan, 150-151.

33. "Extract to the Editors, Dated "Rock Island, Sept. 18, 1829." Galena *Advertiser*, September 21, 1829.

34. No title. Galena *Advertiser*. August 31,1829.

35. *Black Hawk*, 104.

36. *Black Hawk*, 104.

37. It was sold for just $100 more than the original purchase price. Deed: George Davenport and wife, Russel Farnham and wife to Josiah H. Case, May 31, 1831, Jo Daviess County Deed Record Book 58, 366-367. Galena, Illinois.

38. *Black Hawk*, 104 -105.

39. Ferry Rates for George Davenport, December 4, 1828. Jo Daviess County Commissioners, Jo Daviess County Record Book A, 1827 – 1832. Galena, Illinois.

40. *The Daily Argus,* January 26, 1874.

41. In 1828 Davenport had purchased Portage Place or farm from Dr. Samuel Muir, a more permanent accommodation on private land rather on public land. Jo Daviess County Record Book A, 223-227.

42. *Miner's Journal,* Galena, Illinois. 16 May 1829; "Partnership of Farrar, Farnham, and Davenport." May 29,1829. Jo Daviess County Record Book A, 9.

43. Bickel, R.J. "'Rat Row' in Keokuk." *Annals of Iowa* 33 (1956): 450-453; also, VanderZee, Jacob. "The Opening of the Des Moines Valley." *Iowa Journal of History and Politics*, Vol XIV, No 4(1916): 483-484.

44. "Keokuk, Foot of the Des Moines Rapids, July 4, 1829" Galena *Advertiser*, Aug. 19, 1829; Coues, Elliott. *Forty Years a Fur Trader on the Upper Missouri: the Personal Narrative of Charles Larpenteur, 1833-1872.* Vol 1. N.Y.:Francis P. Harper, 1898: 4-6.

Chapter 11 – Escalation to War

1. Black Hawk, 108-109.

2. George Davenport and Russel Farnham, Account Book, 1828. On microfilm, Davenport Collection Reel #2, Davenport Public Library, Davenport, Iowa.

3. "President's Message,: December 6, 1830. Register of Debates, 21st Congress, 2nd Session. A Century of Lawmaking for a New Nation:U.S. Congressional Documents and Debates, 1774 – 1875. https://memory.loc.gov/cgi-bin/mpage?collId=llrd&fileName=010/I

4. Letter: Thomas Forsyth to William Clark, May 22, 1829, Government Letter-books 1818 – 1834, ed. Green and Alvord. Springfield: Illinois State Historical Library, 1909: 144-145.

5. Marriage records, St. Francis Catholic Church, Portage des Sioux, 15 May 1830. microfilm. FHC #1940845.

6. Letter: William Clark to Thomas McKinney, 19 June 1830. Clark Papers, Vol .4: 125-126. Kansas State Historical Society, Topeka, Kansas.

7. Letter: William Clark, Supt of Indian Affairs St Louis, to Col. McKinney, Indian Dept Washington, 12 April 1830, William Clark Papers, Vol. 4: 98-99, Kansas State Historical Society.

8. Stevens, Frank Everett. The Black Hawk War, Chicago: Frank E. Stevens, 1903: 171.

9. Letter: Russel Farnham to Pierre Chouteau Jr, August 1, 1830, Chouteau-Maffitt Collection, Missouri Historical Society, St. Louis, Missouri.

10. License Issued, November 9, 1830. Letters Received by the Office of Indian Affairs, 1824-1851, St. Louis Superintendency, 1824 -1851. NARA M234. Roll #749 (1829 – 1831).

11. Letter: Ramsay Crooks to P. Chouteau Jr. Esq. , New York, March 11, 1831. Chouteau Collection, Missouri Historical Society, St. Louis, Missouri.

12. Letter: Felix St. Vrain to William Clark, October 30, 1830, Whitney, Ellen, ed. The Black Hawk War, 1831 – 1832. Springfield: Illinois State Historical Library, 1970; Davenport purchases, Illinois Public Domain Land Tract Sales on 6 November 6, 11, 29 of 1830; Letter: Felix St. Vrain to William Clark, October 19, 1830 Clark Papers, Kansas State Historical Society, Volume 6: 50 – 51; The post operated by Gilbert was supplied by Davenport until 1835; Today the Meredosia has been drained and is hardly more than a ditch at the northernmost point of the county near the Mississippi River (now Hwy 84 between Cordova and Albany). Advertisement. Galena Advertiser, 25 Jan 1830, and Galena Gazette, Feb 1830.

13. John Hauberg Papers, u.m. Box 5. Thomas Tredway Library, Augustana College, Rock Island, Illinois.

14. Newell, Linda King and Valeen Tippetts Avery. Mormon Enigma: Emma Hale Smith, Univ. of Illinois Press, 1994. Chapter 3, 37.

15. Goble, Benjamin. Narrative of Incidents In the Life of an Illinois Pioneer. 1881 reprinted Knightstown: The Bookmark, 1977: 17, 19.

16. Letter: George Davenport, Rock Island, to Pierre Chouteau Esq., March 2, 1831. P. Chouteau - Maffitt Collection, Missouri Historical Society, St. Louis, Missouri.

17. Letter: George Davenport to Russel Farnham, April 2, 1831, P. Chouteau-Maffitt Collection, Missouri Historical Society, St. Louis, Missouri; also, Letter: George Davenport to Pierre Chouteau, Jr., April 26, 1831. P. Chouteau-Maffitt Collection, Missouri Historical Society, St. Louis, Missouri.

18. Rouse, May Belle and Margaret F. Gardner. Galena's Old Stockade and Underground Refuge. Galena: Ellsworth W. Glick, 1970. p. 36-37; also, "Dissolution of Partnership." May 25, 1831. Jo Daviess County, Deed Book A, 148.

19. Letter: Felix St. Vrain to General William Clark, May 15, 1831. Greene, Evarts Boutell and Clarence Walworth Alvord, eds. Governors' Letter-Books, 1818-1834, Executive Series, Volume 1, Springfield: Illinois State Historical Library, 1909: 178.

20. Governor's Letter-books. May 26, 1831: 165-166.

21. Letter: Edmund P. Gaines to John Reynolds, May 29, 1831. Governors' Letter-books, p. 168; also, Letter: Gaines to Reynolds, June 5, 1831, Whitney, Vol. II: 35.
22. Black Hawk, 115.

23. Black Hawk, 114; also, Letter: Felix St. Vrain to William Clark, July 23, 1831, in Whitney, 112.

24. "Articles of Agreement and Capitulation," signed on the 30th June 1831. Illinois Advocate, Edwardsville, Illinois, July 15, 1831.

25. Letter: George Davenport to Pierre Chouteau Jr., 5 June 1831, Whitney, II, 33; Letter: George Davenport to Russel Farnham, July 4, 1831, P. Chouteau-Maffitt Collection, Missouri Historical Society, St. Louis, Missouri.

26. Rock Island Council with Sac and Fox, September 5, 1831, in Report of the Indian Bureau, November 19, 1831, 22 Cong. 1 Sess. Senate Ex. Doc. No. 2, Vol. 1, Serial 216: 202-204.

27. William Jones, "Notes on the Fox Indians," Iowa Journal of History and Politics, Iowa City: State Historical Society of Iowa, Volume 10: 111.

Chapter 12 – The Black Hawk War and The End of the Indian Trade

1. Letter: Felix St. Vrain to William Clark, October 16, 1831, William Clark Papers, Vol 6, 320, MS 95. Kansas Historical Society; License issued by John B. Sarpy to Davenport and Farnham for year ending 1 October 1832, P. Chouteau-Maffitt Collection, Missouri Historical Society, St. Louis, Missouri.

2. Goble, Benjamin, Narrative of Incidents in the Life of an Illinois Pioneer. 1881 Knightstown, Indiana: The Bookmark, 1977: 20.

3. Davenport's Petition to House of Representatives, January 30, 1832, 22nd Congress, 1st Session, p. 192; Bill #337, 22 Congress, 1st Session, 337.

4. Letter: George Davenport to Hon. Joseph Duncan, Washington City, February 11, 1832. Indian Office Files, Sac and Fox, 1832 - 1839. Typed transcript in Stock Transcripts, Wisconsin Historical Society, Madison, Wisconsin.

5. Letter: George Davenport to the President, Senate Doc. 512, Vol 9, 23rd Congress, 1st Session, 221-223.

6. Whitney, II, 224.

7. Goble, 20.

8. Letter: George Davenport to Henry Atkinson, April 13, 1832 Whitney, II, Part I: 247; Letter: Felix St. Vrain to William Clark, 20 April 1832, Letters received by the Office of Indian Affairs, St. Louis Superintendency, NARA M234, Reel # 750.

9. Missouri Republican, St. Louis, Missouri. 19 April 1832.
10. Black Hawk, 56.

11. The Galenian, May 23, 1832.

12. Goble, 20.

13. Letter: Thomas Forsyth to George Davenport, May 23, 1832, Forsyth Papers, State Historical Society of Iowa, Des Moines. Photocopy in Special Collections, Tredway Library, Augustana College, Rock Island, Illinois.

14. Letter: George Davenport to William Clark, May 27, 1832, NARA, M234, Reel #750.

15. Letter: George Davenport to William Clark, 27 May 1832, in Whitney, 459; Letter: Davenport to Russel Farnham, June 8, 1832, in Whitney, 551.

16. Extract from "Seat of War," The Galenian, Wed. May 23, 1832.

17. Letter: Russel Farnham to George Davenport, July 11, 1832. Missouri Historical Society; also, State Historical Society Iowa, Des Moines, Photocopy in Special Collections. Tredway Library, Augustana College, Rock Island, Illinois.

18. Letter: Russel Farnham to George Davenport, May 21 1832, Augustana Special Collections; Letter: Thomas Forsyth to George Davenport, July 11, 1832. SHSI, Des Moines, Photocopy in Special Collections, Tredway Library, Augustana College, Rock Island, Illinois.

19. Meese, William A. Early Rock Island. Moline, Illinois: Desaulniers & Co., 1905: 86; Letter: George Davenport to Russel Farnham, June 8, 1832, P. Chouteau – Maffitt Collection, Missouri Historical Society, St. Louis, Missouri.

20. "An Abstract of Expenditures by Joshua Pilcher Acting Agent for the Sacs & Foxes during the half year Ending 30 September 1832"; "Abstract of Articles purchased for Presents to Indians by Joshua Pilcher Acting Agent at Rock Island for the 2nd and 3rd Quarters ending the 30th day of September 1832." William Clark Papers. U.S. Superintendent of Indian Affairs, St. Louis. "Records of accounts of Indian Agents, Sac and Fox Indian Agency, Rock Island, 1822 - 1834." Kansas State Historical Society, MS 98. Vol. 24.

21. Letter: W. B. Astor to Pierre Chouteau, August 17, 1833, Chouteau Collection, cited in Lavender, David. Fist in the Wilderness, 479, footnote #4.

22. Letter: George Davenport to Pierre Chouteau Jr, August 22, 1832, Chouteau-Maffitt Collection, Missouri Historical Society.

23. Major-General Scott. Order No. 16, August 28, 1832. Annals of Iowa, 3rd Series, Vol.II: 232 -233; Letter: George Davenport to Pierre Chouteau Jr. September 10, 1832. P. Chouteau-Maffitt Collection, Missouri Historical Society, St. Louis, Missouri.

24. Wilkie, p. 161; also, Holt, Orrin S. "Story of the Pioneers Who Blazed the Trail For Us in This Community." The Moline Dispatch, Chapter VIII, April 1916; The Argus, August 23, 1838; Letter: George Davenport to Russel Farnham, September 2, 1832, P. Chouteau-Maffitt Collection, Missouri Historical Society, St. Louis, Missouri.

25. Letter: Joseph M. Street to Winfield Scott. 6 September 1832. Whitney Vol. II Pt II:1114; Letter: George Davenport to Pierre Chouteau Jr., September 29,1832. Chouteau-Maffitt Collection, Missouri Historical Society, St. Louis, Missouri.

26. Letters: Joshua Pilcher to William Clark, Superintendent of Indian Affairs, October 16, and November 13, 1832. Letters Received by Office of Indian Affairs, Sac & Fox Agency, 1824 – 1880, NARA M234, Reel 728.

27. Treaty of 1832, Library of Congress, Washington, D.C.; Letter: George Davenport to Pierre Chouteau, September 24, 1832. Whitney, II: 1191; Lavender, 404, 415, 479; Letter: Pierre Chouteau, Jr. to Elbert Herring, Commissioner of Indian Affairs, May 2, 1833, Letters Received by the Office of Indian Affairs, Sac & Fox Agency, 1824 – 1880,NARA 234, Reel 728.

28. Letter: H.H. Gear, Administrator of the Estate of Amos Farrar, to Hon. Lewis Cass, Secretary of War, March 19, 1834, NARA M234, Reel 729, Letters Rec'd by OIA, Sac & Fox Agency, 1824 -1880.

29. Salter, William. "Iowa in Unorganized Territory of the United States, August 10, 1821 – June 28, 1834." *Annals of Iowa*, Third Series. Vol VI (1903-1905): 157.

30. Reynolds, John. "State of the State Address," *Western Observer*, Jacksonville, Illinois. December 18, 1830.

31. Letter to Editor, *American Railroad Journal*, January 28, 1832.

32. John Connolly died in October 1832. Amos Farrar died in November 1832. Letter: Ramsay Crooks to Pierre Chouteau Jr., November 16,1832. Missouri Historical Society, St Louis, Missouri; "George Davenport Account Book, May 30, 1835 - July 27, 1835." Rock Island County Historical Society; "Probate Record of Joshua Palen." filed July 5, 1833, Hancock County, Illinois.

33. "Articles of Agreement Between Russel Farnham and Stephen Phelps & Co." August 22, 1832. Chouteau-Maffitt Collection, Missouri Historical Society.

34. "Abstract of Expenditures & Disbursements by M.S. Davenport, Indian Agent at Rock Island in the half year ending 30th June 1833 -- Under the Stipulation of the 10th part, Treaty of 21 September 1832 with Sacs & Foxes Providing for the delivery of corn and under appropriation of 2 March 1833." William Clark Papers. MS 98. Vol 24. Kansas State Historical Society.

Chapter 13 – Laying New Foundations

1. Anderson, K.T. "Some Reminiscences of Pioneer Rock Island Women," *Transactions of the Illinois State Historical Society*, 17(1912): 66. According to the Dictionary of American Biography, the island home of Harman Blennerhassett was a sylvan retreat built in the Ohio River, near Parkersburg, West Virginia, in 1798. It was richly furnished with frescoes, paintings, silver, and imported furniture.

2. Letter: George Davenport to Pierre Chouteau Jr, November 3, 1827, P. Chouteau-Maffitt Collection, Missouri Historical Society, St. Louis, Missouri.

3. Goble, 20; also, Elbert, E. Duane and Keith A. Sculle. "Log Buildings in Illinois: Their Interpretations and Preservation." Illinois Preservation Series, No. 3, Illinois Department of Conservation, Springfield, Illinois.

4. HABS No. IL – 158: The Davenport House, Rock Island, Illinois." Historic American Buildings Survey, Library of Congress, Prints and Photographs Division, Washington, D.C.

5. Letter: George Davenport to J.B. Sarpy Esq., September 1833 and October 29, 1833. P. Chouteau-Maffitt Collection, Missouri Historical Society, St. Louis, Missouri.

6. Shaw, Henry. "George Davenport Account." April 6, 1833; "Bills of Lading." P. Chouteau-Maffitt Collection, Missouri Historical Society, St. Louis, Missouri.

7. The pistols are part of the permanent collection "Ya Gotta Know the Territory," State Historical Society of Iowa, Des Moines, Iowa.

8. Letter: George Davenport to J.B. Sarpy Esq. May 2, 1834, P. Chouteau-Maffitt Collection, Missouri Historical Society, St. Louis, Missouri.

9. Letter: George Davenport to Pierre Chouteau Esq. March 22, 1834. P. Chouteau-Maffitt Collection, Missouri Historical Society, St. Louis, Missouri.

10. Last Will and Testimony of Naomi Davenport, Scott County Probate File # 11633, September 16, 1820. On microfilm, Davenport Public Library, Davenport, Iowa.

11. Author interview with Mrs. Free, Free Studio, Davenport, Iowa.

12. The portraits, furniture, and scrapbook are part of the George L. Davenport Collection in the State Historical Society of Iowa, Division of History and Archives, Des Moines, Iowa. The collection was established by the Will of Naomi Davenport, 1924.

13. Dodge, Ellen Holmes. *Fiftieth Anniversary of the Settlement of Hon. George E. Holmes*, Christmas, A.D. 1896, privately published, 17. It is not clear whether Ellen Dodge's remembrance of an imported spinet and the family piano in the George L. Davenport collection are one and the same. The family piano was made in Cincinnati region.

14. Letter: George Davenport to Messrs Pratte, Chouteau & Co., May 28, 1834. P. Chouteau-Maffitt Collection, Missouri Historical Society, St. Louis, Missouri; also, George Davenport Ledger, 1834-1835, Special Collections, Tredway Library, Augustana College, Rock Island, Illinois.

15. Davenport *Gazette*, July 10, 1845; also, Davis, Fern R. "Davenport House, Scene of 1843(sic) Murder, Has Personal Interest for Rock Island Resident: Mrs. Totten Tells Early Times." *The Rock Island Argus*, November 27, 1951.

16. Lange, Frederick W. "Test Excavations at the Colonel Davenport House, Arsenal Island, Illinois," unpublished report, August 8, 1983, 24; also. Dennis Naglich and Mary Jo Cramer. "Davenport House Site, 2003 Archaeological Investigations," Report # 267. Prepared for Colonel Davenport Historical Foundation. March 2004; also, Marriage record of George L. Davenport and Sarah Grace Clarke, St. Anthony's Catholic Church, Davenport, Iowa. The obituary of Joseph A. Davenport clearly states that his family was living in the island home at the time of his birth in 1841, "Remains of Joseph A. Davenport Brought to Home of His Youth," photocopy of clipping found in the scrapbook belonging to Mrs. Joseph Dietrich of Kansas City, Missouri, Colonel Davenport Historical Foundation files.

17. "Davenport Home Remarkable," *The Argus*, January 5, 1907; Notes from Archie Allen, Port Byron, Illinois, January 10, 1867, Hauberg Collection, Box 50, No. 32, Special Collections, Tredway Library, Augustana College, Rock Island, Illinois; also, Faye E. Dudden, in her study, *Serving Women: Household Service in Nineteenth-Century America* (Middletown, Conn: Wesleyan University Press, 1983) argues that the meaning of help changed over time from an informal, short-term relationship between women to that of a formal relationship between women hired to work and the woman of the household who supervised from a distance. The shift in meaning paralleled the change from a rural, agricultural base to an urban, industrial base. As the middle class became more defined, women found "help" less and less desirable and "domestic" became a necessity.

18. Gleason, George. "Architectural Summary." Unpublished report, August 1987, Colonel Davenport Historical Foundation files; also, Andrew Bruzewicz, "A Color Infra-Red Photographic Reconnaissance of the Davenport House and Its Surroundings, " unpublished report, June 1989, Colonel Davenport Historical Foundation files.

19. Letter; George Davenport to O.N. Bostwick, October 24, 1824, Chouteau-Papin Collection, Missouri Historical Society, St. Louis, Missouri; Hauberg interview with Ellen Lynch, Hauberg Collection, Special Collections, Tredway Library, Augustana College, Rock Island, Illinois.

20. Iowa State Department of Agriculture, Forty-first Annual Iowa Year Book of Agriculture, Des Moines: The State of Iowa, 1940: 214; "Whose Life was History." *The Rock Island Argus*, January 10, 1890.

21. *Black Hawk*, 142.

22. "An Act To Establish a Permanent Seat of Justice for Rock Island County." March 1, 1833. *Laws of a Private Nature, Eighth General Assembly*, Kaskaskia: R.K. Fleming, 1833: 17.

23. Portrait and Biographical History of Rock Island County, 688; Hauberg, John. Untitled and Unpublished manuscript, Hauberg Collection, Box 58, Notebook 17, Special Collections, Tredway Library, Augustana College, Rock Island, Illinois.

24. Special Term, July 1836, Rock Island County Commissioners' Record Book A, 165.

25. Letter: William Davenport to Brigadier H. Atkinson, June 10, 1833, Document #35, William Davenport Papers, P.K. Yonge Library of Florida History, University of Florida; also, Field Notes for Township 18 North, Ranges 2 and 3 West of the 4th Principal Meridian. Photocopy, Rock Island County Historical Society, Moline, Illinois.

26. "Recollections of Suel Foster." No. 79. Walton, J.P. *Pioneer Papers*, Muscatine, Iowa, 1899: 256.

27. Letter: George Davenport to Messrs. Pratte, Chouteau and Co., November 22, 1834, Ayer Collection, Newberry Library, Chicago, Illinois.

28. In 1854 the house became the station house for the M & M Rail Road and the Le Claire's built their grand mansion at Sixth and Farnum in 1855.

29. Wilkie, 171. The small house was on land later known as the Watkins Farm, near the border of Davenport and Bettendorf, and still stands. Its present location is on College Avenue, Davenport, Iowa. It has been enlarged and modernized.

30. Lage, Dorothy. *Le Claire, Iowa, a Mississippi River Town*, Published by Dorothy Lage, 1976: 15; also, Deed: Antoine Le Claire to George Davenport, October 8, 1833, Recorded 8th September 1840. Scott County Deed Book A, 272.

31. Letter: S.E. McCoy to Editor of *Annals of Iowa*. Le Claire, Iowa. February 12, 1864. Manuscript Department. SHSI, Iowa City, Iowa.

32. Richter, Auguste P. *Richter Describes the Early Events in Scott County History*, originally published in a series of articles in the *Davenport Daily Times* Beginning on May 3, 1924.

33. Benjamin Drake. *The Great Indian Chief of the West: or, Life and Adventures of Black Hawk*. Philadelphia: H.M. Rulison, 1856: 213-228.

34. "Sixth Article -- Proceedings of County Court and Inference." *Daily Union*. July 5, 1867.

35. March term of the County Commissioners, 1834. County Supervisor's Record Book A, 19.

36. June Term of the County Commissioners, 1834. R.I. County Supervisors' Book A, 24.

37. Marsh, Cutting. "Expedition to the Sacs and Foxes." Entry for June 30, 1834. *Wisconsin Historical Collections*, Madison: Democrat Printing Company, 1900, Vol. XV: 104- 155.

38. Salter, William. "Iowa in Unorganized Territory of the United States, August 10, 1821 – June 28, 1834." *Annals of Iowa*, Third Series. Vol VI (1903-1905), 202-203; also, "Marsh, 111-112.

39. Farnham and Davenport, November 20, 1831.

40. Letter: Joseph M. Street to William Clark, Rock Island, 7 October 1835, Office of Indian Affairs, 1824-1881, St. Louis Superintendency. 1824 - 1851, NA Microcopy 234, Roll #750, 1832 - 1835.

41. Lippincott, Isaac. "A Century and a Half of Fur Trade at St. Louis." *Washington University Studies,* 3: 205-242.

42. Five Ledgers. George L. Davenport Papers, SHSI Microfilm, Reel #3.

43. Letter: George Davenport to Pierre Chouteau Jr, March 22, 1834, P. Chouteau-Maffitt Collection, Missouri Historical Society, St. Louis, Missouri.

44. Kett, H.F., Past and Present of Rock Island County, Illinois, 126; "Death Of Miles W. Conway Esq." *The (Rock Island, Illinois)Union*, January 24, 1866.; "An Act to

Establish the County Seat of Rock Island County." *Laws of the State of Illinois, Ninth General Assembly, 1ˢᵗ Session..* Vandalia: Sawyer, Public Printers, 1835: 159 – 160.

45. *Miner's Journal*, 23 August 1828 and 12 June 1830; *The Galenian*, 23 May 23, 1832.

46. License Granted by the County Commissioners of Rock Island County, June 6, 1835. Vol. A, 56-57. In Superintendent Record Book A, transcribed by Mabel Ballon. November 25, 1936. State Archives of Illinois, Springfield, Illinois.

47. "Town Plats." *Laws of Illinois*. 4th Illinois General Assembly, 1st session, Nov 1824 - Jan 1825: 184; Walters, William D. Jr. "The Fanciful Geography of 1836." *The Old Northwest*, Vol. 9, No. 4(Winter 1983 -1984): 333.

48.*NW Advertiser and Galena Gazette*, June 13, 1835.

49. Rock Island County Commissioners Book A, 66-71.

50. "Purchase of Lots in Stephenson." Rock Island County Commissioners Record Book A., 70 - 71. Transcribed by Mabel Ballon. Illinois State Archives; License Granted, 6 June 1835. Rock Island County Commissioners Record Book A, 56 -57. Transcribed by Mabel Ballon, State Archives of Illinois, Springfield, Illinois.

51. Rock Island County Commissioners to Susannah Lewis, October 22, 1836, Lots 4 and 7 in Block 6 in the town of Stephenson, Deed Book A, 293; Deed: Susan M. Goldsmith to Joseph A. Brackett, filed and recorded November 18, 1856, Rock Island County Deed Book V, 433. NOTE: Davenport's provision of a trust for Elizabeth in his will suggests that she may very well have been his child, but his relationship to her was never as clearly defined as was his relationship to his sons. After Bailey's death in 1890, Elizabeth tried unsuccessfully to prove that she was Davenport's daughter and therefore half-sister to Bailey, but the State of Illinois denied her claim to the Davenport estate. See, Elizabeth Ferkler(sic) v. Davenport Heirs." Case #3295, February term 1891. R.I. Co. Circuit Court Records, Rock Island, Illinois.

52. Letter: Wiiliam. T. Brashar to General Elias Langham, March 29 1835. also, Letter: Joel Wells Jr. to General Elias Langham, June 19, 1835. Both in Letters to the Surveyor General from the Public, 1834 - 1835. U.S. Surveyors Records for Illinois, RG 953.001 Incoming Correspondence, Ca 1816 - 1862, Illinois State Archives, Springfield, Illinois.

53. Letter: John Emerson to J. Lovell,M.D. Surgeon General of the U.S. Army. Fort Armstrong (Ills.), August 7, 1835. Fort Armstrong papers, NARA, Washington, D.C.

54. "Auction at Fort Armstrong." *The North Western Gazette and Galena Advertiser*, Galena, Illinois. 27 August 1836; John Hauberg interview with Tom Bollman, Hauberg Collection, Box 47– 5, No. 46, Special Collections, Tredway Library, Augustana College, Rock Island, Illinois; From the Report of Capt, A. Bell, Commanding Fort at St. Louis, November 23, 1840. Wisconsin Territorial Papers, Reel # 7.

55. Letter: J.R. Poinsett to George Davenport, Washington City. March 19, 1837. Harlan Papers, State Historical Society of Iowa, Des Moines, Iowa.

56. Letters: Joseph M. Street to Clark, July through November 1838. Street papers. State Historical Society of Iowa, Des Moines, Iowa.

57. Letter: Joseph M. Street, to Mr. David J. Baker, U.S. Attorney at Kaskaskia, Il. in Flagler, 42-43.

58. Rock Island Circuit Court Case: George Davenport v. Asel C. Case, August 22, 1839.

59. Letter: Joseph M. Street to His Excellency Henry Dodge, Governor of Wisconsin Territory and Superintendent of Indian Affairs, Rock Island, October 6, 1836. Letters Received by the Office of Indian Affairs, 1824 - 1881, Sac and Fox Agency, 1824 - 1880. NA M234, Roll#729, 1834 - 1837.

60. Letter: Joel R. Poinsett to James Whitcomb Esq., Commissioner, General Land Office, July 19, 1837, Letters Sent by the Sec of War Relating to Military Affairs, 1800 - 1889, M6 Roll 17, p. 336; Letter: Joel R. Poinsett to George Davenport, July 27, 1837, M6 Roll 17: 349.

61. Letter: Joseph M. Street to Henry Dodge, November 29, 1838. M234. Reel #730; Letter: Joseph M. Street to Henry Dodge, July 17, 1838, M234, Reel #730.

62. Ft. Madison, Iowa, *Patriot*, 11 July 1838; Salter, William. *Iowa: The First Free State in the Louisiana Purchase, 1673-1846.* Chicago: A.C. McClury & Co., 1905, 233; Hagan, 220.

Chapter 14 – Dwindling Indian Trade

1. Deposition, Alexis Phelps for S. Phelps & Co. July 6, 1837. On microfilm. NARA M234, Reel 729, Letters Rec'd by OIA. Sac and Fox Agency, 1824 – 1880.

2. Settlers Accounts 1833, Davenport Collection, on microfilm, original at Tredway Library, Archives, Augustana College, Rock Island, Illinois.

3. Letter: St. Vrain to Clark, October 16, 1831, Clark Papers, Kansas State Historical Society; Letter: George L. Davenport to Henry Sibley. October 8, 1839. Sibley Papers. Minnesota Historical Society, M164, Reel 2, #557; William Phelps was the youngest of the Phelps Brothers. He and his wife Caroline lived with Keokuk's village.

4. Letter: Davenport to Pratte, Chouteau & Co. May 28, 1834, P. Chouteau-Maffitt Collection, Missouri Historical Society, St. Louis, Missouri.

5. Letter; Davenport to P. Chouteau Jr. Esq., June 22, 1834, P. Chouteau Collection; also, Letter: Pierre Chouteau, Jr. to Hon. Elbert Herring, Commissioner of Indian Affairs, May 2, 1833. NARA, M234, Reel 728, Letters Rec'd by OIA, Sac & Fox Agency, 1824 – 1880.

6. Shipping Invoice, April, 1834, P. Chouteau Maffitt Collection; also, George Davenport Accounts. Volume Y: Invoices Outward, P.Chouteau Jr. & Co., Feb – 1834 – October 1839, Chouteau Papers, on microfilm, Reel 8. Missouri Historical Society, St. Louis, Missouri.

7. George Davenport Account Book, June 5 and16, 1835. George L. Davenport Collection. On microfilm. Reels #2 qnd #3 SHSI; Letter: Street, Joseph M. to Governor Henry Dodge, Rock Island, 22 December 1836, Correspondence of the Office of Indian Affairs (Central) and Related records, NARA M234, Letters Received, 1824 - 1891. Reel No. 729 Doc. # 217.

8. Downer, Harry E. *History of Scott County Iowa*, Vol. 1. Chicago: The S.J. Clarke Publishing Co., 1910: 155.

9. Letter: George Davenport to Mrsser Pratte, Chouteau & Co., November 22, 1834, Ayer Collection, Newberry Library, Chicago, Illinois; also, Deposition of Alexis Phelps; The Sac Outfits for 1836, 1837 and 1838 were identified as belonging to Davenport and Phelps. "Volume Y: Invoices Outward, Pierre Chouteau Jr. & Co., February 1834 - October 1839." American Fur Company Papers, Missouri Historical Society.

10. Deposition re: Claim against Treaty of 1832, September, 1834, NARA M234 Reel #729, Letters Rec'd by OIA, Sac and Fox Agency, 1824 – 1880. Also, Letter: Davenport to Mrsser Pratte, Chouteau & Co., Rock Island, November 22, 1834. Mnss #217. Ayer Collection, Newberry Library, Chicago, Illinois.

11. Council with Poweshiek and His People with Indian Agent Street and Colonel William Davenport, June 2, 3, 4 June 1835. On microfilm. NARA M234, Reel 729, Letters Rec's by OIA, Sac and Fox Agency, 1824 – 1880.

12. Davenport Account Book, May 20, 1835 – July, 1835. Special Collections, Tredway Library, Augustana College. On microfilm. Note: Davenport began business with the Pratte, Chouteau & Co. on April 24, 1834.

13. Report: Indian Agent Joseph M. Street to General William Clark, October 7, 1835. NARA M234, Reel #750, Letters Rec'd by OIA, 1824 – 1881, St. Louis Superintendency, 1824 – 1851.

14. *History of Muscatine County Iowa.* Chicago: S.J. Clarke Pub. Co., 1911: 446.

15. Downer, Harry E., *History of Scott County Iowa.* Chicago: The S.J. Clarke Publishing Co., 1910. Vol. 1: 118.

16. "Indian – The Rumor." *North Western Gazette and Galena Advertiser*, March 12, 1836; "Auction." *North Western Gazette and Galena Advertiser*, August 27, 1836.

17. "Original Journal of Cyrus Dickson Western Journey with His Father, 1836. Journal and Letters of Cyrus Dickson." The Learned T. Bulman '48 Historic Archives and Museum, Washington and Jefferson College, Washington, Pennsylvania.

18. Letter: George Davenport to George W. Jones, Dec 20, 1835. Henry Dodge Collection, on microfilm. SHSI, Des Moines.

19. Council of 1836. 1 June 1836. U.S. Office of Indian Affairs, Letter Rec'd, 1824 - 1880. Sac and Fox Agency, 1824 - 1880. NARA. M234. Reel #883 - 884 (1824 - 1851): 759.

20. Treaty With the Sauk and Foxes, 1836. September 28, 1836. in Kappler, Charles J. compiler and editor. *Indian Affairs: Laws and Treaties.* Vol. 2: 474–475.

21. Wilkie, 162.

22. No title, *Galena (Illinois) Advertiser*, 9 September 1837.

23. Letter: Cyrus Dickson to William Dickson, 29th September 1837. Cyrus Dickson File. U. Grant Miller Library. Washington-Jefferson College; Hagan, 216-217; also, Kappler, Charles J. "Treaty with the Sauk and Foxes, 1837." *Indian Affairs: Laws and Treaties.* Washington: GPO, 1904. Vol. II: 495-496.

24. Letter: Joseph Street to William Clark, October 7, 1835. Letters Received by Office of Indian Affairs, 1824 – 1881. St. Louis Superintendency, 1824 – 1851. National Archives and Records Administration, M234, Reel #750 (1832 – 1835).

25. Letter: Street to Governor Henry Dodge, August 27, 1837. Carter, ed. Territorial Papers of the United States, Wisconsin Territory, Vol. XXVII: 841–843.

26. Kappler, Charles J. *Indian Treaties*, 1778-1883, N.Y.:Interland Pub, 1972: 495-498.

27. *NW Gazette and Galena (Illinois) Advertiser*, August 19, 1837.

28. Wilkie, 177-180.

29. VanderZee, Jacob. "Fur Trade in Iowa Country, Iowa." *Iowa Journal of History and Politics*, Iowa City, Iowa: State Historical Society of Iowa, Volume 12, No. 4: 558.

30. Letter: Davenport to Cary Harris, Commissioner of Indian Affairs, Indian Lodge, Rock Island, Sept. 14, 1838, Nat. Archives microcopy 234, Roll 730, pp. 397-400, Letters Received by Office of Indian Affairs, 1828-81.

Chapter 15 – New Town in Iowa

1. Pre emption Claim by Antoine Le Claire, Dubuque Land Office Records, NARA, Record Group 49.

2. Rock Island County Commissioners to Antoine LeClaire, R.I. Co. Deed Book A, July 11, 1835: 5.

3. Stuve, Dr. Bernard. "The States Internal Improvement Venture of 1837 - 1838." *Transactions of the Illinois State Historical Society.* Springfield. 1902: 117.

4. Agreement to Found City of Davenport, Newberry Library, Graft collection, MNSS #1008.

5. Darby, John F. *Personal Recollections of John F. Darby*, NY:Arco Press, 1975,:276-277.

6. Barrows, *Annals of Iowa*, 47; Obit, *Davenport Gazette*, June 25, 1857; "Descendants and collateral families of the 1630 immigrant William Cheesbrough." available on-line: CHEESBRO' Genealogy@RootsWeb.

7. "Geo. Davenport Esqr. A/C Dr," July 21st, 1837. Le Claire Papers, Putnam Museum, Davenport, Iowa.

8. Reps, John William. *The Making of Urban America: a history of city planning in the United States*. Princeton University Press, 1965:174.

9. "Davenport." *Northwestern Gazette and Galena Advertiser*, 12 March 1836.

10. Wilkie, 33-35.

11. Virginia Macklot pedigree. available on-line. http://genealogy.kathihill.com/Person/pedigree/235342.

12. "In Chancery," *Gazette*, Davenport, Iowa. February 16, 1843.

13. "Petition to Congress By Citizens of Davenport," *Territorial Papers of the United States, Territory of Wisconsin, Executive Journal, 1836 - 1848*. Vol. 27. edited by John Porter Bloom. Washington, D.C.: National Archives, 1969,:920, 921, 922.

14. Burrows, *Annals of Iowa* Volume One – 1863: 45-46.

15. George Parker Map, dated February 1837, George Parker Collection, Putnam Museum, Davenport, Iowa.

16. Letter: George Parker to Mr. J.A. Crandall, no date, and map dated February 1837. George Parker Collection, Putnam Museum, Davenport, Iowa.

17. "Cook Home is Approaching Own Centennial," *Davenport Times*, July 11, 1936.

18. "Pioneer Gavitt," *The Morning Democrat Gazette*, November 8, 1887; "Davenport: For Whom Was Our Fair City Named," *Davenport Sunday Democrat*, December 16, 1894.

19. "An Old Settler of Scott County Becomes Reminiscent," *The Davenport Democrat and Leader*, August 22, 1920.

Chapter 16 – Out on the Rock and RIC

1. "Lo, The Poor Indian!" *Iowa News*. Published at Upper Mississippi Lead Mines, Wisconsin Territory. 15 July 1837; Rock Island *Argus Anniversary Issue*. 31 December 1925.

2. Partition. Deed Book B, 12. Rock Island County Recorder's Office, Rock Island, Illinois.

3. "Peter Cartwright's Visits to the Rock Island Mission." Rock Island *Argus*, August 15, 1915.

4. Ferry Licenses. George Davenport and Joshua Vandruff, Rinnah Wells, Benjamin Carr. March Term, 1834. Rock Island County Supervisors Book A, 1833 – 1838: 15–18.

5. *NW Gazette and Galena Advertiser*, 10 June 1837.

6. Deed: George Davenport to John H. Sullivan, March 12, 1836, Book A, 245, Rock Island County Recorder's Office; Deed: William Carr to John H. Sullivan , June 21, 1836, Deed Book A, 106. Rock Island County recorder's Office, Rock Island, Illinois.

7. Dickson, William, "A Few Short Sketches of My Eventful Life." Mnss, August 1853. Rock Island County Historical Society, Moline, Illinois; Turner, Levi Crosby. *Autobiography*. Cooperstown, N.Y.: Douglas Turner Johnston, 1954: 14.

8. "New Towns." *Chicago American*, 2 July 1836; Letter: Cooley to Munn, Bronson, June 14, 1836. E.G. Munn Papers. University of Rochester Library, Rochester, New York.

9. Davenport, George, to Levi C. Turner, July 1, 1836, Rock Island County Deeds, Book A, 46–49. Rock Island County Recorder's Office, Rock Island, Illinois.

10. Clark, Benjamin to Lewis Moss and Levi C. Turner, July 4 1836, Scott County, Iowa, Deed Book B, 198-199, Davenport, Iowa; William Carr to Levi C. Turner and William C. Dickson, July 6, 1836. Deed Book A, 197, Rock Island County Recorder's Office, Rock Island, Illinois.

11. Rock Island City." *Northwestern Gazette and Galena Advertiser*. July 9, 1836; "The Foundation of a City." *The Otsego Republican*, Cooperstown, New York. August 22, 1836.

12. In 1830, the Census for Illinois showed 157,445 people. Stuve, Dr. Bernard. "The State's Internal Improvement Venture of 1837-38*." Transactions of the Illinois State Historical Society For the Year 1902*. Springfield: 1902: 117; "New Towns." *Galena Advertiser*, May 14,1836.

13. *Western Gazette and Galena Advertiser*, 13 May 1837.

14. Rock Island City Plat, Deed Book A, 68, filed July 22, 1836.

15. Letter: G.W. Featherstonhaugh to John James Abert, 19 May 1837. Abert Family Papers. Missouri Historical Society St. Louis, Missouri.

16. "Items, Galena, August 20," *Cincinnati (Ohio) Daily Gazette*, September 4, 1839.

17. *Galena Advertiser*, 14 May 1836. (Note: The *Gipsy* was sternwheeler with an open deck and a small cabin, and measured 100 feet long and thirty feet wide and 79 tons. Larson, Gustav. E. "Notes on Rock River Navigation. *Journal of the Illinois Historical Society*. Vol. 33, No. 3 (September 1940): 341–358.

18. "Navigation of the Rock River." *Peoria (Illinois) Register and Northwestern Gazette*, April 17, 1840.

19. Most of Turner's investors had been affected by the fire. "Great Fire in New York -- MIllions of Property Destroyed." *Northwestern Gazette and Galena Advertiser.* January 16,1836; Deed: Davenport and wife, Levi C. Turner and wife to J.P. Coffin, C. Carlton, Edwards W. Fiske and L. Allen. August 6, 1836, Deed Book A, 196, 198, Rock Island County Recorder's Office.

20. Davenport and wife, Turner and wife to Charles A. Spring, August 29, 1836. Deed Book A, 527 – 528; Davenport and wife, Levi C. Turner and Wife to Charles A. Spring, Deed Book A, 340-341; Davenport and wife, Turner and wife to Nathaniel Norton. September 14, 1836. Deed Book B, 114, Rock Island County.

21. Correspondence with descendant Marilyn Gerard-Hartman, October 2004.

22. *Rock Island Banner*, 13 February 1840. In 1853 Norton moved to Chicago where he entered the lumber business and was a successful capitalist; Deed: Levi C. Turner to Robert Campbell, Rock Island County Recorder's Office, July16, 1837, Deed Book A, 507-508.

23. Letter Henry L. Kinney to Daniel Webster, Peru July 18th,1836. published in *Daniel Webster Papers*, Correspondence 1836. edited by Wiltse, Charles M. and Harold D. Mosier, University Press of New England, 1974, p. 149; Letter concerning Indian Affairs written to Geo. W. Jones in the City on February 6, 1837. Henry Dodge Collection, SHSI; Deed, Levi C. Turner and George Davenport to Daniel C. Webster, February13, 1837, Book A, 311, Rock Island County Recorder's Office.

24. "An Act to Incorporate the Rock Island City Bridge Company." *Incorporation Laws of the State of Illinois*. Vandalia: William Walters, Public Printer, 1837: 29 - 31; *Peoria (Illinois) Register and North-Western Gazetteer*, September28, 1839.

25. Letter: Anthony Cooley to E.G. Munn. Bronson, Michigan. April 27, 1836; Letter: Cooley to Munn, Kalamazoo, November 28, 1836. E.G. Munn Papers, University of Rochester Library; Neilson, Chris. "The Life of Anthony Cooley, January7, 1958. Unpublished paper in Kalamazoo Public Library, Kalamazoo, Michigan.

26. *Historic Rock Island County*, Rock Island, Illinois: Kramer & Co., 1908: 67; Also, Ellsworth, H.L. : *Illinois in 1837:A Sketch*. Philadelphia: S. Augustus Mitchell, 1837: 25; Plat Book #1, 5 July 5, 1836, Rock Island County Recorder's Office.

27. Deed: Joshua Vandruff to Daniel G. Garnsey. Rock Island County Recorder's Office, Book A, 144; Letter: A. Cooley to Edwin George Munn, Kalamazoo, August 11, 1839. E.G. Munn Papers, University of Rochester Library, Rochester, New York.

28. "Rock Island and Its Prospects." reprinted from the *New York Evening Star* in the *Iowa News*, 22 July 1837.

29. "George Templeton Strong: The Panic of 1837." *The Annals of America*, Vol. 6, 1833-1840: 311. William Benton, Publisher. Chicago: Encyclopedia Britannica, Inc., 1968.

30. Power of Attorney: Antoine Le Claire and George Davenport To Levi C. Turner October 31, 1837, Scott County Deed Book B, 12-13, Scott County Courthouse, Davenport, Iowa.

31. Gates, Paul W. 'Frontier Land Business in Wisconsin." *Wisconsin Magazine of History*, Vol. 51: 310- 311.

32. William C. Dickson died the previous October.

33. Hauberg, John. "Rock Island County Sawmills." Hauberg collection. Rock Island County Historical Society; Benjamin Carr to Levi Turner and William C. Dickson, Deed Book A,197, dated 20 July 1836; Agreement between George Davenport and wife, Daniel Webster by Levi C. Turner, and Levi C. Turner, of the first part and William Dickson of the second part, Deed Book D,23. Rock Island County Recorder's Office.

34. No Title. *The Western Voice*, Shawneetown, Illinois, 6 January 1838; *Northwestern Gazette*, February 24, 1838; Letter: John Dixon to The Honorable James W. Stephenson, Commissioner of Public Works for the Sixth Judicial District, Engineer's Office, May 15th 1838, in Illinois Record Book and Report 1837 - 1841. Auditor of Public Accounts. Springfield, Illinois: 292-293.

35. Ellsworth, H.L. *Illinois in 1837*. Philadelphia: S. Augustus Mitchell, 1837:102.

36. "An Act to Incorporate the Mississippi and Rock River Canal." Approved by the Illinois Legislature, in force, 21 Feb. 1837. *Incorporation Laws of the State of Illinois*, Vandalia: William Walters, Public Printer, 1837: 72 -77. Also Bill S.96, 25th Congress, 3rd Session.

37. Letter: James Seymour to The Honorable the Board of Public Works, State of Illinois. Chicago, November 26, 1837. Senate Doc. #259. *Documents in Relation to Internal Improvements, in the State of Illinois, March 5, 1838*. 25th Congress, 2nd Session.

38. *Northwester Gazette and Galena Advertiser*, 10 March 1838; also, Kett's *Past and Present of Rock Island County*, 1877: 473; Payroll of A. Blanc, Daybook, Illinois State Archives, Springfield, Illinois; *Iowa Sun*, December 6,1838.

39. Deed: Joshua Vandruff to State of Illinois April 6, 1839, Rock Island County Deed Book C, 146; "An Act to Authorize Joshua VanDruff to establish a Ferry across Rock River at Vandruff's Island." March 2,1839. *Laws of the State of Illinois*: 268 – 269.

40. Deeds: Thomas Harris to John Dement and H.B. Truett. January 7 and 11, 1838. R.I. Co Deed Book C, 361- 363; Deed: Joshua and Elizabeth Vandruff to James Craig and Daniel H. Whitney, February 23, 1839, Rock Island County Deed Book C, 142, 144.

41. Dement et al, by Sheriff to George Davenport, December 14, 1844, Rock Island County Deed Book F, 398.

42. *Milan (Illinois)Weekly Independent*, September 17, 1903: 8.

43. Record of Public Works, 1837 – 1843, Auditor of Public Works, Illinois State Archives, Springfield, Illinois; *Rock Island Banner and Stephenson Gazette*, September 5, 1839. NOTE: In 1843, after four years of inactivity, the State ordered the canal works be sold at public auction. All stone, timber iron and any other useable materials were sold. See, "Died in This Place." *Rock Island Banner and Stephenson Gazette*, Sept. 5, 1839; Letter: Governor Thomas Ford to Lemuel Andrews, Sheriff of Rock Island County, July 13, 1843. *Governor's Letter-Books, 1840 -1853*. Executive Series II, editor Evarts Boutell Green and Charles Manfred Thompson. Springfield, Il.: Illinois State Historical Library, 1911: 96.

44. Obituary. *New York Herald*, 28 January 1841; Shepard, Edward M. "The Panic of 1837." from *Life of Martin Van Buren*, Houghton, Miflin Company. 1888-1889. on-line: www.usgennet.org/usa/topic/preservation/epochs/vol6/pg178.htm); Power of Attorney, Daniel Webster to Nathaniel Ray Thomas, 5 March 1838. Mnss. Illinois State Historical Library, Springfield, Illinois.

45. Bill in Chancery. Hubbard v. Turner. 19 Feb 1838. Rock Island County; September Term 1839 and April term 1840, Law Record, on microfilm, Illinois Regional Archives Department (IRAD), Western Illinois University Library, Macomb, Illinois; Letter: Turner to Daniel Webster, Cleveland, Ohio. March 13, 1840, microfilm copy, Webster Papers, Library of Congress.

46. Some of the RIC investors mortgaged their shares to Turner, who eventually mortgaged all to Samuel Blackwell. Mortgage Book A, 105, 107; Mortgage Book B, 114. Rock Island County Recorder's Office, Rock Island, Illinois; Spring and his sons held onto the RIC land until selling to Blackwell in 1855. Deed Book T, 259.

47 Letter: Anthony Cooley to E.G. Munn, Kalamazoo, August 11, 1839. Munn Papers, University of Rochester, New York.

48. *Iowa Sun*, May 22, 1839; also, *Peoria (Illinois) Register and Northwestern Gazetteer*, June 22, 1839; "Items," *Cincinnati Daily Gazette*, September 4, 1839.

49. "Vacation of part of Plat of Rock Island City." Deed Book E, 104, Rock Island County Recorder's Office, Rock Island, Illinois.

Chapter 17 – Harnessing the Waterpower

1. "Rock Island." *The Iowa Sun.*, published in Davenport, Iowa, December 11, 1839 and December 6, 1872.

2. "A Reminiscence of Early Days." *The(Rock Island) Daily Argus*. December 6, 1872.

3. "Stephenson." *The Upper Mississippian*, November 19, 1839, and "Stephenson." *The Mississippian, published in Rock Island, Illinois,* November 19, 1840.

4. *Rock Island Banner and Stephenson Gazette*, 31, October 1839; *The Davenport Gazette*, 1840; "An Act to Incorporate the seminaries of learning therein named."

Incorporation Laws Illinois of the State of Illinois, 11th General Assembly, Vandalia: March 2, 1839. Section 16: 240.

5. "Scott County Saw-Mill History." *Daily Davenport Democrat*. December 14 and 17, 1868; "Scott County Flour Mills." *Daily Davenport Democrat*. December 19, 1868; 1840 Federal Census for Rock Island County, Illinois.

6. "A Memorial to Congress." *Davenport Gazette*, 17 February 1842.

7. "Public Meeting." *The Iowa News*. Dubuque, Iowa. 20 September 1837; H.R.403. "A Bill to provide for the registration of vessels ... the collection of hospital money ... the erection of marine hospitals ... on western rivers and lakes ..." 25th Congress, 2nd Session. January 12, 1838.

8. Flagler, Major D.W. *History of Rock Island Arsenal*. Ordnance Dept. 1877: 31; "National Armory in the West," *Upper Mississippian*, 7 January 1841.

9. Bell Report, printed in Flagler, Daniel. *History of Rock Island Arsenal*. Ordinance Department,1877: 27 -35; "The Upper Mississippi." *The Gazette*. February 8, 1844.

10. "The Upper Mississippi" *Gazette*, Feb 8, 1844; "Loss of the Steam Boat Brazil." *Upper Mississippian*, 13 May 1841. NOTE: In 1838 and again in 1839 Lt. Robert E. Lee had supervised work on the Des Moines Rapids, deepening and straightening the main channels of the river, but no work was done on the Rock Island Rapids. Source: Roald Tweet. *A History of Navigation Improvements on the Rock Island Rapids*. Rock Island District, U.S. Army Corps of Engineers, April 1980: 3.

11. "Rock-Island, -- Arsenal, &tc." *The Upper Mississippian*, 5 November 1840; *Davenport Gazette*, March 23, 1843.

12. Petition found in RS 600.00: Folder 472. "Bills, Resolutions, and Related General Assembly Records. Twelfth General Assembly 1840-1841 Session; also, *Rock Island Banner and Stephenson Gazette*, January 23, 1840, February 4, 1840, and April 24, 1841; Vandruff, Joshua. Land Purchases. September 25, 1839. Illinois Public Domain Land Tract Sales Database, available on-line: http://www2.sos.state.il.us/cgi-bin/land.

13. "An Act to authorize John W. Spencer and David B. Sears, to build a mill dam across Rock Island Slough." In force, 11 February 1837. *Laws of the State of Illinois passed by the Tenth General Assembly*. Vandalia: William Walters, Public printers, 1837: 161.

14. Letter: Hon. John Buford to John W. Spencer, Burlington, Iowa Territory, 18 July 1838, printed in Kett, H.F. *Past and Present of Rock Island County*, 1877: 176-177.

15. "A Foundry." *Upper Mississippian*. September 14, 1842. This mill when finished in January 1845 was five stories high and one of the biggest and grandest mills around.

16. Plat of Davenport's Addition to Moline, July 5,1843, Deed Book F, 54-55. Rock Island County Recorder's Office, Rock Island, Illinois.

17. Deed: Davenport to Charles Atkinson, August 10, 1844, Deed Record Book F, 160. Rock Island County Recorder's Office, Rock Ilsand, Illinois.

18. Rock Island County Supervisor's Record Book B, 298; also, Hauberg Interview with David Sears, Hauberg manuscripts, Rock Island County Historical Society, Moline, Illinois.

19. September 1844. Rock Island County Commissioners' Book C, 58. Rock Island County Clerk's Office, Rock Island, Illinois.

20. Plat of Moline, Deed Book F, 54 - 55. Rock Island County Recorder's Office, Rock Island, Illinois.

21. "Public Meeting." Davenport *Gazette*, January12, 1843; "A Bill." Davenport *Gazette*. March 2, 1843, and "Scott County Hydraulic Company. Davenport *Gazette*. September 14, 1843; "To the Citizens of Scott County." Davenport *Gazette*. December 23, 1843; "Scott Co. Hydraulic Company." Davenport *Gazette*, 18 January 1844; "The Candidates - Hydraulic Company." Davenport *Gazette*, April 3, 1845.

22. Letter: Ford, Thomas to Lemuel Andrews, Sheriff of Rock Island County. July 13, 1843. Governor's Letter-Books, 1840 - 1853. ed. Everts Boutelle Greene and Charles Manford Thompson, Executive Series II. Illinois State Historical Library. Springfield, Ill.:96; "Rock River Meeting." *The Upper Mississippian*, October 23, 1841.

23. Buford, N.B. "Report on the Survey of the Des Moines and Rock River Rapids, in the Mississippi River," July 12, 1829. Doc No 7, 21st Congress, 1st Session, 1829: 17; "Improvement of the Rapids." *Galena Advertiser*, 25 February 1837; Letter: Henry M. Shreve to Brigadier General C. Gratiot, Chief Engineer, Louisville, September 16, 1836. Senate Doc. #699: 892–894. 24th Congress, 2nd Session,

24. Letter: Lee, R.E. Lieutenant Engineers to Gen. C. Gratiot, Chief Engineer, St Louis, December 6, 1837; Excerpt from Report of W.H. Bell to A.G. Gano, November 23, 1840, *Territorial Papers of the United States, Territorial Papers of Iowa, 1838 – 1846*. NARA RG 156, M325, Reel # 7; Report from the Secretary of War. January 29, 1838. Senate Doc. #139. 25th Congress. 2nd Session.

25. Le Claire and Davenport to Levi C. Turner, October 31, 1837. Deed Book B, 12-13, Scott County Recorder's Records. The POA was revoked in 1840.

26. Plat of Port Byron, Deed Book A, p.81; also, Deed; Walter Phillips and wife to C.R. Bennett, August 2, 1836; Deed Book A, 83; Deed: Walter Phillips and wife to George Davenport, Deed Book B, 324. Rock Island County Recorder's Office; "Notice." *The Davenport Gazette*, 18 November 1841.

27. Deed: Rinnah Wells, Senior, and Luke Wells to John H. Sullivan and Albert Moyer, November 23, 1842, Rock Island County Deed Book E, 217.

28. "Dissolution of Partnership," Rock Island County Mortgage Book A, 384-385; "Award of Arbitration." John H. Sullivan v. Albert Moyer." September 9, 1844. Scott County District Court Book B, 485; "Camden." *Upper Mississippian*. May 22, 1845; *Journal of the Illinois State Senate*, January and February, 1843, 206, 294, 301, 303, 312, 340, 355, 368, 482 – 483; R.I. Co. deed records pertaining to Sullivan's sale of lots on Big Island.

29. Dement et al, by Sheriff to George Davenport, September 16, 1843. Rock Island County, Illinois, Deed Book F, 398 – 399; An Act to authorize …", in force February 23,1843. *Journal of the Illinois State Senate*, 46, 47; "Rock River." *Upper Mississippian*. July 20, 1844. NOTE: After some difficulty in procuring funding and a competent contractor to build it, the bridge was finally completed, but proved expensive to operate and maintain. Eventually ownership was transferred to The Rock Island and Plank Road Company in 1852 and then to the city of Rock Island in 1859. See, *Rock Island County Portrait and Biographical*, 736.

Chapter 18 – Digging Out and Digging In

1. No title. The *Upper Mississippian*, December 23, 1841.

2. Mortgage: William B. Watts to Antoine Le Claire, Date October 6,1840. Deed Book A, 299. Scott Co. Iowa Recorder's Office, Davenport, Iowa.

3. No heading. *Gazette*, Davenport, Iowa. October 13, 1842.

4. Letter: George Davenport to George L. Davenport, St. Louis, March 1, 1843, Davenport Collection. State Historical Society of Iowa, Des Moines, Iowa.

5. Letter: George Davenport to George L. Davenport, St. Louis. February 7, 1842. Davenport Collection. SHSI. On microfilm. See also, list of properties to be offered. "Tax sale." *Davenport Gazette*. January 11, 1843;"Lists of properties offered at Tax Sale," Book G, 162-163. Rock Island County Recorder's Office, Rock Island, Illinois.

6. "Award to Daniel C. Doty," April 6, 1841, and "Daniel C. Doty v. George Davenport," October Term 1841, and "Dismissal of Suit," June 20, 1842, all filed in Rock Island County Circuit Court, Rock Island, Illinois.

7. Young, John. "Interview with John Hauberg," July 19, 1916. Hauberg Collection. Rock Island County Historical Society, Rock Island, Illinois.

8. Letter: George Davenport to George L. Davenport. St. Louis, February 7, 1842. Davenport Collection, Davenport Public Library, Davenport, Iowa.

9. No title. *The Mississippian*, November 5, 1840 "Rapid Settlement of Iowa." The *Gazette*, Davenport, Iowa, October 28, 1841.

10. *The Gazette*, Davenport, Iowa. November 4, 1841, 2; "Rapid Settlement of Iowa." *The Gazette*. Davenport, Iowa. October 28, 1841.

11. *41st Annual Iowa Year Book of Agriculture*, Des Moines: Iowa State Department of Agriculture, 1940: 214-15; "40 Years Ago." The *Daily Union*, Rock Island, July 17, 1867.

12. "Land Sales at Dubuque," *Iowa Sun*, June 6, 1840

13. Advertisement. Davenport *Gazette*, 26 August 1841.

14. *Iowa Sun*, 13 October 1839.

15. Davenport *Gazette*, Sept. 2, 1841.

16. October Term, A.D. 1842. "In Chancery. George Davenport, James May, Thomas F. Smith, William Gordon, Alexander W. McGregor, Levi S. Colton, and Antoine Le Claire, Complainants vs. Neil Cameron, defendant." February 16, 1843. *The Davenport Gazette;* Scott County District Ct Records B, 526 on microfilm, Special Collections. Davenport Public Library, Davenport, Iowa.

17. October Term, A.D. October 1841. "In Chancery. George Davenport and Antoine Le Claire vs James K. Goodwin," *The Davenport Gazette*, December 16 and 23, 1841 Scott County, Iowa, District Ct Records B, 231 -232. April 9, 1842 on microfilm, Special Collections. Davenport Public Library. Davenport, Iowa.

18. October Term, A.D. 1841. "In Chancery. George Davenport and Antoine Le Claire vs William E. McLellan," The *Davenport Gazette,* December 16 and 23, 1841; Scott County District Ct Records B, 233, April 9, 1842. on microfilm Special Collections. Davenport Public Library, Davenport, Iowa.

19. Barrows, Willard. "History of Scott County, Iowa." *Annals of the State Historical Society of Iowa*. Iowa City, Iowa: Jerome & Duncan, 1863. 65, 72; "Died." *Iowa Sun*. September 26, 1840

20. "Administrator's Sale." *Iowa Sun*. November 26, 1840 and "Terms of Sale." *Iowa Sun*. November 18, 1840. Scott County, Ia., Court of Probate, 24th May 1841, Book A, 211, on microfilm. Special Collections. Davenport Public Library. Davenport, Iowa.

21. Case #423. "George Davenport vs. Gershom Biddle and Elizabeth Nichols." Scott County Circuit Court records, on microfilm, Special Collections, Davenport Public Library, Davenport, Iowa.

22. "People of the State of Illinois vs. George Davenport, Michael Bartlett, and Joel Wells Jr." September 1839 through May 1843. Rock Island County Civil Suits; also, "People for the use of Rock Island County v. Davenport et al," May 1843, and "Davenport et al vs. People of the State of Illinois, Appeal. Illinois Supreme Court." December 1843. File # L02364. Lincoln Legal Papers, Illinois State Archives, Springfield, Illinois.

23. Stambaugh, Samuel C. "Iowa Copper Mines." *Niles Weekly Register*, January 14, 1837; Case #429: "Alexander Hunter, Marshall of the District of Columbia vs John D. Ansley, Jno P. Sheldon, George Davenport and Samuel C. Stambaugh," September 9, 1844. Scott County District Court Book B, 482.

24. Scott County Case # 627 and # 579, Microfilm Reel No. 1851924. Note: thank you to Judge D. Hobart Darbyshire for help deciphering this case.

25. Stambaugh, Samuel C. "Iowa Copper Mines." *Niles Weekly Register*, January 14, 1837; Case #429: "Alexander Hunter, Marshall of the District of Columbia vs John D. Ansley, Jno P. Sheldon, George Davenport and Samuel C. Stambaugh," September 9, 1844. Scott County District Court Book B, 482.

26. Scott County Case # 627 and # 579, Microfilm Reel No. 1851924. Note: thank you to Judge D. Hobart Darbyshire for help deciphering this case.

27. "In the Matter of Partition." Jo Daviess Circuit Court Record Book C, 1834 – 1848: 172, 373-374, 379 -380. Also Book E, p. 179; "George Davenport, James Bennett, Horatio Newhall, John Bolles, and Charles Farnham, appellants v. Sophia Farrar, appellee. Appeal from Jo Daviess." December Term, 1836. Scammon, J Young. *Ed. Cases Argued and Determined in the Supreme Court of State of Illinois*, Vol. 2, St. Louis, 1870: 314 – 317; Letter: Alexander Hamilton to Peter Chouteau Jr., March 29, 1838, Chouteau-Papin Collection; "George Davenport, appellant, v. Hezekiah H. Gear, administrator, and Sophia Farrar, administratix of the estate of Amos Farrar, deceased." December Term, 1840. Scammon. *Illinois Reports*, Vol. 3: 495 – 499; "Sophia Farrar, Administratix of Estate of Amos Farrar, Deceased, v. George Davenport et al," May 5, 1845, Rock Island County Circuit Court Documents.

Chapter 19 – Wrapping Up the Indian Trade

1. Letter: Davenport, George to C.A. Harris, Commissioner of Indian Affairs, Sept 14, 1838, National Archives and Records Administration, M234, Reel # 730, Letters Rec'd by OIA, 1824 – 1881, Sac and Fox Agency.

2. Sac Outfit 1836, Volume Y: Invoices Outward. Reel 8. also, Pierre Chouteau Jr. & Co. February 1834 - October 1839 and Volume BB: Ledger Pierre Chouteau Jr. & Co., 1839 - 1842, Reel 8. Fur Trade Papers, Missouri Historical Society, St. Louis; also, Kurtz, Royce Delbert. *Economic and Political History of the Sauk and Mesquakie, 1780s - 1845,* unpublished dissertation. University of Iowa, 1986: 31 -34; Letter: Davenport to C.A. Harris, September14, 1838.

3. Letter: Joseph M. Street, to Governor Henry Dodge, Rock Island, 27 August 1837. *Territorial Papers of the US, Territory of Wisconsin, 1836 - 1839*, compiled by John Porter Bloom. Vol XXVII: 841 – 843; "Communication." George Davenport to editor. Dated August 10, 1837. Published August 19, 1837 and "The Indians." September 9, 1837. *NW Gazette and Galena Advertiser.*

4. Viola, Herman J. *Diplomats in Bucksins: A History of Indian Delegations in Washington City.* Washington, D.C.: Smithsonian Institution Press, 1981; Kappler, Charles J. compiler and editor. "Treaty with the Sauk and Foxes," Held at Washington City, 21ˢᵗ October 1837, *Indian Affairs: Laws and Treaties.* Volume II. Washington: Government Printing Office, 1904: 495–496.

5. Hagan, William T. *The Sac and Fox Indians*, Norman: University of Oklahoma Press, 1980: 205–206 and 220 – 221.

6. Green, Michael D. "The Sac-Fox Annuity Crisis of 1840 in Iowa Territory." *Arizona and the West.* 16(Summer 1974): 14–156.

7. Green, p. 155; "Treaty at Sac & Fox Agency." October 15, 1841. 27 Cong. 2 Sess. Senate Document. pp. 270 - 75; *Burlington Hawkeye & Iowa Patriot.* October 21, 28, 1841; "The Treaty." *Davenport Gazette*, October 20, 1842.

8. Sauk and Fox Treaty of 1842, October 11, 1842. Kappler. 546, 549; Annual Report of T. Hartley Crawford. November 25 1843. 25th Cong. 1 Sess. House Ex. Docs. Serial 439: 271.

9. Hagan, 221.

10. "The Treaty." *Davenport Gazette*, 20 October 1842; Davenport *Gazette*, January 25, 1844.

11. Cash book, Pierre Chouteau Jr. & Co., 1842-1846. Volume HH: Reel 10. Fur Trade Papers, Missouri Historical Society; Wilkie, 163; also, Davenport *Gazette*, October 13,1842: 2.

12. "Treaty at Sac & Fox Agency." *The Gazette*, October 28, 1841; Treaty at Sac & Fox Agency, 27th Congress, 2 Session. Senate Document 270-275.

Chapter 20 – Frontier Is Passing

1. Deed: Margaret and George Davenport to Bailey Davenport, Rock Island County Deed Book F, 148.

2. Deed: George Davenport to Stickney, Benjamin, Rock Island County Recorder's Deed Book E, 301- 302.

3. Davenport *Gazette*, 30 March 1843; Letter: George Davenport to George L. Davenport, St. Louis, March 30, 1843, Davenport Collection, State Historical Society of Iowa, Des Moines, Iowa; Letter: Benjamin Clapp to Pierre Chouteau Sen, Esq., March 23, 1843, P. Chouteau-Maffitt Collection, Missouri Historical Society, St. Louis, Missouri; Letter George Davenport to The Commissioner of General Land Office in Washington City, St. Louis, April 3, 1843. On microfilm. Davenport Collection. State Historical Society of Iowa.

4. "Rock Island Improvements." *Iowa Sun*, August 23, 1841.

5. Letter: Davenport to the Commissioners of the Government Land Office.

6. The Davenport *Gazette*, March 10, 1842.

7. Letter: George Davenport to Commissioners of the Government Land Office. Note: A copy of the original bill Is in the Davenport Family Scrapbook, Davenport Collection, State Historical Society of Iowa, Des Moines, Iowa; also, "Notice to Pre-Emption Claimants," Davenport *Gazette*, June 23, 1843.

8. "List of Private Claims Presented to the House of Representatives of the United States from the 1st to the 31st Congress, Inclusive," U. S. Congress, American State Papers, Class IX (1834, Omaha: Nebraska *Journal of Genealogy*, Vol. 4, Nos. 6 – 9, 1979; also, Davenport *Gazette*. May 16, 1844.

9. "Rock Island and the Rock River Country." *Upper Mississippian*, August 14, 1845.

10. "An Act to vacate the town of Rock Island City." February 20, 1843. *Laws of the State of Illinois passed by the Thirteenth General Assembly*, Springfield: Walters and Weber, 1843: 299.

11. Neilson, Chris. "The Life of Anthony Cooley." unpublished mnss. 1958, Kalamazoo Public Library, Kalamazoo, Michigan.

12. "Letters from the West. Number Five." *Upper Mississippian*. February 11, 1841.

13. Rock Island County Deed Book A, 206 - 209 and Book C, 181, and 184, Deed Book D, 200 - 204, 213 and Mortgage Book A, 75 -77 and 206 – 209; the November 5, 1840, issue of *The Upper Mississippian* carried several articles written by Mr. Wentworth of the *Chicago Democrat* that give a broad view of the development of the area.

14. "The New Purchase." Davenport *Gazette*, May 11, 1843.

15. *Iowa Sun*, May 1, 1841.

16. There are many stories that tell of pioneer experiences with wolves. Rock Island County Pioneer Archie Allen wrote that he and his wife often killed their hogs by the river's edge. One time they watched as 15 wolves gathered to eat the offal. Another time he had been given 24 chickens for which he had built a small house with a door about two feet off the ground. One evening when he was gone until nine o'clock he returned to find a wolf had been there and killed twenty of the hens Most frightening was the call of wolves heard throughout the night and many pioneers recalled times when as children they lay awake at night in fear of what those wolves might do. Only the Wells family seemed to enjoy the wolf. Stories were told of Joel Wells Sr. who was a great horseman and
used to hunt wolves on horseback for sport. He and David B. Sears would ride across the country on their thoroughbred horses, jumping fences, dashing down banks, all in the pursuit of wolves. Davenport Gazette, Jan 1843; "Circular Wolf-Hunt." *Upper Mississippian and Rock Island Republican*, 6 March 1845; Hauberg Interviews with David Sears and with Archie Allen, 1875, Hauberg Collection, Rock Island County Historical Society.

17. "Valuable Lands for Sale." *The Upper Mississippian*, April 1, 1841; "Steam Boilers for Sale." *The Upper Mississippian*, April 13, 1841; "Affairs in Cincinnati," The *Upper Mississippian,* April 14, 1842; "Steam Mills at Davenport, Iowa." *The Upper Mississippian*, April 15, 1841.

18. "Davenport*." Upper Mississippian*, February 11,1841.

19. "Extensive Sale of Town Lots*, " Iowa Sun*, February 13, 1841.

20. John Thorington was elected mayor. Frazier Wilson was elected Recorder. The Trustees for the town were Seth Whiting, J.W. Parker, John Forrest, William Nichols, and George L. Davenport.

21. Sheriff to Davenport, George L. and James Bowling, Scott County, Iowa, Deed Book C, 29-30, on microfilm, Davenport Public Library, Davenport, Iowa; also, "Davenport," *Davenport Gazette*. December 16, 1841.

22. Advertisement. *Iowa Sun*, May 1841.

23. Fulton, Ambrose Cowperthwaite. *A Life's Voyage*. New York:The Author, 1898: 122.

Chapter 21 – The Iron Horse

1. Crumrin, Timothy. Road Through Wilderness: The Making of the National Road. 1994. Available on-line: http://www.connerprairie.org/Learn-And-Do/Indiana-History/America-1800-1860/The-National-Road.aspx

2. Reynolds, Governor John. Address to the People of Illinois (1830 State of the Union Address), January 4, 1830, The Galena Advertiser, Galena, Illinois; Letter signed CHICA: "Canals & Railways. To the People of Illinois." Galena Advertiser, March 22, 1830.

3. Redfield, W.C. Sketch of the Geographical Rout(sic) of a Great Railway, New York . G. & C .& H. Carvill1830; George Armroyd. A Connected View of the Whole Internal Navigation of the United States. Philadelphia: Lydia R. Bailey, 1830.

4. Nicewarner, Gladys Bull. Michigan City, Indiana: The Life of a Town, Michigan City, Indiana: Whipporwill, 1980, 46; "Petition Presented, January 16, 1832. Journal of the House of Representatives of the Unites States 22 Congress, 1st Session, 192. http://memory.loc.gov/cgi-bin/query/r?ammem/hlaw:@field(DOCID+@lit(hj02529)).

5. "Davenport." Iowa Sun. January 22, 1840.

6.Fulton, A. C. A Life's Voyage. Nee York: Published by author, 1898: 448-449; Davenport Daily Times, January 24, 1898; Also, "Demise of A.C. Fulton." Davenport Republican. October 17, 1903.

7. Fulton also made the first survey for the Milwaukee & St. Paul, and the Davenport, Iowa, & Dakota which later became the Burlington, Cedar Rapids, & Northern Railroad. See, "Demise," October 17, 1903.

8. NOTE: Galena to the mouth of Ohio, from Alton to Shawneetown, from Alton to Mount Carmel, from Alton to the eastern boundary of the state towards Terre Haute, from Quincy through Springfield and on to the Wabash River, from Bloomington to Pekin, and from Peoria to Warsaw. McGrane, Reginald.The Panic of 1837, Chicago: University of Chicago Press, 1924: 31; Krenkel, John H. Illinois Internal Improvements, 1818-1848. Cedar Rapids, Iowa: The Torch Press, 1958: 202.

9. "Moline." Davenport Gazette, October 26, 1843; also, "Moline, Ill." The Davenport Gazette, September 4, 1845.

10. Hon. John King. "John Plumbe Originator of the Pacific Railroad." Annals of Iowa. Vol VI, Third Series, Vol. 4: 289–296.

11. Whitney, A. "The Oregon Rail Road." Letter written 22 September 1845 and printed in The Upper Mississippian and Rock-Island Republican. October 23, 1845.

12. "Demise of A.C. Fulton." Davenport Republican, October 17,1903.

13. Price, Hiram. "Recollections of Iowa Men and Affairs." Annals of Iowa, Volume One, April 1893: 13.

14. Deed: George Davenport, by George L. Davenport, executor, to James Eads, August 1845, Scott Deed Book D, 389. On microfilm. Davenport Public Library, Davenport, Iowa.

15. "Valuable Land for Sale." Upper Mississippian, September 4, 1845.

16. Tax Sales in RIC, various deeds in Rock Island Deed Books D and F. Rock Island County Recorder's Office, Rock Island, Illinois.

17. Henry McNeal Preemption Claim #3649, Galena Land Office, National Archives and Record Administration, Record Group #49, Records of Land Management; Deed: McNeal to Charles Hempstead, Deed Book F, 318, Rock Island County Recorder's Office; Deed: Hempstead to George Davenport, Deed Book A, 35, Rock Island County Recorder's Office, Rock Island, Illinois.

18. Lease: George Davenport to H & M Powars, Deed Book C, 92-93; Deed Book F, 148-151; Deed Book F, 457, Rock Island County Recorder's Office, Rock Island, Illinois.

19. McNeal Patent #480 issued February 15, 1844, Book E, 460; McNeal to Babcock, August 13, 1844, Deed Book F, 131; McNeal to Belcher, 8 Feb 1844. Book E, 461; McNeal to Andrews, Feb 8, 1844, Deed Book E, 462, all in Rock Island County Recorder's Office, Rock Island, Illinois.

19. Deed: Belcher to Davenport; Andrews and wife to George Davenport; and Babcock to Davenport, Deed Book F, 350, 351, 352. Rock Island County Recorder's Office., Rock Island, Illinois.

20. Gazette, May 16, 1844.

21. Gazette, December 18, 1845.

22. Krenkel, 9-10.

23. Shambaugh, Benjamin, Old Stone Capitol Remembers. Iowa City, Iowa: State Historical Society of Iowa, 1939, 379; Rock Island Advertiser, December 1, 1853 and February 9, 1853.

Chapter 22 – Seduced By The Devil

1. "Our Town," *Davenport Gazette*, February 20, 1845; "Trip Through the Country," *Davenport Gazette*, May 15, 1845.

2. "Fire," *Davenport Gazette*, May 15, 1845; "Removal of Munitions." *Davenport Gazette*, June 5, 1845.

3. Sanders, Alfred. "Our Town," *Davenport Gazette*, February 20, 1845; also, Sanders, Alfred. "Weekly Gossip," *Davenport Gazette*, May 15, 1845.

4. Sanders, Alfred. "Weekly Gossip," *Davenport Gazette*, July 3, 1845.

5. Holt, Orrin S. "The Fourth of July Celebration," *Moline Daily Dispatch*, April 12, 1916.

6. *History of Scott County, Iowa*. Chicago: Inter-state Publishing Co., 1882: 969.

7. "Another Witness," *Davenport Democrat*, August 5, 1901.

8. Today his death would be attributed to shock, loss of blood, complicated by the beating and his advanced age.

9. *The Davenport Gazette*, issues dated July 10, 17, 24, 31, 1845.

10. Hauberg interview of Mrs. Mary McKown, Hauberg Collection. Notebook 17, Box 58. Special Collections, Tredway Library, Augustana College, Rock Island, Illinois.

11. Joseph and Hiram Smith had been murdered the previous year and the Mormons were preparing to move west. *Bible of Susan Lewis*. Rock Island County Historical Society, Moline, Illinois.

12. Hauberg Interview with Ellen Lloyd Lynch, Hauberg Collection, Rocks Island County Historical Society, Moline, Illinois.

13. Sanders, Addison. "An Indian Ceremony." *Davenport Gazette,* July 31, 1845; Sanders, Addison H. "Davenport in the Forties: When the Up-River Country Was Wilderness," *The Half-Century Democrat*, October 22, 1905: 47; *Davenport Gazette*, July 31, 1845; A clipping of this article also appears in Susan Lewis' bible.

14. Letter: Joseph Knox to E. Bonney, August 6, 1845, handwritten manuscript believed to be Edward Bonney's draft of *Banditti of the Prairie*. Ellison Manuscripts. Lilly Library. University of Indiana, Bloomington, Indiana.

15. For Bonney's Account of the search, see Bonney, Edward. *Banditti of the Prairie*. Norman: University of Oklahoma Press, 1963; "No Cure, No Pay," *Upper Mississippian*, September 14, 1844.

16. Records of the Town of Rock Island, Book 2, April 6, 1841-November 2, 1845, City Hall, Rock Island, Illinois.

17. "Indictment for Murder." filed October 11,1845, Rock Island County Circuit Court, Rock Island, Illinois.

18. Bonney, Edward. *Banditti of the Prairie*; also, untitled article, October 14, 1845, *Upper Mississippian and Rock Island Republican*.

19. "Execution of John Long, Aaron Long, and Granville Young." October 30, 1845, *The Upper Mississippian & Rock Island Republican*.

20. Untitled articles, December 18, 1845 and January 23, 1846, *Davenport Gazette*.

21."A Few Matters Connected With Execution of the Murderers," November 14, 1845, *Davenport Gazette*.

22. "Edward Bonney." Wilson, James Grant, and John Fiske eds. *Appleton's Cyclopaedia of American Biography*, Vol. VII. New York: D. Appleton, 1900: 29.

Epilogue

1. Rock Island County Supervisor's Record Book C, 126, 133, 134, 140, Rock Island County Clerk's Office, Rock Island, Illinois.

2. "Reminiscences of Early Days in This County." October 26, 1877, Rock Island *Argus*.

3. Downer, 648; "Harry Davenport, Pioneer Indian, Grandson of Col. George Davenport is Dead," September 16, 1928, *Davenport Democrat and Leader*.

4. *Davenport Gazette*, August 26, 1847; Last Will and Testimony of Naomi L'Oste, Scott County Probate file # 11633, September 16, 1920, on-microfilm, Davenport Public Library; Late Will and Testament of George Davenport, October 1844, Rock Island County Probate, Rock Island, Illinois.

5. *Davenport Gazette*, June 28, 1849.

6. Hauberg interview with David Sears, November 5, 1917, Hauberg Collection; Records: October 14, 1841 – November 4, 1867," Trinity Episcopalian Church, Davenport, Iowa.

7. "Trust Agreement between Zachariah Goldsmith, Susan M. Lewis, and George L. Davenport," June 15, 1849, Rock Island County Deed Records, Rock Island, Illinois;

8. MacDonald and Mack Partnership. "Colonel George Davenport House: Architectural Report," unpublished report, July 15, 1985, in files of Colonel Davenport Historical Foundation.

9. Church Documents in possession of author.

10. Lot #3, Block 46; Lot 8, Block 8; Lot 10, Block 50; Lot 6, Block 11; Lot 11, Block 14. Rock Island County Deed #414, 8 August 8, 1850, Rock Island County Record; "An Old Citizen Gone," August 10, 1854, *Davenport Gazette.*

11. Seventh Federal Population Census (1850), Rock Island County, and Scott County, Iowa.

12. Marriage record of Nicholas Ferkle to Elizabeth Dumboth(sic), March 5, 1852. Monroe County Clerk's Records, Waterloo, IL; Rock Island Circuit Court Bill #3265.

13. "Susan Lewis Goldsmith Household Account Book," restored manuscript, Rock Island County Historical Society.

14. "Trinity (Episcopal) Church," *The Past and Present of R.I. County, Illinois. Chicago:* H.F. Kett & Co., 1877: 169.

15. *Annals of Iowa*, 118-125.

16. Nothstein, 78.

17. Nothstein, 79-80.

18. "Settlement of Rock Island," C.T. Church, unpublished mnss in Phil Mitchell's Notebook, #110, Box 49-2, Hauberg Collection, Tredway Library, Augustana College.

19. Untitled article, July 9, 1856, *The Rock Island Advertiser*; April 3, 1858, *Davenport Democrat.*

18. "Old Times, And Now," July 17, 1858, *Port Byron Messenger.*

20. Nothstein, 88.

21. Rock Island County Deed Book G, September 2, 1845: 233, Recorder's Office, Rock Island County Courthouse, Rock Island, Illinois.

22. Letter: Lewis Gokey to Enoch Hoag, July 15, 1879, Hoag Indian Papers, Haverford College Library, Haverford, Pennsylvania.

Bibliography

Archives and Manuscript Collections

Abraham Lincoln Presidential Library, Springfield, Illinois
Lincoln Legal Papers – Appeal of Davenport, et al.

Beinicke Rare Books and Manuscripts Library, Yale University, New Haven, CT
Western Americana Collection – Amos Farrar Letters.

Chicago Historical Society, Chicago, Illinois
William Clark Papers.

Colonel Davenport Historical Foundation, Rock Island, Illinois
Marston, Major Morrell "Extract from Report to Major General Macomb,"
September 10, 1819, photocopy.
HABS No. IL – 158: The Davenport House, Rock Island, Illinois." Historic
American Buildings Survey, Library of Congress, Prints and Photographs
Division, Washington, D.C.
Bruzewicz, "A Color Infra-Red Photographic Reconnaissance of the
Davenport   House and Its Surroundings, " unpublished report, June 1989
Gleason, George. "Architectural Summary." Unpublished report, August
1987.
Lange, Frederick W. "Test Excavations at the Colonel Davenport House,
Arsenal Island, Illinois," unpublished report, August 8, 1983.

Naglich, Dennis, and Mary Jo Cramer. "Davenport House Site, 2003

Archaeological Investigations," Report # 267. March 2004.
MacDonald and Mack Partnership. "Colonel George Davenport House:
Architectural Report," unpublished report, July 15, 1985.

Davenport Public Library, Special Collections
Scott County District Court Records, on microfilm.
Davenport Collection, on microfilm.
Church records, St. Anthony Catholic Church, Davenport, Iowa, on
microfilm.
Territorial Papers of Iowa, 1838 – 1846, M721, Roll # 7, containing Bell
Report from RG 156: Records of Office of Chief of Ordinance.
Letters Received .

Detroit Public Library, Detroit, Michigan
Burton Historical Collection --"Garrison Orderly Book, Fifth Infantry.
Josiah Snelling Papers.

Haverford College Library, Haverford, Pennsylvania
Hoag Indian Papers -- Lewis Gokey letter.

Illinois Regional Archives Division at Western Illinois University Archives, Macomb

Marston Estate Packet, Hancock County, Illinois.
Palen Estate Packet, Hancock County, Illinois.

Illinois State Archives, Springfield, Illinois
Calendar. Official Bond – Indian Traders.
RG 953.001,Letters to the Surveyor General from the Public, 1834 - 1835.
U.S. Surveyors Records for Illinois, Incoming Correspondence, Ca 1816 –
1862.
Letter: John Dixon to The Honorable James W. Stephenson, Commissioner
of
Public Works for the Sixth Judicial District, Engineer's Office, May 15th
1838, in Illinois Record Book and Report 1837 - 1841. Auditor of
Public Accounts. Springfield, Illinois. p.292-293.
Letter: James Seymour to The Honorable the Board of Public Works, State of
Illinois. Chicago, November 26, 1837. Senate Doc. #259. *Documents in
Relation to Internal Improvements, in the State of Illinois, March 5,
1838.* 25th Congress, 2nd Session.

Kalamazoo Public Library, Kalamazoo, Michigan
Neilson, Chris. "The Life of Anthony Cooley."

Kansas State Historical Society
Records of the Superintendency of Indian Affairs at St. Louis -- William
Clark
Papers.
Library of Congress, Washington, D.C.
Henry Clay Papers – James Morrison Papers

Lilly Library, University of Indiana, Bloomington, Indiana
Ellison Manuscripts -- Edward Bonney's draft of *Banditti of the Prairie*

Lincolnshire County Historical Library, Lincoln, Lincolnshire, England
Lindsey Quarter Session Land Tax Records.
Wills of King and L'Oste Families.

Louth, Lincolnshire, England
St. James Church Records

Minnesota Historical Society, Minneapolis, Minnesota.
John Connolly Papers.
Henry Sibley Papers.

Missouri Historical Society, St. Louis, Missouri
Abert Family Papers .
American Fur Company Letterbook, Ramsey Crooks,
Chouteau Collection.
Pierre Chouteau-Maffitt Collection.
Chouteau-Papin Collection.
Tesson Collection – Forsyth Papers.
Richard Graham papers.
Daniel G. Bissell Papers.
National Archives and Records Administration

RG 29, Records of the Bureau of Census,
   Seventh Federal Population Census (1850), Rock Island County, and Scott
County, Iowa.
   Sixth Federal Population Census (1840), Rock Island County, Illinois.
RG 49, Pre emption Claim by Antoine Le Claire, Dubuque Land Office
   Records.
RG 75, Letters Received by the Office of the Supt of Indian Trade, 1806 –
   1824, Microfilm T58.
RG 75. Office of Indian Affairs, Records Pertaining to Factory at Fort
   Edwards. Transcript of the Journal of the United States Factory at Fort
   Edwards for the Quarter Ending Thirty-first day of March, 1821."
RG 75, Office of Indian Affairs, Prairie du Chien Indian Agency 1824 - 1842.
   M234, Reel #696.
RG 75, Letters Received by OIA, Sac & Fox Indian Agency, 1824 – 1880, Reel
   #728.
RG 92, Fort Armstrong Consolidated Correspondence File.
RG 92, Quartermaster General, Consolidated Correspondence File.
RG 98, Records of U.S. Army Continental Commands, 1784 – 1821, James
   Wilkinson, James. General Order Book, M654, Reel 3.
RG 98, Records of U.S. Army Commands, 1789 – 1821, Company Books, Fort
   · Adams, November 1807 - October 1808.
RG 98, Records of U.S. Army Commands, 1789 – 1821, Company Books
   Company Book of Captain Simon Owens of the First Infantry, 1810 – 1814.
RG 107, Letters Sent by the Secretary of War Relating to Military Affairs,
   1800 - 1889,M6, Roll 17.
RG 153. Records of the Office of the Judge Advocate General (Army), Trial of
   Captain Peter Pelham, W15, Court Martial Case Files, 1809 – 1894.
RG 156, Territorial Papers of the United States, Territorial Papers of Iowa,
   1838 – 1846M325, Reel # 7.
RG 217, Settled Paymaster Accounts, Military Pay Records.
RG 393, Department of War, Letters Sent, Pt 1, 1825 - 26, 3 of 12, Entry
   #5568.

Newberry Library, Chicago, Illinois
   Ayer Collection.
   Graft Collection.

P.K. Yonge Library of Florida History, University of Florida
   William Davenport Papers.

Public Record Office, Kew, London, England
   Correspondence of Alexander and Stephen Shairp.
   "Claims Not Yet Accepted by the Russian Government, but Settled by the
   Commissioners to be Recommended." 31 October 1802. Class
   FO65/51 and Class FO65/47 - 48.

Putnam Museum, Davenport, Iowa
   Le Claire Papers,
   George Parker Collection, Putnam Museum, Davenport, Iowa.

Rock Island Arsenal Museum Archives, Rock Island, Illinois.
   Ft. Armstrong Weather Diary.

Fort Armstrong Post Returns, photographic copy.
William Dickson memoir, "A Few Short Sketches of My Eventful Life."

Rock Island Arsenal, National Cemetery, Rock Island, Illinois
Fort Armstrong Post Cemetery records.

Rock Island County Historical Society , Rock Island, Illinois
Hauberg interviews, Hauberg Collection,
Hauberg, John. "Rock Island County Sawmills."
Field Notes for Township 18 North, Ranges 2 and 3 West of the 4th Principal
Meridian.
George Davenport 1828 Day Book.
Susan Lewis Goldsmith Account Book.
Susan Lewis Goldsmith's Bible.

State Historical Society of Iowa, Division of History and Archives, Des Moines, Iowa
George L. Davenport Collection.

State Historical Society of Wisconsin, Madison, Wisconsin
American Fur Company Papers -- Crooks-Stuart Letterbook, 1816 -1820.
AFC Northern Dept. Michilimackinac Vol. 2,
Draper Manuscript Collection (Symmes Papers and Thomas Forsyth Papers)
Stock Transcripts.

The Learned T. Bulman '48 Historic Archives and Museum, Washington-Jefferson
College, Washington, Pennsylvania.
Cyrus Dickson File.

Thomas Tredway Library, Augustana College, Rock Island, Illinois.
Hauberg Collection.

Univ. of Illinois, Champaign, Illinois, Illinois Historical Survey
Bryan and Morrison Ledgers, Kaskaskia Ledger D (1805 - 1831)
Daybook # 23.

University of Missouri – Columbia
Western Historical Manuscript Collection --Thomas Adams Smith
Collection.

University of Rochester Library, Rochester, New York
E.G. Munn Papers.

W.H. Smith Memorial Library, Indiana Historical Society, Indianapolis, Indiana
Henry Swearingen Letter.

Haverford College Library, Haverford, Pennsylvania
Hoag Indian Papers. Letter: Lewis Gokey to Enoch Hoag, July 15, 1879.

Congressional Records

S. 74. A Bill To Enable the President to carry into effect March 18, 1824.

18ᵗʰ Congress, 1ˢᵗ Session.

Documents Pertaining to Internal Improvements in the State of Illinois, March 5, 1838, Senate Document 259, 25ᵗʰ Congress, 2ⁿᵈ Session,

Petition of George Davenport to House of Representatives, April 13, 1838, Executive Document No. 331, 25 Congress 2 Session. Volume X: 1-2,

Petition of George Davenport to House of Representatives, January 30, 1832. 22ⁿᵈ Congress, 1ˢᵗ Session, p. 192; also, Bill #337, 22 Congress, 1st Session: 337,

Letter of George Davenport to the President, Senate Document 512, 23rd Congress, 1st Session, Volume 9:221-223.

Report from the Secretary of War in Relation to Rock River and Des Moines Rapids on the Mississippi River. January 29, 1838. Senate Document 139, 25ᵗʰ Congress, 2ⁿᵈ Session: 1-38.

H. R. Bill 189. A Bill for the Better Regulation of Trade and Intercourse with the Indian Tribes. March 29, 1826. 19th Congress, 1st Session.

Rock Island Council with Sac and Fox, September 5, 1831, in Report of the Indian Bureau, November 19, 1831, 22 Congress, 1 Session. Senate Ex. Doc. No. 2, Vol. 1, Serial 216:202-204.

Buford, N.B. "Report on the Survey of the Des Moines and Rock River Rapids, in the Mississippi River," July 12, 1829. House Document 7, 21st Congress, 1st Session, 1829:17.

Letter: Henry M. Shreve to Brigadier General C. Gratiot, Chief Engineer, Louisville, September 16, 1836. 24th Congress, 2nd Session, Senate Document 699:892 – 894.

Annual Report of T. Harley Crawford, Commissioner of Indian Affairs, November 25, 1843. 28ᵗʰ Congress. 1ˢᵗ Session. House Executive Documents. Serial 439:271.

County Governmental Sources

Deed Records of Hancock, Fulton, Adams, Pike, Henderson, Jo Daviess, Madison, Mercer, McDonough, and Rock Island Counties, Illinois and Scott County, Iowa.

Plat Books, of Rock Island County, Recorder's Office.

Marriage Records, Monroe County Clerk's Records, Waterloo, IL

Marriage records, St. Francis Catholic Church, Portage des Sioux, LDS Church

microfilm. FHC #1940845.

Rock Island County Circuit Court Records, Rock Island, Illinois.

Rock Island County Commissioners' Records.

Dissertations

Gillson, Gordon E. The Development of a Military Frontier: The Story of Fort Adams and its Hinterland. Unpublished M.A. Thesis, Louisiana State University, 1954.

Johnston, Oda B. History of Fort Armstrong, 1816 - 1836. Unpublished M.A. Thesis, University of Iowa, 1940.

Haeger, John. Western Town Growth: A Study of the Development of Towns on the Western Shore of Lake Michigan, 1815 – 1843. Unpublished dissertation, Loyola University, 1969.

Kurtz, Royce. Economic and Political History of the Sauk and Mesquakie: 1780s-1845. Unpublished dissertation, University of Iowa, 1986.

Silton, Graham Stanley. Life of the Enlisted Soldier on the Western Frontier, 1815-1845. Unpublished Dissertation. North Texas State University, 1972.

Tevebaugh, J.L. Merchant on the Western Frontier: William Morrison of Kakskaskia, 1790 - 1837. Unpublished dissertation, University of Illinois, 1962.

Newspapers

American Railroad Journal, New York City
Argus, Rock Island, Illinois
Burlington Hawkeye & Iowa Patriot, Burlington, Iowa
Cincinnati Daily Gazette, Cincinnati, Ohio
Daily Democrat, Davenport, Iowa
Daily Dispatch, Moline, Illinois,
Daily Union, Rock Island, Illinois
Davenport Times, Davenport, Iowa
Davenport Republican, Davenport, Iowa
Davenport Sunday Democrat, Davenport, Iowa
Davenport Democrat and Leader, Davenport, Iowa
Galenian, Galena, Illinois
Illinois Advocate, Edwardsville, Illinois
Iowa Sun and Davenport-Rock Island News
Iowa Territorial Gazette, Burlington, Iowa
Milan Weekly Independent, Milan, Illinois
Miner's Journal, Galena, Illinois
Missouri Gazette, St. Louis, Missouri
Missouri Republican, St. Louis, Missouri
Niles Register, Baltimore, Maryland
NW Advertiser and Galena Gazette, Galena, Illinois
Otsego Republican, Cooperstown, New York
Patriot, Ft. Madison, Iowa
Peoria Register and North-western Gazetteer, Peoria, Illinois
Rock Island Banner and Stephenson Gazette, Rock Island, Illinois
St. Louis Enquirer, St. Louis, Missouri
Upper Mississippian and Rock Island Republican, Rock Island, Illinois
Western Gazette and Galena Advertiser, Galena, Illinois
Western Intelligencer, Kaskaskia, Illinois Territory, Nov. 6, 1817. printed in Early
        Kaskaskia, Illinois, Newspapers, 1814 -1832 by Lola Frazer Crowder.
Frontier
        Press, Galveston, Texas, 1994
Western Observer, Jacksonville, Illinois
Western Voice, Shawneetown, Illinois

Published Sources

Allaman, John Lee. "The 1831 Probate Inventories of Daniel Harris and Morrill Marston: Early Documents of Warren and Hancock Counties," *Western Illinois Regional Studies*, Vol. XIV, Spring 1991, No.1.

"An Act to Establish the County Seat of Rock Island County." *Laws of the State of Illinois, Ninth General Assembly, 1st Session.* Vandalia: Sawyer, Public Printers, 1835, pp. 159 – 160.

Anderson, Mrs. K.T., "some Reminiscences of Pioneer Rock Island Women," *Transactions of the Illinois State Historical Society*, 17(1912).

Appleton's Cyclopaedia of American Biography, Vol. VII, New York: D. Appleton, 1900.

Armroyd, George. *A Connected View of the Whole Internal Navigation of the United States.* Philadelphia: Lydia R. Bailey, 1830.

Atlas of Indian Villages of the Illinois Country, 1670-1830, Springfield, IL: Illinois State Museum.

Atwater, Caleb. *Remarks Made on a Tour to Prairie du Chien: thence to Washington City in 1829*, New York: Arno Press, 1975.

Baldwin, Leland D. *Keelboat Age on Western Waters.* Pittsburgh: University of Pittsburgh Press, 1941.

Barrows, Willard. "History of Scott County, Iowa." *Annals of Iowa*, Iowa City, Iowa: Jerome & Duncan, January 1863.

Beckwith, Ian, ed. and comp. *The Louth Riverhead, a case study of the development of an industrial and commercial quarter in a LIncolnshire Market Town in the period 1750 -1850.* Published by Louth WEA Branch, 1976.

Beltrami, Giacomo. *A Pilgrimage in America.* Chicago: Quadrangle Books, 1962.

Bickel, R.J. "'Rat Row' in Keokuk," *Annals of Iowa.* 3(1956).

Black Hawk, *Black Hawk: An Autobiography of Black Hawk*, ed. Donald Jackson, Urbana: University of Illinois Press, 1964.

Blair, Emma, ed., *Indian Tribes of Upper Mississippi Valley and Region* of the Great Lakes, New York: Kraus Reprint Co., 1969.

Bloom, John Porter, ed. *Territorial Papers of the United States*, Vol 27 Territory of Wisconsin, Executive Journal, 1836 - 1848. Washington, D.C.: National Archives, 1969.

Bonney, Edward. *Banditti of the Prairie.* Norman: University of Oklahoma Press, 1963.

Brown, Lizzie M. "The Pacification of the Indians After the War of 1812," *Journal of Illinois State Historical Society*, VIII, Oct 1915.

Brown, Jennifer S.H. *Strangers in Blood: Fur Trade Company Families in Indian Country*, Norman: University of Oklahoma Press, 1996.

Buck, Solon. *Illinois in 1818,* revised edition, Chicago, 1918.

Buck, Solon J. ed. "Pioneer Letters of Gershom Flagg." *Transactions of the Illinois State Historical Society*, Vol. 15. Illinois State Historical Library: Phillips Bros, State Printers, 1912.

Caldwell, Norman W. "The Frontier Army Officer, 1794-1814." *Mid-America: An Historical Review*. Vol XXXVII, No. 2 (April 1955).

Carlson, Theodore L. *The Illinois Military Tract.* New York: Arno Press, 1979.

Carter, Clarence Alvord, ed. *Territorial Papers of the United States.* U.S. Government Printing Office, 1934:
        Territory of Illinois, 1809 – 1818, Vol. XVII.
        Territory of Louisiana - Missouri, 1815 - 1821, Vol. XV.
        Territory of Wisconsin, 1836 - 1839, Volume XXVII.

Clark, William. "William Clark's Diary, Part I." *Kansas Historical Quarterly*, February 1948. Footnote #50.

Coffman, Edward M. *The Old Army: A Portrait of the American Army in Peacetime, 1784 – 1898.* New York: Oxford University Press, 1988.

Coues, Elliott. *Forty Years a Fur Trader on the Upper Missouri: the Personal Narrative of Charles Larpenteur, 1833-1872.* Volume 1. New York: Francis P. Harper, 1898.

Cramton, Willa G. *Women Beyond The Frontier: A Distaff View Of Life At Fort Wayne.* Historic Fort Wayne, Inc. 1977.

Cunliffe, *Soldiers and Civilians: The Martial Spirit in America, 1775-1865.* Boston: Little, Brown and Company, 1968.

Darby, John F. *Personal Recollections of John F. Darby*, New York: Arco Press, 1975.

Davis, Ralph. *The Rise of the Shipping Industry in the 17th and 18th Centuries.* Chapter VI: The Merchant Seaman, New York: St. Martin's Press, 1962.

Delo, David M., "The Army Sutler: Regimental Rip-Off Artist Supreme," *Army*, January 1989.

Dodge, Ellen Holmes. *Fiftieth Anniversary of the Settlement of Hon. George E. Holmes*, Christmas, A.D. 1896, privately published

Downer, Harry E. *History of Scott County Iowa*, Volume 1. Chicago: The S.J. Clarke Publishing Co., 1910.

Downer, Harry E. "Territorial Days," Chapter XIII, *History of Davenport and Scott County, Iowa*, Volume 1, Chicago: S.J. Clarke Publishing Company, 1910.

Drake, Benjamin. *The Great Indian Chief of the West: or, Life and Adventures of Black Hawk.* Philadelphia: H.M. Rulison, 1856.

Draper, Lyman Copeland, ed. "Additions and Corrections." Wisconsin Historical Collections, X, 1888.

"Dr. Erich Bollman," *Concise Dictionary of American Biography*, New York: Scribners, 1964.

Dudden, Faye E. *Serving Women: Household Service in Nineteenth-Century America.* Middletown, Conn: Wesleyan University Press, 1983.

Dunn, Mrs. Julia Mills, "Saukenuk." *Transactions of the Illinois State Historical Society* (1902) VII.

Ellsworth, H.L. *Illinois in 1837:A Sketch.* Philadelphia: S. Augustus Mitchell, 1837.

Emerson, Thomas E. and Floyd Mansberger. "The Search for French Peoria." *French Colonial Archaeology: The Illinois Country and the Western Great Lakes*, edited by John A. Walthall. Urbana: University of Illinois Press, 1991.

Fisher, Robert L., "The Treaty of Portage des Sioux," *Mississippi Valley Historical Review*, 19, 1933.

Flagler, Major Daniel W. *A History of Rock Island Arsenal from its establishment in 1836 to December, 1876 : and of the island of Rock Island, the site of the arsenal, from 1804 to 1863 : prepared under the instructions of Brig. Gen. Stephen V. Benét .* Washington: Government Printing Office, 1877.

Forsyth, Thomas. "The French, British and Spanish Methods of Treating Indians &c -" Ethnohistory, 4(2) Spring 1957.

Forsyth, Thomas and Lyman Copeland Draper. ed. "Journal of a Voyage From St. Louis to the Falls of St. Anthony in 1819." *Collections of the State Historical Society of Wisconsin*, VI. Madison: Wisconsin State Historical Society, 1872.

Forsyth, Thomas and Lyman Copeland Draper, ed. "Letter-book of Thomas Forsyth." *Wisconsin Historical Collections*, XI, 1872.

Franklin, Pauline. *The L'Oste Family of Lincolnshire.* Birmingham, England: *Keyway Communications, 1994.*

Fulton, Ambrose Cowperthwaite. *A Life's Voyage.* N.Y., published by the author, 1898.

Gallaher, Ruth A. "The Military-Indian Frontier, 1830-1835." *Iowa Journal of History and Politics.* (July 1917): 15.

Gates, Paul W. 'Frontier Land Business in Wisconsin. " *Wisconsin Magazine of History*, Vol. 51.

Gilman, Rhoda, "How Henry Sibley Took the Road to New Hope," *Minnesota History*, Vol 52, No. 6, 220-229.

Goble, Benjamin. *Narrative of Incidents In the Life of an Illinois Pioneer.* 1881 reprinted Knightstown: The Bookmark, 1977.

Goodrich, James W. "Richard Campbell." *Missouri Historical Review* LXXII, October 1977 - July 1978.

Greene, Evarts Boutell and Clarence Walworth Alvord, eds. Governors' Letter-Books, 1818-1834, Executive Series, Volume 1, Springfield: Illinois State Historical Library, 1909.

Green, Michael D. "The Sac-Fox Annuity Crisis of 1840 in Iowa Territory." *Arizona and the West.* 16(Summer 1974).

Green, Michael. "'We Dance in Opposite Directions': Mesquakie (Fox) Separatism From the Sac and Fox Tribe," *Ethnohistory* 30 (3).

Gussow, Zachary, "An Ethnological Report of the Historic Habitat of the Sauk, Fox, and Iowa Indians," *Sac, Fox, and Iowa Indians*, Vol I, New York: Garland Pub. Inc., 1974.

Haeger, John D. "A Time of Change: Green Bay, 1815 - 834." *Wisconsin Magazine of History*, 54. Summer 1971.

Hagan, William T. *The Sac and Fox Indians*, Norman: University of Oklahoma Press, 1980.

Hansman, John. *Everyday Life at Old Fort Madison.* no publishing co., 1990.

Harlan, Edgar R., ed. *Annals of Iowa*, XII, No. 7, January 1921.

Hayne, A.P. "Report of Inspection of the Ninth Military Dept., 1819." *Mississippi Valley Historical Review*, Vol. 7 (1920 -1921).

Hemphill, W. Edwin, ed. *The Papers of John C. Calhoun*, Vol. II, Columbus, S.C., 1964.

Hemphill, W. Edwin, ed. *The Papers of John C. Calhoun*, Vol. III, Columbus, S.C., 1967.

Hendrickson, Walter Brookfield. *David Dale Owen, Pioneer Geologist of the Middle West.* Indianapolis: Indiana Historical Bureau, 1943.

Historic Rock Island County, Rock Island, Illinois: Kramer & Co., 1908.

History of Lafayette County, Wisconsin: Containing an Account of Its Settlement, Growth, Development and Resources; An Extensive and Minute Sketch of Its Cities, Towns and Villages – their Improvements, Industries, Manufactories, Churches, Schools and Societies; Its Ware Record, Biographical Sketches, Portraits of Prominent Men and Early Settlers; The whole preceded By a History of Wisconsin, Statistics of the State, and An Abstract of Its Laws and Constitution and of the Constitution of the United States. Chicago: Western Historical Company, 1881.

History of Muscatine County Iowa. Chicago: S.J. Clarke Pub. Co., 1911.

History of Pike County, Illinois, Chicago: Chas. C. Chapman & Co., 1880: 259.

History of Scott County, Iowa. Chicago: Inter-state Publishing Co., 1882.

Holt, Orrin S. "Story of the Pioneers Who Blazed the Trail For Us in This Community." *The Moline Dispatch,* April 6, 1916.

Illinois Laws of a Private Nature, Eighth General Assembly, Kaskaskia: R.K. Fleming, 1833.

Incorporation Laws of the State of Illinois. Vandalia: William Walters, Public Printer, 1837.

Iowa State Department of Agriculture, *Forty-first Annual Iowa Year Book of Agriculture,* Des Moines: The State of Iowa, 1940.

Jackson, Donald. "Appendix B, The 1832 Roster." *Voyage of the Yellow Stone.* New York: Ticknor & Fields, 1985.

Jo Daviess County Commissioners, Jo Daviess County Record Book "A", 1827 – 1832. Galena, Illinois.

Jones, Charles T. Jr, *George Champlin Sibley: The Prairie Puritan, 1782-1863.* Jackson County Historical Society, Independence, Mo., 1970.

Jones, William. "Notes on the Fox Indians," *Iowa Journal of History and Politics,* Iowa City: State Historical Society of Iowa, Volumes 10 and 12.

Journal of the Illinois State Senate., XXXXX1843 (Vandruff Canal).

Journal of the Thirteenth General Assembly of the State of Illinois, December 5, 1842. Springfield: William Walter, Public Printers, Volume 13, 1842

Kane, Lucille M., June D. Holmquist, and Carolyn Gilman, eds. *The Northern Expeditions of Stephen H. Long: The Journals of 1817 and 1823 and Related Documents.* Minneapolis: Minnesota Historical Society Press, 1978.

Kappler, Charles J. compiler and editor. *Indian Affairs: Laws and Treaties, 1778-1883,* New York:Interland Pub, 1972.

Kett, H.F., ed. *History of Jo Daviess County,* Illinois. Chicago: H.F. Kett & Co., 1878.

Kett, H.F. ed. *Past and Present of Rock Island County, Illinois.* Chicago: H.F. Kett & Co., 1877.

Krenkel, John H. *Illinois Internal Improvements, 1818-1848.* Cedar Rapids, Iowa: The Torch Press, 1958.

Lage, Dorothy. *Le Claire, Iowa, a Mississippi River Town,* Published by Dorothy Lage, 1976.

Larson, Gustav. E. "Notes on Rock River Navigation. *Journal of the Illinois Historical Society*. Vol. 33, No. 3 (September 1940).

Lavender, David. *Fist in Wilderness*, Albuquerque: University of New Mexico Press, 1979.

Laws of the State of Illinois passed by the Tenth General Assembly. Vandalia: William Walters, Public printers, 1837.

Laws of the State of Illinois passed by the Thirteenth General Assembly, Springfield: Walters and Weber, 1843.

Leuck, Barbara K. *Feeding the Frontier Army, 1775 – 1865*. Eagan, MN: Grenadier Publications, 1990.

Lippincott, Isaac. "A Century and a Half of Fur Trade at St. Louis." *Washington University Studies*, April 1916, Vol. 3: 205 – 242.

Lippincott, Isaac. "Industrial Influence of Lead in Missouri," *The Journal of Political Economy*, Vol. 20, No 7, July 1912.

List of Private Claims Presented to the House of Representatives of the United States from the 1st to the 31st Congress, Inclusive. U. S. Congress, American State Papers, Class IX. 1834, Omaha: Nebraska *Journal of Genealogy*, Vol. 4, Nos. 6 – 9, 1979.

Lockwood, James H. "Early Times and Events in Wisconsin." Second Annual Report and Collections of the State Historical Society of Wisconsin. Madison: Calkins and Proudfit, 1856.

Lytle, William M. *Merchant Steam Vessels of United States, 1807 – 1868. Rhode Island: Steamship Historical Society of America, 1952.*

Mahan, Bruce E.. *Old Fort Crawford and the Frontier*. Iowa City: SHS, 1926.

Marsh, Cutting. "Expedition to the Sacs and Foxes." Entry for June 30, 1834. *Wisconsin Historical Collections*, Vol. XV, Madison: Democrat Printing Company, 1900.

McGrane, Reginald.*The Panic of 1837*, Chicago: University of Chicago Press, 1924.

Meese, William A.. *Early Rock Island*. Moline: Desaulniers & Co., 1905.

Newell, Linda King and Valeen Tippetts Avery. *Mormon Enigma: Emma Hale Smith*, Univ. of Illinois Press, 1994.

Nicewarner, Gladys Bull. *Michigan City, Indiana: The Life of a Town*, Michigan City, Indiana: Whippoorwill, 1980.

Norton, W.T. "Old Fort Bellefontaine." *Journal of the Illinois State Historical Society* 4: 334-339.

Nothstein, Ira O., *History of Rock Island Arsenal From Earliest Times to 1954*, Volume 1 to 1958. Rock Island: U.S. Army, Armament, Munitions, and Chemical Command, 1985.

Olney, R.J. *Rural Society and County Government in Nineteenth Century Lincolnshire*, Volume X, History of Lincolnshire Committee, 1979.

Painter, Bill. *Upon the Poor Rate: The Story of Louth Workhouse and the Paupers of East Lindsey*. Louth Naturalist's, Antiquarian and Literary Society, 2000.

Park, Siyoung. "Land Speculation in Western Illinois Pike County, 1821-1835." *Journal of Illinois State Historical Society*, Vol. LXXVII, Summer, 1984.

Peake, Ora Brooks. *History Of U.S. Indian Factory System*, Denver: Sage Books, 1954.

Perkins, J.A. "Working-Class Housing in Lindsey, 1780 -1870." Lincolnshire History and Archaeology, Vol. 10, 1975).

Petersen, William J. *Steamboating on the Upper Mississippi*. Iowa City: State Historical Society of Iowa, 1968.

Phelps, Caroline. "Mrs. Caroline Phelps' Diary." *Journal of the Illinois State Historical Society*, Vol. 23, No. 2, (1930): 202-239'

Portrait and Biographical Album of Rock Island County. Chicago: Biographical Publishing Co., 1885'

Powell, William H., comp. *List of Army Officers of the United States from 1790 to 1900*. Philadelphia: L.R. Hamersly & Co., 1900'

Prucha, Francis Paul. *The Sword of the Republic. New York:* MacMillan, 1969'

Quarles, Garland R. and Lewis N. Barton, editors. *What I Know About Winchester: Recollections of William Greenway Russell, 1800 – 189'1*

Redfield, W.C. *Sketch of the Geographical Rout(sic) of a Great Railway*, New York . G. & C .& H. Carvill, 1830.

Remini, Robert. *Henry Clay: Statesman for the Union*. New York: W.W.Norton & Company, 1991.

Reps, John William. *The Making of Urban America: a history of city planning in the United States*. Princeton University Press, 1965.

Richter, Auguste P. *Dr. August P. Richter Describes the Early Events in Scott County History*. Davenport, Iowa, 1926.

Robinson, David, N. *The Book of Louth: The Story of a Market Town*, Buckingham, England: Barracuda Books Limited, 1979.

Rouse, May Belle and Margaret F. Gardner. *Galena's Old Stockade and Underground Refuge*. Galena: Ellsworth W. Glick, 1970.

Salter, William. *Iowa: The First Free State in the Louisiana Purchase, 1673-1846.* Chicago: A.C. McClury & Co., 1905.

Salter, William. "Iowa in Unorganized Territory of the United States, August 10, 1821 – June 28, 1834." *Annals of Iowa,* Third Series, VI (1903-1905),

Scammon, J Young. *Cases Argued and Determined in the Supreme Court of State of Illinois,* 2, St. Louis, 1870.

Schoolcraft. Henry Rowe, *Personal Memoirs of a Residence of Thirty Years with Indian Tribes on the American Frontiers,* New York: Arno Press, 1975.

Schoolcraft, Henry. *Narrative Journal of Travels ... American Lakes to Mississippi River in Year 1820.* Albany: E. & E. Hosford, 1821.

Shambaugh, Benjamin. *Old Stone Capitol Remembers.* Iowa City, Iowa: State Historical Society of Iowa, 1939.

Shaw, Colonel John. "Personal Narrative." Lyman Draper Copeland, ed. *Wisconsin Historical Collections,* II, 1856.

Sifferd, Calvin S.,Jr. "The First Permanent Settlement in Hancock County, Illinois," *Journal of the Illinois State Historical Society.* Vol. XVIII, No 4, January 1926 .

Snyder, Rev. Charles. "Antoine LeClaire, The First Proprietor of Davenport." Annals of Iowa, XXIII (1941-1942).

Snyder, Rev. Charles E. Litt.D, L.L.D. "John Emerson, Owner of Dred Scott." *Annals of Iowa,* XXI (1937 – 1939).

Spencer, J. W. "Reminiscences of Pioneer Life in the Mississippi Valley." *The Early Days of Rock Island and Davenport* ,edited by Milo Milton Quaife, The Lakeside Press, Chicago: R.R. Donnelley & Sons Co, 1942.

Stambaugh, Samuel C. "Iowa Copper Mines." *Niles Weekly Register,* January 14, 1837.

State Historical Society of Wisconsin. *Dictionary of Wisconsin Biography.* Madison, 1960.

"Statement of Operations at U.S. Lead Mines." 20th Cong. 1st Sess. *American State Papers. Military Affairs,* 3. Washington, D.C.: Government Printing Office.

Stevens, Frank Everett. *The Black Hawk War,* Chicago: Frank E. Stevens, 1903.

Stuve, Dr. Bernard. "The States Internal Improvement Venture of 1837 - 1838." *Transactions of the Illinois State Historical Society.* Springfield. 1902.

Temple, Wayne C. *Indian Villages in Illinois Country,* Scientific Papers, Volume 2, Part 2, Illinois State Museum, 1977.

Thwaites, Rueben Gold, ed. "Difficulties of Wisconsin Traders." Wisconsin Historical Collections, XIX, 1910.

Thwaites, Rueben Gold, ed. "Licenses for Wisconsin Traders, " July 27, 1819. Wisconsin manuscript # 55B72, Wisconsin Historical Collection, XX (1911).

Thwaites, Rueben Gold, ed. "The Fur Trade in Wisconsin, 1812 – 1825." *Wisconsin Historical Collections*. XX, 1911.

Tillinghast, B. F. *Rock Island Arsenal in Peace and In War*. Chicago: The Henry O. Shepard Co., 1898.

"Town Plats." *Laws of Illinois*. 4th Illinois General Assembly, 1st session, Nov 1824 - Jan 1825.

Turner, Levi Crosby. *Autobiography*. Cooperstown, N.Y.: Douglas Turner Johnston, 1954.

Tweet, Roald. *A History of Navigation Improvements on the Rock Island Rapids*. Rock Island District, U.S. Army Corps of Engineers, April 1980.

Tweet, Roald. *A History of the Rock Island District U.S. Army Corps of Engineers 1866 - 1983*. Rock Island, 1984.

Tyler, C.C. *Reminiscences of Fountain Green, Illinois*. Fountain Green: Illinois. Vol. 8, No 1, April 1915.

VanderZee, Jacob. "Fur Trade in Iowa Country, Iowa." *Iowa Journal of History and Politics*, Iowa City, Iowa: State Historical Society of Iowa, Volume 12, No. 4.

VanderZee, Jacob. "The Opening of the Des Moines Valley." *Iowa Journal of History and Politics*, XIV, No 4(1916).

Van Kirk, Sylvia. *Many Tender Ties: Women in Fur-Trade Society in Western Canada, 1607 – 1870*. Winnepeg, Manitoba: Watson and Dwyer Publishing, Ltd., 1980.

Viola, Herman J. *Diplomats in Buckskins: A History of Indian Delegations in Washington City*. Washington, D.C.: Smithsonian Institution Press, 1981.

Wade, Richard C. *The Urban Frontier: the Rise of Western Cities, 1790-1830*. Cambridge: Harvard University Press, 1967.

Wagner, Mark J. and Mary R. McCowie. *The Archeology of Frontier Taverns on the St. Louis-Vincennes Trace*. Illinois state Museum Popular Science Series, XI, 1993.

Walters, William D. Jr. "The Fanciful Geography of 1836." *The Old Northwest*, Vol. 9, No. 4(Winter 1983 -1984).

Walton, J.P. "Recollections of Suel Foster." No. 79. *Pioneer Papers*, Muscatine, Iowa, 1899.

Wesley, Edgar Bruce. *Guarding the Frontier: A Study of Frontier Defense, 1815 – 1825*, Minneapolis: University of Minnesota Press, 1935.

White, Helen McCann. "Frontier Feud, 1819-1820: How Two Officers Quarreled All the Way to the Site of Fort Snelling." *Minnesota History*, Fall 1970.

Whitney, Ellen ed. *The Black Hawk War, 1831 – 1832*. Vol. II. Springfield: Illinois State Historical Library, 1970.

Wilkie, Franc B. *Davenport Past and Present*, Davenport: Luse, Lane & Co., 1858.

Yoder, Patton. *Taverns and Travelers: Inns of the Early Midwest*. Bloomington: Indiana University Press, 1969.

On-Line Sources:

Circuit Ct Case Files, Office of the Circuit Ct, City of St. Louis, Missouri. Available online. http:// stlcourtrecords.wustl.edu.

Smith, Marjorie. "The Winnebago War of 1827 Chronology of Events." available online. www.geocities.com/old lead/winwarchron.htm. Accessed February 26, 2006.

Illinois Public Domain Land Tract Sales, available online: http://www2.sos.state.il.us/cgi-bin/land

"Descendants and collateral families of the 1630 immigrant William Cheesbrough." available on-line: CHEESBRO' Genealogy@RootsWeb

Virginia Macklot pedigree. available online. http://genealogy.kathihill.com/Person/pedigree/235342.

Shepard, Edward M. "The Panic of 1837." from *Life of Martin Van Buren*, Houghton, Miflin Company. 1888-1889. online: www.usgennet.org/usa/topic/preservation/epochs/vol6/pg178.htm).

Crumrin, Timothy. *Road Through Wilderness: The Making of the National Road*. 1994. Available online: http://www.connerprairie.org/Learn-And-Do/Indiana-History/America-1800-1860/The-National-Road.aspx).

"General Bissell." *The National Register*, Volume 2, No. 10, November 2, 1816 . Available online: https://books.google.com/books?id=35cDAAAAYAAJ&pg=RA1-PA154&lpg=RA1-PA154&dq=General+Bissell+Court+Martial&source=bl&ots=p2EJ9VJoAP&sig=ySFZx415IxbdMj384pN-OonPSRk&hl=en&sa=X&ei=JljnVPWbPMqcygSi4oG4CA&ved=0CCoQ6AEwBQ#v=onepage&q=General%20Bissell%20Court%20Martial&f=false

Marston, Morrill. "Report on Indians of the Upper Mississippi Valley, 1820." *American Journeys Collection*. Wisconsin Historical Society Digital Library and Archives. Available online: www. Americanjourneys.org

New York, 1820 - 1850 Passenger and Immigration Lists. Available online: www.ancestry.com

Oxford Companion to Ships and the Sea, 2006. Available online: http://www. encyclopedia.com

"Petition Presented, January 16, 1832. *Journal of the House of Representatives of the Unites States* 22 Congress,, 1st Session, p. 192. http://memory.loc.gov/cgi-bin/query/r?ammem/hlaw:@field(DOCID+@lit(hj02529))

Image Credits

Anderson, John, "Topographic View of Rock Island in the Mississippi, 1819." Report for Major Morrell Marston, 10 September 1819. RG 92, Fort Armstrong Consolidated Correspondence File. National Archives and Records Administration, Washington, D.C.

Baldwin, Leland. Keel Boat, *Keel Boat Age on Western Waters*, 1941.

Bill S. 44 in the Senate of the United States. 28th Congress, 1st Session, January 11, 1844. A Century of Lawmaking for a New Nation: U.S. Congressional Documents and Debates, 1774 - 1875. Available online: https://memory.loc.gov/cgi-bin/ampage?collid=lisb&fileName=028/lis028.db&recNum-117.
1,500 Dollars Reward. *Davenport (Iowa)Gazette*, July 1845.

Davenport's Obituary. *Davenport (Iowa) Gazette*, July 5, 1845.

Goldsmith, Susan Lewis. Daguerreotype, Item # 97, Book 3, Folder 10, Box 53 in MSS 27 John Henry Hauberg papers, Augustana College Special Collections, Rock Island, Illinois, n.d., Used with permission.

Gordon, William. Plat of City of Davenport (1836), *Quad City Times Centennial Edition*, July 11, 1936.

Gould, M.A. Map of the Village of Moline in the Year 1853, Adapted, *Moline (Illinois) Dispatch*, April, 1916.

Gravepost Detail, Hauberg Museum, Black Hawk State Park, Rock Island, Illinois.

Hannan, William D. *Davenport's Main Trading Posts, 2019.*

Hannan, William D. Rock Island City and Surroundings, 2019.

Holt, Orin. *Early Waterpower Development on Rock River*. Adapted, 2019. *Moline Dispatch*, Moline, Illinois, January 1916.

Melish, John. Map of Illinoise (sic), 1818. Philadelpia: Available Online: http://hdl.loc.gov/loc.gmd/g4100.ct000892

Parker Map of Davenport. George Parker, February 1837. Redrawn by William Hannan, 2019. Putnam Museum Archives, Davenport Iowa. Used with permission.

Proposed Rail Roads, *Rock Island (Illinois)Advertiser*, November 1853.

Royce, Charles C. *Indian Land Cessions in the United States*. 1899. Library of Congress., Washington, D.C. Available online: https://www.loc.gov/resource/g3701em.gct00002/?sp=24

Unknown artist, Portrait of George Davenport, 1844, copy of photo in Colonel Davenport House Historic Site, Rock Island, Illinois.

Unknown Photographer, *Davenport House on Rock Island*, ca 1880.

Untitled and unsigned view of Rock Island, ca. 1844, attributed to John Casper Wilde. Photo courtesy of State Historical Society of Iowa, Des Moines, Iowa/Kay Coats.

Walter, George. *A View of Fort Armstrong, Rock Island, Mississippi River. 1852.* Commissioned by Albert G. Brockett. *Gleason's Drawing Room Companion.* March 2, 1853.

Index

A

Abbott, Samuel, 110, 410, 413
Absolom Baxter, 220
Act of Congress, xix, 398
Ainsworth, 294
Allen, Archie, 150, 427, 445
Allen, Leander, 271–72, 282
Allen, Samuel, 299
American Fur Company, 44–46, 75–79, 89, 92–93, 95, 105, 123, 126–27, 130–32, 152, 212, 305, 318–20
American System, 259
Andrews, Lemuel, 333, 437, 439
Ansley, John D., 442
Armstrong, xvi, 54, 59, 114, 141, 207, 229, 411
Astor, 128, 424
Atkinson, Charles, 297, 346, 439
Atwater, Caleb, 11, 48, 155
Axford, William, 314

B

Babcock, Francis, 350
Bad Axe, 186
Bailey, Moses, 299
Ballard, James H., 408
Barrel, John, 153, 172, 204, 349
Barrel House, 153–54, 205
Barrett, 376
Barrows, 358, 419, 433, 441, 457

Barrows, Willard, 413
Barte, Baptiste, 128
Bartlett, Michael, 215, 442
Baxter brothers, 220
Baxters, 220–21, 365–68
Beach, 219, 323
Belcher, Nathaniel, 299, 350–51, 365
Bell, Captain William H., 291
Bellefontaine, 17, 21–22, 29, 78, 117
Belt, Factor Robert B., 55
Beltrami, 412, 457
Bennet, William, 213
Bennett, 299, 440
Bennett, Charles, 215
Bennett, Charles R., 205
Bennett, James, 442
Beston, Mary, 56
Biddle, Thomas, 125
Bissell, 402
Bissell Papers, Daniel G., 402, 452
Black Hawk, 44–45, 65–67, 148–49, 157–59, 165–67, 169–70, 172, 174–76, 181–86, 203, 208–9, 226, 230–31, 262, 267–68, 402, 418–21, 423–24, 427–28, 457
    appeasing, 169
    confused, 169
    expected, 185
    old friend, 203
    Black Hawk Purchase, 178, 190

Black Hawk's ancient city, 265

Black Hawk's British Band, 173, 182

Black Hawk's city, 266

Black Hawk's people, 155, 211

Black Hawk State Park, 362, 469

Black Hawk's wife, 203

Black Hawk War, 179–95, 199, 204, 206–7, 213–14, 223–35, 289–90, 320, 326, 420, 422–23, 465–66

Black Partridge, 20

Black Snake Hills, 102, 109, 138, 149, 171

Blackwell, 282, 437

Blackwell, Samuel, 282, 437

Blanc, 279, 437

Bliss, John, 176

Blondeau, Catherine, 255

Blondeau, Maurice, 76, 127–28, 412

Bloomington, 252, 397–98, 402, 446, 448, 452, 466

Boilvin, 26

Boilvin, Nicholas, 125, 403

Bollman, Erich, 13, 400, 459

Bollman, Tom, 430

Bonney, 363–64, 368, 448, 457

Bonney, Edward, 362, 365, 368, 448, 452

Bonney's Account, 448

Bonney's search, 363

Bostwick, 123, 127, 141, 412–17, 427

Bostwick, Oliver, 100, 127

Bowling, 249

Bowling, James M., 310, 378

Bowling cousins, 102

Bowling Family, 406

Bowling relatives, 330

Bowling's sisters, 249

Bowling Township, 330

Brashar, 430

Brashar, William, 150, 215

Brashar, William T., 158

Brashar's brother-in-law, 158

Brown County, 240

Brunot, 351

Budd, Charles, 360, 365

Budd's alibi, 360

Buffalo and Mississippi Railroad, 343

Buford, 293, 298, 351, 439, 455

Buford, John, 293, 439

Buford's buoy, 299

Buford's predictions, 294

Bully, John, 272

Burch, 364–68

Burch, Robert, 361, 363, 368

Burr, Aaron, 13

Burr Affair, 13

Burr expedition, 13

Butler, Peter, 213

C

Cabanne, 76

Cabanne & Co, 76

Calhoun, 41, 122, 331, 405, 408

Calhoun, John C., 64, 121–22, 403, 407–8, 414, 460

Calhoun, War John C., 75

Calumet Rivers, 84

Cameron, 312
Cameron, Neil, 312, 441
Campbell, 69–70
Campbell, John, 69, 81, 231, 404
Campbell, Richard, 408, 460
Campbell, Robert, 271–72, 435
Campbell's business, 69
Campbell's Island, xv, 69, 379
Cantonment Davis, 29–30
Carlisle, 9
Carlisle Barracks, 10, 12
Carlton, 435
Carlton, Cyrus, 271
Carr, Benjamin, 263–64, 267, 434, 436
Carr, William, 273, 434
Carr's Island, 264, 277
Case, Asel C., 430
Case, Josiah H., 421
Case's addition, 217
Cass, Lewis, 189, 425
Cass county, 192
Cassner, George, 116
Casteel of Rock Island County, 247
Chamberlain, 207–8
Chambers, 324
Charlotte, 103–5, 112, 138, 202
Chas, 414, 461
Chicago, 264–65, 272, 274, 343–44, 346–47, 355–56, 402–3, 412–16, 419, 430–32, 435–37, 446–47, 451–53, 457–59, 461–65
Chicago American, 265, 434
Chicago and established Fort Armstrong, xvii

Chicago and Rock Island, 351, 378
Chicago and Rock Island Line, 352
Chicago Democrat, 336, 363, 444
Chicago Historical Society, 402, 451
Chicago Land Sales, 265
Chicago Press, 446, 462
Chippiannock Cemetery, 65, 406
Chippiannock gravesite, 362
Chouteau, 212, 225, 231, 242, 419, 422, 424–25, 428
Chouteau, Auguste, xvi, 240, 401
Chouteau, Emilie, 240
Chouteau, Francois, 102
Chouteau, Pierre, 148, 171, 189, 205, 417, 419, 422, 424–25, 431
Chouteau & Co, 427, 431
Chouteau Collection, 411–13, 415–16, 419, 422, 424, 431, 452
Chouteau Company, 206
Chouteau Esq, 418–19
Chouteau family, 240
Chouteau Jr, 418, 422, 431
Chouteau Maffitt Collection, 431
Chouteau- Maffitt Collection, 429
Chouteau-Maffitt Collection, 414–18, 422–27, 431, 444
Chouteau Papers, 431
Chouteau-Papin Collection, 410, 412–13, 415–16, 419, 427, 442, 452

Chouteau Sr, 331
Clapp, Benjamin, 330, 444
Clark, xv–xvi, 2, 11, 76, 151, 167–69, 184, 189, 404–5, 430–31, 434
Clark, Benjamin, 275
Clark, Captain Benjamin W., 151
Clark, William, 43, 167, 171, 182, 184, 189, 401–2, 414–15, 421–25, 429, 432
Clarke Pub, 432, 461
Clarke Publishing Co, 431–32, 459
Clarke Publishing Company, 459
Clark family, 151, 247
Clark Papers, 418, 421–22, 431
Clark property, 151
Clark's assistance, 181
Clark's choice for Forsyth's replacement, 170
Clarks' competition, 247
Clark's Ferry, 275
Clarksville, 34, 74, 81, 410
Clermont County, 102
Coffman, 10–11, 399–400, 403, 458
Cole, Benjamin, 358
Colton, 244, 248
Colton, Levi, 240, 244–45, 334
Colton, Levi S., 239, 441
Connolly, John, 110, 128, 162, 192, 413, 425
Connolly's death, 117
Conway, 213, 251–52, 273
convinced, 252

young, 251
Conway, Joseph, 209
Conway, William B., 251
Conway Esq, 429
Conway of Pittsburgh, 251
Conway's decisions, 252
Cook, William, 245
Cook, William L., 245
Cook Home, 433
Cooley, 274–75, 434, 436
Cooley, Anthony, 265, 274, 333, 436–37, 444, 452
Cooley, James E., 301
Cooper Shop, 244
Cooperstown, 265, 434, 456, 465
Cooperstown newspaper, 267
Copp, James, 249
Copp, Sophia, 378
Copp House, 154
Craig, 280
Craig, James, 280, 437
Cramton, 407, 458
Cramton, Willa, 60
Cramton, Willa G., 406
Crane, 72–73
Crane Dance, 65
Crane's party, 73
Crooks, 46, 76–78, 128, 130–31, 171, 368, 409–10
Crooks-Stuart Letterbook, 405, 454

D
Danforth, John, 150
Darling, 45–46
Darling, Daniel, 44–45
Darling & Edwards, 286

Davenport, 5–13, 19–22, 43–49, 56–61, 63–73, 77–82, 99–112, 118–33, 137–41, 148–62, 170–74, 180–89, 195–221, 223–32, 240–58, 304–23, 329–37, 346–51, 431–36, 438–49
additions to, 257, 346
appointed, 252
blamed, 173
bound, 358
building, 173
congratulating, 189
establishing, 39
first real housing, 17
freed, 192
grand daughter naomi, 389
incorporated, 253
land transactions, 304
ledgers recording, 225
son George L., 99, 306, 309, 313, 346, 384–85
Davenport, Adrian, 205
Davenport, Adrian H., 275
Davenport, Elizabeth, 376, 385, 388, 390
Davenport, George, 4–6, 10–11, 33–34, 59–63, 67–70, 199–201, 216–17, 239–40, 255–57, 266–67, 283–84, 318–19, 346–52, 356–64, 404, 412–16, 418–32, 434–37, 440–44, 446–47
Davenport, George L., 229, 232–34, 248, 254–56, 325–26, 362–63, 374–75, 383–85, 427, 431, 440–41, 444–46, 449
Davenport, Harry, 372, 449
Davenport, Jennie, 375–76
Davenport, Joseph, 388
Davenport, Joseph A., 427
Davenport, Margaret, 52, 372, 385–88
Davenport, Margret, 388–89
Davenport, Naomi, 384, 406, 426
Davenport, William, 220, 428
Davenport Account Book, 431
Davenport and Bailey Davenport, 50
Davenport and Farnham, 84, 109, 128, 153, 156, 158, 170–71, 174, 179, 190, 204
Davenport and Farnham's partner in Galena, 316
Davenport and Farnham's success, 128
Davenport and Gokey children, 117
Davenport and Rock Island, 307, 359
Davenport Brought, Joseph A., 427
Davenport Collection, 89–90, 411, 430, 440–41, 444, 451
George L., 413, 426, 431, 454
Naomi L., 404
Davenport Collection Reel, 421
Davenport Democrat, 411, 434, 447, 449–50, 456
Davenport-Farnham lands, 193
Davenport-Farnham partnership lands in Rock Island County, 263
Davenport Gazette, 324, 326, 332–33, 393, 427, 433, 438–41, 443–49

Davenport Heirs, 429

Davenport home, 53, 100, 137–38

Davenport Hotel, 245, 247, 257, 375–76

Davenport House, 56, 58, 104, 151, 154, 183–84, 194, 196–97, 201, 249, 356, 426–27, 451

Davenport House Site, 427, 451

Davenport Iowa, 469

Davenport lands, 221, 352

Davenport-Le Claire partnership, 248

Davenport Manuscripts, 417

Davenport Papers, George L., 429

Davenport parish, 373

Davenport Public Library, 411, 421, 426, 441–42, 445–46, 449, 451

Davenport Republican, 446, 456

Davenport-Rock Island News, 456

Davenport's business, 119, 148, 152, 226

Davenport's Credit Books, 89, 91, 93, 95, 411

Davenport's death, 44, 125, 216, 359

Davenports' decision, 234

Davenport's family, 184, 195, 197

Davenport's house, 118, 160, 199, 239, 307, 351

Davenport's House Scene of First Sermon, 409

Davenport's land, 209, 308, 350, 352

Davenport's letters, 145, 181, 322

Davenport's murder, 197–98, 358, 372, 385

Davenport's Obituary, 354, 469

Davenport's Petition, 180, 423

Davenport's property, 247, 264, 305

Davenport's trading post, 60, 116, 118, 151

Davenport women, 51–58, 73–74, 103

Davis, 180, 397–99, 427, 458

Davis, Charles G., 397

Davis, Ralph, 6

Davis, Tom, 208

Debutts, 98

Debutts, Henry, 98

Dement, 280, 437, 440

Dement, John, 280, 437

Dickey, Hugh, 272

Dickey, Hugh T., 271

Dickson, 70, 264–65, 270–71, 276–77, 279, 282, 300, 348, 434

Dickson, Cyrus, 229, 432

Dickson, Thomas, 281

Dickson, William, 264, 266, 268, 273, 276, 432, 436, 454

Dickson family, 281

Dickson's brother, William B., 281

Dickson's mill, 277

Dixon, 183, 270, 277, 279

Dixon, John, 436, 452

Dixon resident Sam Fisher, 361

Dixon's Ferry, 184, 279, 331
Dodge, 426, 458
Dodge, Ellen, 426
Dodge, Henry, 226, 430
Doty, 305–6
Doty, Daniel C., 305, 441
Downey, 55, 110, 129, 131
Downey, William, 34, 55, 110, 129
Downey in opposition to Davenport, 128
Drury, 281, 371
Duncan, Joseph, 423
Duncan, Mathew, 403

E
Eads, James, 347, 446
Early, Robert, 371
Edwards, 3, 62, 147, 271, 281, 435, 437, 448, 453, 457, 466
Eldridge, 245–46, 250, 257
Emerson, 218, 254, 407, 459
Emerson, John, 57, 218, 254, 430, 464

F
Farnham, 45–46, 75–77, 92–93, 106–7, 109, 126–28, 130–31, 144–46, 158–62, 170–74, 179, 184–87, 189–90, 192–93, 225, 409–10
    death of, 192, 212
Farnham, Charles, 388, 442
Farnham, Russel, 45, 78, 92, 95, 109, 126, 138, 409, 411–13, 415–16, 418–25
Farnham-Davenport partnership, 318

Farnhamsburg, 154, 159–61, 172, 204, 295, 415, 420
Farrar, 55, 60, 85, 111, 127, 161, 173, 190, 316–18, 407, 410
Farrar, Amos, 54, 60, 82, 85, 160, 189, 192, 406, 413, 425, 442
Farrar, Jacob, 406
Farrar, Sophia, 316, 413, 442
Farrar & Co, 111, 138, 161
Featherstonehaugh, George, 269
Ferris, 200
Fever River, 62, 69, 85, 110, 127, 132, 136, 138, 417
Fever River and Farnhamsburg, 160
Fever River area, 144
Fever River trade in Galena, 193
Fever River trading post, 85
Fisher, 401–2, 459
Fisher, Robert L., 402
Fisher Ames Harding, 272
Fiske, 271, 281, 435
Fiske, John, 448
Flying Betsy, 64, 101, 111
Forsyth, 40–43, 46–47, 71, 116–20, 123, 128, 166, 169–70, 183–85, 404–5, 408–10, 415, 459
Forsyth, John, 162, 168
Forsyth, Robert, 125
Forsyth, Thomas, 105, 110, 116, 120–21, 125, 168, 183–84, 404, 407, 410, 413–15, 421, 424
Forsyth Papers, 414–15, 424, 452
Forsyth's Indian Agency, 150
Forsyth to Secretary of War, 405

Fort Adams, 12–15, 400, 455
Fort Clark, 18, 36, 403–4
Fort Crawford, 30, 36, 44, 46, 70, 94, 122, 125, 135, 149, 181
Fort Crawford Factory, 69
Fort Drummond, 26
Fort Edwards, 30, 32, 67, 69–70, 75, 79–83, 94, 124, 128, 130, 404, 407–8
Fort Edwards and Flint Hills, 95
Fort Edwards and Fort Crawford, 94
Fort Edwards Indian Territory, 408
Fort Edwards trade, 69
Fort Erie, 21, 411
Fort Malden, 42
Fort Snelling, 34, 55, 57, 98–99, 122, 125, 135, 229, 232, 403, 406
Fox, 82, 84, 91, 146–47, 149, 365, 368, 404, 410, 413, 420, 423, 432, 460, 462
Fox, William, 363–64, 369
Fulton, 337–38, 344–46, 351, 415, 445–46, 455, 459
Fulton, Ambrose C., 337
Fulton, Robert, 337
Fulton County, 398

G
Gagnier, 137
Gagnier murders, 137
Gaines, 174–75, 309, 423
Gaines, Edmund P., 423
Gaines, Major General Edmund P., 174
Gaines' soldiers, 175

Galena, 160–61, 189, 191–93, 196, 266, 269, 279–80, 315–17, 421–22, 430, 432, 435, 445–46, 456, 461
Galena Gazette, 214, 363–64, 422, 429, 456
Galena Mounted Volunteers, 214
Galena's Old Stockade, 422, 464
Garnsey, 217
   agent Daniel G., 275
Garnsey, Daniel G., 283, 436
Gates, frontier economics historian Paul W., 276
Gavitt, 246
Gear of Galena, 189
George LOste Davenport, 390
Gerrard, Joseph, 272
Gilbert, John, 212
Gilman, 416, 460
Gleason, 114, 427, 451, 470
Goble, 173, 196, 422–24, 426, 460
Goble, Benjamin, 183, 196
Goble family, 173
Gokey, 43–44, 56, 68, 72, 128, 255, 385
Gokey, Antoine, 44, 68, 72, 128, 141, 385
Gokey, Lewis, 450–51, 454
Gokey, Rosa, 385
Goldsmith, 373–75, 377–78, 380–81, 469
Goldsmith, Susan, 376, 378–79
Goldsmith, Susan M., 429
Goldsmith, Zachariah, 373, 375, 449

Goodwin, 312
Gordon, 240–41, 248, 398, 469
Gordon, William, 236, 240, 334, 441
Graham, 27, 39–40, 397–98
Graham, George, xvii, 397–98, 414
Graham, Richard, xviii–xix, 27, 39–40, 64, 81, 398, 400–401, 403, 405, 407–8, 419
Graham Papers, 408–9
Grand River, 76, 80–81, 95, 107, 109, 144
Grant, James, 448
Grant Miller Library, 432
Gratiot, Charles, 243
Great Council, 125
Great Salt, xiv
Green Mountain Boys, 367
Gregg, 358–59, 363, 371–72
Gregg, Patrick, 299, 371
Gregory, Shannon, 279

H
Haines, John, 83
Hambaugh, 232, 240, 312, 334
   Philip, 239–40
Haney, 151, 367
   John, 151
Hardfish, 322
Harland, George, 150
Harris, Cary, 233–34, 432
Harris, Daniel, 411, 457
Harris, Thomas, 437
Haskill, James, 208
Haydon, 199
Hebert, 255, 414
   Louis, 117, 233, 255, 414

   Nicholas, 128
Hempstead, 87, 349, 446
   Charles, 155, 446
   William, 349
Hesperia, 288–89, 294
Hesperians, 288
Hewet, Maria, 56
Hianope, 372, 375
Hilbrings, 216
Hollister, Edmund, 277
Holt, 333, 407–8, 420, 425, 447, 461, 469
Hubbard, 282, 437
   Thomas, 150
Hummer's school, 254
hunt, 38, 64–66, 82, 91–92, 94–95, 102, 106–7, 143, 146–49, 170–71, 173, 211–12, 224–28, 320–21, 324

I
Illinois, xiv–xv, xvii–xix, 104, 122–24, 173–74, 180–83, 226–27, 238, 265, 272–73, 278–83, 342–43, 351, 397, 401–17, 419–32, 434–42, 444–62, 464–65, 469
Illinois Rangers, 20
Indian Agency, 46, 48, 116–17, 119–21, 131–32, 184, 186, 193, 218, 221, 414–15, 419
Indian Boundary land, 348
Indian Boundary Line, xvi, xx, 45, 76, 156–57, 348, 397
Indian Lodge, 68, 99, 102, 149, 196, 406, 432
Internal Improvement Act, 273
Iowa Land Sales on June, 308

Iowa Territory, 207, 222, 251–52, 258, 274–75, 307, 333, 439, 443, 460

Ioway River, 69, 71, 106, 157, 173, 187, 211–12, 224, 227–28, 231, 320

J

Jenks, 288
  William, 288
Jerome, 73
Jerro, 137
Johnston, John W., 122, 414
Joinville, Joseph, 128
Jones, 217, 400, 418, 435, 461
  George W., 230, 432
Jouett, Charles, 404
Jouette, Charles, 42, 402

K

Kansas River, 102, 138
Kelly, James, 244–45
Keocuck, 101
Keokuck, 84
Ke-o-kuck, 158
Keokuk, 84, 156, 161–62, 182, 190, 192–93, 208, 224–25, 227–28, 230–32, 322, 324, 421
  Keokuk's band, 184
  Keokuk's village, 181, 211, 232, 431
Kinney, Henry L., 272
Knox, 213, 301, 363, 371
  Joseph, 333, 351, 363, 448

L

Labussierre, Francois, 130
Labussierre's trade goods, 130

Labussierre's trading plans, 130
Lagoterie, 45–46
LaGoterie, Eduard, 45
LaMott, 35
  Baptiste, 35
Lange, 202, 427, 451
LaPerche, 244
Lavender, 75, 127–28, 405, 409, 416, 424–25, 462
  David, 75, 189
Le Claire, 207
LeClaire, 230, 381
  Antoine, 433, 464
Lee, 439
  John, 457
  Patrick, 409
  Robert E., 299, 438
Lee County, 363–64
Lee County Sheriff Estes, 362
Leonard, 255
  Harvey, 250, 255, 257, 314, 336
Lewis, 2, 11, 50, 60, 241
  Susan, 35–36, 57, 59–61, 100, 102, 199–200, 216–17, 360, 362, 372–74, 384, 386, 388–89, 448
  Susana, 388
  Susan M., 449
  Susannah, 429
  Susanna M., 50
Lincolnshire, 2, 5, 8, 372, 399, 406, 452, 459
  Lincolnshire County Historical Library, 452
  Lincolnshire heritage, 2
  Lincolnshire Wolds, 2
Lindsey, 417, 463

Lindsey Quarter Session Land Tax Records, 452
Litch, 245
Litch's whiskey establishment, 246
Locke, John, 257
Lockwood, 403, 405, 462
  James, 38
Lockwood companies, 15
Logan, 250–51, 315
  Andrew, 250, 336
Long, Aaron, 363–64, 366–67, 371, 448
Long, John, 363–64, 366–67, 448
Long, Lieutenant Stephen H., 42
Long, Stephen H., 404, 461
Louth, 2–6, 132, 138–41, 372, 398–99, 406, 417, 452, 464
Lynch, Ellen, 427
Lynde, 294
  Cornelius, 380

M
MacDonald, 374–75, 449, 451
Mackinac, 27, 39, 45, 70, 75, 77–78, 99, 405, 409
Mackinac Island, 75, 91
Maganno, 85
Mallette, Joseph, 255
March, Colonel Enoch C., 183
Marsh, 209–11, 428–29, 462
Marston, 37, 85, 403, 406, 411, 451, 467
Marston Estate Packet, 451
Mason, John, 270
Mathilda, 104, 216, 377
Mathilda Barrett, 216, 375

Mathilda wages, 377
May, James, 441
McCabe, 125
McClary, 13
McCloud, Solomon, 237
McCormick, Cyrus, 272
McGee, 196
McGregor, 239, 241
  Alexander, 239, 241, 335
  Alexander W., 441
McGregor's share, 246
McIntosh, 244
  James, 245
McLellan, 312–13
  William, 312
  William E., 441
McNeal, 349–50, 446–47
  Henry, 349
McNeal Patent, 447
Menard, Pierre, 43
Merchant Flour Mill, 294
Methode, 137
Military Tract, xix, 124–25
Mill Creek, 264, 277, 279, 348
Miller, John, 81
Miller, John S., 273
Mitchell, Augustus, 436, 459
Mitchell, David, 168
Moline, 286, 293–97, 330, 332–33, 345–46, 351–52, 407, 409, 419–20, 439, 446, 448, 469
Moore, Henry, 272
Morehouse, 266
Morgan, 39–40, 146
Morrison, 22, 27–28, 33, 38, 401–2
  James, 22, 28, 33, 401
  William, 33, 401, 456
Morrison Ledgers, 405, 454

Moss, Lewis, 267, 434
Motie, Joseph, 255
Moyer, 300–301
　Albert, 440
Muir, 79, 84–85, 161
　Samuel, 79, 128, 192, 421
　Samuel C., 407
Munn, 274, 434, 436–37
　Edwin G., 274

N
Neapope, 159, 230
Ne-a-pope, 158
New Orleans, 12–14, 16, 22, 199, 268, 337, 343
New Purchase, 333
　the, 444
Nicholas, Colonel Robert C., 29
Nichols, 314, 318
　Elizabeth, 313–14, 317, 442
Norton, 271–72, 276, 400, 435, 463
　Nathaniel, 271–72, 282, 435

O
Oakley, 283
　Charles, 278
O'Fallon, 408
　Benjamin, 70, 404
　William, 11
Ogden, Henry, 278
Old Wataico, 72
Owen, 257–58
　Simon, 16
Owen's base camp, 258

P

Palen, Joshua, 107, 127, 162, 168, 192, 413, 425
Palen Estate Packet, 451
panic, 137, 250, 260, 276, 283, 330, 359, 436
Parker, 245, 402, 445
　Daniel, 403
　George, 244–45, 433, 469
Parkhurst, 300, 347
partition, 263, 283, 434, 442
　official, 263
Pashepaho, 182, 208, 231
pettle, 123, 131
Pettle, Louis, 116, 123, 131, 415
Phelps, 58, 187, 192, 226, 407, 431, 463
　Alexis, 430–31
　Caroline, 58
　Stephen, 171, 192, 425
　William, 227, 431
Phelps & Co, 430
Phelps Brothers, 146–47, 223, 226, 431
Phelps Company, 187
Phelps trading post, 226
Phillips, 299
　Walter, 299, 440
Pike, 124, 283, 415, 455
　Benjamin, 215
Pilcher, 186, 189
　Joshua, 184, 232, 425
Planter House, 330
platting, 204, 214, 268, 296
Plumbe, 345
　John, 345
Poinsett, 221, 430
　Joel R., 430
　War Joel R., 221

Pollock, Joseph, 274

Portage Farm, 79, 193

Portage Place, 85, 161, 174, 421

Pouit, Catherine, 388

Powers, Edward, 247

Poweshiek, 224, 227, 231, 233, 320, 322, 326, 431

prairie, the Banditti of the, 365

preemption, xiv, 203, 221, 331, 404

Price, Hiram, 347

Prophet, 176, 183, 186, 230

Prophetstown, 43

Proprietor Levi Colton, 245

proprietors, 239–41, 248, 251, 253, 268, 274, 278, 311–13, 330, 335

R

Rahway, 9

Rat Row, 162, 193, 410, 421, 457

Reddings, 364–65, 368

Reed, 287–88

Silas, 287

Removal Act, 167

Reps, 433, 464

John, 241

Reynolds, 174, 191, 423, 425, 445

John, 423

Reynolds PJP, Harman G., 391

Robidoux, 149

Joseph, 102

Robinson, 398–99, 417, 464

Rockingham, 239, 248–51, 253, 274–75, 290, 300, 337

Rock Island and LaSalle Railroad Co, 351

Rock Island City (RIC), 258, 260–85, 288–89, 332–33, 343, 347–48, 352, 434, 438, 440, 444, 446

Rock River and Mississippi Steam Navigation Company, 283

Rock River Improvements, 281

Rock River Land Company, 262

Rollette, 131

Joseph, 130, 144

Rosa, 44

Russel, 233

S

Sabine River, 12

Saganosh, 72

Sanborn, John G., 213

Sanders, 337, 344–45, 356, 362, 447–48

Alfred, 343

Sargent, 356

Saukenuk, 31–32, 41, 46, 80, 87, 169, 172–74, 181, 183, 208–9, 212

Sausignon, Pierre, 128

Schoolcraft, 38, 410, 415, 464

Henry, 125

Scott, 187–88, 375

Scott County Hydraulic Company, 439

seaman, 6, 335

Sears, 56, 154, 293–94, 296–97, 345, 357

David, 56, 286, 293, 296, 332, 385, 407, 416, 439, 445, 449

Seymour, James, 277, 437, 452

Shairp, Alexander, 7, 399

Shairp, Stephen, 399, 453

Shaw, 426, 464

Shawnee Prophet, 44

Shawneetown, xiii, xix, 436, 446, 456

Sheldon, 442

John P., 315

Shoemaker, 331

William R., 331

Sholes, 241, 245–46, 335

Stanton, 246, 335

Shreve, 298–99, 348

Henry, 299

Henry M., 439, 455

Shull, 79

Sibley, 379

Harriet, 205

Henry, 224, 431

Sibley Papers, 431

Singing Bird, 203

Smith, xviii, 31, 37, 39, 45, 196, 240, 335, 402, 405, 418

Henry, 375

Martin, 196

Thomas A., 403

Thomas F., 334, 441

son George Loste Davenport, 387, 390

Spencer, 213, 217, 237, 293–94, 406, 419, 464

John, 55, 205, 293

John W., 237, 273, 439

Sprague, 118

Spring, Charles A., 271, 435

Squire, Nathaniel, 257

Stambaugh, 232, 315, 442, 464

Samuel C., 315, 442

St. Anthony, 409–10, 459

St. Anthony Catholic Church, 451

St. Anthony's Catholic Church, 243, 254, 427

St. Anthony's Church, 256

Starr, Jacob, 371

steamboat Agnes, 331

Steamboat Ariel, 316

steamboat Clarion, 294

steamboat Dove, 240

steamboat Pike, 283

Steamboat Winnebago, 189

Stephenson, 213–14, 216–17, 238–39, 248–49, 256, 258, 261–62, 272, 274, 278–79, 287–89, 350–51, 366, 438

Honorable James W., 436, 452

James, 213

James W., 214

Stickney, Benjamin, 330

Stillman, 183, 214

St. Jean, 45

Stockbridge Indians, 209

Straub, 335

Isaac, 335

Street, Joseph, 221, 231, 432

Street, Joseph M., 188, 425, 429–30, 443

Strode, 214

Sturdevant, 233, 255

Harvey, 245, 255

St. Vrain, 111, 138, 142, 161, 170–72, 175, 181, 184–85, 431

Charles, 181

Charles D., 111, 418
Felix, 111, 169, 422–24
Sullivan, 275, 300–301, 348, 355, 409
John, 335
John C., 397
John H., 253, 300, 434, 440
Rockingham John H., 253
Sullivan brothers, 264
Sullivan's brother David, 301
summer hunt, 65–66, 79, 93, 107, 125, 145–46, 168–69, 189, 232, 321, 323
Swan, 15–16, 138
Sylvan Slough, 209, 294, 347
Symmes, 29–30
Marianne, 402

T
Talcott, Sylvester, 283
Taliaferro, Lawrence, 11, 98
Temperance Hall, 257
Thomas, 277, 400, 408–10, 413, 439, 459
Thomas Adams Smith, 401–2
Thomas Adams Smith Collection, 402, 454
Thorn, James, 162
Tolman, John, 162
Totten, 201, 427
treaty, xv–xvi, 26, 31, 108, 147, 156, 169–70, 187–89, 225–26, 230–33, 238, 317–18, 322–23, 397, 413, 420, 425, 431–32, 443
Treaty and white settlement, 228
the Treaty of Ghent, xvi, 26
Truett, 280, 437
Turkey River, 42, 80

Turner, Levi C., 248, 265–66, 269, 276–77, 434–36, 440

V
vacation, 283, 438
Vanatta, 213
John, 205
Vandever, William, 351
Vandruff, Joshua, 148, 150, 209, 260, 263, 274, 279, 281, 293, 434, 436–37
versts, 7
Vose, 117, 119–23, 136
Major Josiah H., 413

W
Wapello, 167, 182, 224, 230–31
Wapsipinicon, 118
Washington City, 13, 16, 180, 230–33, 330–32, 406, 413–14, 423, 430, 443–44, 457
Watts, 385
Julia, 378
Julie, 385
married William B., 249
William B., 248, 255, 385, 440
Waucoshasee, 321
Waucoshausee, 321
Waucoshaushe, 362
Wau-co-shawshe, 394
Webb, 335
Webster, 272–73, 277, 282
Daniel, 272, 281, 435–37
Daniel C., 435
Wells, George, 150
Wells, Luke, 440

Western Addition, 274, 282, 333

Whipple, John, 278

Whitney, Asa, 345

Wilcox, Charles C., 278

Wilkie, 7, 13, 40–41, 242, 399–404, 407–10, 412, 417, 419, 425, 428, 432–33

Wilkie's story, 9

Wilkinson, 13, 400, 453

Williams, Peter, 74

Williamsville, 21